Island Tourism Sustainability and Resiliency

This book provides comprehensive insight into the challenges faced by island tourism destinations and theoretical and practical paths for built in sustainability and resiliency. It explores Island Tourism Resilience within the context of 'Lifecycles, System Decline and Resilience'.

Tourism is a key activity for many islands, and some depend on the tourism sector as a main economic activity. An exploration of islands across the globe that addresses substantial matters of ongoing sustainability and resiliency is ever important. An array of challenges including natural disasters, climate change, economic and political crises among others has been addressed in the book, with additional areas such as overtourism and COVID-19 included at the conclusion. This volume is essential reading for academics, tourism planners and policy makers seeking to develop sustainable and resilient island destinations.

With a new Foreword, Introduction, Conclusion and Afterword, the chapters in this book were originally published in the journal, *Tourism Geographies*.

Michelle McLeod is Senior Lecturer at The University of the West Indies, Mona Campus, Jamaica. Her tourism industry experience spans over 30 years as a tourism professional and academic. Dr. McLeod has conducted and published research about tourism in islands.

Rachel Dodds is Full Professor at Ryerson University's Ted Rogers School of Hospitality and Tourism Management as well as working in industry as a consultant. She has been involved in the tourism industry for over 25 years. Her work focuses on all aspects of sustainable tourism.

Richard Butler is Emeritus Professor at Strathclyde University and has been researching tourism since the 1960s. His main research areas are tourism development and impacts on islands and remote locations. He was awarded the UNWTO Ulysses Medal in 2016 for creation and dissemination of knowledge.

Island Tourism Sustainability and Resiliency

Edited by
**Michelle McLeod, Rachel Dodds
and Richard Butler**

Routledge
Taylor & Francis Group

LONDON AND NEW YORK

First published 2022
by Routledge
4 Park Square, Milton Park, Abingdon, Oxon OX14 4RN

and by Routledge
605 Third Avenue, New York, NY 10158

Routledge is an imprint of the Taylor & Francis Group, an informa business

© 2022 Taylor & Francis

British Library Cataloguing in Publication Data
A catalogue record for this book is available from the British Library

ISBN: 978-1-032-24878-3 (hbk)
ISBN: 978-1-032-24879-0 (pbk)
ISBN: 978-1-003-28052-1 (ebk)

DOI: 10.4324/9781003280521

Typeset in Myriad Pro
by Newgen Publishing UK

Publisher's Note
The publisher accepts responsibility for any inconsistencies that may have arisen during the conversion of this book from journal articles to book chapters, namely the inclusion of journal terminology.

Disclaimer
Every effort has been made to contact copyright holders for their permission to reprint material in this book. The publishers would be grateful to hear from any copyright holder who is not here acknowledged and will undertake to rectify any errors or omissions in future editions of this book.

Contents

Citation Information

The following chapters, except chapter 13, were originally published in the journal *Tourism Geographies*, volume 23, issue 3 (2021). Chapter 13 was originally published in volume 15, issue 1 (2013) of the same journal. When citing this material, please use the original page numbering for each article, as follows:

Chapter 1
Globalisation and cultural change in Pacific Island countries: the role of tourism
Denis Tolkach and Stephen Pratt
Tourism Geographies, volume 23, issue 3 (2021), pp. 371–396

Chapter 2
Critiques of island sustainability in tourism
Ilan Kelman
Tourism Geographies, volume 23, issue 3 (2021), pp. 397–414

Chapter 3
Contributions to sustainable tourism in small islands: an analysis of the Cittàslow movement
Therez B. Walker and Timothy J. Lee
Tourism Geographies, volume 23, issue 3 (2021), pp. 415–435

Chapter 4
Modelling tourism resilience in small island states: a tale of two countries
Prosper F. Bangwayo-Skeete and Ryan W. Skeete
Tourism Geographies, volume 23, issue 3 (2021), pp. 436–457

Chapter 5
Social-ecological resilience and community-based tourism in the commonwealth of Dominica
Kristin Weis, Catherine Chambers and Patrick J. Holladay
Tourism Geographies, volume 23, issue 3 (2021), pp. 458–478

For any permission-related enquiries please visit:
www.tandfonline.com/page/help/permissions

Notes on Contributors

Maria Amoamo, Department of Management, University of Otago, Dunedin, New Zealand.

Godfrey Baldacchino, President, International Small Islands Studies Association, Thematic Malta Ambassador for Islands and Small States.

Prosper F. Bangwayo-Skeete, Department of Economics and Finance, University of North Carolina Wilmington, Wilmington, USA; Department of Economics, University of the West Indies, Cave Hill, Barbados.

I Komang Gde Bendesa, University of Udayana, Denpasar Bali, Indonesia.

Richard Butler, Department of Management, School of Business, Strathclyde University, Scotland, United Kingdom.

Pedro Calero-Lemes, Lanzarote University School of Tourism, University of Las Palmas de Gran Canaria, Lanzarote, Spain.

Robert Charles G. Capistrano, School of Community Resources and Development, HAITC HNU-ASU Joint International Tourism College, Arizona State University, Phoenix, AZ, USA.

Catherine Chambers, Stefansson Arctic Institute, University Centre of the Westfjords, Isafjorður, Iceland.

Joan Carles Cirer-Costa, UNIR, Logrono, Spain.

Anthony Clayton, Professor of Caribbean Sustainable Development, University of West Indies.

Rachel Dodds, School of Hospitality and Tourism Management, Ryerson University, Toronto, Canada.

Desiderio Juan Garcıa-Almeida, Department of Management, University of Las Palmas de Gran Canaria, Las Palmas de Gran Canaria, Spain.

Mark P. Hampton, Kent Business School, University of Kent, Canterbury, UK.

Amran Hamzah, Faculty of Built Environment, Universiti Teknologi Malaysia, Johor Bahru, Malaysia.

Patrick J. Holladay, School of Hospitality, Sport, and Tourism Management, Sorrell College of Business, Troy University – Brunswick, Brunswick, GA, USA.

Patricia Johnson, Newcastle Business School, The University of Newcastle, Australia.

Ilan Kelman, Institute for Global Health and Institute for Risk and Disaster Reduction, University College London, London, UK; University of Agder, Kristiansand, Norway.

Mary Stephanie E. King-Chan, Camiguin Polytechnic State College, Institute of Arts and Sciences, Mambajao, Philippines.

Laura Lawton, Dongbei University of Finance and Economics, Dalian, China.

Timothy J. Lee, University of the Sunshine Coast, Brisbane, Australia.

Emma Lina F. Lopez, Asian Institute of Tourism, University of the Philippines Diliman, Quezon City, Philippines.

Yang Liu, School of Engineering and Built Environment, Griffith University, Brisbane, Australia.

Kevin Lyons, Newcastle Business School, The University of Newcastle, Australia.

Michelle McLeod, Centre for Hotel and Tourism, The University of the West Indies, Nassau, The Bahamas.

Sylvine Pickel-Chevalier, ESTHUA (Department of Tourism and Hospitality), University of Angers, Laboratory ESO CNRS UMR 6590, Angers, France.

Stephen Pratt, School of Tourism and Hospitality Management, The University of the South Pacific, Suva, Fiji

I Nyoman Darma Putra, University of Udayana, Denpasar Bali, Indonesia.

Dian Yulie Reindrawati, Airlangga University, Surabaya, Indonesia.

Ryan W. Skeete, Research and Information Technology, Caribbean Tourism Organization, Warrens, Barbados.

Chuanzhong Tang, Dongbei University of Finance and Economics, Dalian, China.

Denis Tolkach, School of Hotel and Tourism Management, The Hong Kong Polytechnic University, Kowloon, Hong Kong.

Therez B. Walker, Tourism and Hospitality, Ritsumeikan Asia Pacific University (APU), Beppu, Japan.

David Weaver, Dongbei University of Finance and Economics, Dalian, China.

Kristin Weis, Jimmy and Rosalynn Carter School for Peace and Conflict Resolution, George Mason University, Arlington, VA, USA.

Tamara Young, Newcastle Business School, The University of Newcastle, Australia.

Foreword

Godfrey Baldacchino

Seen with the lens of geological time, most islands exist but for a little while. They arise dramatically from volcanic eruptions, or patiently via the accretionary actions of coral. Former peninsulas or headlands get eroded into islands. But those very same processes keep nibbling away; while sea level rise poses challenges to all enisled and coastal geographies.

And yet, much can happen in that little while. Once islands get 'discovered' by outsiders, they invariably become tourism destinations: not only for sun, sea and sand (sex and shopping?) but also for ice, Indigenous encounters and charismatic megafauna (whale spotting, polar bear watching, etc.). The smaller the island and the smaller its resident population, the faster, deeper and more significant becomes the tourism effect.

The examination of island tourism is a well-trodden path in academia: and its pursuers secure the envious eyes of their colleagues. Yet, positioning the island condition at the centre of one's research is not a foregone conclusion. We often see disappointing disconnects between 'island as backdrop' (locus) and the condition of being an island – islandness – as an intermediate variable to be considered in one's analysis (focus).

This special issue of *Tourism Geographies* helps to bring back the geography of island tourism, this time by focusing on three inter-related longitudinal processes, all of which are rendered idiosyncratic by the island condition. Rapid and extreme lurches in tourist arrival numbers to islands are common; and the recent experience with Covid-19 has made this abundantly clear. Once established, island tourism – and especially its warm water variety – is heavily coastal; and drawing tourists away from heavily impacted beaches and towards alternative, higher value added activities and experiences is a challenge, often involving a multiplicity of factors, such as road infrastructure, public safety and the availability of visitor attractions. And islanders, immigrant workers plus the island diaspora beyond, must somehow understand and cope with these flows and dynamics, and manage the inevitable changes. The mantra of Green Jobs and Blue Growth, by which international aid and foreign investment have become attracted of late, may suggest useful directions towards which a sustainable island tourism industry may wish to align and transform itself; although one should expect vested politico-economic interests to mount resistance.

I commend the editors and the various article contributors for such a fascinating treasure trove of island tourism insights, drawn from diverse parts of our planet.

Introduction to island tourism sustainability and resiliency

Michelle McLeod, Rachel Dodds and Richard Butler

The purpose of this book is to frame island tourism research while bringing to the forefront the myriad of challenges facing islands to develop successful tourism destinations. Islands are special geographic formations spread all across the globe, and tourism has been an important economic activity for many of these often resource constrained territories. If tourism is a means to economic prosperity, then island destinations need to explore several considerations and build resilient tourism economies that can overcome external shocks. While tourism researchers have noted island tourism research in book and article titles, when addressing the occurrence of tourism in islands, the body of work surrounding tourism in islands requires framing, as a wide array of concepts has been explored including sustainability, resilience, development, economies, impact, destinations, trends, planning and prospects. With such variety, island tourism research has seemed to lack direction or form. Herein, this book addresses this by framing island tourism research around the themes of *Lifecycles, System Decline and Resilience*. Tourism growth and development occur as a process over a period of time and this flow can be illustrated using tourism arrivals. Ongoing flows of visitors are expected to take a particular course and understanding changes in that course relates to identification of system decline. Finally, building resilience means gaining the capacity to adapt to and successfully manage changes in the dimensions and nature of tourism.

Island tourism destinations: lifecycles, system decline and resilience

Research studies about island tourism destinations have grown over the years from the early discussions of island tourism issues in the 1990s (Briguglio, Archer, et al., 1996; Briguglio, Butler, et al., 1996; Conlin & Baum, 1995; Drakakis-Smith et al., 1993) to the more recent works (Baldacchino, 2013; Croes, 2006; Dodds & Graci, 2012; Hamzah & Hampton, 2013; Harrison, 2001; Lim & Cooper, 2009; McLeod & Croes, 2018; Weaver, 2017). Framing island tourism as a field in its own right is an important step towards building island tourism research studies. The distinction of being an island has been an attractive context for tourism researchers, with the context being viewed as a laboratory. Hall (2010) argues that islands are 'natural laboratories' for the observation and study of tourism because of its bounded nature. With the possibility of a bounded island research area under study, the advent of tourism on an island takes a particular path that may be delineated as a 'Tourist Area Life Cycle' (TALC) (Butler, 1980). The TALC within island destinations provides a framework to monitor the path of tourism growth and development an island takes. This 'lifecycle' concept within a tourism area has been clarified by Singh (2011). Research directed to understand the growth and development of tourism in islands has the benefit of guiding policy guidelines and management practices to sustain such growth and at the same time averting any prolonged period of consistent decline.

Resilience of island destinations has drawn attention (Alberts & Baldacchino, 2017; Hall, 2012; Hayle, Singh, & Wright, 2010; McLeod, 2020) to understand the theoretical, facilitating factors and changing circumstances that affect island tourism resilience. In itself, embarking on tourism activities may be viewed as a means by which an island economy can be diversified and become resilient (Alberts & Baldacchino, 2017) and resiliency in tourism destinations builds resistance to the effects of global changes (Cheer & Lew, 2017). The capacity of an island destination to adapt to changes in the global environment is constrained by the creation of knowledge, development of resources and the governance systems to implement and monitor. Island tourism destinations evolve and a field of study that will capture the changing dynamics and contribute to an overall sustainable development agenda is a worthwhile research focus. Island destinations have to become agile in capturing and mitigating any possibility of a tourism system decline. Several authors explored the characteristics of island tourism systems in decline (Carlsen & Butler, 2011; Dodds, 2012; McLeod & Scott, 2018), and converting decline to rejuvenation has to be supported by the building of resiliency in island tourism destinations.

Importance of focusing on island tourism as a special form of tourism

Tourism development, particularly in small islands and archipelagos, has unique socio-cultural, historical and political contexts that require some attention. These contexts are built on an existing fragile ecosystem that in the case of smaller islands are vulnerable to heavy traffic by tourist visitation. Transformation of an island into one that is dependent on tourism may in itself create a vulnerability that cannot withstand isolation brought on by being cut-off from the global travel and tourism system. The development and management of tourism systems in island environments are particularly challenged by leakages (Russell, 2020) and governance matters (Rolle et al., 2020) that are directly and indirectly related to the nature of an island, that is, being cut-off from a main land mass. Environmental issues are particularly evident in island tourism (Kuo & Chen, 2009). Human resource development issues in islands are of prime concern as this capacity has to be built for the successful operation of a tourism destination. The non-availability of local labour and the socio-cultural matters relating to the movement of labour and migration to island tourism destinations have to be addressed. Given the subjects to be addressed a layering approach was outlined for the Special Issue topics to allow a wide scope of subject matter, to address the stated context of island tourism as follows:

Island colonization, geographies and tourism;
Island tourism development stages, lifecycles and decline;
Island travel and transportation, inter-island transportation, and cruise shipping within island environments;
Tourist motivation and demand for islands;
Tourism marketing of islands, including new competition and changing feeder markets;
Island hospitality, services and businesses, micro and small businesses, craft markets;
Island tourism economics, financial leakages, inclusive growth and backward linkages;
Island culture and heritage, festivals and event management, cuisine and gastronomy;
Island tourism migration/diaspora issues;
Island tourism environments and environmental quality, including climate change issues;
Island tourism infrastructure development, sustainability and resilience;

Island tourism networks, suppliers, enterprises, intermediaries and organisations;
Policy-making for tourism development in islands and island tourism governance;
Tourism management issues including human resources and operation management;
Tourism education and training in islands, vocational training and curriculum development.

Tourism on islands: towards island resilience

Island tourism researchers utilise a geographic feature of being an island, a piece of land surrounded by water, as the basis for study. With several islands being categorised as Small Island Developing States (SIDS), and facing ongoing challenges relating to global financial, natural disasters and recently a pandemic crisis, some attention has been paid to understanding responses of island economies (e.g. Buultjens et al., 2017). By the very nature of being islands, several unique characteristics result in degrees of fragmentation and disintegration, which place those economies at a disadvantage. Some islands are very remote with limited connectivity to benefit from growing economic activity in travel and tourism. Nonetheless, it is this very economic activity that islands are often left to turn to, because of lack of resources to support other economic activities. Island geographies are integrally connected to the economic activity that is tourism, and yet focused attention, on a perspective of resilience and recovery in island tourism destinations, needs to be made in the tourism literature. The vulnerability of islands has been well documented in journals such as *Island Studies Journal* (Baldacchino, 2006) and other publications (Calgaro & Lloyd, 2008; Hall, 2012; Klint, 2013), however, understandings about island destinations, lifecycles, system decline and resilience require further elaboration. Several authors have considered various aspects such as the social and ecological perspectives of island resilience (Adger et al., 2005; Cheer et al., 2017), governance and resilience (Lebel et al., 2006; Luthe & Wyss, 2016) and limiting vulnerability (Alberts & Baldacchino, 2017). A burgeoning tourism literature about tourism resilience has contributed to the study, however, for island destinations that are increasingly constrained by limited resources, a path to greater island tourism resilience has to be clarified.

This book started as a *Special Issue* in *Tourism Geographies*, and the call for papers in 2017 resulted in 53 abstracts. A summary of information about the topics of abstracts includes some very important topics about island tourism, although many of these did not evolve into full papers. These included various forms of island tourism, such as a nautical destination, cruise, slow transport and mobilities. Marketing related topics were also submitted including branding, destination loyalty, vacation satisfaction, advertising, and social media content analysis. Abstracts around concepts relating to island tourism submitted included concept of islandness (Butler, 2012), resilience, recreating vulnerability, innovation, overtourism, modelling, planning and lifecycle. Natural environmental impacts included cyclones and climate change, while the human and social geographical perspectives were an important group of content for the abstracts and included topics, such as indigenous communities, immigrants, culture, gastronomy, disease, the sharing economy, resident stress and housing. Unfortunately, no abstracts related to cold-water islands, a subset of islands which include a number of significant tourism destinations and which, while not facing the hazards of hurricanes or typhoons, are perhaps more vulnerable to regular unattractive weather (in a tourism context) and share many of the same problems of small scale, resource scarcity, and difficult access that their warm-water counterparts suffer from.

A body of work has emerged with research insights about island tourism destinations across the globe. A summary of the articles follows. Island tourism authenticity is challenged by globalisation on culture. Several Caribbean tourism destinations and the challenges of resilience are contained in this volume. *Tolkach and Pratt's* chapter, about 'Globalisation and cultural change in Pacific Island countries: the role of tourism', explores resiliency to cultural change within the context of Fiji, Tonga and Cook Islands. *Kelman's* chapter about 'Critiques of island sustainability in tourism' is thought provoking with the balance between tourism and sustainability being challenged. The SIDS context is explored by *Walker and Lee* in the 'Contributions to sustainable tourism in small islands: and analysis of the Cittáslow movement' and the benefits derived from Slow Food and Slow Tourism. *Bangwayo-Skeete and Skeete's* modelling of tourism resilience in two small island states, Grenada and Barbados, using the Adaptive Cycle Model pushes the boundary of understanding island resilience in tourism dependent islands. *Weis, Chambers and Holladay's* chapter presents the social-ecological aspects of resilience and explores community-based tourism in six coastal communities in Dominica.

European islands as tourism destinations have a particular historical context and *Cirer-Costa* presents the 'Economic and social resilience accounts for the recovery of Ibiza's tourism sector' showing the historical development of the destination and the contribution of tourism. *Amoamo's* chapter utilises the geopolitical context of Brexit to understand island resilience in Britain's Overseas Island Territories, which is exemplified in the case of Pitcairn Island. An understanding the role of immigrant island communities and the contribution to island resilience has been presented by *Calero-Lemes and Garcia-Almeida* in relation to immigrant entrepreneur knowledge in the tourism industry utilising a case example of the Eastern Canary Islands.

This book includes developing resilient Asian island tourism destinations. *Weaver, Tang, Lawton and Liu's* chapter considers the resilience of the Maldives in relation to cultivating the Chinese market through destination loyalty. *King-Chan, Capistrano and Lopez* focus of the environment in Camiguin Province, Philippines and draw attention to the increasing need for environmentally responsible behaviour (ERB) to avert potential environmental impact as tourist numbers increase. *Young, Reindrawati, Lyons and Johnson's* chapter particularly focuses on the resident perceptions of tourism from an Indonesian island and associations of host meaning of tourism that may influence tourism outcomes. *Pickel-Chevalier, Bendesa and Putra* explore a policy of integrated touristic villages as an archetype of sustainable development in Indonesia. *Hamzah and Hampton* added contribution about resilience and non-linear change in Perhentian Kecil addresses the complexities of tourism in small island destinations.

Tourism lifecycles

Islands are socio-ecological systems with physical and human activity lifecycles. A lifecycle perspective is an approach that can be applied to understand the evolution of a tourism system (Castellani & Sala, 2012; Chapman & Light, 2016), to reinvent a tourism destination (Corak, 2006), for planning (Getz, 1992), for tourism development (Zhong, Deng, & Xiang, 2008), for carrying capacity (Martin & Uysal, 1990) and carbon emissions (Tang, Zhong, & Ng, 2017). In terms of human aspects of tourism, the tourism lifecycle has been utilised to understand resident attitudes towards tourism at the stagnation stage of a destination (Pennington-Gray, 1970), entrepreneurship (Russell & Faulkner, 2004) and a travel lifecycle

(Oppermann, 1995). A gap can be identified on the human activity aspect of lifecycle assessment. Haywood (1986) supports the operationalisation of the lifecycle concept with a review of six major measurement decisions and applies it to tourism forecasting and marketing strategy. In relation to island tourism destinations, the gamut of application of a lifecycle in tourism has had limited application and only one work was noted (Oreja Rodríguez, Parra-López, & Yanes-Estévez, 2008). Island tourism lifecycles occur as tourism development evolves. A bridge is needed to bring about the methodological approaches that can study a bounded system of an island using the lifecycle concept. Chapters in this book illustrate in particular the evolution of activities to build resilient tourism destinations (Bangwayo-Skeete & Skeete, 2020; Cirer-Costa, 2020).

Tourism system decline

A tourism system is one in which tourists move temporarily between origins and destinations using a form of transport and this movement may be categorised as an overnight stay or day visit. It is expected that this flow of visitors will grow over time as the destination is popularised and the policy, planning, development and management frameworks are put in place to increase tourism activities. Tourism decline has been studied on a tangent and not in the context of a system. Baum and O'Gorman (2010) looked at a destination name and its influence on the decline of tourism. Manente and Pechlaner (2006) conducted some promising work about identification and monitoring decline of tourism destinations within the concept of a tourism area lifecycle. Müller and Brouder (2014) considered tourism businesses and the local labour markets to determine decline. Scott and Laws (2006) article about systemic effects of tourism crises and disasters contributes to understand tourism system decline. While evidence exists that tourism flows change over time and decline is one outcome, the body of work surrounding this very important issue has been sparse and lacks application to island tourism.

Tourism resilience

Resilience involves a systemic approach that breaks down a socio-ecological system into components to understand the interactions of those components (McLeod, 2020). Hall (2017) suggests that there has been limited understanding and application resilience concept to tourism and it has been applied much later than in other fields. Resilience has received increasing prominence in tourism research and can provide benefits for the policy and planning of tourism destinations (Lew, 2014; Lew, Wu, Ni, & Ng, 2017). Tourism in the Caribbean has been devastated by a series of catastrophic hurricanes, Irma and Maria in 2017, and Hurricane Dorian that made landfall on two islands of The Bahamas on 1 September 2019. Some work about resilience in natural events have been conducted. Adger et al. (2005) studied resilience in the context of coastal disasters, Calgaro and Lloyd (2008) explored the impact of the 2004 Indian Ocean tsunami on coastal tourism to understand destination vulnerability. Becken and Khazai (2017) discussed the role of tourism in assisting recovery after disasters, and several authors have addressed the resilience of coral reefs (Coghlan & Prideaux, 2009; Grimsditch & Salm, 2006; Phillips, 2015). A growing application of resilience and its associated concept vulnerability has been evident in the island tourism literature (Klint, 2013; Mahon, Becken, & Rennie, 2013). Broader application of resilience to tourism destinations can bring value to move beyond the sustainability concept as destinations build in mechanisms that are able to respond quickly to changes in the tourism system.

A case for further island tourism studies

Global impacts on island destinations, which are often dependent on tourism as a means of income and viability, require new approaches to understand island tourism resilience. Although a small geographic context, island communities are exposed to the dislocation, disruption and disposition of their lives, and such circumstances do not allow islanders to benefit fully from the development of successful tourism destinations. The treatment of island tourism discourses in the tourism literature is a critical and essential component for advanced understandings of tourism as a discipline, and understandings of the island context in particular. Sharpley (2012) and others (Baldacchino, 2013; Butler, 2012) point attention to the long standing fascination of tourists with islands. Island tourism has a distinctive form (Sharpley, 2012). Tourists from generating markets visit islands, and the unique characteristics of these small island gems provide rest and relaxation to the mundane issues of life. Major tourist markets will benefit by the development of island tourism communities that seek to build resilient tourist destinations that are better managed and developed in a manner that sustains the flows of tourists to these islands. Moreover, islanders stand to gain from the benefits of tourism by understanding the nature of island tourism and potential evolutionary changes that result in setting a path towards island resilience. If an island is treated as an ideal laboratory on a small scale, then the examination and exploration of tourism principles and practices are endless, with the potential of providing better understandings about issues relating to climate change, economic vulnerability and sustainable development. While new methodologies develop around island research (McLeod, 2018), new theoretical constructs that guide the development of these land masses are to be examined, and thereby new knowledge emerges about tourism theory, management and development impacts. The burgeoning of papers that this call generated is evidence of the need and interest for island tourism research and justifies its own niche in the tourism literature.

References

Adger, W. N., Hughes, T. P., Folke, C., Carpenter, S. R., & Rockström, J. (2005). Social-ecological resilience to coastal disasters. *Science, 309*(5737), 1036–1039.

Alberts, A., & Baldacchino, G. (2017). Resilience and tourism in islands: insights from the Caribbean. In R. W. Butler (Ed.), *Tourism and resilience* (pp. 150–162). Wallingford: CABI.

Baldacchino, G. (2006). Islands, island studies, island studies journal. *Island Studies Journal, 1*(1), 3–18.

Baldacchino, G. (2013). *Island tourism.* Jeju, Korea: Jeju Development Institute.

Bangwayo-Skeete, P. F., & Skeete, R. W. (2020). Modelling tourism resilience in small island states: A tale of two countries. *Tourism Geographies, 23*(3), 436–457.

Baum, T. G., & O'Gorman, K. D. (2010). Iran or Persia: What's in a name, the decline and fall of a tourism industry? In R. Butler & W. Suntikul (Eds.), *Tourism and political change* (pp. 175–187). Oxford: Goodfellow Publishers.

Becken, S., & Khazai, B. (2017). Resilience, tourism and disasters. In: R. W. Butler, (Ed.) *Tourism and Resilience* (pp. 96–102). Boston, MA: CAB International,.

Briguglio, L., Archer, B., Jafari, J., & Wall, G. (1996). *Sustainable tourism in islands and small states: issues and policies.* London: Cassell.

Briguglio, L., Butler, R. W., Harrison, D., & Filho, W. L. (1996). *Sustainable tourism in islands and small states: case studies.* London: Cassell.

Butler, R. W. (1980). The concept of a tourist area cycle of evolution: implications for management of resources. *Canadian Geographer/Le Géographe canadien, 24*(1), 5–12.

Butler, R. W. (2012). Islandness: It's all in the mind. *Tourism Recreation Research, 37*(2), 173–176.

Buultjens, J., Ratnayake, I., & Gnanapala, A. C. (2017). Sri Lankan tourism development and implications for resilience. In R. W. Butler (Ed.), *Tourism and resilience* (pp. 83–95). Wallingford: CABI.

Calgaro, E., & Lloyd, K. (2008). Sun, sea, sand and tsunami: examining disaster vulnerability in the tourism community of Khao Lak, Thailand. *Singapore Journal of Tropical Geography, 29*(3), 288–306.

Carlsen, J., & Butler, R. (2011). Introducing sustainable perspectives of island tourism. *Island Tourism. Sustainable Perspectives, CABI, Ecotourism Series, 8*(1), 1–7.

Castellani, V., & Sala, S. (2012). Ecological Footprint and Life Cycle Assessment in the sustainability assessment of tourism activities. *Ecological indicators, 16*, 135–147.

Chapman, A., & Light, D. (2016). Exploring the tourist destination as a mosaic: The alternative lifecycles of the seaside amusement arcade sector in Britain. *Tourism Management, 52*, 254–263. doi: https://doi.org/10.1016/j.tourman.2015.06.020

Cheer, J. M., Cole, S., Reeves, K., & Kato, K. (2017). Tourism and Islandscapes-Cultural realignment, social-ecological resilience and change. *Shima, 11*(1), 40–54.

Cheer, J. M., & Lew, A. A. (2017). *Tourism, resilience and sustainability: Adapting to social, political and economic change*. Abingdon: Routledge.

Cirer-Costa, J. C. (2020). Economic and social resilience accounts for the recovery of Ibiza's tourism sector. *Tourism Geographies, 23*(3), 479–500.

Coghlan, A., & Prideaux, B. (2009). Welcome to the Wet Tropics: the importance of weather in reef tourism resilience. *Current Issues in Tourism, 12*(2), 89–104.

Conlin, M. V., & Baum, T. (1995). *Island Tourism: Management Principles and Practice*. New York: John Wiley.

Corak, S. (2006). The modification of the tourism area life cycle model for (re) inventing a destination: The case of the Opatija Riviera, Croatia. In R. W. Butler (Ed.), *The Tourism Area Life Cycle: Applications and Modifications* (Vol. 1, pp. 271–286). Clevedon: Channel View Publications.

Croes, R. R. (2006). A paradigm shift to a new strategy for small island economies: Embracing demand side economics for value enhancement and long term economic stability. *Tourism Management, 27*(3), 453–465.

Dodds, R. (2012). Sustainable tourism: a hope or a necessity? The case of Tofino, British Columbia, Canada. *Journal of Sustainable Development, 5*(5), 54.

Dodds, R., & Graci, S. (2012). *Sustainable tourism in island destinations*. Routledge.

Drakakis-Smith, D., Lockhart, D., & Schembri, J. (1993). *The Development Process in Small Island States*. Abingdon: Routledge.

Getz, D. (1992). Tourism planning and destination life cycle. *Annals of tourism research, 19*(4), 752–770.

Grimsditch, G. D., & Salm, R. V. (2006). *Coral reef resilience and resistance to bleaching*.: Citeseer.

Hall, M. C. (2010). Island destinations: A natural laboratory for tourism: Introduction. *Asia Pacific Journal of Tourism Research, 15*(3), 245–249.

Hall, M. C. (2012). Island, islandness, vulnerability and resilience. *Tourism Recreation Research, 37*(2), 177–181.

Hall, M. C. (2017). Resilience in tourism: development, theory, and application. In J. Cheer & A. A. Lew (Eds.), *Tourism, Resilience and Sustainability* (pp. 18–33). Oxon: Routledge.

Hamzah, A., & Hampton, M. P. (2013). Resilience and non-linear change in island tourism. *Tourism Geographies, 15*(1), 43–67.

Harrison, D. (2001). Islands, image and tourism. *Tourism Recreation Research, 26*(3), 9–14.

Hayle, C., Singh, D. R., & Wright, A. (2010). Planning for tourism resilience in the Caribbean. *Journal of Eastern Caribbean Studies, 35*(1), 36–59.

Haywood, K. M. (1986). Can the tourist-area life cycle be made operational? *Tourism Management, 7*(3), 154–167. doi: https://doi.org/10.1016/0261-5177(86)90002-6

Klint, L. M. (2013). *"Buoyancy–bifo and afta": a climate change vulnerability/resilience framework for tourism–the case study of Vanuatu dive tourism*. Centre for Tourism and Services Research.

Kuo, N.-W., & Chen, P.-H. (2009). Quantifying energy use, carbon dioxide emission, and other environmental loads from island tourism based on a life cycle assessment approach. *Journal of Cleaner Production, 17*(15), 1324–1330. doi: https://doi.org/10.1016/j.jclepro.2009.04.012

Lebel, L., Anderies, J. M., Campbell, B., Folke, C., Hatfield-Dodds, S., Hughes, T. P., & Wilson, J. (2006). Governance and the capacity to manage resilience in regional social-ecological systems. *Ecology and Society, 11*(1). http://dx.doi.org/10.5751/ES-01606-110119

Lew, A. A. (2014). Scale, change and resilience in community tourism planning. *Tourism Geographies, 16*(1), 14–22.

Lew, A. A., Wu, T., Ni, C., & Ng, P. T. (2017). Community tourism resilience: some applications of the scale, change and resilience (SCR) model. In R. Butler (Ed.), *Tourism and resilience* (pp. 23–31). Oxfordshire: CABI.

Lim, C. C., & Cooper, C. (2009). Beyond sustainability: optimising island tourism development. *International Journal of Tourism Research, 11*(1), 89–103.

Luthe, T., & Wyss, R. (2016). Resilience to climate change in a cross-scale tourism governance context: a combined quantitative-qualitative network analysis. *Ecology and Society, 21*(1). http://dx.doi.org/10.5751/ES-08234-210127

Mahon, R., Becken, S., & Rennie, H. (2013). *Evaluating the business case for investment in the resilience of the tourism sector of small island developing states.* Christchurch, New Zealand: Lincoln University.

Manente, M., & Pechlaner, H. (2006). How to define, identify and monitor the decline of tourist destinations: Towards an early warning system. In R. W. Butler (Ed.), *The tourism area life cycle: Conceptual and theoretical issues* (Vol. 2, pp. 235–253). Clevedon: Channel View Publications.

Martin, B. S., & Uysal, M. (1990). An examination of the relationship between carrying capacity and the tourism lifecycle: Management and policy implications. *Journal of Environmental Management, 31*(4), 327–333. doi: https://doi.org/10.1016/S0301-4797(05)80061-1

McLeod, M. (2018). Developing a network analysis methodology for island tourism research. In M. McLeod & R. R. Croes (Eds.), *Tourism Management in Warm-water Island Destinations* (pp. 178–191). Oxfordshire: CABI.

McLeod, M. (2020). Tourism governance, panarchy and resilience in The Bahamas. In S. Rolle, J. Minnis, & I. Bethell-Bennett (Eds.), *Tourism Development, Governance and Sustainability in The Bahamas* (pp. 103–113). Oxon: Routledge.

McLeod, M., & Croes, R. R. (2018). *Tourism management in warm-water island destinations* (Vol. 6). Wallingford: CABI.

McLeod, M., & Scott, N. (2018). Destination management: A network perspective. *Tourism Management in Warm-water Island Destinations, 147*–162. Wallingford, UK.

Müller, D. K., & Brouder, P. (2014). Dynamic development or destined to decline? The case of Arctic tourism businesses and local labour markets in Jokkmokk, Sweden. In A. Viken & B. Granas (Eds.), *Tourism destination development: Turns and tactics* (pp. 227–244). Oxon: Routledge.

Oppermann, M. (1995). Travel life cycle. *Annals of tourism research, 22*(3), 535–552. doi: https://doi.org/10.1016/0160-7383(95)00004-P

Oreja Rodríguez, J. R., Parra-López, E., & Yanes-Estévez, V. (2008). The sustainability of island destinations: Tourism area life cycle and teleological perspectives. The case of Tenerife. *Tourism Management, 29*(1), 53–65. doi: https://doi.org/10.1016/j.tourman.2007.04.007

Pennington-Gray, L. (1970). Resident attitudes towards tourism in a destination in the stagnation stage of the tourism life cycle. *Sustainable Development and Planning II, 2*, 1411–1418.

Phillips, W. N. (2015). Tourism threats to coral reef resilience at Koh Sak, Pattaya bay. *Environment and Natural Resources Journal, 13*(1), 47–60.

Rolle, S., Minnis, J., & Bethell-Bennett, I. (2020). *Tourism Development, Governance and Sustainability in The Bahamas.* Abingdon: Routledge.

Russell, C. D. (2020). *Addressing Leakages between the Tourism Hotel Sector and Other Sectors in The Bahamas.* (PhD), Walden University, Minneapolis. Retrieved from https://scholarworks.waldenu.edu/dissertations/9638 (9638)

Russell, R., & Faulkner, B. (2004). Entrepreneurship, Chaos and the Tourism Area Lifecycle. *Annals of tourism research, 31*(3), 556–579. doi: https://doi.org/10.1016/j.annals.2004.01.008

Scott, N., & Laws, E. (2006). Tourism crises and disasters: enhancing understanding of system effects. *Journal of Travel & Tourism Marketing, 19*(2–3), 149–158.

Sharpley, R. (2012). Island tourism or tourism on islands? *Tourism Recreation Research, 37*(2), 167–172.

Singh, S. (2011). The tourism area 'life cycle': A clarification. *Annals of Tourism Research*, *38*(3), 1185–1187. doi: https://doi.org/10.1016/j.annals.2011.03.005

Tang, C., Zhong, L., & Ng, P. (2017). Factors that influence the tourism industry's carbon emissions: a tourism area life cycle model perspective. *Energy Policy*, *109*, 704–718. doi: https://doi.org/10.1016/j.enpol.2017.07.050

Weaver, D. B. (2017). Core–periphery relationships and the sustainability paradox of small island tourism. *Tourism Recreation Research, 42*(1), 11–21.

Zhong, L., Deng, J., & Xiang, B. (2008). Tourism development and the tourism area life-cycle model: A case study of Zhangjiajie National Forest Park, China. *Tourism Management, 29*(5), 841–856. doi: https://doi.org/10.1016/j.tourman.2007.10.002

Globalisation and cultural change in Pacific Island countries: the role of tourism

Denis Tolkach (iD) and Stephen Pratt (iD)

ABSTRACT

Globalisation is often perceived as a threat to the preservation of traditional cultures. There are various approaches to understanding the impact of globalisation on culture. Pieterse's three paradigms of globalisation and culture, clash of civilisations, McDonaldisation and hybridisation, provide a useful theoretical foundation for understanding how tourism impacts culture. The three paradigms of globalisation assess cultural change holistically. Cultural change in Pacific Island countries (PIC) due to globalisation, especially tourism's role, in this change, is the focus. Data are sourced via interviews with various tourism stakeholders from Fiji, Tonga and Cook Islands. Tourism is only one driver of cultural change. Other forces include mobilities, migration, diaspora, geopolitical change, technology and popular culture. Examples of the clash of civilisations paradigm include geopolitical changes resulting in different tourism markets and the imitation effect from diaspora and tourists. Commodification of cultural performance for both tourist and local consumption and use of popular culture, for example the animated film *Moana*, are viewed as McDonaldisation of culture. Participants' reflections on ongoing evolution of culture including the integration of PIC into the world economy, through increased mobilities and technologies, exemplify hybridisation. In general, the three PIC are found to be culturally resilient. Culture of these PIC is resilient with Pacific Islanders maintaining agency over change, however the impact of various globalisation factors demand effort in preserving culture in the long term.

摘要

全球化经常被认为是对传统文化保护的威胁。有多种方法可以理解全球化对文化的影响。皮特斯（Pieterse）1996年提出了三种全球化影响文化的范式：文明的冲突，文化的麦当劳化和混杂，为理解旅游如何影响文化提供了一个有用的理论基础。本文运用全球化的三种范式从整体上评估文化变迁。全球化对太平洋岛国的文化变迁的影响，尤其旅游业对文化变迁的影响，是本文关注的焦点。本文数据来源于对斐济、汤加和库克群岛旅游利益相关者的采访。旅游业只是文化变迁的一种动力。其他力量包括人口流动、移民、散居、地缘政治变迁、科技和流行文化。文明冲突范式的例子包括影响不同旅游市场的地缘政治变化，以及侨居和游客的模仿效应。为游客和当地消费者提供的商业化的文化表演和流行文化，例如动画片《海洋奇缘》，被视为文化的麦当劳化。参与者反思文化的持续演变, 包括通过日益增加移民和技术将太平洋岛国融入世界经济, 这些是文化杂交的例证。总的来说, 发现这三个太平洋岛国具有文化方面的韧性。这些太平洋岛国的文化如太平洋岛国民对文化变化的维护机构一样是有韧性的, 但是各种全球化因素的影响需要长期努力来保护文化。

Introduction

Culture plays a major role in and for tourism. Culture serves as a major attraction and thus has the ability to preserve or revive cultural practices (McKercher, 2002). However, the adverse effects of tourism on culture, through cultural appropriation and commodification, have been extensively discussed in tourism literature (Root, 2018; Shepherd, 2002). Culture is important for Pacific Island countries (PIC). The unique PIC cultures attract tourists, while tourism impacts their culture. Tourism is also one of the few economic options for many PIC, thus, although there are possible negative cultural impacts of tourism, PIC in many cases need to sustain visitation (Cave, Ryan, & Panakera, 2003). While there are some aspects of culture that are common across national boundaries, many customs and traditions are unique to a particular island state, geographical area or even tribe due to a variety of geographical, historical and social factors. These unique cultures are under external pressure due to a variety of globalisation forces that include, but are not limited to, migration, popular culture, technological advancement and tourism (Crocombe, 2001). As visitor arrival numbers grow across many PIC, tourism becomes more geographically widespread and mature, with new destinations now existing in the region (Cheer et al., 2018). Therefore, it is timely to reassess the socio-cultural impacts of tourism along with other forces of globalisation on PIC.

Culture is defined as 'behaviour and beliefs that are learned and shared: learned so that it is not "instinctual," shared so that it is not individual' (Pieterse, 1995, p. 1390). This definition emphasises the social sharing aspect, but it is not limited by any geographic borders; just a shared common experience. Culture refers as much to behaviour and beliefs held in common as those which are different. The definition of globalisation is much more contested. There is general agreement that globalisation is shaped by technological change, involves the reconfiguration of nation states, accompanies regionalisation and is uneven. There is less consensus about whether globalisation is purely an economic occurrence or multidimensional, whether it is a modern phenomenon or a long-term historical process, whether it is a result of neoliberal capitalism or a much broader social phenomenon, whether it exists or is merely rhetoric? (Pieterse, 2015, p. 8). As this study concerns culture, globalisation is defined from a cultural perspective as 'a social process in which the constraints of geography on social and cultural arrangements recede and in which people are increasingly aware that they are receding' (Waters, 1995, p. 3).

A lot has been written on tourism and globalisation (e.g. Mowforth & Munt, 2015; Wahab & Cooper, 2005) as well as tourism's impact on culture and the host culture's impact on tourism and tourists (Canavan, 2016; Macleod & Carrier, 2009). The main objective of this paper is to examine cultural change in PIC due to globalisation, with a focus on tourism's role as one of the contributors to this change. The context of PIC is appropriate for exploration into tourism's impact on cultural change as the South Pacific is home to diverse cultures, while tourism forms one of the major economic activities for many PIC (Harrison & Pratt, 2013). Different from previous research, various impacts of globalisation on culture and tourism's role in it are discussed using Pieterse's (1996) three paradigms of globalisation, namely clash of civilisations, McDonaldisation and hybridisation. The application of the three paradigms contributes to a more holistic understanding of the complexity of relationships between culture and tourism. The paradigms are based on two contrasting worldviews: modern and postmodern, which allow the discussion of structural issues as well as dynamic cultural changes in the PICs.

The next section briefly outlines Pieterse's (1996) three paradigms of globalisation, clash of civilisations, McDonaldisation and hybridisation, and describes how these paradigms apply to tourism in general. The subsequent methodology section explains the research approach and data collection methods after which the findings section 'Globalisation, tourism and culture of PIC' demonstrates specific examples from PIC of how globalisation through tourism has impacted local culture. The penultimate section, the discussion section, locates the findings from this research back into the wider body of literature and a conclusion section follows.

Globalisation: three paradigms

Increasing global interconnectedness has been associated with cultural change. Cultural change and differences in cultures have been explained by Pieterse (1995, 1996, 2015) with three contrasting paradigms: clash of civilisations, McDonaldisation and hybridisation. The first two paradigms are modernist in that they are static and address an issue of imposition of Western culture in non-Western countries. Hybridisation is thought of in postmodern terms, where cultures affect each other and evolve dynamically.

Clash of civilisations

Huntington (1993) posits that differences in cultures are likely to result in a clash of these cultures. Viewing globalisation from a mainly political viewpoint, Huntington (1993) sees cultural differences as dividing the world into opposing forces, notably the West versus the Rest. The 'Rest' has been the Islamic world, Asian 'yellow peril' and the Iron Curtin and Communist threat (Kavolis, 1988), depending on the era and the issue being discussed. These geopolitics politicise culture and emphasise a national security doctrine. In the modern world system, culture is an ideological tool (Wallerstein, 1990). This paradigm views cultural differentialism as a kind of 'billiard ball' model where cultures are separate entities bumping into one another but not interacting (Pieterse, 1996).

The clash of cultures has been identified in the tourism context. In Deery, Jago, Fredline, (2012), the authors note that social interaction between tourists and local communities, both their positive and negative impacts, has generated a large body of research. In this paradigm, the clash of cultures is often predicated on the overriding Western tourist culture dominating or displacing the host culture (Canavan, 2016). International tourists are often viewed as a threat to local culture, to the local communities' recreation activities and cultural identity, as found by Wray, Espiner, and Perkins (2010) discussing one case in New Zealand. Scholars have documented how tourists threaten deeply held values and beliefs about the local resources, both physical and cultural. For example, Weaver (2010) states that across Australia, Canada, New Zealand and the United States, indigenous peoples have been coerced off their land and relegated to surviving on the periphery, leading to economic and social deprivation of the indigenous community. Lew and Kennedy (2002) note that in the case of Native Americans, tourism is a means of forced assimilation. Native American culture was perceived as second class to the dominant Euro-American culture. Elsewhere, tourists transplant their own culture physically to the host destination, occupying the physical space but enjoying many of imported elements of their own culture, as noted by Hottola (2004) in the case of Finnish package tourists to Spain. Enclave tourism is sometimes representative of this type of globalisation via tourism (Nunkoo & Ramkissoon, 2016).

Others have suggested that tourism is a new form of colonialism (Britton, 1982; Fisher, 2004a; Jaakson, 2004), whereby the historically dominant imperial cultures continue to subjugate these peripheral, usually developing, countries. One way for this to occur is the demonstration effect, which is seen when the hosts of a tourist destination adopt behavioural patterns of tourists. Typically, the examples of demonstration effect include residents in non-Western destinations adopting behaviours of tourists from developed Western countries. Such examples include dress preferences in favour of more open and casual dress, increased consumption of imported goods and alcohol consumption (Fisher, 2004b). Globalisation facilitates this through mass tourism via inexpensive and increasingly accessible transportation. Cultural hegemony is then imposed on the host destination, alluding to the Fukuyama thesis of the 'end of history' (Giampiccoli, 2003). This form of cultural globalisation assumes all cultures are converging into the same, notably Western, global culture.

McDonaldisation

The McDonaldisation paradigm posits the worldwide homogenisation of cultures through the impact of multi-national corporations (Pieterse, 1996). This type of modernisation is essentially Americanisation and alludes to the spread of global capitalism. This phenomenon was foreshadowed in Marx's thesis with the world-system theory being the latest version of this perspective (Peet & Hawick, 2015). The McDonalds formula is built on efficiency (rapid service), is calculable (fast and inexpensive), is predictable (no surprises), and controls labour and customers (Ritzer, 2004). However, Pieterse (2015, p. 52) highlights several examples where multi-national global expansion has not resulted in a homogenisation of cultures but global localisation (glocalisation). McDonalds in Moscow adjusted its services to cater for local tastes, that is, the procedures and some products and services are standardised globally throughout a corporation with adjustments for the preferences of the local market. Yet the idea of McDonaldisation has been applied in many areas: McJobs, McInformation, McCitizens, McUniversity, McTourism, McCulture, McPrisons, McCourts. The idea describes the rationalisation and optimisation of various institutions and aspects of life (Gottdiener, 2000).

McDonaldisation has been highlighted in the tourism literature. Highly predictable, highly efficient and highly controlled package tours of mass tourism help to create McTourists, who want predictable, minimal cost, efficient entertainment with low levels of risk (Ritzer & Liska, 1997). They explain how Disney World is a prime example of McTourism, providing a fully rationalized, highly commoditised, inauthentic experience. Weaver (2005) illustrates the McDonaldisation of cruise tourism. In Alaska, Zegre, Needham, Kruger, and Rosenberger (2012) associate the commercial outdoor recreation and tourism industry with McDonaldisation because of characteristics such as efficiency, calculability, predictability and control.

Associated with global homogenisation is the commodification of culture. Cultural commodification, as it is presented and 'consumed' by tourists has been a fertile area for tourism research. The commodification of culture is essentially perceived as negative, where traditional ceremonies, handicrafts and language are changed to suit tourists (Kirtsoglou & Theodossopoulos, 2004; Macleod, 2006; Shepherd, 2002). Some see cultural commodification as disempowering traditional cultures and cultural practices to respond to the demands of global tourism (Ateljevic & Doorne, 2003).

Hybridisation

Differing from the previous two paradigms, hybridisation blurs boundaries and involves cross-over of cultures, recognising that culture is fluid (Pieterse, 1996). Hybridisation sits between the previous two paradigms. It is an answer to cultural differentialism, which may lead to nationalist doctrines of culture (Pieterse, 1995). Hybridisation goes by various terms, such as global localisation, local globalisation, and glocalisation (Swyngedouw, 2004). As a concept, hybridisation does not reveal the contribution of the mix of cultures. Any asymmetries in the mix of cultures are concealed (Pieterse, 2015). There are different types and styles of mixing, emphasising that intercultural mingling is an open and creative process (Pieterse, 2015). The forces of globalisation, such as technology, communication, mobility, migration, trade, investment, tourism, heighten the awareness of cultural differences (Pieterse, 2015).

In tourism literature, scholars have noted examples of hybridisation, describing a number of events and festivals that showcase aspects of the culture of diasporic populations, for example The Notting Hill Carnival in London and The Mela Festival in Edinburgh (Burr, 2006; Carnegie & Smith, 2006). While celebrating the traditional culture of the diasporic communities, there are elements of the host community that are imported into these festivals to provide new hybridised cultural forms. Conversely, the dominant culture also may evolve to include the elements of diasporic cultures. For example, South Asian cuisine in the UK is now popular beyond the diaspora and is arguably part of British culture (Buettner, 2008). Jacobsen (2003) notes, in the age of modernity, international travel around Europe involves glocalisation as there are elements of tourists' home culture as they travel in a 'tourist bubble'. Trau (2012) argues that Vanuatu's World Heritage Site, Chief Roi Mata's Domain, is an example of glocalisation because, at the local community level, the customary landowners negotiate international tourism development while attempting to maintain their traditional culture. Salazar (2005) highlights the case of glocalisation among Indonesian tour guides where the guides tailor 'local (and localized) products (representations of heritage and culture) to changing global audiences (international tourists coming from various parts of the world and with different preferences)' (Salazar, 2005, p. 631). Chang & Pang (2017) suggest that even theme parks such as Universal Studios in Singapore can be analysed in terms of interaction of global and local forces that result in glocalisation.

This brief literature review expounds the three paradigms of globalisation: clash of civilisations, McDonaldisation and hybridisation. Examples of how these paradigms have been applied in a tourism context are provided. While there have been individual applications of each of these paradigms, this paper explores comparisons and contrast examples of each of these paradigms across the common context of the Pacific to provide a contribution to knowledge.

Method

This study is constructivist in its nature (Crotty, 1998; Patton, 2001). It aims to explore and provide an in-depth understanding of a complex social phenomenon, that is, cultural change in the South Pacific. This qualitative study is informed by semi-structured in-depth interviews to allow flexibility for the researchers to react and explore themes emerging from participants in further detail (Jennings, 2011). Such research design is found most suitable to address research objectives, albeit qualitative exploratory studies may lack generalisability and objectivity (Bryman & Bell, 2011). The questions asked participants to provide their background. Participants were then asked to describe tourism impacts on their country as well as how tourism itself has evolved. Research participants were asked to reflect specifically on socio-cultural impacts of tourism. Consequently, participants reflected on the topics of modernisation, international relations, migration, education and employment. These topics allowed freedom for participants to express their opinions in relationship to different aspects of culture, not limited to heritage or representations of culture, but also related to worldviews, beliefs and values.

Fifty interviews with stakeholders representing government agencies, businesses, non-government organisations, community leaders and educators from Fiji (19 participants), Tonga (14 participants) and Cook Islands (17 participants) were conducted. Sixteen participants were female, fourteen were expatriates. See Appendix 1 for full profiles of research participants.

All interviews were conducted in English during July and August 2017. English is one of the official languages in all three countries, therefore there was no language barrier as all participants speak English. The researchers are not native to any of the three countries that are part of this research, which may be a hindrance as the researchers may not be aware of certain cultural practices. The participants' answers may have been different if the researchers were locals rather than outsiders. However, the researchers do not have bias towards any of the researched destinations and participants did not have to be wary of researchers being offended by participants' views regarding their culture. This research study has been approved by the ethics commit-tee of the university the corresponding author is affiliated with (reference number HSEARS20170531001-01).

Consent was sought of research participants to be interviewed and interviews to be audio-recorded. The audio-recorded interviews were then transcribed. The average length of an interview was around 1 h, however the interviews varied in length between 25 min and 2 h 6 min. NVivo qualitative data analysis computer software package was used to manage and analyse data. Thematic analysis was undertaken. Coding was conducted through open and axial coding. Besides the categories emerg-ing from the data, three themes related to paradigms of globalisation's impact on cul-tures were used, namely clash of civilisations, McDonaldisation and hybridisation. A total of 39 categories incorporating 497 codes have been identified. Cluster analysis using Jaccard's co-efficient has been undertaken to identify relationships between codes with particular focus on themes related to the three above mentioned para-digms. Jaccard's co-efficient is commonly applied to analyse the co-occurrence of codes in text and has been used for analysis of cultural concepts in the past (Levandowsky & Winter, 1971; Rogers, Feldman & Ehrlich, 2009).

Globalisation, tourism and culture of Pacific Island countries (PIC)

The following sections discuss impacts of globalisation on culture in the PIC from the three aforementioned paradigms of clash of civilisations, McDonaldisation and hybridisa-tion. The findings and discussion are presented as a narrative, based on the identified cat-egories related to each paradigm. In some cases one quote could be attributed to two paradigms, for example interviewees would reflect on past experience of an issue as a clash of civilisations, and the subsequent solution to that issue is hybridisation. The fol-lowing narrative avoids overlap and therefore issues that emerged in the analysis are allo-cated into only one of the sections. Images are provided to illustrate the discussed issues.

Clash of civilisations

Of the three paradigms, clash of civilisations reflects more participant comments than the other two. A total of 232 quotes from 48 participants relate to this paradigm. Clash of civilisations paradigm envisions clashes between Western and non-Western civilisations (Pieterse, 1996). Generally, the clash of civilisations paradigm focuses on geopolitics. However, the clash of beliefs, worldviews and behaviours indicates the paradigm also includes a cultural aspect.

Tourism interacts with PIC culture in multiple ways. Five participants specifically mentioned the so-called demonstration or imitation effect, where local residents imi-tate behaviours of tourists. The demonstration effect is a prominent concept in tour-ism, although it has attracted various critiques (Fisher, 2004b). As a result of the demonstration effect, new behaviours adopted by local residents from tourists (typic-ally by local people involved in the tourism industry) clash with the local lifestyle and culture. Participants from Tonga, suggest that the demonstration effect from diaspora Tongans who come to visit relatives is much stronger than from tourists. Tongans living in Tonga are more likely to adopt behaviours and attitudes of their relatives who live in New Zealand, Australia or elsewhere, rather than those of tourists who come to Tonga. Many Pacific Islanders work or have worked overseas. The importance of PIC diaspora in New Zealand is exemplified by inclusion of Pacific artefacts into exhibitions of one of the major national museums in New Zealand, the Auckland War Memorial Museum (see Figure 1). While the complexity of relationships between diaspora and Pacific Islanders living in home nations has been explored elsewhere (e.g. Connell, 2010), the demonstration effect studies appear to be limited to tourism and merit further investigation in migration and diaspora studies. Temporary and permanent mobilities of Pacific Islanders represent another important factor for cultural change, with possible clashes with traditional cultures. However, comparisons of the demonstration effect between the three groups, that is, conventional tourists; diaspora and migrant workers, are seldom made.

The tourism sector requires Pacific Islanders to adjust their lifestyle and social practices. In this study, 47 participants commented on work issues as related to the clash of civilisations. Most of these comments related to tourism jobs requiring work according to a schedule, that is, for a certain number of hours every week, making it difficult to fulfil certain traditional obligations, for example, attending a funeral of a distant relative. Work ethic issues (e.g. not showing up at work, being late) were raised by 17 participants representative of all three countries; 14 of them are private sector managers, nine are expatriates and eight are native citizens of these countries. Economic relations are not dominant in PIC. Rather, social relationships are more important in PIC. However, tourism work necessitates this attitude to be changed so staff are available at all times to ensure products and services can be consistently provided. The work ethic issues are not limited

Figure 1. PICs exhibits at Auckland War Memorial Museum.
Source: Authors.

to tourism and can be applied across various industries. However, they are especially evident in tourism as expectations of managers and tourists for punctuality at work clash with local attitudes to hospitality. Hospitality is a social phenomenon in PIC rather than a business model. Life priorities are more social rather than career oriented for Pacific Islanders. An expatriate academic in Cook Islands explains this as follows:

> There is a phenomenon here: people will produce enough to meet some specific need, they don't mind doing a little bit every day, or a month or particular part of the year, but they will not engage in a workshop production, because they get enough money to satisfy their need. And then they stop. The market is not dominant. They engage in the market to meet a particular need … They are not wage slaves. They're not lazy. They have a very sensible attitude towards life and money isn't everything, work isn't everything. It's a balance of those things.

Another clash between the culture of PIC studied here and demands of the tourism sector is religion, especially observing the Sabbath. For example, residents of Aitutaki, Cook Islands, protest flights arriving on Sundays, because no work should be done on the Sabbath (see Figure 2). Similar issues are prominent in Tonga. While the tourism sector demands full operation every day, cultural practice demands restraining from work on Sundays. An expatriate private sector representative in Cook Islands expressed the following:

Figure 2. A protest sign in Aitutaki, Cook Islands.
Source: Authors.

Sunday in the last few years is so different from the Sundays before. Nothing used to happen on Sundays. People were relaxing because they worked six days a week. They believed the seventh day was for rest and now Air New Zealand brings in the planes on Sundays. And it's one of our busiest days and it is playing havoc on a cultural fabric of the Cook Islands.

In all three countries, additional factors disincentivise participation in regular tourism-related work. Land tenure system is one of the important issues of tourism development in the Pacific (Scheyvens & Russell, 2012). The communal landownership system requires foreign investors to lease land from local residents. In Fiji, the resorts contribute to infra-structure, education and employment of communities on whose land the resorts are built. According to participants from Tonga, seasonal farm work in New Zealand attracts many Tongans, who may not wish to work in the part of the year they spend in Tonga. The Cook Islands provide more attractive salaries than most other Pacific Islands, therefore there is a growth of skilled Fijian workers in the Cook Islands, contributing to a shortage of human resources in Fiji's hospitality sector. The Cook Islands also attract workers from other countries to work in tourism and hospitality, notably the Philippines. Together with the existing expatriate communities from New Zealand, Australia and other countries, the multicultural makeup of Cook Islands society is considered a negative. The issue of ethni-city is also relevant for Fiji, as there are two large ethnic groups living in Fiji, native *iTaukei* and Indo-Fijians. There has been political tension between the two groups that previously contributed to military coups. The tourism marketing of Fiji largely portrays the native Fijians, while Indo-Fijian culture is less visible. According to participants from private sector, Indo-Fijians are more likely to occupy back-of-house positions, while iTaukei are more likely to work in the front-of-house. Migration of people to and from the PIC studied in this paper, appears to contribute to difficulties regarding human resources and marketing of tourism, albeit this is only a part of broader issue of adapting to a globalised multicultural environment that many societies struggle with (Cohen, Duncan, & Thulemark, 2015).

Participants suggest that despite an extensive history of international assistance, training programmes and consultancies, overseas agencies aiming to help develop tourism in PIC lack understanding of the aforementioned cultural issues. An expatriate private sector participant suggests the following:

> Consultants have been brought in many, many times, but the consultants also unfortunately lack the knowledge of local traditions, cultures, the way they do things, and very often doesn't take those efficiently into account. Of course they come and ask the Tongans that they speak to how should I do this, how should I do that, and very often it's the Tongans themselves that don't fully understand the whole picture.

Clashes of cultures that affect PIC now include not only Western tourists and Pacific Islanders, but also non-Western tourists (often, but not only, Chinese tourists). Participants from different stakeholder groups in Fiji suggest PIC became accustomed to tourists from major Western markets, for example, Australia, New Zealand and the US, however the entry of new lucrative non-traditional non-western markets, for example China and Russia, is posing a new challenge. An educator from Fiji mentioned the following:

> I hear that [Name of a Resort] is building a whole new other side of their hotel that will just cater for Chinese. But it will be an enclave that would be cut-off from the rest, because yet again when they try to mix markets, it didn't work and their main Australian market just boycotted them… Other luxury resorts that have entered these markets compare the Chinese to the Russians. You know, they find them very difficult to deal with

Figure 3. Chinese workers working on a resort development funded by Chinese investors in Fiji.
Source: Authors.

and so what they have done is that they book off certain weeks and it's all Chinese or all Russian.

A similar situation is reflected in trade and international relations. PIC are experiencing geopolitical challenges between Western countries, China, Japan and other major powers (Cheer et al., 2018). Various participants in this research, across the three countries, are suspicious of their own governments' deals with various foreign countries (see Figure 3). This is especially evident when discussing foreign aid. When questioned about motives of foreign powers in providing assistance to the Cook Islands, a participant from a tourism business said the following: 'They want our fishing rights. We are very suspicious of Spanish, Chinese, Taiwanese and Japanese people coming here'. Therefore, a revision of political economy (e.g. Britton, 1982; Milne, 1992) and research on geopolitics of tourism in PIC (Cheer et al., 2018) is timely.

All of the above examples demonstrate the power dynamic whereby the outside culture attempts to subjugate the local culture. While the tourism sector may appear rather powerful, the above examples demonstrate the resilience of local residents in protecting their lifestyle even though this may diminish economic opportunities.

McDonaldisation

McDonaldisation, Disneyfication or Hollywoodisation of culture refers to homogenisation, standardisation, rationalisation and commodification of culture usually driven by multinational corporations (Liu, 2003; Pieterse, 1996; Weaver, 2005). A total of 93 quotes from 39 participants are attributed to this paradigm. They cover fewer issues than Clashes of Civilisations and predominantly relate to issues of cultural preservation and commodification. Generally, this paradigm is concerned with the loss of genuine cultural practices in tradition in favour of commercially successful demonstrations of culture.

Figure 4. A *Moana* poster at the Royal Agricultural & Fisheries Show in Tonga.
Source: Authors.

PICs are currently experiencing a wave of literal Disneyfication after the release of an animated film *Moana*. Critics of the film have pointed out that Polynesian cultures have been reduced to a single monoculture, which degrades the diversity of Pacific Island peoples (NBC News, 2016). For example, the movie trailer includes Fijian music, Tahitian drumming, and Samoan tattoos. But the movie portrays a single Polynesia. Ka'ili (2016) notes that the Disneyfication of Polynesian tales results in inaccurate and incomplete simplified accounts of indigenous myths that are profoundly multifaceted. *Moana* is nevertheless used by local entrepreneurs to promote their products (see Figure 4).

Research participants express concern over the homogenisation of culture. An expatriate participant from private sector in Fiji, where the majority of the native population is Melanesian, states the following:

> It's more and more of this fire dance, Polynesian singing, and swinging fire dancing, and hula dances, which is South Pacific. It's the Disneyfication, Moana view of the South Pacific... The iTaukei [native Fijian] culture is at risk of being sidelined for other Polynesian cultures just because they're sexy, and we're going to get less and less meke [traditional dance] in the villages, less and less meke in the resorts, and overall less and less cultural meke across the country.

In the Cook Islands, concerns are raised regarding the preservation of dances and performances. A community leader and a private sector operator both observed that the dances have changed not only in performances displayed to tourists, but also in festivals for Cook Islanders. Performance groups are increasingly creative in striving to impress, rather than to preserve traditional culture (see Figure 5). A native Cook Islander from the private sector expressed it as follows:

Figure 5. A cultural show in Rarotonga, Cook Islands (left) and a fire dance in Tonga (right). Source: Authors.

> A classic example is last week: Te Maeva Nui [lit. The Big Celebration, a festival celebrating Cook Islands Constitution]. It's supposed to be our traditional … a celebration for the Cook Islanders, but now they've made it as a big tourist attraction … Back in the day, we used to use just the grass skirt, that would do. But now we've taken the grass skirt, made it look pretty, because some of the audience said 'you need to put some bling on that, some paint, then we'll come and watch you'. Sure enough, everybody has upped their game and made all this pretty stuff. Put on the feathers. We don't have feathers here.

Not only tourism and popular culture contribute to the homogenisation of the culture in the Pacific. For example, one participant mentioned cultural exchange through the Festival of Pacific Arts, which showcases culture from various PIC. Some participating groups borrow elements or techniques they observe during the festival and include them into their repertoire when they return home. Performance groups strive to impress, however it may well be that similar types of dance, moves, dresses or accessories are most 'impressive', thus contributing to the homogenisation of culture. A native Tongan NGO representative commented the following:

> I noticed in the Pacific Arts Festival [a.k.a. Festival of the Pacific Arts] … You could see that some of the actions from that island has been picked up from another island. You can see that there has been some parts picked up by other countries. But at the same time, there is a similarity between us, remember that we are Polynesian (see Figure 5).

Handicrafts is another aspect of culture that can be discussed within the McDonaldisation paradigm. In Tonga, replicas of Maui's [a demi-God from Polynesian mythology and one of the main characters in *Moana*] fishhook, have become prominent souvenirs. It is not clear to what extent handicrafts are affected by such Disneyfication and whether there should be a concern, as Disneyfied handicrafts are often made using traditional skills by local people. Eighteen participants discussed handicrafts and souvenirs, but rarely reflected on whether the designs were traditional. Most of the concerns of participants related to preservation of skills and use of traditional materials when making traditional clothing or woodcarving. In essence, the importance is placed on the preservation of skills as intangible cultural heritage, rather than on the appearance of the tangible artefacts. One native Fijian community leader explained that even at a village level instead of producing artefacts, local residents may opt to purchase imported souvenirs and resell them:

> One thing I must mention that unfortunately, most of the things that are sold here, they buy from Nadi. You know, cheaply made in the Philippines. I know the ladies organisation, they try to bring in people that are experts in the traditional artefacts, some come in and learn, but some prefer just to go to Nadi and buy and sell, which is unfortunate.

The theme of migration to some extent fits the McDonaldisation paradigm for the Cook Islands in particular. As previously described, there has been an influx of foreign labour to fill the labour gap in tourism sector. Many workers are from Fiji. Participants see native Cook Islands Maori people, and their culture, as one of the major tourist attractions. Therefore, the fact that Melanesian Fijian workers service tourists and not the Polynesian Cook Islanders may be interpreted as an inauthentic tourist experience. One expatriate private sector representative said that Fijian staff have to say *Kia Orana* [a local Maori greeting] instead of *Bula* [a Fijian] greeting. Moreover, that participant expressed the following concern:

> We are at a tipping point now, with the Filipino staff and the Fijians… Especially, the Filipino staff, they are most amazing workers. And of course they are here and they don't have to go to funerals and that. They tick all the boxes, except the fact people come here to see Cook Islanders not Filipinos…

The use of local greetings in Fiji and Cook Islands is also seen as McDonaldisation by some participants. One native Cook Islands private sector participant expressed this as part of a lack of understanding of use of culture in tourism, while discussing preservation of local culture:

> What are central elements of the social-cultural milieu that is attractive to tourists? What are those? Because those are the things you lose, if you are not careful. I don't see enough work being done there. For example, you go to Hawaii, and I hated when I listened to the tour guide say 'Aloha, Aloha!', and then 'Bula!' in Fiji. Here they're 'Kia Orana! Kia Orana!' I guess it's okay to do it because it's a greeting, but behind there… What are the central elements?

Nevertheless, while there were 18 categorically negative references to McDonaldisation, eight were positive. Despite changes in dances to make them more appealing to tourists or other cultural manifestations which lack authenticity, seven participants from various backgrounds suggested tourism motivates young generations to learn cultural practices and thus preserves traditional skills and knowledge. Tourism adds an economic value to culture and provides jobs that young people of the PIC need (see Figure 6). A native Tongan academic suggested the following:

> Some of those cultural activities are being performed and maintained mainly because of the tourist dollar. I mean, if we didn't have that demand, the tourists coming in, we'd probably still do it, but let's say once or twice a year. But because there's a demand, there's a financial reward out of it.

Overall, the research participants raise concerns about how culture is represented in tourism and how that affects what cultural practices are preserved and thrive. There are

Figure 6. A young Cook Islands Maori demonstrating a traditional craft to tourists (left) and a Fijian warrior meeting tourists on a village tour (right).
Source: Authors.

signs of homogenisation of culture with respect to the performances in PIC that are consumed by tourists, but also locals. The concern that participants raise is that the culture presented to tourists eventually replaces the genuine traditional culture. The concerns are also mostly related to intangible heritage, that is, knowledge and skills. Not only tourism is at fault in homogenisation of culture in PIC. As research participants explain, some cultural practices are borrowed from other islands simply because they are generally more attractive to both locals and tourists. However, tourism not only brings negative impacts in this regard, commodification of culture places a value on that culture, thus stimulating its preservation through the creation of economic opportunities.

Hybridisation

Pieterse's (2015) perspective is that in a globalised world cultures are not static, they travel and evolve, interact and create hybrids. Comments from participants that relate to such interactions and hybrids of cultures are grouped under the hybridisation paradigm. A total of 123 comments from 43 participants are considered as such. Many of these comments are related to the evolution of Pacific Island culture, changes that are experienced in both culture and tourism domains and in representation of PIC as modern countries integrated into global community.

   Participants of this study often expressed several contrasting opinions at the same time. On the one hand, they do not want to lose the traditions and to some extent are nostalgic about the past. On the other hand, they embrace modernisation and connectedness to the world. Pacific Islanders from Fiji, Tonga and the Cook Islands are generally well-travelled and have personal connections overseas either through their education, work, family ties or personal networks. An expatriate private sector participant from Tonga had concerns about cultural impacts as follows:

   This idea of retaining primitive, is what people are really talking about here as a
   manifestation of cultural things … Is it really trying to say that people should be

encapsulated in a time warp and just be kept there? I call that a zoological approach ... I mean, people go to these countries to look at the animals in the zoo. Except that these animals are two-legged.

Pieterse (1996) suggests that often changes that take place in a culture are superficial. The essence of the culture, that is worldviews and beliefs, is less affected. A government representative from Fiji provides the following comment reflecting this:

I don't want the whole thing to be moved from traditional straight to modern, because I think that there are some traditional aspects that needs to be kept, because that defines uniqueness. I am different from the next boy to me in the village, because of how I speak, how I see the world ... But in terms of marketing of that, in terms of saving the environment through modern technology, I am all for that.

Technological advancements, especially the Internet, have brought the world closer together. They provide many new opportunities, but contribute to modernisation of traditional societies, and thus their cultures. Tourists in this case, are seen as seeking an experience of traditional lifestyles that are perceived as authentic and may be disappointed that Pacific Islanders do not walk around in traditional dress every day and do not live in a *bure/fale* [traditional house]. Instead, they are compelled to do so for tourists, for example during the village tours (see Figure 6).

Tourism as a medium of cultural exchange between people is acknowledged by ten participants. A native Tongan participant from an NGO sees the role of tourism as follows:

I believe that the impact of tourism is good for some of our [Pacific Island] countries. It makes our attitude more positive in accepting people, improves our customer service level, it improves our understanding of different cultures and acceptance of other cultures. So, it makes you a better person.

How Pacific culture will evolve in the future is dependent on the younger generations. Participants from all three countries raise concerns regarding young people's interest in their culture and passing the knowledge on to them. As the previous section suggests, tourism may stimulate the younger generation's interest in traditional culture as tourism adds an economic value to traditional skills and knowledge. However, the migration of young people from PIC overseas is seen as a threat and participants generally do not believe tourism jobs are attractive enough to persuade young people to stay in their communities. The prices tourists are prepared to pay and the wages offered by employers do not satisfy many Pacific Island youth, who find it more economically viable and prestigious to migrate and work in other industries. At the same time, participants suggest that communal structures and extended families ensure most of population is protected from severe material poverty.

In the Cook Islands in particular, and to a lesser extent in Fiji and Tonga, concerns are raised regarding young people's knowledge of native languages. Because the education system operates in English, communication with tourists is in English and many young people want to migrate to English speaking countries, participants are worried that native languages may be threatened. A native Cook Islands public sector representative expressed the fast change in the society and the concern regarding the local language as follows:

The lifestyle is moving so fast. And basically because of New Zealand, we're exposed to New Zealand, to Australia, to the States. And we have high-tech ... We see what's happening overseas and they bring it over here, easy. Easy. And it is changing our mentality and the way we react to what is around us. You see, a lot of people have very little understand of our local language.

Such dramatic changes that take existing cultures in a new direction can be thought of as revolutionary rather than evolutionary. As identified by the research participants in Cook Islands the pace of socio-cultural change is too fast, due to rapid growth of tourism as well as intensity of globalisation through other means including technology.

The continuous evolution of culture and the global melange Pieterse (2015) discusses, can be exemplified in the PIC by their adoption of rugby as a national sport, or Western-style cooking of traditional foods (see Figure 7). Moreover, Christianity is another relevant example of the evolution and change in culture. Prior to the arrival of Christianity and colonisation of much of the Pacific, Pacific Islanders did not cover up their bodies. As Christian beliefs took hold in the Pacific, it became indecent to wear little or no clothes. Now tourists, often from the same countries where Christian missionaries came from, arrive in the Pacific and wear revealing dresses and swimsuits. The following quote from a native community leader in the Cook Islands expresses this as follows:

> We didn't wear skimpy clothes on the road 20 years ago, that was not seen. But now the tourists come in with their swim tops, because maybe it's hot, or how they feel. And it's accepted now. I know there have been notices in the accommodation areas, and in the tourism pamphlets asking tourists not to wear anything too revealing as well. Once upon

Figure 7. Grilled mahi-mahi with coconut lime sauce and breadfruit chips served at a restaurant in Tonga.
Source: Authors.

a time, we were not wearing clothes, and, the Christian missionaries came and told us 'you've got to cover yourself', and then later on they come with no clothes on!

It is important to note that Pacific Islanders are not victims of globalisation and modernisation processes. They do have a choice on which aspects of globalisation to adopt and how to adapt to the constantly changing world. An expatriate academic in the Cook Islands expresses this as follows:

> It's a constant process of evolution depending on the context that you find yourself in, and Cook Islanders do it very well. In terms of this agency determination thing they're very strong on the side of being active agents in what they're doing, you know what I mean? They are not victims of processes.

Generally, research participants acknowledge that cultures evolve and the processes of cultural change are seen positively. The research participants believe integration in the globalised world benefits Pacific Islanders as long as the change is controlled, occurs with Pacific Islanders agency over it, and the pace is not too rapid. However, this should not undermine issues related to preservation of culture that have been discussed in clash of civilisations and McDonaldisation sections. Preservation of unique aspects of local culture and transmitting that culture to younger generations remains of great concern.

Discussion

Participants of this study have raised various themes regarding cultural changes in Fiji, Tonga and the Cook Islands. The three countries have different population sizes, historic backgrounds and level of tourism development, however most comments appear similar. One distinctive difference is that the Cook Islands, a country in Free Association with New Zealand and with the smallest population of the three selected PIC, has higher concerns regarding the native Maori culture. Free movement for both tourism and migration between New Zealand and the Cook Islands contributes to younger generations having less interest in either their culture or in staying in the Cook Islands.

With reference to Pieterse's (1996) three paradigms of globalisation and in the context of the selected PIC, clash of civilisations paradigm seems to fit early encounters with a different culture, while hybridisation is what eventually occurs as PIC adapt to new circumstances. The process of clash and adaptation is ongoing in a same way as the evolution of culture that results from intermingling of cultures (Pieterse, 2015). Changing tourism markets and international relations require adaptation as exemplified by the strengthening relations between China and the PIC (Cheer et al., 2018).

Modernist views about the effects of globalisation on culture, typically view people living in developing countries as passive recipients of change (Pieterse, 1996). This applies for both classical modernisation theory and neo-Marxist dependency theory of development. The first theory suggests that societies move from traditional to modern in a linear progression. The latter theory suggests that developing countries (i.e. the periphery) are culturally dependent on the developed countries (i.e. the core), often former colonial powers, and the culture of the developing countries loses its authenticity and is replaced by that of the core (Peet & Hartwick, 2015). Tourism in such context is seen as a driving force of modernisation and loss of authentic culture (Canavan,

2016; Fisher, 2004a; Jaakson, 2004). This is however not the perception of most participants of this study irrespective of their place of origin or occupation.

Participants of this study are aware of the external pressures on their societies, however they want to be part of the global community, and see many benefits in modern technology and being connected with the rest of the world. Residents of the selected PIC are highly mobile, are educated, do not experience severe material poverty and have relatives living overseas. Lee & Francis (2009) demonstrate various aspects of transnationalism of the PIC, including migration, diaspora, business and governance. In such a setting, access to information and migration are at least as important influences on cultural change as tourism.

Pacific Islanders have an agency over the cultural changes in their communities. The preference is generally towards modernisation of infrastructure and communications. However, participants prefer to preserve traditional social structures and knowledge. Participants note that younger generations are less interested in learning traditional skills, and thus tourism is seen as beneficial in preserving the culture. Tourism as a means of revaluation of traditional culture among youth has been previously identified elsewhere (e.g. Medina, 2003). Nevertheless, the anthropology of youth and study of culture provides many avenues for continued research (Bucholtz, 2002). In the Pacific context, youth culture research is often focused on youth-at-risk (Schoone, 2010), thus a more holistic research into young Pacific Islanders' attitudes towards traditional culture would be beneficial.

Participants are rather pragmatic regarding the issues of cultural authenticity, as they suggest that even though cultural expressions may be less authentic as a response to tourist demands, it is nevertheless better than losing the skills and knowledge of cultural expressions entirely. Participants feel they have less control over the homogenisation of Pacific culture through its representation in the popular media and through the constructed tourist image of the Pacific (Pratt, 2013). However, Pacific Islanders also contribute to this as evidenced by evolution of dances across the Pacific with more 'impressive' dance moves and costumes being borrowed and adopted not only for tourist consumption, but also for the consumption of Pacific Islanders themselves.

Undoubtedly, Pacific Island cultures constantly change and evolve. This process is not necessarily negative, as participants expressed positive opinions about many of the changes occurring. Tourism plays a role in this process on par with other influences, such as other types of mobilities, migration, diaspora, geopolitical change, technology and popular culture (Figure 8).

One dimension that explains the imitation effect is the intensity of contact between the cultures. As research participants suggest, the migration of Pacific Islanders and the communication between the diaspora and the family in PIC is more likely to affect cultural practices than interactions with tourists, as interactions with relatives who live overseas or spend a certain period of time living overseas provide a more intensive interaction with another culture. While the Pacific Island diaspora relations have been extensively studied, such cultural influences of diaspora on the Islands appear less studied than remittances and gift exchanges (Connell, 2010). Jeuring & Diaz-Soria's (2017) conceptualisation of visiting friends and relatives as simultaneously hosts and guests may be useful in further research. Interactions with tourists are also less frequent than, for example, interaction with the world through technology. Popular media and adoption of more

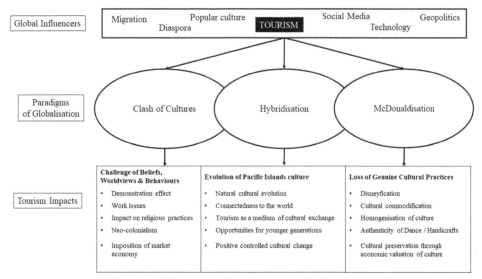

Figure 8. Impacts of Tourism and Globalisation on the Culture of selected PICs.
Source: Authors.

expressive cultural practices lead to homogenisation of PIC cultures both for tourist and internal consumption. The influence of popular culture, in particular popular music, has been studied by Alexeyeff (2004), who suggests Pacific Islanders are anxious about the loss of authentic local music due to globalisation.

The pace of cultural change is also important. PIC have adapted to Australian and New Zealand tourists, the two major tourist markets, which have generally grown steadily over time in Fiji. However, the rapid recent growth of the Chinese tourist market and investment from China diminishes the sense of control and requires a rather more rapid adjustment. As suggested by Cheer et al. (2018), the impact of such geo-political changes on tourism development requires further investigation. At the same time, the rapid growth of the New Zealand tourist market in the Cook Islands still places a lot of strain on the Cook Islands, largely due to the small land and population size. The agency of local people over any change is vitally important. In recognising that change is inevitable, what changes do take place need to be decided by the local population. Therefore, it is important for local residents collectively to have the capacity to withstand the negative changes while embracing the positive influences of globalisation, for example, knowledge and understanding of other cultures and people of different backgrounds.

Conclusion

This study discusses the relationship between the culture of the Pacific Islands and tourism from three different paradigms of globalisation, namely, clash of civilisations, McDonaldisation and hybridisation. This allows identification of the issues of concern among the Pacific Islanders with regards to preservation of their cultural uniqueness, as well as demonstrating the positive impacts of tourism and globalisation on local culture.

This study contributes theoretically to the body of knowledge through applying Pieterse's (1996) three paradigms of globalization and culture to tourism, in general and more specifically to Pacific Island Countries. While previous research has highlighted some of the effects of tourism's socio-cultural impacts, especially on host communities, such as the demonstration effect and the commodification of culture, this research systematically highlights these effects and others, through these three paradigms. Further, the findings of this research discuss the complex and multifaceted impact that globalisation has on host communities. Participants recognise that, while tourism has an influence on their (host) culture (sometimes for the better, sometimes for the worse), it is only one influence. Given that culture is dynamic, it is not possible to say one impact is because of tourism and another impact is due to other factors. The influences occur simultaneously and in varying degrees at different times. It is too reductionist to attribute various changes to one single factor. Therefore from a practical point of view, it is not appropriate for outsiders (e.g. researchers) to argue that culture needs to be preserved; rather there should advocacy for local communities to have the agency to decide for themselves which parts of their culture they want to maintain and pass down to further generations, which parts of their culture they want to adapt or hybridise and which parts of their culture they want to change. In terms of tourism, local ownership and local senior management of tourism businesses help maintain such agency. There is a strong sense of community in the three countries analysed in this paper, which helps protect the culture, although additional efforts may be required to ensure there is enough capacity in communities to maintain traditions and educate youth. Further efforts are required in terms of youth education, both at national level and community level. As the results have shown, Pacific Islanders are aware of the changes their nations are undergoing, and generally PIC have resilient cultures, despite various global influences.

Tourism is only one element affecting the cultures of PIC, others being types of mobilities, migration, diaspora, geopolitical change, technology and popular culture. However, to date comparative studies that discuss impacts of all these factors on culture are rare. Tourism and human geography studies would benefit from further investigations of combined impacts of these forces on cultures. Further research should focus on the intersection between geopolitics, tourism and cultural clashes not only between Western and non-Western civilisations, but also using other geopolitical divisions. While general ideas of McDonaldisation of culture are clearly presented, the process of adoption and internalisation of a homogenised culture by Pacific Islanders merits further investigation. Hybridisation of culture also requires further research to understand how to manage tourism in a culturally responsible manner.

Disclosure statement

No potential conflict of interest was reported by the authors.

ORCID

Denis Tolkach ⓘ http://orcid.org/0000-0002-8820-7764
Stephen Pratt ⓘ http://orcid.org/0000-0002-6550-132X

References

Alexeyeff, K. (2004). Sea breeze: Globalisation and Cook Islands popular music. *The Asia Pacific Journal of Anthropology*, *5*(2), 145–158. doi:10.1080/1444221042000247689

Ateljevic, I., & Doorne, S. (2003). Culture, economy and tourism commodities: Social relations of production and consumption. *Tourist Studies*, *3*(2), 123–141. doi:10.1177/1468797603041629

Britton, S. G. (1982). The political economy of tourism in the Third World. *Annals of Tourism Research*, *9*(3), 331–358. doi:10.1016/0160-7383(82)90018-4

Bryman, A., & Bell, E. (2011). *Business research methods* (3rd ed.). New York: Oxford University Press Inc.

Bucholtz, M. (2002). Youth and cultural practice. *Annual review of anthropology*, *31*(1), 525–552.

Buettner, E. (2008). "Going for an Indian": South Asian restaurants and the limits of multicultural-ism in Britain. *The Journal of Modern History*, *80*(4), 865–901.

Burr, A. (2006). The freedom of slaves to walk the streets: Celebration, spontaneity and revelry versus logistics at the Notting Hill Carnival. In D. Picard & M. Robinson (Eds.), *Festivals, tourism and social change: Remaking worlds* (pp. 84–98). Bristol, UK: Channel View Publications.

Canavan, B. (2016). Tourism culture: Nexus, characteristics, context and sustainability. *Tourism Management*, *53*, 229–243. doi:10.1016/j.tourman.2015.10.002

Chang, T. C., & Pang, J. (2017). Between universal spaces and unique places: heritage in Universal Studios Singapore. *Tourism Geographies*, *19*(2), 208–226.

Carnegie, E., & Smith, M. (2006). Mobility, diaspora and the hybridisation of festivity: The case of the Edinburgh Mela. In D. Picard & M. Robinson (Eds.), *Festivals, tourism and social change: Remaking worlds* (pp. 255–268). Bristol, UK: Channel View Publications.

Cave, J., Ryan, C., & Panakera, C. (2003). Residents' perceptions, migrant groups and culture as an attraction—The case of a proposed Pacific Island cultural centre in New Zealand. *Tourism Management*, *24*(4), 371–385. doi:10.1016/S0261-5177(02)00110-3

Cheer, J. M., Pratt, S., Tolkach, D., Bailey, A., Taumoepeau, S., & Movono, A. (2018). Tourism in Pacific island countries: A status quo round-up. *Asia & The Pacific Policy Studies*, *5*(3), 442–461. doi:10.1002/app5.250

Cohen, S. A., Duncan, T., & Thulemark, M. (2015). Lifestyle mobilities: The crossroads of travel, leisure and migration. *Mobilities*, *10*(1), 155–172. doi:10.1080/17450101.2013.826481

Connell, J. (2010). Pacific islands in the global economy: Paradoxes of migration and culture. *Singapore Journal of Tropical Geography*, *31*(1), 115–129.

Crocombe, R. (2001). *The south Pacific*. Suva, Fiji: University of the South Pacific.

Crotty, M. (1998). *The foundations of social research: Meaning and perspective in the research process*. California: Sage.

Deery, M., Jago, L., & Fredline, L. (2012). Rethinking social impacts of tourism research: A new research agenda. *Tourism Management*, *33*(1), 64–73.

Fisher, D. (2004a). A colonial town for neocolonial tourism. In C. M. Hall & H. Tucker (Eds.), *Tourism and postcolonialism: Contested discourses, identities and representations* (pp. 126–139). London: Routledge.

Fisher, D. (2004b). The demonstration effect revisited. *Annals of Tourism Research, 31*(2), 428–446. doi:10.1016/j.annals.2004.01.001

Giampiccoli, A. (2003). Hegemony, globalisation and tourism policies in developing countries. In Y. Reisinger & L. W. Turner (Eds.), *Cross-cultural behaviour in tourism: Concepts and analysis* (pp. 175–191). Oxford, United Kingdom: Butterworth-Heinemann.

Gottdiener, M. (2000). *New forms of consumption: Consumers, culture, and commodification*. Lanham, Maryland, United States: Rowman & Littlefield.

Harrison, D., & Pratt, S. (2013). Tourism in Pacific Island Countries. In C. Cooper (Ed.), *Contemporary tourism reviews* (pp. 1–24). Oxford, UK: Goodfellows Publishers.

Hottola, P. (2004). Culture confusion: Intercultural adaptation in tourism. *Annals of Tourism Research, 31*(2), 447–466. doi:10.1016/j.annals.2004.01.003

Huntington, S. P. (1993). The clash of civilizations? *Foreign Affairs, 72*(3), 22–49. doi:10.2307/20045621

Jaakson, R. (2004). Globalisation and neocolonialist tourism. In C. M. Hall & H. Tucker (Eds.), *Tourism and postcolonialism: Contested discourses, identities and representations* (pp. 169–183). London: Routledge.

Jacobsen, J. K. S. (2003). The tourist bubble and the Europeanisation of holiday travel. *Journal of Tourism and Cultural Change, 1*(1), 71–87. doi:10.1080/14766820308668160

Jennings, G. (2011). *Tourism research* (2nd ed.). Milton: John Wiley & Sons Australia, Ltd.

Jeuring, J., & Diaz-Soria, I. (2017). Introduction: proximity and intraregional aspects of tourism. *Tourism Geographies, 19*(1), 4–8.

Ka'ili, T. O. (2016). Goddess Hina: The missing heroine from Disney's Moana. Retrieved July 17, 2018. Retrieved from https://www.huffingtonpost.com/entry/goddess-hina-the-missing-heroine-from-disney%CA%BCs-moana_us_5839f343e4b0a79f7433b6e5

Kavolis, V. (1988). Contemporary moral cultures and "the return of the sacred". *Sociological Analysis, 49*(3), 203–216. doi:10.2307/3711585

Kirtsoglou, E., & Theodossopoulos, D. (2004). 'They are taking our culture away': Tourism and culture commodification in the Garifuna community of Roatan. *Critique of Anthropology, 24*(2), 135–157. doi:10.1177/0308275X04042650

Lee, H., & Francis, S. T. (Eds.). (2009). *Migration and transnationalism: Pacific perspectives*. Canberra: ANU Press.

Levandowsky, M., & Winter, D. (1971). Distance between sets. *Nature, 234*(5323), 34.

Lew, A., & Kennedy, C. (2002). Tourism and culture clash in Indian country. In S. Krakover & Y. Gradus (Eds.), *Tourism in frontier areas* (pp. 259–282). Lexington, KY: Lexington Books.

Liu, Z. (2003). Sustainable tourism development: A critique. *Journal of Sustainable Tourism, 11*(6), 459–475. doi:10.1080/09669580308667216

Macleod, D. (2006). Cultural commodification and tourism: A very special relationship. *Tourism Culture & Communication, 6*(2), 71–84. doi:10.3727/109830406777410580

Macleod, D., & Carrier, J. G. (2009). *Tourism, power and culture: Anthropological insights*. Bristol, UK: Channel View Publications.

McKercher, B. (2002). Towards a classification of cultural tourists. *International Journal of Tourism Research, 4*(1), 29–38. doi:10.1002/jtr.346

Medina, L. K. (2003). Commoditizing culture: Tourism and Maya identity. *Annals of tourism research, 30*(2), 353–368.

Milne, S. (1992). Tourism and development in South Pacific microstates. *Annals of Tourism Research, 19*(2), 191–212. doi:10.1016/0160-7383(92)90077-3

Mowforth, M., & Munt, I. (2015). *Tourism and sustainability: Development, globalisation and new tourism in the third world* (4th ed.). London: Routledge.

NBC News. (2016). Critics accuse Disney of 'culture theft' ahead of 'Moana' release. Retrieved from https://www.nbcnews.com/news/asian-america/critics-accuse-disney-culture-theft-ahead-moana-release-n685866

Nunkoo, R., & Ramkissoon, H. (2016). Stakeholders' views of enclave tourism: A grounded theory approach. *Journal of Hospitality & Tourism Research*, *40*(5), 557–558. doi:10.1177/1096348013503997

Patton, M. Q. (2001). *Qualitative research & evaluation methods* (3rd ed.). Thousand Oaks, CA: SAGE Publications, Inc.

Peet, R., & Hartwick, E. (2015). *Theories of development: Contentions, arguments, alternatives*. New York: Guilford Publications.

Pieterse, J. N. (1995). Globalisation as hybridisation. In M. Featherstone, S. Lash, & R. Robertson (Eds.), *Global modernities* (pp. 45–68). London: Sage.

Pieterse, J. N. (1996). Globalisation and culture: Three paradigms. *Economic and Political Weekly*, *31*(23), 1389–1393.

Pieterse, J. N. (2015). *Globalization and culture: Global mélange*. Lanham, MD: Rowman & Littlefield.

Pratt, S. (2013). Same, same but different: Perceptions of South Pacific destinations among Australian travelers. *Journal of Travel & Tourism Marketing*, *30*(6), 595–609.

Ritzer, G. (2004). *The McDonaldisation of society* (revised New Century edition ed.). Thousand Oaks, CA: Pine Forge Press.

Ritzer, G., & Liska, A. (1997). "McDisneyization" and "Post-Tourism": complementary perspectives on contemporary tourism. In C. Rojek & J. Urry (Eds.), *Touring cultures: Transformations of travel and theory* (pp. 96–109). London: Routledge.

Rogers, D. S., Feldman, M. W., & Ehrlich, P. R. (2009). Inferring population histories using cultural data. *Proceedings of the Royal Society B: Biological Sciences*, *276*(1674), 3835–3843.

Root, D. (2018). *Cannibal culture: Art, appropriation, and the commodification of difference* (Reprint ed.). London: Routledge.

Salazar, N. B. (2005). Tourism and glocalization "local" tour guiding. *Annals of Tourism Research*, *32*(3), 628–646. doi:10.1016/j.annals.2004.10.012

Scheyvens, R., & Russell, M. (2012). Tourism, land tenure and poverty alleviation in Fiji. *Tourism Geographies*, *14*(1), 1–25. doi:10.1080/14616688.2011.593188

Schoone, A. (2010). Re-scripting life: New Zealand-born Tongan'youth-at-risk'narratives of return migration. *Mai Review*, *1*, 1–11.

Shepherd, R. (2002). Commodification, culture and tourism. *Tourist Studies*, *2*(2), 183–201. doi:10.1177/146879702761936653

Swyngedouw, E. (2004). Globalisation or 'glocalisation'? Networks, territories and rescaling. *Cambridge Review of International Affairs*, *17*(1), 25–48. doi:10.1080/0955757042000203632

Trau, A. M. (2012). Beyond pro-poor tourism: (Re) interpreting tourism-based approaches to poverty alleviation in Vanuatu. *Tourism Planning & Development*, *9*(2), 149–164. doi:10.1080/21568316.2011.630750

Wahab, S., & Cooper, C. (2005). *Tourism in the age of globalisation*. London: Routledge.

Wallerstein, I. (1990). Culture as the ideological battleground of the modem world-system. In M. Featherstone (Ed.), *Global culture*. London: Sage.

Waters, M. (1995). *Globalization*. London: Routledge.

Weaver, A. (2005). The McDonaldization thesis and cruise tourism. *Annals of Tourism Research*, *32*(2), 346–366. doi:10.1016/j.annals.2004.07.005

Weaver, D. (2010). Indigenous tourism stages and their implications for sustainability. *Journal of Sustainable Tourism*, *18*(1), 43–60. doi:10.1080/09669580903072001

Wray, K., Espiner, S., & Perkins, H. C. (2010). Cultural clash: Interpreting established use and new tourism activities in protected natural areas. *Scandinavian Journal of Hospitality and Tourism*, *10*(3), 272–290. doi:10.1080/15022250.2010.496570

Zegre, S. J., Needham, M. D., Kruger, L. E., & Rosenberger, R. S. (2012). McDonaldization and commercial outdoor recreation and tourism in Alaska. *Managing Leisure*, *17*(4), 333–348. doi:10.1080/13606719.2012.711604

Appendix 1. Interviewee profiles

Country	Gender	Ethnic Background	Sector	Position	Year of arrival into the country	Year of initial involvement with tourism
Fiji	Male	iTaukei	Public	Department Director	Born	2016
	Female	iTaukei	Academia	Faculty	Born	1970s
	Female	iTaukei	Public	Department Director	Born	2000
	Male	European	Academia/Private	Fellow/Consultant	1998	1998
	Male	European	Private Tours	Managing Director	2006	2012
	Male	Chinese Fijian	Private Accommodation	Managing Director	Born	1969
	Female	iTaukei	Non-profit	Chief Executive	Born	1980s
	Male	iTaukei	Public	Chief Executive	Born	1991
	Male	iTaukei	Academia	Faculty	Born	1991
	Male	iTaukei	Public	Member of Parliament	Born	1968
	Male	iTaukei	Community	Community leader	Born	2012 (the village is involved in tourism since 1970s)
	Male	iTaukei	Public	Chief Executive	Born	1991
	Female	iTaukei	Community	Community Leader	Born	2015 (the village is involved in tourism since 1970s)
	Male	Indian Fijian	Private Tours	Owner	Born	1989
	Male	Australian	Private Accommodation	Owner	1989	1970s
	Male	Australian	Private Accommodation	Manager	2002	1982
	Male	Australian	Private Accommodation	General Manager	2015	1982
	Male	iTaukei	Private Accommodation	General Manager	Born	1989
	Female	iTaukei	Public	Manager	Born	1993
Tonga	Male	Tongan	Non-profit	Chief Executive	Born	1988
	Male	Tongan	Private Accommodation	Owner	Born	1995
	Male	Tongan	Private Accommodation	Owner	Born	1970s
	Male	European	Private Accommodation	Owner	1993	1993
	Male	New Zealand	Private Accommodation	Owner	1977	1979
	Female	Tongan	Public	Acting Chief Executive	Born	1999
	Female	Tongan	Private Tours	Manager	Born	1979
	Male	Tongan	Non-profit	Chair	Born	1997
	Male	New Zealand	Private Transport	General Manager	1979	1980
	Male	New Zealand	Private Tours	Owner	1985	1985
	Male	Tongan	Private Food Supplier	Owner	Born	2007
	Male	Tongan	Private Food & beverage	Owner	Born	1970s
	Female	Tongan	Public	Deputy Chief Executive	Born	2015
	Male	Tongan	Academia	Faculty	Born	1976

(continued)

Appendix 1. Continued.

Country	Gender	Ethnic Background	Sector	Position	Year of arrival into the country	Year of initial involvement with tourism
Cook Islands	Female	Cook Islands Maori	Private Accommodation	General Manager	Born	1992
	Male	Cook Islands Maori	Public	Clerk	Born	1987
	Male	Cook Islands Maori	Private Tours	Owner	Born	1992
	Female	Cook Islands Maori	Private Pearls	Owner	Born	1995
	Male	Cook Islands Maori / Fijian iTaukei	Public	Chief Executive	Born	1980s
	Male	New Zealand	Private Accommodation	Chief Executive	2002	1984
	Female	New Zealand	Private Accommodation	General Manager	2005	1987
	Female	Cook Islands Maori / Fijian iTaukei	Public	Policy Advisor	Born	2009
	Male	Australian	Academia	Faculty	1981	NA
	Male	European	Private Pearls	Owner	1992	1992
	Male	Cook Islands Maori / Fijian iTaukei	Public	CEO	Born	1980s
	Female	Cook Islands Maori / Fijian iTaukei	Private Lawyer	Lawyer	Born	1980s
	Female	New Zealand	Private Accommodation	Owner	1973	1972
	Female	Cook Islands	Public	Policy Advisor	Born	2005
	Male	Cook Islands	Private Accommodation	Owner	Born	1980s
	Female	Cook Islands	Public	Manager	Born	2002
	Male	Cook Islands	Private Accommodation	Owner	Born	1974

Critiques of island sustainability in tourism

Ilan Kelman

ABSTRACT

Island sustainability influences and is influenced by tourism resources, such as sun, sea, and sand for warm water destinations and ice and large mammals for cold water destinations. To understand better these influences, some critiques of island sustainability are examined with regard to their relevance for tourism, using principally theoretical discussion supported by empirical examples as exemplified through the small island developing states (SIDS) acronym, pristine nature, and climate change. Energy (including transportation) and waste management, being essential service sectors for tourism, are examined in terms of island sustainability. Tourism-relevant consequences and understandings of island sustainability, especially from island studies literature, cover conspicuous sustainability, the storyline of climate change destroying islands including 'last-chance tourism', and island assemblages. Branding and marketing feature, often trapping tourism into using island sustainability to achieve tourism goals irrespective of any sustainability goals succeeding. Although tourism using island sustainability is not inherently detrimental to tourism or to sustainability, it can distract and detract from working with islanders to seek sustainability including, but not limited to, tourism endeavours.

摘要

岛屿的可持续性影响并受旅游资源的影响, 比如温带水域的阳光、海水和沙滩以及寒带水域的冰山和大型哺乳动物。为了更好地理解这些影响, 本文对岛屿可持续性的一些评论以及与旅游业的相关课题进行了研究, 主要使用理论讨论, 并以小岛屿发展中国家的原始自然和气候变化为例进行了实证研究。能源(包含交通)和废弃物管理是旅游业基本的服务部门, 从岛屿可持续性的角度也对这些方面进行了检讨。旅游相关的后果和对岛屿可持续性的理解, 特别是从岛屿研究文献, 涵盖了显著的可持续性, 气候变化破坏岛屿的故事情节, 包括"告别游"和岛屿组合。旅游品牌和营销的特点, 往往使旅游业陷入利用岛屿可持续性来实现旅游目标, 而不管任何可持续发展目标的成功与否。虽然利用岛屿可持续性的旅游业本身并不对旅游业或可持续性有害, 但它会分散和减损与岛民一起寻求可持续性的努力, 包括但不限于旅游业的努力。

Introduction

Islands have long been subjected to promoting what islanders and non-islanders think an island should be and how islanders should act regarding sustainability (Baldacchino, 2005, 2010, 2012b; Crane & Fletcher, 2017; Gillis, 2007). This literature highlights and deconstructs, for instance, isolation, smallness, marginalization, remoteness, littorality, existential threats, helplessness, lack of opportunity, and vulnerability contrasted with paradise, utopia, resilience, romance, and the idyll. Grydehøj (2019) points out how many of these repeated 'aspects of islandness' are based on the assumptions and expectations of what islands and islanders should be, often as a presumed homogenous and static collective, rather than the reality of diversity and dynamism. Specific examples of island studies disputing the assumptions and expectations are explaining that islands and islanders (i) are connected by water as much as they are separated by the disconnectedness of land (Hau'ofa, 1993; Hay, 2013) and (ii) are members of integrated and diverse networks rather than necessarily being remote and isolated (Chandler & Pugh, 2019).

Presumed features of islands and islandness, and challenges to them, are discussed for island tourism (Crick, 1989; Graci & Dodds, 2010). One baseline for island tourism can be, and is frequently assumed to be, 3S (sun, sea, and sand) or sometimes 4S (adding sex) (Butcher 2003; Carrigan, 2011; Crick, 1989; Hobson & Dietrich, 1995; Spencer & Bean, 2017). Another oft-assumed basis for island tourism is sustainable tourism, defined in different ways, with an underlying theme that the island, being an eco-paradise, has pristine nature alongside communities, livelihoods, and lifestyles with low environmental impacts (for examples and critiques, see Graci & Dodds, 2010 for Caribbean islands; Self, Self, & Bell-Haynes, 2010 for Ecuador's Galapagos Islands; and Kokkranikal, McLellan, & Baum, 2003 for Lakshadweep, India).

Efforts to achieve and showcase island sustainability in tourism intersect and connect many notions for each of 'island', 'sustainability', and 'tourism'. Drawing on the analysis of Dodds, Graci, and Holmes (2010) for island tourism in southeast Asia, how much do the management and marketing of sustainability for tourism reflect each other in an island destination? As Gössling, Hansson, Hörstmeier, and Saggel (2002) imply for Seychelles, how might tourists reconcile their desire for eco-friendly tourism with the environmental cost of travelling and being there?

To contribute to answering such questions, critiques of island sustainability are examined with regards to their relevance for tourism. Principally theoretical discussion is supported by empirical examples from the literature and, where uncited, from the author's experience to support the conceptual points identified and critiqued. Methodologically, this approach is pursued and accepted in research on islands, sustainability, and tourism, with some examples combining these areas being:

- From sustainable tourism work, Weaver (2016) combines definitions, key literature, and anecdotal examples for discursively 'reimagining indigenous tourism'.
- From island sustainability studies, Grydehøj and Kelman (2017) conceptualise 'The Eco-Island Trap' with respect to climate change through a critiquing, rather than systematic, review of the literature supported by illustrative examples from peer-reviewed academic work, grey literature, and their own experiences.

- From island tourism research, McLeod, Lewis, and Spencer (2017) adopt a 'state of play' and 'regional spotlight' analysis to set the agenda for research and application in the Caribbean.
- From sustainable island tourism, Scheyvens and Momsen (2008a) apply the approach described above to indicate issues and directions related to pro-poor tourism.

The next section presents and appraises some aspects of island sustainability in tourism followed by a section on two essential tourism sectors: (i) energy including transportation and (ii) waste management. Then, prior to the conclusion, a critiquing discussion engages further with some tourism-relevant consequences and understandings of island sustainability, especially from island studies literature.

Exemplifying island sustainability in tourism

The United Nations grouping of small island developing states (SIDS) epitomises many issues regarding island sustainability in tourism. SIDS were first formalised as a group in 1992 at the United Nations Conference on Environment and Development (the Earth Summit in Rio de Janeiro) in order to link small countries and territories which have ostensibly similar development and sustainability challenges. The number of SIDS has ranged from approximately three dozen to nearly five dozen depending on the year, the context, and the organisation listing them. The sustainability agenda for SIDS was first put forward in UN (1994) and was revisited each decade in UN (2005) and UN (2014).

The name 'SIDS' aims to convey particular island characteristics which are said to create sustainability challenges. The first 'S' in SIDS is for 'small', yet member Papua New Guinea is larger in population and area than New Zealand. Although SIDS represents islands, the mainland countries of Belize, Guyana, and Guinea-Bissau are part of the group. Singapore and Bahrain are not classified as being 'developing' yet are SIDS. Finally, despite the final "S" meaning 'states', non-sovereign territories such as Montserrat in the Caribbean and Cook Islands in the Pacific are part of the group.

None of these examples necessarily denigrates the SIDS' attempts to influence international sustainability policy, notably international treaties for addressing climate change (Betzold, 2010) and implementation for sustainable tourism (Scheyvens & Momsen, 2008b), although these studies discuss and critique the effectiveness of SIDS pushing their interests. Nor do these examples necessarily detract from the exchanges of knowledge and ideas amongst SIDS and the rewards of joint programmes, such as pooling resources to form intergovernmental agencies including the Pacific Regional Environment Programme (https://www.sprep.org) and the Caribbean Community Climate Change Centre (https://www.caribbeanclimate.bz). It does mean that institutions and individuals representing SIDS frequently use this grouping's labels as rhetoric rather than as being fully representative of all members' characteristics. This use spills over into tourism; for instance, in using 'small' and 'developing' as reasons for SIDS governments to pursue tourism, even when the evidence indicates that tourism is far from a social or environmental, including economic, panacea for SIDS (Bojanic & Lo, 2016; Graci & Dodds, 2010; Scheyvens & Momsen, 2008b).

Other such examples are prevalent for island tourism covering both SIDS and non-SIDS, such as New Zealand (Becken, 2005). Warm water destinations market images of white sand beaches, sun, and a tranquil sea (for example, Echtner, 2010; Naidoo, Ramseook-Munhurrun, & Durbarry, 2012 for Mauritius). Cold water island tourism uses ice, glaciers, landscapes, polar bears, sea mammals, and birds (Baldacchino, 2006). Within the sustainability ethos promoted for Svalbard in Norway's High Arctic, 'the world's northernmost' anything is branded, from locomotive to jazz festival. This diversification away from nature-based and adventure tourism would seem to be more about sustaining tourism than necessarily about sustainable tourism. Greenland is similarly trying to diversify from adventure tourism to cultural tourism (Weaver & Lawton, 2017). In such cases, it is an open question regarding the balance amongst a sustainable society and environment, sustaining tourism for the income, and using tourism income and activities to sustain an island's culture, lifestyle, and environment.

For warmer locales, in developing a tourism strategy for Timor-Leste, Currie (2018) tried to avoid the typical 3S approach, yielding some success. Dodds, Dimanche, and Sadowski (2017) describe strategic ambiguity regarding Cuba's expectations for tourism expansion, in terms of balancing cultural and natural heritage with resorts—further complicated since their analysis by the rapid changes in Cuba–USA relations. Nelson (2005) analysed images from Grenada presenting itself as an eco-tourism and nature tourism destination, finding a common theme of promoting something different, such as spices and rain forest, from the tourists' assumed home lives. For both Timor-Leste and Grenada, images of ostensibly pristine, palm-fringed beaches were still used to appeal to assumed traditional tourist expectations of islands, even as part of the apparent promotion of 'sustainable tourism'.

This island sustainability vision for tourism of perfect, untouched nature is being affected by another island sustainability issue: climate change. Contemporary climate change is witnessed as rapid changes in weather statistics over decades measured particularly by a rise in global mean air temperature (IPCC, 2013–2014). It arises from two main anthropogenic sources: (i) greenhouse gas emissions into the atmosphere, including carbon dioxide and methane, such as from burning fossil fuels, including oil and coal, and (ii) land use changes reducing greenhouse gas uptake such as from deforestation. Many human systems emit and fail to absorb greenhouse gases, such as for food, freshwater, waste management, and energy supply, the latter being notable for transportation and electricity generation.

Projections of climate change impacts have led to global catastrophe narratives (Nisbet, 2009). Some authors raise the spectre of possible human extinction from climate change (Matheny, 2007; Tonn, 2003) without robust conceptualisation, evidenced argumentation, or predictive modelling results of how climate change could actually destroy all of humanity. These catastrophe and extinction narratives are projected onto islands, framing climate change as an existential threat (Lilley, 2008), particularly for low-lying tropical islands and for polar islands such as Svalbard and Greenland.

The threat highlighted for polar locations tends to be disappearance of the cryosphere and animals, particularly polar bears, although many campaigns have been aiming to reduce the influence of these images by making peoples and cultures the central concern (Manzo, 2010; Watt-Cloutier, 2015). The threat highlighted for the tropics is typically sea-level rise which is assumed to be inevitably destructive to atolls (Locke, 2009; Wyett, 2014). Currently, social and physical theories and evidence of island and islander responses to climate change do not support this contention of tropical island countries and territories definitely vanishing under climate change (Albert et al., 2016; Perry et al., 2015; Webb & Kench, 2010; Yates, Le Cozannet, Garcin, Salai, & Walker, 2013). Nevertheless, no doubt exists that islands, including in the Arctic (ACIA, 2005; AHDR, 2004; AMAP, 2011), are experiencing major social and environmental shifts from climate change (IPCC, 2013-2014) with extinction-level threats being a plausible, but far from definite, outcome. The importance is acknowledging the nuances, provisos, and misleading representations in the physical and social responses of islands and islanders to climate change impacts (Connell, 2016; Farbotko, 2005, 2010; Gaillard, 2012; McLean & Kench, 2015) rather than accepting the assumptions of destruction without question.

Climate change within tourism has entered into the island sustainability discourse as being damaging to what tourists are assumed to be travelling for, namely beaches for warm water islands (e.g. Belle & Bramwell, 2005 for Barbados) and nature for cold water islands (e.g. Snyder & Stonehouse, 2007 for the polar regions). Yet for islands, coastal tourism might not be impacted by climate change any more or any less than non-coastal tourism, as Hyman (2014) shows for Jamaica. As with SIDS, climate change exemplifies island sustainability suggestions with respect to tourism which do not necessarily stand up to close scrutiny.

Sectoral perspectives of island sustainability in tourism

Island sustainability appears for essential service sectors which are part of tourism, here examined for energy including transportation and waste management.

Energy

Climate change within island sustainability and tourism has placed islands at the forefront of energy-related efforts (Praene, Payet, & Bénard-Sora, 2018; Weir, 2018), given electricity generation's contribution to climate change, especially with many islands relying on diesel generators. Yet many islands experience energy overuse due to tourism (Dodds, 2007b; Ioannides & Holcomb, 2003). For SIDS, Surroop, Raghoo, and Bundhoo (2018) provide an overview of energy systems, indicating how renewable energy sources for generating electricity are frequently highlighted for island sustainability. Hydropower and geothermal are particularly prominent for tourists, being promoted as sustainable sources as well as sites to visit.

For Mauritius, for which tourism generates about one quarter of the economy (WTTC, 2017), approximately 5% of electricity comes from in-country hydropower with significant prospects for expansion (Elahee, 2013). Hydropower has been implicated as inhibiting sustainability in numerous ways, such as through forced displacement and ecosystem damage (World Commission on Dams, 2000). The potential environmental damage from dams has long been noted as a concern for Mauritius (Ramjeawon, 1994), but most of the sites are distant from main tourist locations. Hydropower for Mauritius could be seen as sustainable given that it is local, renewable, and generates jobs, while the costs of construction, maintenance, and changed ecosystems would rarely be visible to visitors.

Surroop et al. (2018) report that only one SIDS, Papua New Guinea, was found to have geothermal electricity generation, providing 11% of the country's electricity production. Mauritius is planning to implement geothermal while many other SIDS, from Vanuatu to St. Lucia, have potential for it. Non-SIDS island countries, particularly Iceland, Indonesia, and New Zealand, are much further along the geothermal path than SIDS including using the geothermal infrastructure for some tourism (Erfurt-Cooper & Cooper, 2010). The main disadvantage of geothermal energy is perhaps that infrastructure is often required in comparatively remote locations, adding costs such as the transmission system and disturbing ecosystems. Another potential drawback is that local people might feel exploration of and resource extraction from their lands are against or interfere with their culture or livelihoods. On these bases, around the slopes of Mount Pinatubo in the Philippines, the indigenous Aeta objected to geothermal exploration (Goertzen, 1991).

More overt energy-related symbolism of island sustainability which appeals to tourists relates to 'carbon neutrality', referring to no net greenhouse gas emissions by reducing their release and increasing their uptake. Mohamed Nasheed's Presidency of Maldives from 2008 to 2012 led to the movie *The Island President* (2011) representing his views of impacts from and measures to tackle climate change. One initiative aimed to make his country carbon neutral by 2020. Given the sectoral distribution of energy demand in the country, a major overhaul of the culture and economy would be essential to reach this target.

At the time of Nasheed's commitment, Bernard, Khelil, Pichon, and Tissot (2010) provided a national audit for Maldives demonstrating how the tourism industry is the largest producer of Maldivian greenhouse gases, emitting 36% of domestic emissions. In fact, greenhouse gas emissions from international flights to and from the country (the method by which most tourists reach Maldives) were calculated to equal all domestic emissions (Bernard et al., 2010)—although these calculations do not include shipping which covers yachts, cruise ships, and cargo.

Following Nasheed's ousting in 2012, successive Maldivian governments have tended to downplay his environmental initiatives while not repudiating them entirely. Recent decisions in Maldives have encouraged even more tourism through permitting tourist facilities on inhabited islands, rather than on resort-only islands which frequently aimed to fulfill the promise and image (even if not reality) of idyllic eco-tourism (Ayala, 1996; King, 1997). The country now also allows foreign ownership of land provided that the owner reclaims land from the sea (CIA, 2018). Maldives is still marketed as an eco-tourism idyll, reinforcing warm water island sustainability in tourism, despite 96% of electricity being generated through fossil fuels (and the remainder by non-hydro renewables) (CIA, 2018). Solar water heating is used, as it is on many warm water islands, which would not be reflected in the electricity generation numbers.

Coconut biofuels have long been promoted as a potential contribution from SIDS to energy systems, for both electricity generation and vehicle operation, especially in the Pacific (Solly, 1980). It has not yet succeeded at a large scale and concerns are continually raised for all attempts at increasing biofuel use (Cloin, 2007; Gardebroek, Reimer, & Baller, 2017). If it did succeed at a large scale, then coconut plantations would need to expand, exacerbating already existing problems of food-related land being taken over for commercial products. Meanwhile, perceptions of coconut biofuel being local, eco-friendly, and plentiful could lead to an increase in consumption, especially if it were cheap. Ioannides and Holcomb (2003) already noted that aiming for fewer tourists to islands to reduce consumption loads made the destinations more upmarket, translating into more resource consumption per tourist. Should a coconut biofuel leader such as Vanuatu change all in-country transportation to a local fossil-fuel-free product, then the publicity might induce more tourists to fly there to witness energy futures and to use the local biofuel extensively because it is deemed to be eco-friendly.

The examples here thus far have been mainly supply side rather than reducing energy demand. One of the most common demand reduction initiatives across SIDS is solar energy for heating water which is typically taken as a given rather than as being for island sustainability. Given how much energy is required to heat water, the sustainability gains from solar heating are substantive, even on a life cycle basis (e.g. Lin, Chang, & Chung, 2015 for an isolated part of Taiwan).

Meanwhile, sustainable transport is not always a priority. Many buses in island countries such as Fiji and Barbados are old, spewing out noxious particulates and gases. For inter-island travel in Maldives, slow ferries exist, but most visitors end up on sea planes or motor boats. Meanwhile, in warm water destinations, year-round air conditioning is increasingly expected for visitor (and resident) comfort, yielding high energy consumption.

Islands not connected to external grids frequently depend on diesel-powered electricity generation plants, meaning that fuel and spare parts require a supply chain tending to extend far from the island. Even island countries which extract fossil fuels, such as Timor-Leste, do not typically have the in-country processing and refining facilities to provide for their own needs (Raghoo, Surroop, Wolf, Filho, & Jeetah, 2018). Meanwhile, as noted by Doraisami (2018), the (mis)management of the resource has led to development and economic troubles. Maintaining an electricity grid, such as over the mountains of St. Lucia, undersea across an archipelago, or to a mainland increases supply costs for parts and expertise for construction, maintenance, and decommissioning, even where the operations are run entirely on-island. After Hurricane Maria swept through Puerto Rico in 2017, external assistance was required for months afterwards in order to restore power (de Onís, 2018).

In Iceland, bitter tension emerges between assumed needs of nature-based tourism and energy production based on the natural resources from this same nature, namely hydro and geothermal electricity generation (Karlsdóttir, 2013). Renewable energy is promoted as being clean, green, and sustainable, as is nature-based tourism, so that the two clash with each other. It is not easy to determine which might be more sustainable in any specific context: being self-sufficient for electricity supply or bringing in tourists to see nature and then using the income to import electricity? Much might depend on the definition of 'sustainable' and perhaps neither would be sustainable in some situations. It is also unclear whether energy infrastructure or nature would pro-vide more overall tourist income.

Consequently, while many islands have sought be innovators in energy systems on both the supply and demand sides (Lenzen et al., 2014; Raturi, Singh, & Prasad, 2016), mixed degrees of success are witnessed. Tourists might not always be aware of the difficulties or apparent trade-offs, meaning that energy systems including transporta-tion, ostensibly to tackle climate change, can be used to represent island sustainability in tourism.

Waste management

Tourism-related waste has long been a concern for island sustainability (Pantin, 1999) with analyses hampered by lack of data and varying analysis methods (Eckelman et al., 2014). Using different parameters, Georges (2006) implies that tourists in Caribbean hotels generate twice as much waste as locals, along with different forms of waste, whilst Mateu-Sbert, Ricci-Cabello, Villalonga-Olives, and Cabeza-Irigoyen (2013) calculate that an extra tourist on Menorca produces less extra waste than an extra resident. Across islands, for residents and tourists, typical waste management sustainability focuses on the 3Rs of reduce, reuse, and recycle which, in turn, have their own implementation challenges.

Outer islands of Åland, Finland have recycling stations rather than home pickup. Residents collect their recyclables at home, they generally drive to the recycling sta-tions, the deposited material is collected by a lorry which drives onto a ferry, and thus the material is taken off-island for processing and recycling—an intensive use of fossil fuels. Vehicle tires pose an especial problem for recycling or reusing. Part of the prob-lem, as shown for Taiwan converting tires to energy (Tsai, 2015), is that the technology still requires substantive improvements. Part of the problem, as for Dominica (Sarkar, Chamberlain, & Miller, 2011), is that the annual volume of tires available apparently does not justify operating and maintaining the tire recycling equipment needed, although as always, the method of calculating costs and benefits affects the results. Malta had just started a household recycling programme when Dodds (2007a) pub-lished her analysis of sustainable tourism for the island country.

Without suitable and efficient 3 R programmes, waste accumulates leading to situa-tions such as in Maldives where burning solid waste is visible to many tourists. Lal and Takau (2006) noted how some Tongan islands have a household collection system for which a charge is levied by either the government or a private company. Not everyone can afford or wishes to pay the fee, so older practices of 'solid waste man-agement' are reverted to by throwing rubbish into the mangroves where it would not be seen. This approach for Tonga has not necessarily been detrimental when the waste was principally local and organic, such as coconut husks and fish bones. Difficulties emerge for modern, imported waste such as plastics and batteries which do not decompose rapidly and can release toxic substances, in addition to the increas-ing volumes of solid waste being produced. From a tourism perspective, waste bob-bing in the ocean or being left on the beach by high tide contradicts expectations of pristine nature and clean environments.

Where these aspects of island sustainability in tourism are sought to be maintained, waste management issues might be hidden from tourists. Managing e-waste from devices such as laptops and mobile phones is a growing problem internationally, so some islands step into the breach. Indonesia's Batam and Wakatobi Islands illegally import e-waste from Europe and the USA, for recycling or refurbishment and resale (Panambunan-Ferse & Breiter, 2013), but the sites are not those where tourists typically go. Conversely, Kassa Island is mainly used as a day trip for tourists from Conakry, Guinea and in 1989 received a shipment labelled as being brick material which turned out to be illegally dumped and poisonous incinerator ash from Philadelphia (Vir, 1989). Caribbean SIDS have long fought the US over transporting through their region nuclear waste for processing without asking permission or verifying the type of waste (Rodríguez-Rivera, 2009).

Where tourists cannot see these waste management issues, many island sustainability presumptions can be maintained, plus there are examples where waste management is used for island sustainability in tourism. The Future Centre Trust in Barbados is a local sustainability centre and a tourist attraction. Waste tires hold soil forming a garden of small tire-sized compartments where fruit and vegetables are grown. The Future Centre Trust also organised volunteers to collect rubbish from walkers around the country, demonstrating to tourists and locals that Barbados has a clean ethic (Raffoul, Mahon, & Goodridge, 2006).

Other social and technical innovations for island waste sustainability are being tested and implemented (Eckelman et al., 2014), although few have much connection to tourism or even could be tourist attractions. Instead, the absence of visible waste and waste management is likely to be most appealing for tourists, apart from standard items in many places, such as recycling bins which tourists can point to as evidence of island sustainability, even if the techniques provide few results, especially over a life cycle.

Critiquing island sustainability in tourism

The sectoral analysis of energy and waste management shows that island sustainability efforts sometimes have genuine sustainability aims, including in tourism, and sometimes are more for show, including in tourism. Meanwhile, some island sustainability issues are not dealt with, to large degree because they are out of sight.

One critique of promoting island sustainability for garnering attention is 'conspicuous sustainability' (Grydehøj & Kelman, 2017). Conspicuous sustainability means engaging in initiatives which appear to support sustainability irrespective of their real contribution to sustainability. Although the literature has not yet applied conspicuous sustainability to tourism, research and practice have long examined whether or not tourism itself is inherently unsustainable alongside analyses of the promotion and marketing used to highlight claimed sustainability traits (Becken & Hay, 2007; Buckley, 2012; Graci & Dodds, 2010). Consequently, tourism case studies involving island sustainability can exemplify conspicuous sustainability.

Dodds et al. (2010) discuss sustainability initiatives for the islands of Koh Phi Phi, Thailand and Gili Trawangan, Indonesia showing how practical as well as nebulous notions of sustainability are being examined for tourism marketing and tourism man-agement. Involving tourists in the sustainability practices is part of both islands' initia-tives, yet tourists seem to support the endeavours because they are visible rather than due to sustainability results from them. In effect, whether or not island sustainability is progressed with tourists and through tourism, the marketing and the tourists' percep-tions of contributing to sustainability continue.

The sustainability initiatives become conspicuous, used to illustrate how much islands are engaging with sustainability, even when the activities achieve little (Baldacchino & Kelman, 2014; Grydehøj & Kelman, 2017). At times, conspicuous sus-tainability endeavours, rather than merely failing to advance sustainability, can regress it. An example from island tourism is creating branding or expectations which draw in tourists who then damage what they come to see. Graci and Dodds (2010) describe overtourism in Maldives and the Galapagos Islands harming the wildlife, ecosystems, and beaches which attract visitors, especially due to successful marketing aiming to highlight the supposed sustainability; that is, to make it conspicuous.

Island sustainability branding has become important for tourism around the world. Khamis (2007) describes how tourists are attracted by the reputation of King Island, Tasmania for gourmet cuisine, tranquillity, and gorgeous landscapes, despite this repu-tation being significantly manufactured through careful and clever branding. For Shetland, Scotland, tourism branding not only presents contradictory elements creat-ing visitor expectations which cannot always be met, but also conflicts with some local identities and islander interests for their own communities (Grydehøj, 2008). Self et al. (2010) detail how ecotourism has become an important marketing ploy for the Galapagos Islands with many tour operators greenwashing their operations rather than providing legitimately eco-friendly products and services.

The storyline of climate change destruction has yielded further contradictions in island sustainability. Within tourism, a 'last-chance' narrative has emerged, marketing island destinations as the last chance to see them before them are irrevocably ruined by social shifts or anthropogenic environmental changes (Lemelin, Dawson, & Stewart, 2012). One dimension is that these supposedly pristine, natural destinations would be sustainable without climate change. Now, however, the destinations will not last—that is, they are not sustainable—so they should be visited as soon as possible, no matter what the resource consumption required for doing so, which itself contributes to cli-mate change. Last-chance tourism for islands is often marketed with island sustainabil-ity, while not apparently increasing environmental awareness or actions amongst the tourists (Eijgelaar, Thaper, & Peeters, 2010). As such, last-chance tourism contradicts sustainable tourism, feeding into the discussions of tourism contributing to climate change and of climate change affecting tourism positively and negatively (Becken, 2013; Scott & Becken, 2010).

Similarly, as discussed earlier, climate change is used for island sustainability through the energy sector, but does not necessarily encourage tourists to reduce their own energy use by avoiding travel to island destinations or when visiting islands. The focus on renewable energy supplies which are ostensibly sustainable also distracts from the well-known points (Lovins, 1976, 2011) that (i) for sustainability, energy demand reduction must be implemented in conjunction with sustainable energy supplies and (ii) these actions are required for many reasons other than climate change, such as health, livelihoods, cost-effectiveness, safety, and durability.

For tourism, island sustainability for energy supply, to a large degree, detracts from the priority action of reducing energy consumption. Climate change has supported conspicuous sustainability more than sustainability. Meanwhile, visible aspects of waste management might not be the most effective island sustainability endeavours in tourism, as tourists do not usually encounter some of the most damaging waste-related consequences for islands. Again, conspicuousness is more prominent than actual sustainability.

Is moving beyond conspicuous sustainability, such as for energy and waste management, feasible without sacrificing important aspects of sustainability? One step might be recognising that island assemblages can have as much forcefulness in attracting tourists as single island entities. SIDS are an example of an island assemblage. For island tourism, three other significant forms of assemblages from the literature are discussed here.

First, grouped islands are archipelagos, with archipelagicity being examined for tourism (Baldacchino, 2013). Baldacchino and Ferreira (2013) look at the Azores as an example of promoting the archipelago for tourism, indicating how advantages include expanding the tourist base, distributing tourism income throughout the archipelago, and increasing the value of visits with a variety of experiences. Drawbacks include simplifying inter-island differences which can detrimentally impact island and archipelagic identity while providing archipelago tourism products which presume what the visitors and residents seek.

The second assemblage discussed by island studies is aquapelagos (Hayward, 2012, p. 5) defined as 'an assemblage of the marine and land spaces of a group of islands and their adjacent waters'. That is, an aquapelago is an island group and its waters. The response is that the term 'archipelago' suffices for this assemblage (Baldacchino, 2012a). From an island tourism perspective, repackaging the same offerings in different vocabulary is not necessarily detrimental (Buckley, 2002). That is, aquapelagic tourism might generate interest to complement archipelagic tourism even while offering the same products, services, and experiences, but just using a neologism. The concept then becomes a representation in its own right, being imagined, explored, and promoted—including for and in tourism—with Hayward (2015) analysing an example of the archipelago/aquapelago of New York City.

Hayward's (2015) work demonstrates the third assemblage: that of the island or archipelago (or aquapelago) in relation to the mainland. As with Grenada appealing to tourists by 'othering' the images offered (Nelson, 2005)—that is, promoting them as being different or an 'other' to what people typically experience—islands are often presented as being the 'other' to the mainland. This viewpoint bolsters on mainland terms the assumed island traits of remoteness, marginality, and isolation (Baldacchino, 2008). Sustainability is assumed to be more difficult on these island 'others' of (or 'outliers' from) the mainland/continental assemblage. Yet these alleged sustainability challenges are purported to bring advantages for tourists seeking a holiday escape, whether 3S, 4S, eco-resorts, adventure, and/or pristine nature.

In this regard, assemblages of islands produce, in effect, the same issues for sustainability in tourism as islands do. Whether archipelagos, aquapelagos, or mainland-exception constructions, island assemblages do not necessarily produce different sustainability representations or assumptions in tourism than islands.

Perhaps there is an inevitable return to the long-discussed definitions of "sustainability" for tourism and "sustainable tourism" (Becken, 2013; Buckley, 2012; Butler, 1999; Carlsen & Butler, 2011; Dodds, 2007b; Graci & Dodds, 2010; Liu, 2003). The oft-asked questions include (i) whether or not sustainable tourism, not just conspicuousness thereof, is a realistic goal for islands and (ii) how much tourism undermines sustainability—of tourists and of destinations. Attempts have been made to answer such questions by actively embracing public diplomacy and public relations as for Cuba (L'Etang, Falkheimer, & Lugo, 2007) and aiming for conflict resolution as has been proposed for Cyprus (Sonmez & Apostolopoulos, 2000).

Care is needed not to overplay such issues or to expect everyone to respond to them similarly. Examining island sustainability in tourism has demonstrated how often, such as for energy and waste management, actions can be focused more on presenting sustainability than on achieving aspects of it. Applying conspicuous sustainability to island tourism demonstrates that the eco-island trap is prevalent for a variety of island destinations, not limited to 3S or 4S locations, including island assemblages. The viability of other pathways, as Currie (2018) tried for Timor-Leste, remains an open question.

Conclusion

Some critiques of island sustainability have been examined with regards to their relevance for tourism, showing how tourism can become trapped (eco-trapped, from Grydehøj & Kelman, 2017) by island sustainability—and vice versa—despite, or perhaps because of, many contradictions and inconsistencies. As with typical conspicuous sustainability for islands (Grydehøj & Kelman, 2017), tourism uses island sustainability for its own interests, no matter what the contribution to sustainability is or the real feasibility of achieving some form or process of sustainability. The labels used might also emphasise a specific direction irrespective of sustainability rather than strategically selecting the pathway(s) desired for sustainability and then labelling it/them. For instance, Scheyvens and Momsen (2008b) explain how stating that SIDS are vulnerable, ostensibly invoking assumed island traits, inhibits sustainable tourism development through this assumption of vulnerability.

The discussion here shows how the situation is not inherently deleterious to island sustainability in tourism. It can distract and detract from (i) working with islanders to seek sustainability including, but not limited to, tourism endeavours and (ii) enquiring about and testing the realism of sustainability involving tourism. Moreover, islanders collectively and in a specific location are not a single-minded, homogenous, static group, instead holding and acting on a variety of viewpoints of islands, sustainability, and tourism. Being aware of images, views, expectations, and assumptions which are present and absent, how they arise, why they remain, and what they do and do not represent to different internal and external groups would yield opportunities for constructively using island sustainability in and through tourism.

References

ACIA (2005). *Arctic climate impacts assessment*. Cambridge, UK: Cambridge University Press.

AHDR (2004). *Arctic human development report*. Akureyri, Iceland: Stefansson Arctic Institute.

Albert, S., Leon, J. X., Grinham, A. R., Church, J. A., Gibbes, B. R., & Woodroffe, C. D. (2016). Interactions between sea-level rise and wave exposure on reef island dynamics in the Solomon Islands. *Environmental Research Letters, 11*, paper 054011. doi:10.1088/1748-9326/11/5/054011

AMAP (2011). *Snow, water, ice and permafrost in the Arctic*. Oslo: AMAP (Arctic Monitoring and Assessment Programme) Secretariat.

Ayala, H. (1996). Resort ecotourism: A paradigm for the 21st century. *The Cornell Hotel and Restaurant Administration Quarterly, 37*(5), 46–53. doi:10.1177/001088049603700523

Baldacchino, G. (2005). Islands: objects of representation. *Geografiska Annaler, Series B: Human Geography, 87*(4), 247–251. doi:10.1111/j.0435-3684.2005.00196.x

Baldacchino, G. (Ed.). (2006). *Extreme tourism: Lessons from the World's Cold Water Islands*. Oxford: Elsevier.

Baldacchino, G. (2008). Some epistemological and methodological challenges to the pursuit of Island Studies. Studying Islands: on whose terms? *Island Studies Journal, 3*, 37–56.

Baldacchino, G. (2010). Island brands and 'the Island' as a brand: insights from immigrant entrepreneurs on Prince Edward Island. *International Journal of Entrepreneurship and Small Business, 9*(4), 378–393. doi:10.1504/IJESB.2010.032400

Baldacchino, G. (2012a). Getting wet: A response to Hayward's concept of Aquapelagos. *Shima, 6*, 22–26.

Baldacchino, G. (2012b). The lure of the island: A spatial analysis of power relations. *Journal of Marine and Island Cultures, 1*(2), 55–62. doi:10.1016/j.imic.2012.11.003

Baldacchino, G. (Ed.). (2013). *Archipelago tourism: Policies and practices*. London: Routledge.

Baldacchino, G., & Ferreira, E. C. D. (2013). Competing notions of diversity in archipelago tourism: Transport logistics, official rhetoric and inter-island rivalry in the azores. *Island Studies Journal, 8*(1), 84–104.

Baldacchino, G., & Kelman, I. (2014). Critiquing the pursuit of island sustainability: Blue and Green, with hardly a colour in between. *Shima, 8*, 1–21.

Becken, S. (2005). The role of tourist icons for sustainable tourism. *Journal of Vacation Marketing, 11*(1), 21–30. doi:10.1177/1356766705050840

Becken, S. (2013). A review of tourism and climate change as an evolving knowledge domain. *Tourism Management Perspectives, 6*, 53–62. doi:10.1016/j.tmp.2012.11.006

Becken, S., & Hay, J. E. (2007). *Tourism and climate change: Risks and opportunities*. Toronto: Channel View.

Belle, N., & Bramwell, B. (2005). Climate change and small island tourism: Policy maker and industry perspectives in Barbados. *Journal of Travel Research, 44*(1), 32–41. doi:10.1177/0047287505276589

Bernard, F., Khelil, T. B., Pichon, V., & Tissot, L. (2010). *The Maldives' 2009 carbon audit*. Paris: BeCitizen.

Betzold, C. (2010). 'Borrowing' power to influence international negotiations: AOSIS in the climate change regime, 1990–1997. *Politics, 30*(3), 131–148. doi:10.1111/j.1467-9256.2010.01377.x

Bojanic, D. C., & Lo, M. (2016). A comparison of the moderating effect of tourism reliance on the economic development for islands and other countries. *Tourism Management, 53*, 207–214. doi:10.1016/j.tourman.2015.10.006

Buckley, R. (2002). Surf tourism and sustainable development in Indo-Pacific Islands. I. The Industry and the Islands. *Journal of Sustainable Tourism, 10*(5), 405–424. doi:10.1080/09669580208667176

Buckley, R. (2012). Sustainable tourism: Research and reality. *Annals of Tourism Research, 39*(2), 528–546. doi:10.1016/j.annals.2012.02.003

Butcher, J. (2003). *The Moralisation of Tourism: Sun, Sand and… Saving the World*. London: Routledge.

Butler, R. (1999). Sustainable tourism: A state-of-the-art review. *Tourism Geographies, 1*(1), 7–25. doi:10.1080/14616689908721291

Carlsen, J., & Butler, R. (2011). *Island tourism: Sustainable perspectives.* Wallingford: CAB International.

Carrigan, A. (2011). *Postcolonial tourism: Literature, culture and environment.* New York: Routledge.

Chandler, D., & Pugh, J. (2019). Islands of relationality and resilience: The shifting stakes of the Anthropocene. *Area.* doi:10.1111/area.12459

CIA (2018). *CIA World fact book.* Washington, DC: Central Intelligence Agency, Retrieved from https://www.cia.gov/library/publications/the-world-factbook/geos/mv.html accessed on 7 October 2018.

Cloin, J. (2007). Coconut oil as a fuel in the Pacific Islands. *Natural Resources Forum, 31*(2), 119–127. doi:10.1111/j.1477-8947.2007.00145.x

Connell, J. (2016). Last days in the Carteret Islands? Climate change, livelihoods and migration on coral atolls. *Asia Pacific Viewpoint, 5*, 3–15. doi:10.1111/apv.12118

Crane, R., & Fletcher, L. (2017). *Island genres, genre Islands: Conceptualisation and representation in popular.* London: Rowman and Littlefield.

Crick, M. (1989). Representations of international tourism in the social sciences: Sun, sex, sights, savings, and servility. *Annual Review of Anthropology, 18*(1), 307–344. doi:10.1146/annurev.an.18.100189.001515

Currie, S. (2018). Beyond a 3s approach to marketing Island Nations? Destination marketing and experiences from Timor-Leste. *The Contemporary Pacific, 30*(2), 438–459. doi:10.1353/cp.2018.0034

de Onís, C. M. (2018). Energy colonialism powers the ongoing unnatural disaster in Puerto Rico. *Frontiers in Communication, 3.* https://www.frontiersin.org/articles/10.3389/fcomm.2018.00002/full

Dodds, R. (2007a). Malta's tourism policy: Standing still or advancing towards sustainability? *Island Studies Journal, 2*, 47–66.

Dodds, R. (2007). Sustainable tourism policy—rejuvenation or a critical strategic initiative. *Anatolia, 18*(2), 277–298. doi:10.1080/13032917.2007.9687206

Dodds, R., Dimanche, F., & Sadowski, M. (2017). Planning for growth in islands: The case of Cuba (Chapter 7). In M. McLeod & R. Croes (Eds.), *Tourism management in warm-water island destinations* (pp 95–107). Wallingford: CABI.

Dodds, R., Graci, S. R., & Holmes, M. (2010). Does the tourist care? A comparison of tourists in Koh Phi Phi, Thailand and Gili Trawangan, Indonesia. *Journal of Sustainable Tourism, 18*(2), 207–222. doi:10.1080/09669580903215162

Doraisami, A. (2018). The Timor Leste Petroleum Fund, veterans and white elephants: Fostering intergenerational equity? *Resources Policy, 58*, 250–256. doi:10.1016/j.resourpol.2018.05.013

Echtner, C. (2010). Paradise without people: Exclusive destination promotion. *Tourism Culture & Communication, 10*, 83–99. doi:10.3727/109830410X12815527582747

Eckelman, M. J., Ashton, W., Arakaki, Y., Hanaki, K., Nagashima, S., & Malone-Lee, L. C. (2014). Island waste management systems: Statistics, challenges, and opportunities for applied. *Industrial Ecology. Journal of Industrial Ecology, 18*(2), 306–317. doi:10.1111/jiec.12113

Eijgelaar, E., Thaper, C., & Peeters, P. (2010). Antarctic cruise tourism: The paradoxes of ambassadorship, "last chance tourism" and greenhouse gas emissions. *Journal of Sustainable Tourism, 18*(3), 337–354. doi:10.1080/09669581003653534

Elahee, M. K. (2013). Potential of hydropower in Mauritius: Myth or reality? *Energy Sources, Part A: Recovery, Utilization, and Environmental Effects, 35*(10), 921–925. doi:10.1080/15567036.2010.514592

Erfurt-Cooper, P., & Cooper, M. (Eds.). (2010). *Volcano and geothermal tourism: Sustainable geo-resources for leisure and recreation.* London: Earthscan.

Farbotko, C. (2005). Tuvalu and climate change: Constructions of environmental displacement in the Sydney Morning Herald. *Geografiska Annaler – Series B: Human Geography, 87*(4), 279–293. doi:10.1111/j.0435-3684.2005.00199.x

Farbotko, C. (2010). Wishful sinking: Disappearing islands, climate refugees and cosmopolitan experimentation. *Asia Pacific Viewpoint, 51*(1), 47–60. doi:10.1111/j.1467-8373.2010.001413.x

Gaillard, J. C. (2012). The climate gap. *Climate and Development, 4*(4), 261–264. doi:10.1080/17565529.2012.742846

Gardebroek, C., Reimer, J. J., & Baller, L. (2017). The impact of biofuel policies on crop acreages in Germany and France. *Journal of Agricultural Economics, 68*(3), 839–860. doi:10.1111/1477-9552.12218

Georges, N. M. (2006). Solid waste as an indicator of sustainable development in Tortola, British Virgin Islands. *Sustainable Development, 14*(2), 126–138. doi:10.1002/sd.300

Gillis, J. R. (2007). Island sojourns. *Geographical Review, 97*(2), 274–287. doi:10.1111/j.1931-0846.2007.tb00403.x

Goertzen, D. (1991). Valour under fire (tribe trusted in Mt. Pinatubo's protection). *Far Eastern Economic Review*, 25–26.

Gössling, S., Hansson, C. B., Hörstmeier, O., & Saggel, S. (2002). Ecological footprint analysis as a tool to assess tourism sustainability. *Ecological Economics, 43*(2-3), 199–211. doi:10.1016/S0921-8009(02)00211-2

Graci, S., & Dodds, R. (2010). *Sustainable tourism in Island destinations.* London: Earthscan.

Grydehøj, A. (2008). Branding from above: Generic cultural branding in Shetland and other islands. *Island Studies Journal, 3*(2), 175–198.

Grydehøj, A. (2019). Aspects of Islandness. *Special section in* Area, forthcoming.

Grydehøj, A., & Kelman, I. (2017). The Eco-Island trap: Climate change mitigation and conspicuous sustainability. *Area, 49*(1), 106–113. doi:10.1111/area.12300

Hau'ofa, E. (1993). Our sea of Islands. In V. Naidu, E. Waddell, and E. Hau'ofa (Eds.), *A New Oceania: Rediscovering our sea of Islands* (pp 2–17). Suva: School of Social and Economic Development, The University of the South Pacific.

Hay, P. (2013). What the sea portends: A reconsideration of contested Island Tropes. *Island Studies Journal, 8*(2), 209–232.

Hayward, P. (2012). Aquapelagos and aquapelagic assemblages. *Shima, 6*, 1–11.

Hayward, P. (2015). The aquapelago and the Estuarine City: Reflections on Manhattan. *Urban Island Studies, 1*, 81–95. doi:10.20958/uis.2015.5

Hobson, J. S. P., & Dietrich, U. C. (1995). Tourism, health and quality of life: Challenging the responsibility of using the traditional tenets of Sun, Sea, Sand, and Sex in tourism. *Journal of Travel & Tourism Marketing, 3*, 21–38. doi:10.1300/J073v03n04_02

Hyman, T.-A. (2014). Assessing the vulnerability of beach tourism and non-beach tourism to climate change: A case study from Jamaica. *Journal of Sustainable Tourism, 22*(8), 1197–1215. doi:10.1080/09669582.2013.855220

Ioannides, D., & Holcomb, B. (2003). Misguided policy initiatives in small-island destinations: Why do up-market tourism policies fail?. *Tourism Geographies, 5*(1), 39–48. doi:10.1080/1461668032000034051

IPCC (2013). *Fifth assessment report.* Geneva: IPCC (Intergovernmental Panel on Climate Change).

Karlsdóttir, U. (2013). Nature worth seeing! The tourist gaze as a factor in shaping views on nature in Iceland. *Tourist Studies, 13*, 139–155.

Khamis, S. (2007). Gourmet and Green: The branding of King Island. *Shima, 1*, 14–29.

King, B. E. M. (1997). *Creating island resorts.* London: Routledge.

Kokkranikal, J., McLellan, R., & Baum, T. (2003). Island tourism and sustainability: A case study of the Lakshadweep Islands. *Journal of Sustainable Tourism, 11*(5), 426–447. doi:10.1080/09669580308667214

Lal, P., & Takau, L. (2006). *Economic Costs of Waste in Tonga.* Nuku'alofa and Suva: Government of Tonga, PIFS (Pacific Islands Forum Secretariat), and SPREP (Pacific Regional Environment Programme).

Lemelin, H., Dawson, J., & Stewart, E. J. (Eds.). (2012). *Last chance tourism: Adapting tourism opportunities in a changing world.* Abingdon: Routledge.

Lenzen, M., Krishnapillai, M., Talagi, D., Quintal, J., Quintal, D., Grant, R., ... Murray, J. (2014). Cultural and socio-economic determinants of energy consumption on small remote islands. *Natural Resources Forum, 38*(1), 27–46. doi:10.1111/1477-8947.12030

L'Etang, J., Falkheimer, J., & Lugo, J. (2007). Public relations and tourism: Critical reflections and a research agenda. *Public Relations Review, 33*, 68–76. doi:10.1016/j.pubrev.2006.11.008

Lilley, I. (2008). Apocalypse now (and avoid the rush): Human dimensions of climate change in the Indo-Pacific. *Archaeology in Oceania, 43*(1), 35–40. doi:10.1002/j.1834-4453.2008.tb00028.x

Lin, W. M., Chang, K. C., & Chung, K. M. (2015). Payback period for residential solar water heaters in Taiwan. *Renewable and Sustainable Energy Reviews, 41*, 901–906. doi:10.1016/j.rser.2014.09.005

Liu, Z. (2003). Sustainable tourism development: A critique. *Journal of Sustainable Tourism, 11*(6), 459–475. doi:10.1080/09669580308667216

Locke, J. T. (2009). Climate change-induced migration in the Pacific Region: Sudden crisis and long-term developments. *Geographical Journal, 175*(3), 171–180. doi:10.1111/j.1475-4959.2008.00317.x

Lovins, A. B. (1976). Energy strategy: The road not taken. *Foreign Affairs, 55*(1), 65–96. doi: 10.2307/20039628

Lovins, A. B. (2011). *Reinventing fire: Bold business solutions for the new energy era.* Boulder, CO: Rocky Mountain Institute.

Manzo, K. (2010). Beyond polar bears? Re-envisioning climate change. *Meteorological Applications, 17*(2), 196–208. doi:10.1002/met.193

Mateu-Sbert, J., Ricci-Cabello, I., Villalonga-Olives, E., & Cabeza-Irigoyen, E. (2013). The impact of tourism on municipal solid waste generation: The case of Menorca Island (Spain). *Waste Management, 33*(12), 2589–2593. doi:10.1016/j.wasman.2013.08.007

Matheny, J. G. (2007). Reducing the risk of human extinction. *Risk Analysis, 27*(5), 1335–1344. doi: 10.1111/j.1539-6924.2007.00960.x

McLean, R., & Kench, P. (2015). Destruction or persistence of coral atoll islands in the face of 20th and 21st century sea-level rise? *Wiley Interdisciplinary Reviews: Climate Change, 6*(5), 445–463. doi:10.1002/wcc.350

McLeod, M., Lewis, E. H., & Spencer, A. (2017). Re-inventing, revolutionizing and transforming Caribbean tourism: Multicountry regional institutions and a research agenda. *Journal of Destination Marketing & Management, 6*, 1–4. doi:10.1016/j.jdmm.2016.08.009

Naidoo, P., Ramseook-Munhurrun, P., & Durbarry, R. (2012). The brand image of a small Island destination. *Tourismos, 7*, 261–278.

Nelson, V. (2005). Representation and images of people, place and nature in Grenada's tourism. *Geografiska Annaler: Series B, Human Geography, 87*(2), 131–143. doi:10.1111/j.0435-3684.2005.00187.x

Nisbet, M. C. (2009). Communicating climate change: Why frames matter for public engagement. *Environment: Science and Policy for Sustainable Development, 51*(2), 12–23. doi:10.3200/ENVT.51.2.12-23

Panambunan-Ferse, M., & Breiter, A. (2013). Assessing the side-effects of ICT development: E-waste production and management: A case study about cell phone end-of-life in Manado, Indonesia. *Technology in Society, 35*(3), 223–231. doi:10.1016/j.techsoc.2013.04.002

Pantin, D. A. (1999). The challenge of sustainable development in small island developing states: Case study on tourism in the Caribbean. *Natural Resources Forum, 23*(3), 221–233. doi:10.1111/j.1477-8947.1999.tb00911.x

Perry, C. T., Murphy, G. N., Graham, N. A. J., Wilson, S. K., Januchowski-Hartley, F. A., & East, H. K. (2015). Remote coral reefs can sustain high growth potential and may match future sea-level trends. *Nature Scientific Reports, 5*. Article number: 18289.

Praene, J. P., Payet, M., & Bénard-Sora, F. (2018). Sustainable transition in small island developing states: Assessing the current situation. *Utilities Policy, 54*, 86–91. doi:10.1016/j.jup.2018.08.006

Raffoul, L., Mahon, R., & Goodridge, R. (2006). *Roadside Litter in Barbados: Sources and solutions.* CERMES Technical Report No 1. Cave Hill Campus, Barbados: University of the West Indies.

Raghoo, P., Surroop, D., Wolf, F., Leal Filho, W., Jeetah, P., & Delakowitz, B. (2018). Dimensions of energy security in small Island developing states. *Utilities Policy*, *53*, 94–101. doi:10.1016/j.jup.2018.06.007

Ramjeawon, T. (1994). Water resources management on the small Island of Mauritius. *International Journal of Water Resources Development*, *10*(2), 143–155. doi:10.1080/07900629408722619

Raturi, A., Singh, A., & Prasad, R. D. (2016). Grid-connected PV systems in the Pacific Island Countries. *Renewable and Sustainable Energy Reviews*, *58*, 419–428. doi:10.1016/j.rser.2015.12.141

Rodríguez-Rivera, L. E. (2009). Transportation of radioactive materials through the Caribbean Sea: The development of a nuclear-free zone. In D. D. Caron & H. N. Scheiber (Eds.), *The Oceans in the Nuclear Age: Legacies and Risks* (pp. 169–195). Boston: Brill.

Sarkar, S., Chamberlain, J. F., & Miller, S. A. (2011). A comparison of two methods to conduct material flow analysis on waste tires in a small Island developing state. *Journal of Industrial Ecology*, *15*(2), 300–314. doi:10.1111/j.1530-9290.2010.00323.x

Scheyvens, R., & Momsen, J. H. (2008a). Tourism and poverty reduction: Issues for small Island states. *Tourism Geographies*, *10*(1), 22–41. doi:10.1080/14616680701825115

Scheyvens, R., & Momsen, J. H. (2008b). Tourism in small Island states: From vulnerability to strengths. *Journal of Sustainable Tourism*, *16*(5), 491–510. doi:10.2167/jost821.0

Scott, D., & Becken, S. (2010). Adapting to climate change and climate policy: Progress, problems and potentials. *Journal of Sustainable Tourism*, *18*(3), 283–295. doi:10.1080/09669581003668540

Self, R. M., Self, D. R., & Bell-Haynes, J. (2010). Marketing tourism in The Galapagos Islands: Ecotourism or greenwashing?. *International Business & Economics Research Journal (IBER)*, *9*(6). doi:10.19030/iber.v9i6.590

Snyder, J. & Stonehouse, B. (Eds.). (2007). *Prospects for polar tourism*. Wallingford: CAB International.

Solly, R. K. (1980). Coconut oil and coconut oil-ethanol derivatives as fuel for diesel engines. *Fiji Agricultural Journal*, *42*, 1–6.

Sonmez, S. F., & Apostolopoulos, Y. (2000). Conflict resolution through tourism cooperation? The case of the partitioned Island-State of Cyprus. *Journal of Travel & Tourism Marketing*, *9*, 35–48. doi:10.1300/J073v09n03_03

Spencer, A., & Bean, D. (2017). Female sex tourism in Jamaica: An assessment of perceptions. *Journal of Destination Marketing & Management*, *6*, 13–21. doi:10.1016/j.jdmm.2016.10.002

Surroop, D., Raghoo, P., & Bundhoo, Z. M. A. (2018). Comparison of energy systems in Small Island developing states. *Utilities Policy*, *54*, 46–54. doi:10.1016/j.jup.2018.07.006

Tonn, B. (2003). An equity first, risk-based framework for managing global climate change. *Global Environmental Change*, *13*(4), 295–306. doi:10.1016/S0959-3780(03)00051-7

Tsai, W.-T. (2015). The utilization of scrap tires as an energy source and its environmental benefit analysis in Taiwan. *Energy Sources, Part B: Economics, Planning, and Policy*, *10*(4), 333–339. doi:10.1080/15567249.2010.551825

UN (1994). Report of the Global Conference on the Sustainable Development of Small Island Developing States. Document A/CONF.167/9 (October, 1994) from Global Conference on the Sustainable Development of Small Island Developing States. Bridgetown, Barbados: United Nations.

UN (2005). Draft Mauritius Strategy for the further Implementation of the Programme of Action for the Sustainable Development of Small Island Developing States, Document A/CONF.207/CRP.7 (13 January 2005) from the International Meeting to Review the Implementation of the Programme of Action for the Sustainable Development of Small Island Developing States. Port Louis, Mauritius: United Nations.

UN (2014). *Draft Outcome Document of the Third International Conference on Small Island Developing States. Apia, 1–4 September 2014*. Apia, Samoa: United Nations.

Vir, A. K. (1989). Toxic trade with Africa. *Environmental Science & Technology*, *23*(1), 23–25. doi:10.1021/es00178a600

Watt-Cloutier, S. (2015). *The right to be cold*. Toronto: Penguin Random House.

Weaver, D. B. (2016). Beyond convention: Reimagining indigenous tourism. *Tourism Geographies*, *18*(1), 28–37. doi:10.1080/14616688.2015.1122077

Weaver, D. B., & Lawton, L. J. (2017). Degrees of peripherality in the production and consumption of leisure tourism in Greenland. In Y.-S. Lee, D. Weaver, & N.K Prebensen (Eds.), *Arctic Tourism Experiences: Production, Consumption and Sustainability* (pp 56–66). Wallingford: CAB International.

Webb, A. P., & Kench, P. S. (2010). The dynamic response of reef islands to sea-level rise: Evidence from multi-decadal analysis of island change in the Central Pacific. *Global and Planetary Change*, *72*(3), 234–246. doi:10.1016/j.gloplacha.2010.05.003

Weir, T. (2018). Renewable energy in the Pacific Islands: Its role and status. *Renewable and Sustainable Energy Reviews*, *94*, 762–771. doi:10.1016/j.rser.2018.05.069

World Commission on Dams. (2000). *Dams and development: A new framework for decision-making*. London: Earthscan.

WTTC. (2017). *Travel & tourism: Economic Impact 2017, Mauritius*. London: Author .

Wyett, K. (2014). Escaping a rising tide: Sea level rise and migration in Kiribati. *Asia & the Pacific Policy Studies*, *1*(1), 171–185. doi:10.1002/app5.7

Yates, M. L., Le Cozannet, G., Garcin, M., Salai, E., & Walker, P. (2013). Multidecadal atoll shoreline change on Manihi and Manuae, French Polynesia. *Journal of Coastal Research*, *29*, 870–882. doi:10.2112/JCOASTRES-D-12-00129.1

Contributions to sustainable tourism in small islands: an analysis of the Cittàslow movement

Therez B. Walker and Timothy J. Lee

ABSTRACT

The Cittàslow philosophy aims to preserve the unique characteristics of places, people, products, food and the environment. Inclusive participation is the focus of the movement for small communities that aim to improve residents' quality of life and share in one of a kind experiences with visitors. Discussion of the Cittàslow movement has been increasing in recent years, and the conceptualization offered in this paper adds to that discourse by showing how the movement, with its unique approach to sustainability and local governance, has the potential to be beneficial to Small Island Developing States (SIDS) by directly and indirectly contributing to sustainable tourism development. Slow Food, Slow Tourism, and sustainability in relation to tourism are discussed to clarify how they all fit into the slow tourism ethos and influence the Cittàslow movement. Interestingly, by examining some of the essentials of the Cittàslow movement, we can ascertain how the quality of life and experience value of tourism complements the Cittàslow approach to sustainable tourism development for SIDS. Sustainability from an island perspective is conceptualized in the context of the Cittàslow model, and the varying elements that are contributors to sustainable tourism development in SIDS are discussed. These include its marketing potential, environmental and agricultural benefits, as well as the definitive socio-economic advances that may come about from implementing such an initiative. Ultimately, our analysis illustrates the SIDS specific impacts that the strategies of the Cittàslow model facilitate, while it also highlights some of the potential barriers to SIDS seamlessly adopting such a concept.

摘要

慢城市的理念旨在保护地方、人、产品、食物和环境的独特特征。包容性参与是小型社区运动的重点,旨在提高居民的生活质量,并与游客分享他们独一无二的体验。"慢城运动"运动的讨论近年来一直在增加,本文对这个概念的界定增进了对这个话题了解。本文通过研究运动对可持续性和地方治理的作用过程,进而促进小岛发展中国家(SIDS)的发展,最终直接或间接促进了可持续旅游的发展。 本文通过对慢食、慢旅游和与旅游业相关的可持续性的讨论,阐明它们是如何融入慢旅游精神并影响慢城市运动的。有趣的是,通过审查慢城市运动的一些要点,我们可以确定旅游业的生活质量和体验价值如何促进慢城市对小岛屿发展中国家可持续旅游发展的做法。从岛屿角度的可持续性是在慢城市模型的脉络下概念化的，并讨论了对小岛屿发展中国家可持续旅游发展作出贡献的各种因素。这些因素包括其市场潜力、环境和农业效益，以及执行这一倡议可能产生的明确的社会经济进步。最后，我们的分析说明了慢城市模式的战略所促进的小岛屿发展中国家的具体影响，同时也强调了小岛屿发展中国家无缝采用这一概念的一些潜在障碍。

1. Introduction

Cittàslow, Città Lenta, Slow City, and Slow Town are terms used to describe the various aspects of a movement that tries to spread an awareness on how important it is to reduce the pace of everyday life. This originated from an earlier movement that stressed the importance of Slow Food as an anti-fast food and fast-life philosophy and has now evolved to include the Cittàslow (Slow City) and Slow Tourism concepts. Although these concepts are distinct, they complement each other in several ways. Cittàslow and Slow Tourism both build on the philosophy of Slow Food, and while the Cittàslow movement focuses on portraying local distinctiveness through sustainability and local governance, all three slow movements (food, city and tourism) are based on a philosophy that aims to change the mindset of people by fostering better connections between people, places and life. Although tourism is typically viewed as a negative force in many local communities, Slow Tourism aims to ameliorate the potential problems associated with it by introducing slowness, harmony and sustainability (Chemli, Nunes, & Toanoglou, 2018; Fullagar, Markwell, & Wilson, 2012). In addition, even though Slow Tourism has evolved from the slow ethos, it can be discussed from several different perspectives such as marketing, consumer behavior and sustainable tourism. Slow Food and Cittàslow have also inspired local sustainability based on other concepts such as fair trade (Heitmann, Robinson, & Povey, 2011).

The Cittàslow initiative is a 'grassroots movement' and it has been effectively adopted across all continents (Nilsson, Svärd, Widarsson, & Wirell, 2011). While its adoption has been effective in small communities and especially in island communities, the unique sensitivities of sovereign nations such as 'small island developing states' (SIDS) to it have not been addressed. Our analysis investigates the relationship between the Cittàslow initiative and sustainability as it relates to tourism, to allow the discovery of appropriate tourism approaches in local communities, and to study potential benefits and impacts in the context of small islands (Eusébio, Luís Vieira, & Lima, 2018; Okonkwo & Odey, 2018). The Cittàslow approach to sustainability and local governance in small communities provides a highly suitable method to investigate tourism development along with community empowerment in a small island context (Lee, Jan, Tseng, & Lin, 2018). The Cittàslow movement is primarily concerned with social economy, conservation of local heritage and the environment (Nilsson et al., 2011). Nonetheless, while Cittàslow is not aimed at promoting tourism, the visibility of the movement can stimulate sustainable tourism, which in turn boosts the local economy and community led tourism developments (Heitmann et al., 2011). Furthermore, while the Cittàslow organization does not explicitly speak on issues such as tourism, its policies reflect this alternative development approach (Croes, 2012).

Interestingly, the fluidity of the movement suggests that communities should aim to achieve development that is local and self-supporting based on their own unique characteristics (Miele, 2008), and although Semmens and Freeman (2012) have raised the question of the applicability of the Cittàslow movement outside of its Eurocentric affluent and urban origins, the success of the movement, its fluidity and the philosophy behind it, negates queries regarding transferability. The fluidity of the movement as prescribed by Miele (2008) has become evident, however the existing literature has yet to examine how the Cittàslow philosophy can impact small island economies. To rectify this situation, we discuss in this paper how the Cittàslow model serves as a framework for small societies to realize the practical implications of sustainable development theory, to indirectly enhance the tourism product by improving quality of life, and to do so while addressing wider sustainability concerns (Ridderstaat, Croes, & Nijkamp, 2016a). Our analysis introduces theoretical and conceptual considerations that are relevant when discussing the Cittàslow model as a suitable method for sustainable tourism development in SIDS. This analysis enhances our understanding of Cittàslow and explores some of the key issues relating to sustainability in SIDS. The Cittàslow approach can therefore be seen as an opportunity for SIDS to use their unique characteristics, strengthen local networks and encourage further inclusive participation within the national tourism industry (Pratt, 2015).

Ultimately, the Cittàslow movement has gained popularity as more and more countries implement sustainable initiatives and seek a Cittàslow designation (Coşar & Kozak, 2014). Given this, Cittàslow can be used as a guideline that inspires a change in people's attitudes towards sustainability and creates places that can practically implement sustainable development practices (Nilsson et al., 2011; Okonkwo & Odey, 2018). Slow travel has also emerged as a local social movement (Lumsdon & McGrath, 2011), however, this is limited to countries or regions where borders are land locked or infrastructure developments such as railways allow for this to occur. Slow tourism goes a little further and allows for international travel across borders where there may be sincere involvement with the local community (Conway & Timms, 2012). This allows tourism to link with the quality of life in the host community and the visitor experience, and through this, the goals of sustainable tourism are realized (Ridderstaat, Croes, & Nijkamp, 2016b). There is a demand for Slow Tourism and Slow Cities to give destinations the ability to supply various aspects of local distinctiveness as a part of a sustainability agenda while striving at the same time to achieve sustainable tourism goals (Moltz, 2009).

2. Literature review

2.1. Key features and practical applications of the cittàslow model

The Cittàslow philosophy is part of the *slow* ethos and one of the main features of a Cittàslow destination is the requirement to be *small*. To become a designated town within the Cittàslow network, the population needs to be below 50,000 and the community must comply with 72 quality criteria covering seven main areas. These criteria are guidelines to a *sustainable* self-assessment for all prospective towns (Karabag, Yucel, & Inal, 2012). While the requirements of the Cittàslow movement are that they are *slow*, *small* and *sustainable*, its aims collectively frame a model that operates as a form of grassroots activism (see Table 1). Typically, the push to join the Cittàslow network is initiated at the grass-roots level through the mayor, local business representatives or the local Slow Food convivium, and is in keeping with the slow ethos relating to the movement, locally oriented responses and action plans that have been developed to preserve the uniqueness of a place (Mayer & Knox, 2009). The Cittàslow model helps to facilitate a 'bottom up' approach to governance, enabling individuals to achieve sustainable living while at the same time, maintaining local distinctiveness, improving local businesses and enhancing the overall visitor experience by creating a sense of place (Li & Li, 2014).

The Cittàslow movement also promotes the eating of local in-season produce/food, supporting locally owned businesses and preserving cultural heritage (Nilsson et al., 2011). Local Cittàslow towns adopt various approaches to achieve these requirements. In Hersbruck (Germany), for example, the community has effectively connected the three components of sustainability as follows: the local environmental protection groups have collaborated with farmers, small businesses and the government to protect traditional pasture lands that are used for the growing of organic crops that are later used to make local products, and the community has also formed a network of farmers who sell their products directly from their farms (Mayer & Knox, 2006). This farm to table project is just one of many, while additional projects have also incorporated food education, as well as alternative energy production that is utilized by local businesses. This illustrates how communities can implement strategies that promote environmental conservation as well as creating income-generating opportunities for local residents (Budruk & Phillips, 2011).

Similarly, while the implementation strategies that have been used in many of the UK Cittàslow towns have not been uniform, Pink (2009) discussed how local Cittàslow organizers have viewed the model as a practical tool that can assist UK market towns to maintain a particular model of economic sustainability that encourages a diverse range of small businesses. Likewise, Milutinovic (2007) provided a detailed examination of the Cittàslow community in Ludlow (UK). The author concluded that once citizens become committed to local development, and the preservation of agricultural and or handcraft traditions with historical heritage, the journey towards enhancing and protecting the environment, boosting the social economy and improving resident's quality of life will prove to be successful regardless of the strategies used. The Cittàslow approach to sustainability is easily transferrable once this framework is in place, and

Table 1. Key features of Cittàslow.

Key features of Cittàslow	
Requirements	Slow ethos
	Total population of less than 50,000
	Sustainable self-assessment
Aims/Objectives	Grassroots, social movement
	Local distinctiveness
	Local governance
	Encourage a change in mindset and philosophy
	Preservation of local culture, heritage and traditions
	Integration of local production and support of local businesses

Source: The authors (2019).

these collective and progressive approaches to local sustainability highlight the various attitudes that small communities can take using grassroot collaborative efforts to harness commitment to local development. This not only increases the community's awareness of self-sustaining practices, but it creates local pride and a local identity (Okonkwo & Odey, 2018).

The quality of life and sustainability indicator point system embodied in the Cittàslow methodology acknowledges the importance of local development and the goal of creating self-supporting, and authentic places that are worth visiting (Lee et al., 2018). A unique visitor experience occurs as a direct result of sustainable place making. Varying levels of sustainability can be achieved, and the flexibility gained in doing so opens tremendous opportunities for small communities that are interested in sustainable practices (Bjelland, 2010).

2.2. Experience values in tourism and the cittàslow movement

While previous studies have emphasized the connection between Cittàslow and urban development (Jamal, Camargo, Sandlin, & Segrado, 2010; Knox, 2005; Mayer & Knox, 2006; Mayer & Knox, 2010; Pink, 2009), others have explored its fundamental roots with Slow Food, and discussed Cittàslow from a gastronomic point of view (Nilsson et al., 2011; Yurtseven & Karakas, 2013). And, although many have specified that Cittàslow is more concerned with sustainable communities, several authors have discussed the Cittàslow movement from a tourism marketing perspective (Coşar & Kozak, 2014; Karabag et al., 2012). The general fluidity of the movement also allows for cross disciplinary research (Miele, 2008). The commonality in all this research has been its connection to sustainability (Baldemir, Kaya, & Şahin, 2013; Ekinci, 2014; Grzelak-Kostulska, Hołowiecka, & Kwiatkowski, 2011; Semmens & Freeman, 2012). So, while Hatipoglu (2015) focused on the contribution that the Cittàslow philosophy has on the community's quality of life and visitor experience there has been little focus on the social dimensions of the Cittàslow movement, and by extension, how this can positively impact on social exchange between a community and its visitors.

Nevertheless, exploring Cittàslow through various disciplines allows for an insightful analysis of the philosophy, and it also allows for an identification of gaps in our treatment of sustainable tourism development. This has led to an understanding that slowing down the pace of a destination, while attempting to improve its living standards or quality of life for residents, requires that a destination continually improve the scope and quality of the tourism experience (Pink & Lewis, 2014). Moreover, where tourism is concerned, buying local, saving energy, using public transportation and protecting heritage is always commendable (Andereck & Jurowski, 2006). This goes beyond economic benefits and incorporates quality of life issues (Carmichael, 2006). Likewise, the quality of life of the host community can also be positively or negatively affected by environmental (crowding, air, water, and noise pollution), economic (inflation, tax, job availability) and/or social (image, awareness, preservation of heritage) perspectives (Figure 1). Thus, gaining experience value has been recognized as important as an integrated process between hosts and guests in a setting where their

Figure 1. The Cittàslow tourism exchange.

respective meanings of value are shared and recognized (Prebensen, Chen, & Uysal, 2014).

It is important therefore that quality of life becomes a major part of the sustainable development agenda, and although defining and measuring quality of life as a multi-dimensional construct is outside the scope of this paper, satisfying the various needs of a community that fall within the broad spectrum of sustainability (environmental conservation, economic efficiency, social equity) can lead to a better society (Karabag et al., 2012). Practical approaches to local small-scale sustainability have been encouraged within the Cittàslow network. Cittàslow sustainability indicators are directly linked to action plans (Mayer & Knox, 2009), and although the goals do not allow for a quantifiable measure of quality of life, actual improvements in policies make it easier for stakeholders to implement projects and events that affect the everyday lives of the community, resulting in a higher quality of life for residents and a better visitor experience (Hatipoglu, 2015).

2.3. Island resilience and cittàslow

2.3.1. Community vulnerability and resilience

Resilience in the face of problems is important, and this concept has become a part of policy and academic debate internationally, especially as it relates to climate change (Christopherson, Michie, & Tyler, 2010; Pink & Lewis, 2014). However, resilience from an island perspective also needs to take community resilience into account (Walker & Salt, 2006). Caribbean SIDS have been recently devastated by natural disasters, and according to a Post Disaster Needs Assessment (2017), during the recovery process the SIDS in the Caribbean need to strengthen the resilience of agriculture and fisheries as key production sectors. The community level capacity building and partnerships that the Cittàslow movement encourages can assist with a more climate resilient sector that supports the creation of value chains (Christopherson et al., 2010; United Nations Development Programme, 2017). It is therefore paramount that resilience in SIDS focuses on empowering communities and individuals to become self-sufficient by way of putting better systems in place for times of crisis. Community planning, sustainability and resilience become even more important in the effort to reduce damage to livelihoods and foster faster recovery (Pratt, 2015; de Bruijn, Buurman, Mens, Dahm, & Klijn, 2017). With the need for Caribbean SIDS to safeguard productive sectors that integrate and compliment the main economic sector (the tourism industry), the principles that guide Cittàslow offer an opportunity that should be explored (Coşar & Kozak, 2014).

2.3.2. The importance of local produce and products

The history of the development of SIDS is quite complex. For example, as many Caribbean islands moved away from a plantation economy, the share of agricultural production gradually weakened as the share of industries such as tourism increased (Apostolopoulos & Gayle, 2002; Duval, 2004). However, the growth and expansion of the tourism industry in each country varied, and while tourism has generally been used as a mechanism to offset the decline in the agriculture sector, its development has largely been dependent on the interests of stakeholders. The history of small islands has also been marked by the postwar development factors of decolonization and the global spread of international tourism (McElroy, 2003). Since then, the tourism industry has played a vital role in the economic growth of many Caribbean islands (Punnett & Morrison, 2006). Although many Caribbean islands have had favorable infrastructural developments that align with tourism development, such development in small islands may merely have shifted the burden of dependence from one form of production (agriculture) to another one (experiences), even though this move is not surprising when the restricted economic alternatives are considered (Grzelak-Kostulska et al., 2011).

The dynamics of the tourism industry in many SIDS are quite unique. In the Caribbean group of SIDS, Dominica may be categorized as a low-revenue - low-leakage destination (Weaver, 1991). On the other hand, while leakage rates vary across the Caribbean, figures as high as 85% has been recorded (Conway & Timms, 2010; Ramjee-Singh, 2006). But, there is a demand for locally grown produce in Dominica (Boys, Willis, & Carpio, 2014), thus researchers such as Milne (2008), Potter and Lloyd-Evans (1997) and Pratt (2015) have suggested that coupled with a high level of indigenous participation within the Dominican tourism industry, this is indicative to how economic leakages from Dominica may not be as high as those recorded in other SIDS.

2.3.3. Local communities, local resilience and cittàslow

In addressing what makes resilience possible, (McManus et al., 2012) outlined that it is the notion of belonging. With this at the heart of resilience, is the appreciation that it is something about a local community that enables it to cope with change by developing itself as a whole. Community development can therefore be seen as important for resilience, along with the underlying principles of Cittàslow. As noted by Pink and Lewis (2014), there is now growing attention being placed on resilient communities being a model for sustainability, and researchers have explored a 'community study' approach to resilience. The slow movement provides a practical way for local communities to increase local resilience in accordance with the slow philosophy that is rooted in the local environment, people and economy. The Cittàslow movement therefore allows for a way forward in the planning of local communities and resilience. Slow living is about how we live now and in the future. It allows for a contemporary interpretation of the past of places, communities and mobilization of their traditions, principles and values, so that the present can be critiqued as a way to plan alternatives for the future (Parkins & Craig, 2006).

The argument put forward thus far has looked at the relationships and elements that make up the slow philosophy. Cittàslow was originally conceived as a network of towns promoting a sustainable way of living, providing an example of the ways that these objectives can be achieved (Ball, 2015). Resilience requires a societal capacity to take impacts into account as it relates to everyday decision making (Carp, 2012), at the same time, Walker and Salt (2006) suggest that resilience thinking can prove beneficial. Cittàslow leaders have been using the global network to pool resources and create future oriented accounts of recovery in the face of crisis or threats (Pink & Lewis, 2014). According to these researchers, the essential element of the Cittàslow approach is its focus on capacity building and they highlight the movement's mode of activism through a revised concept of resilience. Essentially, resilience is not based on a single factor, but instead needs to take the physical environment, people's sense of belonging, and their job opportunities into consideration (McManus et al., 2012). Cittàslow promotes places that are rich in uniqueness, sustainable economies, and pleasant living environments (Li & Li, 2014). These elements ultimately contribute to the resilience of communities.

2.4. Sustainability, the cittàslow movement, and island tourism

The tourism industry is an important global industry and for many parts of the world, it is the dominant economic sector. Small island economies rely on the tourism industry as a key contributor, providing jobs for most of the local population and being the main source of foreign exchange (Briguglio, 1995; Lee et al., 2018; McElroy, 2003; Pratt, 2015; Scheyvens & Momsen, 2008a; Scheyvens & Momsen, 2008b). This type of dependence means that these societies need to ensure that sustainability is achieved, resources conserved, human resources constantly upgraded, skills enhanced, and relevant policies for these critical issues are developed. There are many challenges associated with achieving sustainability, yet it provides an immense opportunity for maximizing its potential because tourism can facilitate a way for host societies to create sustainable livelihoods and inclusive development (Singh, 2008). Furthermore, as progress is made towards achieving sustainability, societies become more stable, continue to raise their awareness, and develop new ways of solving problems. Thus, the tourism industry has proven to be one of the most important economic sectors for SIDS (Clarke, 1997); if it is managed in a responsible and ethical manner, it will positively affect society and the economy as a whole (Jayawardena, 2002).

Tourism has thus been economically beneficial for many SIDS however they have also been subject to negative impacts on nature and local communities in terms of uncontrolled development, unfair practices, and inequalities in employment (Pratt, 2015). For such small countries, these impacts can be extreme and far-reaching. The main challenge for SIDS is to create appropriate policies and strategies that can enhance the approach to achieving sustainable tourism development, while adding value to the tourism product (Ball, 2015; Bjelland, 2010). For developed and developing countries across the globe, the issue of sustainability is not new, just as the concept of corporate social responsibility is not new to the business world. However, given that the tourism industry is often a lifeline for SIDS, the time has come for societies in these tourism dependent economies to be proactive and approach the issues of sustainable development effectively (environmental conservation, economic efficiency and social equity) (Oriande & Evans, 2011). This may in many cases require a different approach to the usual top-down decision-making process that has to date given priority to only macro-economic benefits.

Sustainability is a complex phenomenon and while the environmental, economic and social dimensions create a holistic framework of defining it, there are additional and more detailed characteristics that can be associated with sustainability and the practical approach to achieving it (Oriande & Evans, 2011). As there are different types of countries with a variety of priorities and approaches to tourism development, there is no "one size fits all" when it comes to sustainable development. Nonetheless, while a framework can provide a universal guideline that countries can adopt, flexibility is important, and sustainability should be monitored to assess its impact on all stakeholders at the different levels of planning and development (Semmens & Freeman, 2012). Stakeholders must develop systems to monitor and adjust planning and destination management, and long-term goals should achieve economic linkages between destination communities and industries to improve the social wellbeing of host communities (Budruk & Phillips, 2011). This paper is primarily concerned with how sustainable tourism development in SIDS can lead to an improved quality of life, visitor experience and a balance of economic benefits from the tourism industry among all stakeholders, and the discussion throughout this paper emphasizes this (Ridderstaat, Croes, & Nijkamp, 2016a).

Where sustainability is concerned, the Cittàslow movement can only serve as a guiding framework. The practical applications have varied, and small towns have tailored their approaches (Mayer & Knox, 2006; Mayer & Knox, 2009; Miele, 2008; Milutinovic, 2007). This hands-on approach to local development has been effective because the movement is essentially a grassroots one, designed by local people and aimed at improving their quality of life. Thus, for SIDS, the Cittàslow philosophy can serve as an alternative or even as an additional approach to advancing sustainable development to not only secure local people's livelihood but also to ensure that the tourism industry continues to develop in a holistic manner (Jayawardena & Ramajeesingh, 2003; Li & Li, 2014).

The existing literature on the Cittàslow movement has explored its implementation in a range of countries and highlights a diverse array of strategies that various small towns have introduced. However, the literature has yet to fully examine how the Cittàslow philosophy can impact upon small island economies (Nilsson et al., 2011). To this point, our analysis has emphasized the social aspects of sustainability, and how this can impact on sustainable tourism development in tourism dependent economies. It has also addressed the significance that tourism has for the environmental aspect of sustainability (Mayer & Knox, 2009). We have examined how sustainable agriculture might lead to the promotion of more local food and products, while the economic and social aspects have been combined to highlight how efficiency and equity can be achieved by encouraging inclusion, social progress and other ways of enhancing quality of life for its residents (Pink, 2009). The overlapping environmental and socio-economic segments in destinations identify common locally oriented responses for Cittàslow towns, while tourism marketing and national branding segments have introduced the indirect impacts of Cittàslow and identified how the visibility of being a part of the slow movement can contribute to their overall sustainable tourism development (Yurtseven & Kaya, 2011).

Based on this analysis, Figure 2 combines the various approaches that have been applied internationally to show how the Cittàslow movement can positively impact SIDS (Coşar & Kozak, 2014). Interestingly, the strategies that Cittàslow towns implement are geared towards creating peaceful, visitor friendly spaces, which are characteristics that islands have traditionally had. Thus, it should be remembered that Cittàslow originated in industrialized Europe where the need to slow down acts as a motivator to travel to smaller locations or rural areas (Ekinci, 2014). Slow Tourism also falls within the overall slow movement alongside Cittàslow, and according to Conway and Timms (2012), Slow Tourism allows for the concept of inclusive growth in developing regions such as the Caribbean, Latin America, Oceania, Africa and Asia. The concept is also relevant to destinations in wealthier parts of the world. Without placing limitations on travel movements, the impacts of sustainability can be examined from a tourism perspective where visitors are interested in authentic experiences and gaining a sense of place by engaging with the destination (nature, heritage, people, culture, food), while at the same time avoiding negative environmental, economic and social impacts to host communities (Baldemir et al., 2013).

Finally, the underlying concept of sustainability and Cittàslow appeals to environmentally conscious tourists who are attentive to various forms of responsible tourism, or who reflect on the intrinsic value of the travel experience (Fullagar et al., 2012). In Mauritius, for example, although sun, sea and sand are the main tourism products, Ramkissoon and Uysal (2014) have shown how authenticity adds value to the tourism experience at cultural and natural heritage sites and suggested that authenticity appeals to high-order needs of satisfaction and motivation, and in particular novelty seeking, prestige and learning. However, in contrast, Bricker and Kerstetter (2006) examined what 'sense of place' means to Fijians. Preserving the unique characteristics

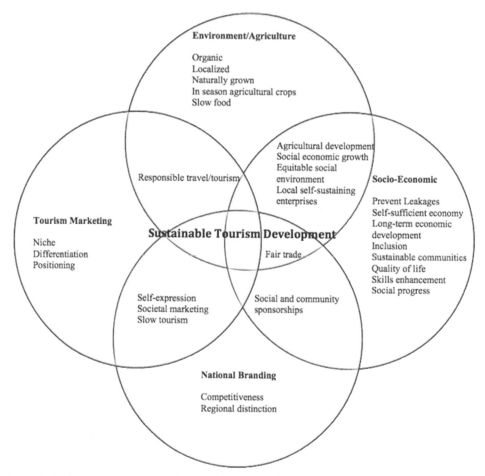

Figure 2. Cittàslow impact analysis for small island developing states (SIDS).

of a destination that incorporates its people, food, products as well as environmental surroundings, and the continuity of its local traditions thus plays a vital role in ensuring that a destination maintains an authentic presence.

3. Analysis

3.1. Impact analysis for small island developing states (SIDS)

The main objective of investigating the ways in which the Cittàslow model of sustainable development and local governance can impact on SIDS, was to identify the most effective way to bring about a change in attitude towards achieving sustainability as part of a long-term sustainable agenda in small tourism dependent islands (Eusébio et al., 2018). Figure 2 illustrates some of the major potential impacts that a Cittàslow affiliation can have on SIDS and explores how the underlying philosophy of Cittàslow can help to fill the gap in the planning framework for sustainable tourism development in SIDS (Duval, 2004). The main impact areas illustrated in Figure 2 are environment/agriculture, socio-economic, tourism marketing and national branding. The environmental considerations are primarily associated with the promotion of agriculture and how links can be made to the tourism industry. The Cittàslow movement promotes the preservation of local agricultural production, and this can serve as a way for SIDS to supply indigenous agricultural produce to the tourism industry. According to Bowen, Cox, and Fox (1991), greater integration of the agriculture and tourism industries will help to reduce leakage from the local economy. In keeping with the principles of Cittàslow, providing local, naturally grown, organic and in season produce to visitors serves many purposes. Firstly, sustainability can be gained from the form of agricultural development that goes beyond local consumption, giving farmers a means of creating co-operatives and owning self-sufficient enterprises. This in turn would lead to a greater sense of social equity, progress and satisfaction.

From a different perspective, visitors can feel engaged with the authenticity of the destination and appreciate a sense of place (Mayer & Knox, 2006). Unfortunately, as the tourism industry has developed in many SIDS, the agricultural industry has declined as mentioned previously (Apostolopoulos & Gayle, 2002; Duval, 2004; Gössling, 2003). Therefore, because of the limited scope for economic diversification (Jayawardena & Ramajeesingh, 2003), to achieve sustainability, SIDS need to develop sectoral linkages with the tourism industry, and not just be limited to the agricultural industry. According to Conway (2002), there has been a growing demand for local foods from hotels and restaurant businesses in the Caribbean, and with advances in new large-scale farming technologies and improved tourism-agriculture supplier relationships, this acts as an encouraging factor in implementing some of the environmental/agricultural elements of Cittàslow. There are indeed huge benefits from creating networks and developing inter-sectoral linkages that work through cooperation (Hall, Kirkpatrick, & Mitchell, 2005; Kim, 2017), and this is another main feature of Cittàslow.

Traditionally, economic linkages have always been essential for sustainable development, and these need to be enhanced if the tourism industry is to contribute to the well-being of its residents (Semmens & Freeman, 2012). Endorsed in the Cittàslow philosophy is the right of all citizens to enjoy good, clean and fair food that is sustainably produced with consideration for all stakeholders (Heitmann et al., 2011). This further enhances the quality of life of residents, and the trickle-down effect from these practices essentially creates a progressive means of achieving sustainability for communities and the tourism industry, while at the same time also contributing to wider sustainability concerns (Pink & Lewis, 2014).

The overlapping of the components of environment/agriculture with the socio-economic aspect ensures that there is an optimistic outlook for the development of local enterprises that benefit communities and the social economy (Budruk & Phillips, 2011). As the Cittàslow bottom up approach to sustainability tackles issues of equity and shifts the balance of power to complementary sectors of society, the promise of self-sustaining communities extends to other specialized niche markets (Hatipoglu, 2015). Niche markets provide an alternative for small producers in SIDS who are otherwise unable to compete in the global market due to their small size, high manufacturing costs and lack of economies of scale. Punnett and Morrison (2006) outlined several specialized niche markets such as natural organic produce/products, pottery and fair-trade products, yet while their research focused on access to the North American market, these can also appeal to visitors to the islands through Cittàslow projects or events that promote local products. Fair trade emerges as a potential brand, and although fair trade tourism is not a product, it addresses the issue of equity and is seen by many as a contributive initiative to the sustainable agenda while also benefiting from improved image and potential tourism promotion (Oriande & Evans, 2011). Creating awareness of this potential for both residents and visitors alike can be achieved in a variety of ways, and stakeholder cooperation is imperative for these developments to be successful.

Because sustainable development in small islands has been largely concentrated on sectoral and macro-policy shifts (Lee et al., 2018; Singh, 2008), more attention needs to be placed on people and societal concerns. Furthermore, the top down leadership style in SIDS leaves a wide gap between policy makers and the rest of society (Briguglio, Butler, Harrison, & Filho, 1996), and it is for this reason that grassroots movements such as Cittàslow are important. It is unfortunate that policy makers in SIDS place most of their resources into attracting tourists in large numbers rather than formulating ways of benefiting from the "tourism multiplier effect" (Apostolopoulos & Gayle, 2002). Sustainable development is a holistic framework, yet tourism development is often implemented in top-down approaches by international, private sector organizations in cooperation with local policy makers (Gössling, 2003). These approaches usually negatively impact on host communities, and because these communities are rarely consulted about how they can contribute to economic activity, they associate tourism with unfair and unethical practices. Nonetheless, while small islands should diversify their economies, tourism has a comparative advantage for many of them, and therefore has a place in local development plans (Eusébio et al., 2018). Moreover, the tourism life cycle in islands needs to be supported by all stakeholders including local residents (Graci & Dodds, 2010). The relevant stakeholders within a dynamic tourism system need to be considered within the sustainable tourism framework, and the Cittàslow underlying philosophy helps to facilitate initiatives that allow for mutual benefits for various stakeholder groups. With the objective being to attain community goals, forging partnerships helps to enrich stakeholder relationships within the tourism industry (Scheyvens & Momsen, 2008a).

Tropical destinations are similar in their offerings (sun, sea and sand), therefore many have embarked on diversifying the tourism product to include other forms of tourism such as cultural heritage. The Cittàslow philosophy of promoting local heritage adds to this aspiration. Additionally, by promoting alternatives, SIDS effectively control negative impacts that are associated with tourism, and address competitiveness (Duval, 2004; McElroy & de Albuquerque, 1998). The enhanced localized characteristics that can be accomplished because of continued implementation of Cittàslow policies can complement already established tourism products. Abundant beaches and limited attractions in tropical destinations usually invite rest and relaxation, where visitors from industrialized countries can feel happy in a laid-back environment (Gössling, 2003). Ultimately, the traditional purpose of a holiday or vacation is precisely this, and thus is the reason why so many people are fascinated with island destinations.

The main attractions of island tourism are not likely to change in the near future. However, considering the changing dynamics of the tourism industry, SIDS can benefit from positioning themselves so that there is a positive spillover effect from being a part of a progressive movement such as Cittàslow. Positive associations help to shape the perception of a place (Clifton, 2014), and because some visitors travel to satisfy their need for self-esteem or even self-actualization in accordance to Maslow's hierarchy of needs, their destination of choice may enhance their sense of self-identity (Kolb, 2006). The source market for many SIDS (Europe and North America) may fall into the target market for the slow movement, and being a part of the Cittàslow network or creating value for the established tourism product can only be beneficial. Essentially, the majority of SIDS is only capable of small-scale tourism in absolute terms, therefore the most important factor is differentiation through the advancement of a sustainability agenda, and the Cittàslow approach offers a practical way to achieve this (Semmens & Freeman, 2012).

The United Nations (2019) categorizes SIDS by geographical regions: the Caribbean, the Atlantic, Indian Ocean, Mediterranean and South China Sea (AIMS), and the Pacific, and there are thirty-nine (39) countries in total, with the largest number of countries belonging to the Caribbean group. Interestingly, the Cittàslow movement is not present in any country within the SIDS group, yet the Slow Food movement has in recent years been adopted, particularly in the Caribbean. There are currently 12 SIDS that promote Slow Food (Slow Food, 2019), and the Slow Fish with particular focus on Slow Fish Caribe is a network of Slow Food members in the Caribbean region, although this has a wider reach that the United Nations categorized SIDS. Caribbean SIDS, such as Slow Food Barbados, have adopted the movement to create dramatic and lasting change in the national food system by facilitating the development of food sovereignty and food security initiatives on the island of Barbados (Slow Food Barbados, 2019). Initiatives include the Chef Alliance, and in a tourism dependent country such as Barbados, chefs across various hotels and restaurants that source and promote local produce directly and indirectly contribute to sustainability, reduce the food import bill as well as the leakages that are often associated with the tourism industry.

Greater integration of agriculture in the tourism industry will reduce leakages from the local economy and expand export earnings (Bowen et al., 1991). Conway and Timms (2012) also mentioned that Slow Tourism helps to reduce capital leakages through the provision of local agricultural products, handicrafts, furnishings, and service activities that capture a great amount of tourist expenditure at the destination. Research on Turkey's first Cittàslow area also showed that, from a marketing perspective, there is a close link between the Slow Food and Cittàslow movements that can influence Slow Tourism (Yurtseven & Kaya, 2011). Cittàslow was in fact born out of the Slow Food movement and has morphed into a progressive approach to sustainability and local governance for small communities. The concept behind Cittàslow is simple: it emphasizes good living, which stresses the quality of the local environment, and gastronomic resources (Miele, 2008). However, promoting local distinctiveness and a sense of place is just as important as enjoying good local food, wine or beer (Knox, 2005). The movement provides a brand that symbolizes authenticity and individuality. Most significantly, the Cittàslow movement encourages endogenous community and economic development opportunities that are embedded in local products, habits and traditions (Mayer & Knox, 2009). In brief, the Cittàslow approach to development supports 'slow' sustainable development at the local level by incorporating a social movement and a model for local governance, while also potentially creating an indirect impact for tourism development by improving product development and increased visibility (Nilsson et al., 2011).

3.2. Barriers to adapting the cittàslow approach in SIDS

Whether the Slow Food movement can be the start of the Cittàslow movement in SIDS is yet to be seen. Nonetheless, it is important to note that, unlike Slow Food providers, Cittàslow designated towns need to go through registration with a 72-point set of sustainable policies already in place, or to be implemented. For many SIDS, a top down style of leadership has historically been a widely adopted practice, and a grassroots type movement may not be very familiar to many. This coupled with the economic interest of government officials that are motivated towards fast results aimed at satisfying voters with figures that highlight economic growth during their tenure, may introduce additional challenges for the adoption of Cittàslow in SIDS (Semmens & Freeman, 2012). With this political environment being a reality for many SIDS, adapting the Cittàslow philosophy to the social economy and tourism activities will require a bottom up approach much like that of activist groups or grassroots movements and this will need to be an integral part of the process for successful implementation. Consideration should be given to all stakeholder groups and relative power should be neutralized (Sautter & Leisen, 1999).

If balance of power issues is excluded for the collaboration process of stakeholders, those with economic value and those with quality of life values such as residents and activist groups will be able to voice concerns and seek co-operation in line with the overall mandate within the sustainable tourism development agenda. Ultimately, these activist groups or grassroots movements are made up of residents, who also double as voters, and government officials need to take their quality of life, wellbeing and socio-economic progress into consideration as much as they do for hoteliers and other investors. The barriers to seamlessly adopting a movement like Cittàslow in SIDS are complex, in much the same way that tourism itself represents significant sustainable development policy dilemmas and some researchers see tourism's role in sustainable development as a complex one that highlights contradictions (Hall, Scott, & Gössling, 2013). Considerations such as information and awareness may therefore be a prerequisite, but a more detailed assessment is also necessary to examine why some approaches are successful in some contexts and not in others. Local attributes such as the marginalized locations or historical factors may have some influence on the successful adaptability, however, minimizing some of the impediments in achieving sustainability is the main concern of this paper and the aim is to discover how the positive attributes of a progressive movement aimed at achieving inclusive sustainability for small communities can be achieved.

While this is the case, it is still important that we do not avoid a critique of the feasibility of Cittàslow for SIDS. Although barriers may not be obvious, mentioning them in this section enriches our analysis, and allows for them to be more meaningfully applied. A number of barriers to adopting the Cittàslow movement in SIDS may stem from local challenges such as the high presence of agricultural imports, and local stakeholders would need to encourage a wider use of locally produced food, even for the local population, and actively seek to promote a buy local campaign. This can then extend to the tourism industry, although other challenges may arise when identifying and accessing the tourism market, and key players would need to gain knowledge about this market through research (Ekinci, 2014). Additionally, building a destination brand based on local produce, products and a strong local identity away from the sun, sea, sand brand that many SIDS are well known for, will take a considerable amount of effort and time, as well as a carefully planned and executed destination management strategy, and the cooperation of a diverse range of stakeholders. Stakeholder collaboration and networking may also pose challenges for producers and hospitality businesses, since different stakeholders that span across a number of sectors have varying needs and challenges (Punnett & Morrison, 2006).

These stakeholders vary from small enterprises to large resorts, yet while introducing Cittàslow principles in SIDS may not address the popularity of all-inclusive resorts, the increased collaboration amongst these stakeholders can benefit many and provide alternative solutions to complex issues. At the same time, any effort that advances stakeholder collaboration would be beneficial in many ways beyond the tourism industry and would help in advancing the sustainable development agenda.

As previously stated, the three key elements of the Cittàslow network are small size, a slowdown ethos and sustainable practices. In the context of SIDS, while the small and slow essentials are already in existence, sustainable practices that support an efficient and productive business environment are not as common. Our analysis has put forward the argument that SIDS usually possess the fundamental characteristics of the Cittàslow movement and coupled with the fluidity of the initiative (Miele, 2008), SIDS are essentially at a stage in development where they should create their own version of small, slow and sustainable. The overall academic discourse on the Cittàslow movement in varying contexts suggests that the benefits resulting from this approach to sustainability outweigh the difficulties. However, Bjelland (2010) implied that the success of the Cittàslow movement in small Italian towns did not guarantee its applicability elsewhere. Semmens and Freeman (2012) have also indicated that due to the strong Italian identity, many towns may not have the ideal characteristics such as community cohesion, local business environment and produce, heritage, architecture and culture.

There may not be as much awareness of the phenomenon of sustainability among residents in the developing world, and the question of whether affluence is a prerequisite for the movement, or that it creates improved quality of life from implementing sustainable policies, becomes an important outcome for the analysis of SIDS. Nevertheless, the aim of the Cittàslow movement is to achieve sustainability, and as a result sustainability as a construct may very well be an ongoing achievement to strive towards (Yurtseven & Kaya, 2011).

4. Conclusions

The dynamic nature of the tourism industry provides a far-reaching opportunity for SIDS to propel the sustainability agenda by implementing a progressive approach such as Cittàslow. Our analysis introduces a few theoretical and conceptual considerations that are relevant when discussing the Cittàslow model as a suitable one for sustainable tourism development in SIDS. While the tourism dynamic in SIDS is complex, varying levels of tourism development and the general maturity of the industry in these states allows for a wide range of conclusions regarding the tourism area life cycle (TALC) and the needs of various destinations. In addition, contemporary forces mean that tourist destinations need to be more flexible to changing consumer demand, and Cittàslow branding would be beneficial for SIDS. With an already vibrant tourism industry, the people of SIDS can use these opportunities to further the sustainability agenda and increasingly contribute to their livelihoods, making their society more resilient and sustainable.

Nevertheless, although this analysis has sought to understand and evaluate the impact of an innovative approach to sustainability in tourism development in small places such as SIDS, several limitations were identified. The first is that this analysis has treated SIDS as a group, even though the level of economic development and maturity of the tourism industry varies between destinations, and this will greatly determine how the Cittàslow approach would be implemented in practice. Furthermore, since the Cittàslow movement is not currently present in any destination within the SIDS group, a complete evaluation of its impact on sustainable tourism development could not be made. There is the potential that some unexpected situations could occur that would introduce additional factors. Nevertheless, there is scope for research on how a movement such as Cittàslow and its policies could operate in these geographical locations. More specifically, further research would help to highlight mechanisms to minimize negative voices and to maximize the positive outcomes of the Cittàslow approach.

When considering this analysis, we recommend that communities in the SIDS group begin to regenerate their communities in ways that lead to socially desirable outcomes. Given the current situation, examples of such initiatives may start with economic zones aimed at reducing food import bills, where communities begin to produce locally and adopt a local intervention policy on food security. A realization of the Cittàslow spirit in this way can help motivate residents to find inclusive solutions to difficult problems, because ultimately, societies cannot afford to dismiss progressive approaches to development. The goal should be to invest and build on social capital for long-term growth. Our analysis also enhances the understanding of Cittàslow tourism as a new niche opportunity, while at the same time it identifies key developmental characteristics and makes valuable suggestions for the tourism industry that could be adopted by many countries. The study has contributed both theoretically and practically by examining the unique and updated characteristics of this recently emerging field in the global tourism industry. As for the limitations of the research, given that we specifically focused on a particular SIDS context the results may well remain contingent on the specific industrial environments, and socio-political characteristics of this group. To build on this study, further comparative analyses of the industrial formation and development of Cittàslow tourism in other contexts is essential. Providing empirical survey data with the main stakeholders on the discussed themes and issues would also add to the contribution of this study.

Disclosure statement

No potential conflict of interest was reported by the authors.

References

Andereck, K., & Jurowski, C. (2006). Tourism and quality of life. In G. Jennings & N. P. Nickerson (Eds.) *Quality tourism experiences*, (pp. 136–154). Oxford: Elsevier.
Apostolopoulos, Y., & Gayle, D. J. (Eds.). (2002). *Island tourism and sustainable development: Caribbean, pacific, and mediterranean experiences*. Westport, CT: Greenwood.
Baldemir, E., Kaya, F., & Şahin, T. K. (2013). A management strategy within sustainable city context: Cittaslow. *Procedia - Social and Behavioral Sciences*, *99*, 75–84. doi:10.1016/j.sbspro.2013.10.473
Ball, S. (2015). Slow cities. In: W. K. D. Davies (Ed.), *Theme Cities: Solutions for urban problems*, (pp. 563–585). New York: Springer.
Bjelland, M. D. (2010). Small town sustainability: Economic, social, and environmental innovation [Review of the book *Small town sustainability: Economic, social, and environmental innovation*, by Paul Knox and Heike Mayer]. *Urban Geography*, *31*(8), 1150–1151. doi:10.2747/0272-3638.31.8.1150
Bowen, R. L., Cox, L. J., & Fox, M. (1991). The interface between tourism and agriculture. *Journal of Tourism Studies*, *2*(2), 43–54.
Boys, K. A., Willis, D. B., & Carpio, C. E. (2014). Consumer willingness to pay for organic and locally grown produce on Dominica: Insights into the potential for an "Organic Island." *Environment, Development and Sustainability*, *16*(3), 595–617. doi:10.1007/s10668-013-9496-3
Bricker, K. S., & Kerstetter, D. (2006). Saravanua ni vanua: Exploring sense of place in the rural highlands of Fiji. In G. Jennings & N. P. Nickerson (Eds.), *Quality tourism experiences*, (pp. 99–114). Oxford: Elsevier.
Briguglio, L. (1995). Small island developing states and their economic vulnerabilities. *World Development*, *23*(9), 1615–1632. doi:10.1016/0305-750X(95)00065-K
Briguglio, L., Butler, R., Harrison, D., & Filho, W. L. (1996). *Sustainable tourism in islands and small states: Case studies*. London: Pinter.
Budruk, M., & Phillips, R. (2011). *Quality-of-life community indicators for parks, recreation and tourism management*. London, U.K. Springer.
Carmichael, B. A. (2006). Linking quality tourism experiences, residents' quality of life, and quality experiences for tourists. In G. Jennings & N. P. Nickerson (Eds.), *Quality tourism experiences*, (pp. 115–135). Oxford: Elsevier.
Carp, J. (2012). The Town's Abuzz: Collaborative opportunities for environmental professionals in the slow city movement. *Environmental Practice*, *14*(2), 130–142. doi:10.1017/S1466046612000014
Chemli, S., Nunes, S., & Toanoglou, M. (2018). Sustainable economies by the time of crisis: Snowball effect on medium and small companies. *International Journal of Tourism Sciences*, *18*(3), 153–169. doi:10.1080/15980634.2018.1517933
Christopherson, S., Michie, M., & Tyler, P. (2010). Regional resilience: Theoretical and empirical perspectives. *Cambridge Journal of Regions, Economy and Society*, *3*(1), 3–10. doi:10.1093/cjres/rsq004

Clarke, J. (1997). A framework of approaches to sustainable tourism. *Journal of Sustainable Tourism, 5*(3), 224–233. doi:10.1080/09669589708667287

Clifton, N. (2014). Towards a holistic understanding of country of origin effects? Branding of the region, branding from the region. *Journal of Destination Marketing & Management, 3*(2), 122–132. doi:10.1016/j.jdmm.2014.02.003

Conway, D. (2002). Tourism, agriculture, and sustainability of terrestrial ecosystems in small islands. In Y. Apostolopoulos & D. J. Gayle (Eds.), *Island tourism and sustainable development: Caribbean, pacific, and mediterranean experiences,* (pp. 113–129). Westport, CT: Greenwood.

Conway, D., & Timms, B. F. (2010). Re-branding alternative tourism in the Caribbean: The case for 'slow tourism. *Tourism and Hospitality Research, 10*(4), 329–344. doi:10.1057/thr.2010.12

Conway, D., & Timms, B. F. (2012). Are slow travel and slow tourism misfits, compadres or different genres?. *Tourism Recreation Research, 37*(1), 71–76. doi:10.1080/02508281.2012.11081689

Coşar, Y., & Kozak, M. (2014). Slow tourism (Cittaslow) influence over visitors' behavior. In A. G. Woodside & M. Kozak (Eds.), *Tourists' behaviors and evaluations* (Vol. 9, pp. 21–29). UK: Emerald.

Croes, R. (2012). Assessing tourism development from Sen's capability approach. *Journal of Travel Research, 51*(5), 542–554. doi:10.1177/0047287511431323

de Bruijn, K., Buurman, J., Mens, M., Dahm, R., & Klijn, F. (2017). Resilience in practice: Five principles to enable societies to cope with extreme weather events. *Environmental Science & Policy, 70,* 21–30.

Duval, D. T. (2004). *Tourism in the Caribbean: Development, management, prospects,* London: Routledge.

Ekinci, M. B. (2014). The Cittaslow philosophy in the context of sustainable tourism development: The case of Turkey. *Tourism Management, 41,* 178–189. doi:10.1016/j.tourman.2013.08.013

Eusébio, C., Luís Vieira, A., & Lima, S. (2018). Place attachment, host–tourist interactions, and residents' attitudes towards tourism development: The case of Boa Vista Island in Cape Verde. *Journal of Sustainable Tourism, 26*(6), 890–909. doi:10.1080/09669582.2018.1425695

Fullagar, S., Markwell, K., & Wilson, E. (2012). *Slow tourism: Experiences and mobilities.* U.K.: Channel View.

Gössling, S. (2003). *Tourism and development in tropical islands: Political ecology perspectives.* Cheltenham, U.K.: Edward Elgar.

Graci, S., & Dodds, R. (2010). *Sustainable Tourism in Island Destinations.* London: Earthscan.

Grzelak-Kostulska, E., Hołowiecka, B., & Kwiatkowski, G. (2011). Cittaslow international network: An example of a globalization idea? Paper presented at The Scale of Globalization: Think Globally, Act Locally. University of Ostrava: Ostrava, Czech Republic.

Hall, D., Kirkpatrick, I., & Mitchell, M. (2005). *Rural tourism and sustainable business.* Clevedon, U.K.: Channel View.

Hall, C. M., Scott, D., & Gössling, S. (2013). The primacy of climate change for sustainable international tourism. *Sustainable Development, 21*(2), 112–121. doi:10.1002/sd.1562

Hatipoglu, B. (2015). Cittaslow": Quality of life and visitor experience. *Tourism Planning & Development, 12*(1), 20–36. doi:10.1080/21568316.2014.960601

Heitmann, S., Robinson, P., & Povey, G. (2011). Slow food, slow cities and slow tourism. In P. Robinson, S. Heitmann, & P. Dieke (Eds.), *Research themes for tourism,* (pp. 114–127). Wallingford: CAB International.

Jamal, T., Camargo, B., Sandlin, J., & Segrado, R. (2010). Tourism and cultural sustainability: Towards an eco-cultural justice for place and people. *Tourism Recreation Research, 35*(3), 269–279. doi:10.1080/02508281.2010.11081643

Jayawardena, C. (2002). Mastering Caribbean tourism. *International Journal of Contemporary Hospitality Management, 14*(2), 88–93. doi:10.1108/09596110210419273

Jayawardena, C., & Ramajeesingh, D. (2003). Performance of tourism analysis: A Caribbean perspective. *International Journal of Contemporary Hospitality Management, 15*(3), 176–179. doi:10.1108/09596110310470239

Karabag, O., Yucel, F., & Inal, M. E. (2012). Cittaslow movement: An opportunity for branding small towns and economic development in Turkey. *International Journal of Economics and Research*, *3*(3), 64–75.

Kim, J. J. (2017). Theoretical foundations underpinning supply chain management and supply chain level sustainable performance. *International Journal of Tourism Sciences*, *17*(3), 213–229. doi:10.1080/15980634.2017.1351155

Knox, P. (2005). Creating ordinary places: Slow cities in a fast world. *Journal of Urban Design*, *10*(1), 1–11. doi:10.1080/13574800500062221

Kolb, B. M. (2006). *Tourism marketing for cities and towns: Using branding and events to attract tourists*. Oxford: Elsevier.

Lee, T. H., Jan, F.-H., Tseng, C. H., & Lin, Y. F. (2018). Segmentation by recreation experience in island-based tourism: A case study of Taiwan's Liuqiu Island. *Journal of Sustainable Tourism*, *26*(3), 362–378. doi:10.1080/09669582.2017.1354865

Li, Y., & Li, H. (2014). The Slow City concept and its inspiration for local culture protection in domestic urbanization process. *Advanced Materials Research*, *1079-1080*, 1286–1289. doi:10. 4028/www.scientific.net/AMR.1079-1080.1286

Lumsdon, L. M., & McGrath, P. (2011). Developing a conceptual framework for slow travel: A grounded theory approach. *Journal of Sustainable Tourism*, *19*(3), 265–279. doi:10.1080/09669582.2010.519438

Mayer, H., & Knox, P. (2006). Slow cities: Sustainable places in a fast world. *Journal of Urban Affairs*, *28*(4), 321–334. doi:10.1111/j.1467-9906.2006.00298.x

Mayer, H., & Knox, P. (2009). Pace of life and quality of life: The slow city charter. In M. J. Sirgy, R. Phillips, & D. R. Rahtz (Eds.), *Community quality-of-life indicators: Best cases III*, (pp. 21–40). New York: Springer.

Mayer, H., & Knox, P. (2010). Small-town sustainability: Prospects in the second modernity. *European Planning Studies*, *18*(10), 1545–1565. doi:10.1080/09654313.2010.504336

McElroy, J. L. (2003). Tourism development in small islands across the world. *Geografiska Annaler, 85B*, *85*(4), 231–242. doi:10.1111/j.0435-3684.2003.00145.x

McElroy, J. L., & de Albuquerque, K. (1998). Tourism penetration index in small Caribbean islands. *Annals of Tourism Research*, *25*(1), 145–168. doi:10.1016/S0160-7383(97)00068-6

McManus, P., Walmsley, J., Argent, N., Baum, S., Bourke, L., Martin, J., … Sorensen, T. (2012). Rural community and rural resilience: What is important to farmers in keeping their country towns alive?. *Journal of Rural Studies*, *28*(1), 20–29. doi:10.1016/j.jrurstud.2011.09.003

Miele, M. (2008). Cittaslow: Producing slowness against the fast life. *Space and Polity*, *12*(1), 135–156. doi:10.1080/13562570801969572

Milne, S. (2008). The impact of tourism development in small Pacific island states: An overview. *New Zealand Journal of Geography*, *89*(1), 16–21. doi:10.1111/j.0028-8292.1990.tb00283.x

Milutinovic, S. (2007). 'Citta Slow' movement: Case study of Ludlow, UK, unpublished. Retrieved from http://upenn-envs667660.webs.com/Case%20studies/CittaSlow.pdf. 28 July 2016

Moltz, J. G. (2009). Representing pace in tourism mobilities: Staycations, slow travel and the amazing race. *Journal of Tourism and Cultural Change*, *7*(4), 270–286.

Nilsson, H. J., Svärd, A.-C., Widarsson, Å., & Wirell, T. (2011). Cittáslow' eco-gastronomic heritage as a tool for destination development. *Current Issues in Tourism*, *14*(4), 373–386. doi:10.1080/13683500.2010.511709

Okonkwo, E. E., & Odey, A. O. (2018). Impact of sustainability on tourism development in Nigeria: A case study of cross river state, Nigeria. *International Journal of Tourism Sciences*, *18*(2), 89–109. doi:10.1080/15980634.2018.1471878

Oriande, A., & Evans, M. (2011). Sustainable and alternative tourism. In P. Robinson, S. Heitmann, & P. Dieke (Eds.), *Research Themes for Tourism*, (pp. 69–86). Wallingford, CAB International.

Parkins, W., & Craig, G. (2006). *Slow living*. Oxford: Berg.

Pink, S. (2009). Urban social movement and small places: Slow cities as sites of activism. *City*, *13*(4), 451–465. doi:10.1080/13604810903298557

Pink, S., & Lewis, T. (2014). Making resilience: Everyday affect and global affiliation in Australian Slow Cities. *Cultural Geographies*, *21*(4), 695–710. doi:10.1177/1474474014520761

Post Disaster Needs Assessment. (2017). Hurricane Maria september 2017. The government of the Commonwealth of Dominica [Website] Retrieved from https://resilientcaribbean.caricom.org/wp-content/uploads/2017/11/DOMINICA-EXECUTIVE-SUMMARY.pdf. October 13, 2018.

Potter, R. B., & Lloyd-Evans, S. (1997). Sun, fun & a rum deal: Perspectives on development in the commonwealth Caribbean. *Focus on Geography*, *44*(4), 19–26. doi:10.1111/j.1949-8535.1997.tb00096.x

Pratt, S. (2015). The economic impact of tourism on SIDS. *Annals of Tourism Research*, *52*, 148–160. doi:10.1016/j.annals.2015.03.005

Prebensen, N. K., Chen, J. S., & Uysal, M. (2014). Co-creation of tourist experience: Scope, definition and structure. In N. K. Prebensen, J. S. Chen, & M. Uysal (Eds.), *Creating Experiences Value in Tourism*, (pp. 1–10). Wallingford: CAB International.

Punnett, B. J., & Morrison, A. (2006). Niche markets and small Caribbean producers: A match made in heaven?. *Journal of Small Business & Entrepreneurship*, *19*(4), 341–353. doi:10.1080/08276331.2006.10593375

Ramjee-Singh, D. H. (2006). Import content of tourism: Explaining differences among island states. *Tourism Analysis*, *11*, 33–44.

Ramkissoon, H., & Uysal, M. (2014). Authenticity as a value co-creator of tourism experiences. In N. K. Prebensen, J. S. Chen, & M. Uysal (Eds.). *Creating experiences value in tourism*, (pp. 113–124). Wallingford, CAB International.

Ridderstaat, J., Croes, R., & Nijkamp, P. (2016a). A two-way causal chain between tourism development and quality of life in a small island destination: An empirical analysis. *Journal of Sustainable Tourism*, *24*(10), 1461–1479. doi:10.1080/09669582.2015.1122016

Ridderstaat, J., Croes, R., & Nijkamp, P. (2016b). The tourism development: Quality of life nexus in a small island destination. *Journal of Travel Research*, *55*(1), 79–94. doi:10.1177/0047287514532372

Sautter, E. T., & Leisen, B. (1999). Managing stakeholders: A tourism planning model. *Annals of Tourism Research*, *26*(2), 312–328. doi:10.1016/S0160-7383(98)00097-8

Scheyvens, R., & Momsen, J. (2008a). Tourism and poverty reduction: Issues for small island states. *Tourism Geographies*, *10*(1), 22–41. doi:10.1080/14616680701825115

Scheyvens, R., & Momsen, J. (2008b). Tourism in small island states: From vulnerability to strengths. *Journal of Sustainable Tourism*, *16*(5), 491–510. doi:10.2167/jost821.0

Semmens, J., & Freeman, C. (2012). The value of Cittaslow as an approach to local sustainable development: A New Zealand perspective. *International Planning Studies*, *17*(4), 353–375. doi:10.1080/13563475.2012.726851

Singh, N. (2008). Sustainable development in the Caribbean: From policies to people. *The Caribbean Environment*, *1*(1), 50–53.

Slow Food Barbados. (2019). Our philosophy. [Website]. Retrieved from http://www.slowfoodbarbados.org/slowfood2016/mission/. April 12, 2019.

Slow Food. (2019). Where we are. [Website]. Retrieved from https://www.slowfood.com/about-us/where-we-are/. April 12, 2019.

United Nations Development Programme. (2017). UNDP regional overview impact of Hurricanes Irma and Maria. Conference Supporting Document. [Website} Retrieved from http://www.latinamerica.undp.org/content/rblac/en/home/library/environment_energy/regional-overview–impact-of-hurricanes-irma-and-maria.html December 8, 2018.

United Nations. (2019). About small island developing states [Website]. Retrieved from http://www.sids2014.org/index.php?menu=1496. April 8, 2019.

Walker, B., & Salt, D. (2006). *Resilience thinking: Sustaining ecosystems and people in a changing world*. Washington, DC: Island Press.

Weaver, D. B. (1991). Alternative to mass tourism in Dominica. *Annals of Tourism Research*, *18*(3), 414–432. doi:10.1016/0160-7383(91)90049-H

Yurtseven, H. R., & Kaya, O. (2011). Slow tourists: A comparative research based on Cittaslow principles. *American International Journal of Contemporary Research*, *1*(2), 91–98.

Yurtseven, H. R., & Karakas, N. (2013). Creating a sustainable gastronomic destination: The case of Cittaslow Gokceada-Turkey. *American International Journal of Contemporary Research*, *3*(3), 91–100.

Modelling tourism resilience in small island states: a tale of two countries

Prosper F. Bangwayo-Skeete and Ryan W. Skeete

ABSTRACT

The rising incidence and consequences of natural disasters, global economic crises, climate change, and socio-political upheavals have raised interest in resilience, particularly in small island economies. Their small size and high tourism-dependency make these small island states more vulnerable to such disruptions. Hence, understanding resilience or adaptive capacity to withstand shocks is fundamental to their sustainable development. The emerging literature uses the Adaptive Cycle Model to qualitatively analyse resilience through the evolution of tourism destinations. Nevertheless, the absence of quantitative studies using the Adaptive Cycle Model makes it a daunting task to adequately advise policymakers about the scope and scale of intervention necessary to facilitate the rebuilding of a stronger tourism industry. We, therefore, pioneer the use of Markov Switching Autoregressive Model to test the model's applicability using four decades of data on tourist arrivals in two Caribbean destinations, Barbados and Grenada. The results reveal untapped opportunities for transformation and regeneration in both countries' tourism industries, but highlight sharp contrast in their resilience capability. Grenada exhibits greater resilience as its adverse shocks, though deeper, are relatively transitory, while Barbados despite experiencing fewer external shocks faces prolonged repercussions from global recessions. For small islands, we conclude that the factors impacting lower resilience are the industry's management deficiencies, inadequate cohesion among stakeholders, and lack of innovation. Overall, the findings present a modelling framework for tourism-dependent economies to determine how quickly they recover from major stress events, the associated strategies necessary to strengthen tourism resilience, and the potential to innovate in the tourism industry.

摘要

自然灾害、全球经济危机、气候变化和社会政治动荡的发生频率不断增加, 后果更为严重, 提高了人们对恢复力的兴趣, 特别是小岛屿经济恢复力。这些小岛屿国家面积小, 对旅游业的依存程度高, 使它们更容易受到这种破坏。因此, 了解应对冲击的恢复力或适应能力对它们的可持续发展至关重要。新近文献采用适应性循环模型, 采用旅游目的地的演变的途径定性地分析了目的地的恢复力。然而, 由于缺乏使用适应性循环模型的定量研究, 因此向决策者提供促进重建更强大的旅游业所需的干预尺度和范围的充分建议是一项艰巨的任务。因此，我们率先使用马尔科夫转换自回归模型来测试该模型的适用性，该模型使用了四十年来两个加勒比海旅游目的地巴巴多斯和格林纳达的游客人数数据。调查结果揭示了两国旅游业尚未开发的转型和复兴机会，但也突显了两国在恢复力方面的鲜明对比。格林纳达表现出了更强的恢复力，因为其负面冲击虽然更深，但相对短暂，而巴巴多斯尽管经历的外部冲击较少，但仍面临全球衰退的长期影响。对于小岛屿国家，我们得出的结论是，影响恢复力低的因素是行业管理的缺陷，利益相关者之间的凝聚力不足，以及缺乏创新。总体而言，研究结果为依赖旅游业的经济体提供了一个模型框架，以确定它们从重大压力事件中恢复的速度，增强旅游业恢复力所需的相关战略，以及旅游业创新的潜力。

1. Introduction

The tourism industry is highly exposed to numerous disruptions such as global economic disturbances, extreme natural disasters, climate change, political and social upheavals. Yet, the industry is the primary engine of economic growth in many small island economies. WTTC (2018) featured all small island nations in its top 10 ranking of tourism contribution to GDP. The small islands' lack of economies of scale, geographic isolation, high degree of economic openness, dependency on export concentration (particularly tourism) and strategic imports compound their vulnerability (Briguglio et al., 2009). Hence, their resilience or adaptive capacity to withstand devastating and frequent shocks is fundamental to their sustainable development, the core objective of the United Nations' Sustainable Development Goals.

Like social-ecological systems, tourism systems evolve in a non-linear fashion. The tourism system's resilience refers to its evolutionary capacity to absorb disturbances (or perturbations) and reorganize while undergoing change in order to maintain its fundamental function, structure, identity, and feedbacks (Bristow and Healy 2014; Walker and Salt, 2012; Walker et al. 2004). However, in the case of tourism-dependent destinations, of paramount interest are the idea of resilience as 'adaptive ability'. Adaptability is superior in its evolutionary scope (McGlade et al., 2006). It is the differential ability of an island to adapt to shocks that shape the complex tourism dynamics and trajectories over time (Simmie and Martin, 2010). The paper, therefore, focuses on the adaptive cycle model which postulates that tourism systems evolve in non-linear patterns, through repeated cycles or loops with diverse characteristics at each phase as well as distinct recovery speeds from the destabilizing events (Alberts and Baldachinno, 2017; Cochrane, 2010; Simmie and Martin, 2010). The recovery speeds are dependent on the system's adaptive capacity to a stress event. The adaptive cycle model can help envision the organization of the complex dynamics in the tourism system/industry.

The adaptive cycle posits the existence of different stages of growth, yet no studies have quantitatively tested the model's applicability and identified the stages for validation of its structure. Episodic stress events cause the tourism system to adapt from one regime to another. Understanding how the model's regime shifts occur helps policymakers and resource managers not only to avoid, manage, mitigate or retool the industry after disruptive events (Cochrane, 2010), but as a process to managing continuous change (Hall, Prayag and Amore, 2018). Consequently, and uniquely, this study primarily uses the non-linear econometric methods (regime-switching models) to investigate the adaptive cycle model through identification of the stages and stressors of the tourism system. Regime switching models account for both short memory and structural breaks in time series data. The study also determines the path time to restoring tourism activity from a shock using two Caribbean Islands as case studies. Tourism is considerably more significant to the Caribbean economic development than any other region. Its proportion in regional output is 15% relative to 12% in Oceania and South East Asia, 10% in Europe and other regions account for less than 10% each (WTTC, 2018). The industry further creates 3 to 4 in every 10 jobs, and generates about 21% of total exports in the region (WTTC, 2018). Hence, two Caribbean countries' monthly tourist arrivals data spanning four decades, 1978–2017, were collected and analysed.

Barbados and Grenada present a fascinating story of two island countries with similar economic, historical and social characteristics: tourism-based economies, small sovereign islands with long-standing fixed exchange rates and former British colonies which both drifted from agricultural-based to tourism-based in the 1980s. Barbados was primarily sugarcane oriented while Grenada primarily cultivated bananas and spices (cinnamon, nutmeg, and cocoa). Throughout their tourism development, each island faced various shocks. Grenada was severely hit by a major hurricane in 2004, a revolution and the USA invasion of Grenada during the 1980s in addition to impacts from common global recessions and the 9/11 terrorist attack. Barbados, on the other hand, never experienced a major hurricane (category 3 or higher) nor political upheaval yet the evolution of tourist arrivals growth were significantly higher in Grenada than Barbados as the two series diverged over time. The tourism sector is the prime source of foreign currency with the year 2017 constituting 68.2% and 60.8% of total exports in Barbados' and Grenada's respectively (WTTC, 2018). Furthermore, the tourism industry represents an important source of job creation.

The factors leading to adaptive and regenerative capacity are revealed. Emphasis is on highlighting the fundamental elements and change agents necessary for innovation, adaptation, and structural transformation that contribute to sustainable tourism systems. Ultimately, the study will improve the planning for and management of resilience in tourism-dependent destinations and sub-regions. It also presents opportunities for learning from previous cycles and other island experiences that are crucial in developing interventions which facilitate achievement of the desired growth path.

The study of tourism resilience is trending though several research gaps are still evident in the literature. Previous research is exclusively qualitative. After explaining the cyclical tourism resilience process while drawing inferences from the 2014 Tsunami in Sri Lanka and Thailand, Cochrane (2010) constructed 'the Sphere of Tourism Resilience' model. Alberts and Baldachinno (2017) historically and narratively discussed the resilience mechanisms utilized in three Caribbean countries: Aruba, United States Virgin Islands, and St. Maarten during dramatic stress events. The concept was also used to identify relationships between stakeholders in a tourism destination in Western

Australia (McDonald, 2009). Although qualitative studies are useful in revealing new processes, quantitative approaches validate the robustness of the theories and concepts. Qualitative studies are better integrated with the systemic insights provided by quantitative methods to gain a more complete assessment of resilience factors in tourism (Luthe and Wyss, 2014). Scant resilience studies in tourism complement quantitative analyses with qualitative data to allow for validation of metric interpretations. Yet this validation is principal to understanding the nexus between tourism growth paths and tourism resilience. A quantitative resilience study informs policymakers of the required planning, designing, and intervention which facilitate the rebuilding of a stronger tourism industry. It also provides opportunities to cope with the intricacies and uncertainties associated with tourism activities. Additional contribution towards the concept's applicability and quantitative testing of the adaptive cycle model presents a novelty approach.

The next section discusses stylized facts in the tourism industry of the nations studied. Section 3 presents the adaptive cycle model. The Markov-Switching model utilized and the associated data are dealt with in section 4. Section 5 empirically evaluates the adaptive cycle model as section 5 provides conclusions and recommendations.

2. Stylized facts: Barbados and Grenada

Barbados is located far easterly of the tropical Caribbean island chain at latitude 13.2 degrees north and longitude 59.5 degrees west. Unlike most volcanic origins of its neighbouring islands, Barbados evolved as an accretionary prism. The Pleistocene coral reef limestone cap covers about 85% of the island while tertiary sedimentary rocks of marine origin make up the rest (Donovan & Harper 2005). As of 2018, the island has a population of 286,388 living in an area of only 431 square kilometres, placing it among the ten most densely-populated countries in the world. That represents a density of 664 persons per square kilometre. At latitude 12.1 degrees north and longitude 61.7 degrees west or 261 km south west of Barbados lies Grenada with 108,339 people, as of 2018, covering 310 square kilometres. The resultant population density of 349 persons per square kilometre is nearly half of Barbados'. Grenada is part of the Lesser Antilles volcanic island arc. The island is mostly covered in alkaline, magnesium-rich basaltic rocks (Donovan and Jackson, 1994).

Tourism in the Caribbean is viewed as a means of transforming formerly agrarian economies into service-based economies to improve the livelihood of its citizens. The tourism industry creates thousands of jobs, drives foreign exchange earnings, and generates prosperity in the two economies. Barbados' tourism sector contributed 40.6% of GDP, generated 40.5% of total employment, and brought in 68.2% of total exports in 2017. In comparison, Grenada's proportion of tourism in GDP tallied at 23% as the sector generated 21% of total employment and 60.8% of total exports (WTTC, 2018). Grenada has consistently been a desirable destination for American visitors attracting 46% of total arrivals in 2017. In contrast, Barbados' main source markets have changed at least three times in the last four decades. The 1970s were dominated by Canadian tourists, 1980s by Americans, and since the mid-1990s British tourists took over. To be exact, in 2017, 33% of the island's market share originated from the United Kingdom.

Both countries were chosen due to their similar socio-economic structures and history, common adversities yet varied outcomes in favour of the more disadvantaged nation, Grenada, which underwent through more disasters. Grenada and Barbados are former British colonies, small island tourism-dependent economies (that drifted from agriculture) operating long-standing fixed exchange rates and are both "sun, sand and sea" destinations. Nevertheless, Grenada experienced more devastating events than Barbados in the past 40 years. The standards of living, however, are converging in the two islands. Barbados citizens consistently enjoy higher standards of living than Grenada, with 2017 average annual GDP per capita totalling US$16,788 relative to US$10,376 in Grenada. By World Bank classifications, Barbados falls into the high-income group, and Grenada is in the upper-middle income group. At the onset of the analysis, in 1978, Grenada's GDP per person was US$992 compared to US$2,616 in Barbados (World Bank, 2018). Grenada's incomes skyrocketed almost ten-fold and Barbados' in excess of six-fold growth over the study period. Consequently, Grenada is catching-up to Barbados' living standards. This can be argued to be consistent with the neoclassical growth theory that predicts developed countries grow slower than developing countries due to diminishing returns of capital in wealthy economies and technological advances in the latter (Keefer and Knack, 1997). If that holds, then a more developed country is expected to be more resilient than a lesser developed nation due to superior infrastructure and macro-fiscal management, yet there is an anomaly in these countries tourist development. The lesser developed country, Grenada, outpaces Barbados in tourism adaptability.

A look at 1978 figures show Barbados received 316, 883 tourist arrivals which grew to 661,160 in 2017, doubling the arrivals in 40 years. Grenada had 32,336 visitor arrivals in 1978 and 146,375 in 2017, more than quadrupling the arrivals over the period, and basically three times faster than Barbados. Over time, similar to income paths, visitor arrivals trajectories show strong signs of converging as Grenada catches-up to Barbados.

An interesting picture emerges when plotting the indices of annual tourist arrivals for the two islands from 1978 through 2017 (see Figure 1). By construction, the value of the index is 100 in 1978 for both countries. Thereafter the indices reveal the growth paths of each nation with time. Beginning late 1970s to early 1980s, Barbados outperformed Grenada by a modest margin. This could be attributed to Barbados only experiencing the 1980-82 global recession relative to Grenada which was subjected to three concurrent major shocks: 1980-82 global recession, the revolution (1979–1983) and the subsequent USA invasion of Grenada, which occurred from October 25, 1983 to December 15, 1983. Post shocks, Grenada recovered remarkably faster than Barbados leading to the two indices coinciding again in 1983. Thereafter, Grenada experienced a tourism growth miracle for two decades, even withstanding the 1990-91 recessions and a swift rebound from the 2001 global recession, a clear divergence to Barbados' relatively slower growth. Grenada's tourist growth was slowed by the 2004 Hurricane Ivan, though remained higher than Barbados' tourist growth which was spared by the same natural disaster.

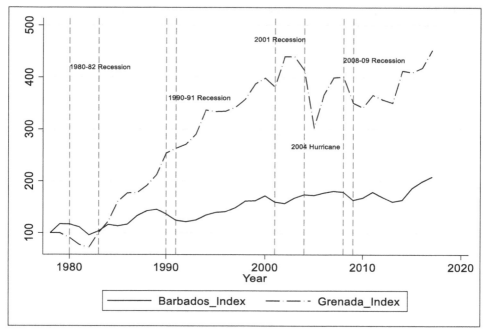

Figure 1. Annual tourist arrivals growth paths in Barbados and Grenada (1978–2017).
Source: Authors
Notes: • The information in Table 4 is depicted here.

Another striking feature is the varied resilience of the two economies following the 2008/2009 global economic downturn. According to Figure 1, the recession impacted Grenada's tourist arrivals more severely than Barbados as Grenada's tourist arrivals declined by about 12.5% in 2009 compared to 8.6% fall-off in Barbados' tourist arrivals. Nevertheless, Grenada recovered faster and much more strongly than the latter. Further, after the recession, the arrivals-growth-gap even widened. These shocks exposed the different nature of adaptation and resilience in the two case-study economies motivating us to undertake an in depth analysis of each series' precise regimes, a closer study of the impact of shocks and the recovery periods using monthly data covering 40 years while testing the adaptive cycle model is discussed next.

3. Theoretical framework

Tourism is considered a "system" functioning under diverse environments such as humans, social, cultural, economic, technological, physical, political, and legal environment. The tourism system is comprised of five related elements: tourists, three geographical elements (traveller-generating region, transit route region and traveller-destination region) and a tourist industry (Leiper, 1979; 1990).

3.1. Resilience schematic representation

The long-run success of a tourist economy is the ability of the island to adapt to the changing climate, weather, political, economic and social disruptions. Adaptability is

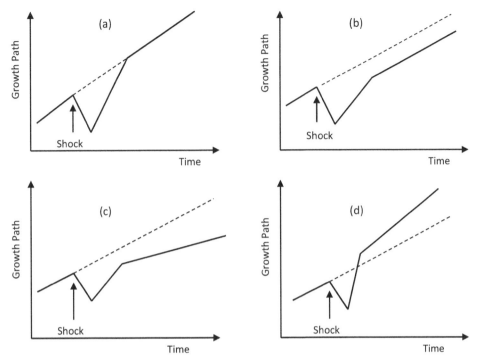

Figure 2. Schematic representation of adaptive resilience.
Notes: (a) Return of region to its pre-existing steady growth path following the shock;
(b) and (c) region fails to resume former steady growth path after the shock, but settles on inferior path
(d) region recovers from shock and assumes an improved growth path.
Source: Simmie and Martin, 2010.

an evolutionary economics phenomenon that is contingent on the actions of individual economic agents (stakeholders) capable of learning, innovating and adjusting their behaviour following a dramatic event (Ramlogan and Metcalfe, 2006). Thus, a tourism system evolves following a process of successive steady growth paths, the hysteretic movement between which is triggered by periodic shocks or major perturbations (Simmie and Martin, 2010).

An appeal to evolutionary economics perspective yields four possible tourist industry (arrivals) transformations after a disturbance indicating the adaptive capacity of a tourist destination. The four schematic representations of the transformations are depicted in Figure 2. Though presented linearly, the transformations are non-linear, depict possible impacts of adverse shocks on growth rates. The first possible transformation is when a stress event shifts tourist arrivals off its equilibrium growth path, and self-correcting forces (self-organization) and adjustments eventually restore the system's path (see Figure 2(a)). The resilience of different island economies is measured relative to their susceptibility to being drifted off their equilibrium paths (their 'sensitivity' to shocks) and their response times of recovery to equilibrium. Figure 2(c) resembles the 'ecological resilience' notion where disturbances cause a system to move into another inferior regime of behaviour (Holling, 1973). In Figure 2(b), the system resumes its former steady growth rate after the shock but settles on a lower trajectory. Only (c) is a non-resilient economy which failed to transform itself and became trapped into an outmoded or obsolete structure, with a consequential lowering of its long-run equilibrium growth path. The economy in (b) is more resilient than (c) but settles for a constant output gap after the disturbance. In this case, resilience refers to the magnitude of the shock of disturbance that can be absorbed before the system changes its structure and function and becomes shaped by a different set of processes (Holling, 1973). A resilient tourism economy adapts successfully and either resumes, or improves, its long-run equilibrium growth path (as in Figure 2(d)).

The tourist destination's degree of resilience to shocks depends on the depth of the shocks. An economy that is hardly affected by a shock is much more likely to recover more quickly, than an economy that is severely weakened by the shock such as a deep recession. Thus, the economy's response could be the product of a slower, more cumulative process of adaptation or 'resilience building'.

The graphs show what the possible forms of resilience regardless of phase in the adaptive cycle. Does the form of resilience differ depending on the adaptive cycle phase or depending on the type of shock?

3.2. Adaptive cycle model

The earlier resilient theories developed to describe how socio-ecological systems evolve overtime relied on the equilibristic notion premised on stable and linear development. The conventional economics and engineering theories had this in common. In deviation, Holling (2001) introduced the adaptive cycle model; a dynamic, more connected, complex, and less predictable depiction of systems.

The adaptive cycle model envisions a four-phase continual adjustment in the socio-ecological system, which in this paper is the tourism sector. Tourism involves a strong interplay between ecosystems and society. The consequential effect of tourism on a destination emanates from a complex interaction process among visitors, host communities, destination landscapes (Farrell and Twining-Ward, 2004); tourist business operators, and policymakers. Such interaction can be better understood in the context of complex adaptive socio-ecological system (Holling and Gunderson, 2002). A socio-ecological system goes through four transitional states/periods: reorganization, exploitation, conservation, and release (see Figure 3). The reorganization phase represents a period of innovation and transformation, the exploitation phase is a period of growth and exploiting opportunities, the conservation phase is a period of stability and increasing rigidity, while the release phase is a period of decline and liquidation. Each stage constitutes various degrees of three different dimensions: potential, connectedness, and resilience (see Table 1). Potential refers to the system's capacity to change using resources accumulated from earlier stages. Interconnectedness is the interrelatedness of the system's components, while resilience measures the system's ability to withstand shocks, disturbances, and stresses.

The adaptive cycle can commence with any stage such as **Reorganization and Restructuring** phase, which is characterised by rapid growth. This phase occurs post a destabilizing event when the tourism system experiences substantial/rapid change with regeneration and transformation. Either it reorganizes within the same regime or flips into another regime (with unpredictable connections or with different

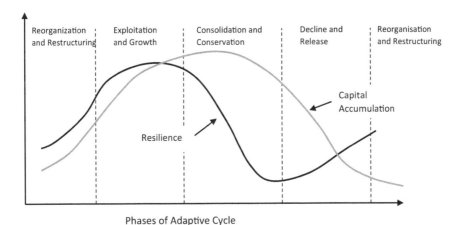

Phases of Adaptive Cycle

Figure 3. Adaptive cycle modelSource: Simmie and Martin, 2010.

Table 1. The four phases and three dimensions of the adaptive cycle.

	DIMENSIONS		
Adaptive cycle PHASES	Potential	Connectedness	Resilience
1. Reorganization and Restructuring	high	low	Increasing
2. Exploitation and Growth	low	increasing	high
3. Consolidation and Conservation	high	high	decreasing
4. Decline and Release	low	decreasing	low

Notes:. **Potential** – capacity to change/alter using accumulated resources.
Connectedness – capacity to control and manage.
Resilience – capacity to innovate and adapt.
Source: Lew (2017).

fundamental functions and structures). While the system does experience growth, it is not able to consolidate the benefits of that growth as it swiftly turns towards restructuring itself. Restructuring involves creativity in building increased/solid resilience. This period/phase of creative and flexible response is associated with increasing resilience and capital accumulation (Peterson, 2000; Holling and Gunderson, 2002; Pendall et al., 2008). Hence, a destination character or outline of new systems takes shape.

During the **Exploitation and Growth** period, new systems emerge through rapid exploitation of resources leading to the formation of inter-dependent institutions in political, cultural, and social spheres. With growing order, high resilience to shocks, and new variables jockeying to control the system, the period experiences stable growth and seizure of opportunities abound for human creativity. "Movers and shakers" may seize the moment and create new forms of entrepreneurial activity resulting in rapid capital accumulation during this phase (Russell and Faulkner, 1999; Weaver and Oppermann, 2000).

The dynamic process proceeds to **Consolidation and Conservation** phase. This phase portrays the gradual construction of a steady state where structures are institutionalized and more capital is initially accumulated (there is incremental accumulation on capital, energy, materials, and investment), quickly reaching a threshold after which it decreases. The ultimate effect is a net decline in capital accumulation driven by a slowdown in visitor arrivals growth rates. Increased interconnection among structures is realised. Consequently, the system becomes more rigid with lower resilience making it vulnerable to threats (Kates and Clark, 1996).

Movement from conservation to **Decline and Release** is a key moment in the underlying dynamics. A disturbance/threatening event (or series of events) which destabilizes the existing tourism system, releases the rigidity of structures such as stored capital with low resilience and negative growth rates. Ultimately, low resistance cause old systems to collapse, readjust, and eventually reorganizing again as the system cycle repeats either in an orderly manner or not.

The afore-discussed stages are shown in Figure 3, indicating the typical paths that systems can take over time as they adapt to changing conditions. The systems may experience all four, three, or two stages of the adaptive cycle, and the cycle might repeat with dissimilar stages altogether. Moreover, systems need not go through all stages of the cycle.

It will be noted that the phases of the resilience cycle concur with Butler's (1980) Tourism Area Life-Cycle (TALC) model (refer to Cochrane, 2010). The reorganization stage roughly aligns with the 'exploration' stage of the TALC, followed by the exploitation stage of increasing orderliness, or the 'developmental' stage. The 'institutionalization' stage aligns with the conservation phase as systems become stable but also somewhat rigid, while the 'decline' or 'rejuvenation' stage can be precipitated by a release event. The TALC's linear narrative fails to rigorously analyse the complexity of the interactions and forces shaping destination areas (Hamzah and Hampton, 2013; Cochrane 2010). Tourism destinations resemble living ecosystems rather than discrete 'products' as depicted in the TALC (McKercher, 2005). The loop/adaptive cycle successfully encapsulates this complexity and extends the TALC in recognizing the agency of individuals to effect significant change and that "seemingly insignificant changes to one part of the system can have dramatic and unexpected ramifications on other parts of the system" (Lepp, 2008). Additionally, the adaptive cycle recognizes the repeats of the cycle, yet TALC is a one-time development path. The study, therefore, ventures on a tour to determine the nature of the adaptive cycle in the Caribbean.

4. Empirical framework

4.1. Markov-Switching model

The stochastic growth process of tourist arrivals is modelled using the Markov Switching - Autoregressive (MS-AR) Model. It is often used to analyse tourism non-linear development (see Lanouar and Goaied, 2019; Moore and Whitehall, 2005). The MS-AR model allows the evolution of the time-series to be state-dependent as follows:

$$\Delta y_t = \mu_{s_t} + \sum_{i=1}^{k} \alpha_i \Delta y_{t-i} + \varepsilon_t, \tag{1}$$

where μ denotes the regime-dependent intercept, s_t represents a regime variable, k is the number of autoregressive coefficients α_i stands for the coefficients on the autoregressive terms and ε_t is an independently, normally distributed error term. The transition between the various unobservable states is modelled by a discrete time and space Markov chain. A statistical description of unobservable states that influence the evolution of time series was popularised by Hamilton (1989).

Table 2. Model selection results.

	BARBADOS		GRENADA	
	Statistic	P-Value	Statistic	P-Value
One versus two regimes				
LL Ratio test (Davies Approx. Upper Bound)	18.44	0.00	132.10	0.00
Two versus three regimes				
LL Ratio test (Davies Approx. Upper Bound)	65.83	0.00	224.36	0.00

Notes: • LL Ratio refers to the log-likelihood ratio.
Source: Authors.

The MS-AR allows tourist arrivals to be in one of n states/regimes at any given time. The probability (P_{ij}) of a transition from regime i at time t to regime j at time $t + 1$ is only dependent on the regime at time t and independent of the regimes at previous times. Hence, this outcome can be represented by the following transition probabilities (see Hamilton, 1989):

$$Prob\{S_t = j | S_{t-1} = i, S_{t-2} = h, \ldots\} = Prob\{S_t = j | S_{t-1} = i\} = P_{ij}$$

$$\text{and } \sum_{j=0}^{N} P_{ij} = 1 \text{ for all } i.$$

The optimal parameters are obtained by performing maximum likelihood estimation of equation 1 given the restrictions on the transition probabilities described above. Additionally, Kim's (1994) smoothing algorithm is employed to derive inferences on the unobserved states.

4.2. Data description

This study employs annual percentage change in monthly tourist arrivals from January 1978 (i.e., 1978:1) to December 2017 (i.e., 2017:12) for Barbados and Grenada. Visitor arrivals are used to indicate the health of the tourism industry, given the unavailability of credible expenditure data over a long period. The data is acquired from the Caribbean Tourism Organization's annual reports and form the basis of this research's estimations. Though few studies provide a comprehensive study of resilience, tourism resilience perspectives on the recovery of tourism industries have also utilized the tourist arrival numbers (Lew, 2014). Tourist arrivals trajectories are largely shaped by a nation's ability to mitigate and respond to stress events. Hence, a detailed examination of the factors that determine adaptability follows next.

5. Results and discussion

A general to specific procedure is undertaken to arrive at the optimal lag length of the Markov Switching Autoregressive (MS-AR) model. Next, a likelihood ratio test using Davies (1987) upper bound test is performed to determine the optimal number of regimes (reported in Table 2). Table 2 shows that three regimes are preferred for both countries. The optimal models selected are presented in Table 3 along with the residuals diagnosis, where the MS(3)-AR(4) is the best model for Grenada tourist arrival growth rate, and the MS(3)-AR(1) is selected for Barbados tourist arrival growth rate.

Table 3. Estimation results from Markov switching auto-regressive model.

	BARBADOS MS(3)-AR(1)		GRENADA MS(3)-AR(4)	
	Coefficient	P-Value	Coefficient	P-Value
Regime-dependent intercepts				
μ_1 (moderate growth)	5.34	0.000	9.30	0.006
μ_2 (decline)	−5.70	0.000	−31.64	0.000
μ_3 (high growth)	23.07	0.000	104.38	0.000
AR Coefficients				
α_1	0.41	0.000	0.30	0.000
α_2			0.26	0.000
α_3			0.12	0.030
α_4			0.14	0.007
Transition Probabilities				
p_{11}	0.93		0.98	
p_{12}	0.04		0.12	
p_{13}	0.44		0.61	
p_{21}	0.03		0.01	
p_{22}	0.94		0.86	
p_{23}	0.05		0.00	
p_{31}	0.04		0.00	
p_{32}	0.02		0.02	
p_{33}	0.51		0.39	
Average Duration of Regimes (months)				
Regime 1	21.21		51.88	
Regime 2	16.67		8.80	
Regime 3	1.82		1.67	
Goodness of Fit Tests				
Log-likelihood	−1628.39		−1926.92	
LR Ratio	47.38		159.50	
AIC	7.02		8.36	
SC	7.12		8.48	
Residual Analysis				
Normality test	2.66	0.26	28.93	0.00
ARCH test	2.44	0.09	1.95	0.08
Portmanteau (36)	32.12	0.61	100.67	0.00
Observations	467		464	

Notes: ● MS(3)-AR(1) – There-regime Markov Switching of first-order Autoregressive model. Thus, has one autoregressive coefficient, α_1.
● MS(3)-AR(4) – There-regime Markov Switching of fourth-order Autoregressive model. Hence, has four autoregressive coefficients: α_1, α_2, α_3 and α_4.
● μ_1, μ_2 and μ_3 represents each regime's intercept referring to its average growth. Regime 1 is of high growth, regime 2 is a decline period and regime 3 refers to high growth episodes.
● p_{11}, p_{22} and p_{33} denote the probability of staying in regime 1, 2 and 3 respectively. p12 is the probability of shifting from regime 1 to 2 and so forth.
● AIC stands for Akaike Information Criterion. It is an estimator measuring the relative fitness of a model to the data under analysis.
● SC – is the chi-square goodness-of-fit test.
● ARCH test is the Autoregressive Conditional Heteroscedastic test for the errors of the lag length.
Source: Authors.

5.1. Grenada

Table 3 results show that all coefficients of the MS-AR model for Grenada are strongly statistically significant at the 5% level. The corresponding transition probabilities, p_{ij}, are also reported. They range from zero to one signifying that the likelihood of shifting from one regime i to another (regime j). Grenada's mean growth rate in regime 1 is 9.3% with high transition probability, p11, of 0.98, which suggests that this regime is very persistent (refer to Table 3 and Figure 4). Figure 4 also illustrates this high probability of remaining in regime 1 and the periods which the country was in this

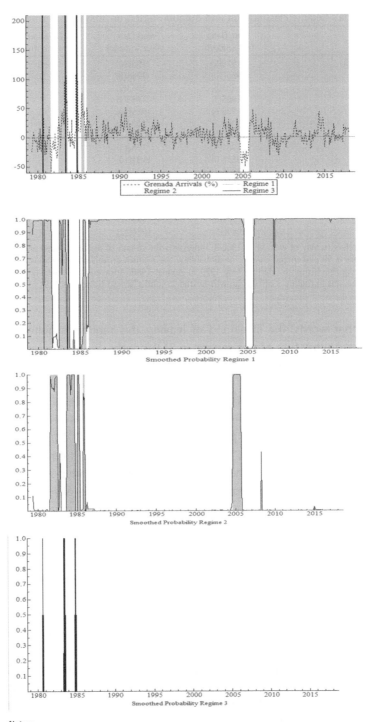

Notes:
- The information in table 4 is depicted here.

Figure 4. Grenada's year-to-year monthly growth of tourist arrivals and probabilities smoothed.
Source: Authors
Notes: • This is a graphical representation of the information in Table 5.

Table 4. Grenada's Regime classification and duration based on smooth probabilities.

Regime	Start Date: Year (month)	End Date: Year (month)	Duration in months	Average Probability
1 (moderate growth)	1979(5)	1980(8)	16	0.99
	1980(10)	1981(8)	11	0.98
	1983(8)	1983(9)	2	1
	1985(1)	1985(1)	1	1
	1985(6)	1985(10)	5	0.99
	1986(2)	2004(8)	223	1
	2005(10)	2017(12)	147	1
2 (decline)	1981(9)	1982(7)	11	0.94
	1983(10)	1984(10)	13	0.99
	1985(2)	1985(5)	4	0.97
	1985(11)	1986(1)	3	0.84
	2004(9)	2005(9)	13	0.96
3 (high growth)	1980(9)	1980(9)	1	1
	1983(6)	1983(7)	2	1
	1984(11)	1984(12)	2	1

Notes: • 1979(5) refers to May of year 1979, 1980(8) represents the month of August in 1980 and so forth.
• 0.99 means there is 99 percentage chance (or probability) the tourism arrivals series remains in regime 1 of moderate growth during the 16 months starting May 1979 to August 1980. An average probability of 1 means it is certain the system remains in regime 3 of high growth for the 2 months lasting November 1984 to December 1984.
Source: Authors.

regime. In other words, the likelihood of leaving this regime is quite low, less than 0.02. The average duration of this regime is 51.9 months, by far the longest regime of the three found. The longest stretch of this regime spanned for 18 continuous years (223 months) from 1986 to 2004 (see Table 4). This moderate growth regime of average 9.3% is quite solid corresponding to the exploitation phase of the Adaptive Cycle model. Hence, high resilience is anticipated in this phase. This prediction is corroborated by the fact that this regime persisted in the face of the 1990/91, 2001 and 2008/9 global economic recessions that interrupted stayover arrivals from the USA, the leading source market for Grenada. The 2001 recession also coincided with the September 11, terrorist attacks. Empirical studies have demonstrated the disruptive effect of terrorist attacks and global economic downturns on destination arrivals and their economies (see for example Kubickova, Kirimhan, and Li, 2019; Lanouar and Goaied, 2019; Ritchie, Amaya Molinar, and Frechtling, 2010).

Focusing on the September 11, 2001 terrorist attacks and the concurrent global recession provide insights into strategies employed by Grenada to hastily escape the deleterious effects and revamped even to surpass the pre-terrorist attack levels though the country's visitor arrivals remained in the moderate growth regime. The sector's swift rebound was due to the determined conjoint response with the international community that sought to prevent the devastation envisioned by the perpetrators of terror (Honourable Elvin Nimrod, Grenada Minister for Foreign Affairs and Cooperation in November 2001, New York at the 56th Session of the United Nations General Assembly). In addition, the Government of Grenada actively supported the tourism sector through vigorous strategic marketing programmes with airlines; intense destination marketing activities; concentration on product enlargement and environment management; small hotels specialized assistance programme and human resource development (Grenade, 2008). This action was supplemented by the Caribbean Tourism Organization's regional marketing campaign launched in 2002 entitled: "Life needs the Caribbean" targeted at the North American, Canadian and U.K. tourists, the regions dominant markets. Grenada also benefitted from the regional body, CARICOM's approved US$18m Joint Public/Private Sector Emergency Tourism Promotion Programme for the Caribbean.

The mean growth rate in regime 2 is negative, −31.6% with a transition probability of 0.86, indicating high persistence though not at as persistent as regime 1. The average duration of this negative regime is 8.8 months. Hence, this regime represents a period of decline and resembles the decline and release phase of the Adaptive Cycle. Most notably, the following disruptions were associated with the negative regime: the 1980/82 global recession and the 1979/83 Grenada military revolution, the USA invasion of Grenada during 1983 and the Hurricane Ivan which struck Grenada as a category 3 storm in 2004. The hurricane destruction was excessive, as the financial cost was estimated at twice the level of GDP. The devastation also adversely impacted 70 percent of the tourism plant (Reliefweb, 2009). Not surprising, the disturbance took the longest to recover from as stayover arrivals were stuck in the decline stage for 13 consecutive months before resuming the moderate growth phase. Of equal effect on arrivals growth rates were the October to December of 1983s USA invasion of Grenada. The invasion destroyed the perception of safety and security in the country. The combined effects of the 1979/83 revolution and the 1980/82 recession took 11 months of negative growth to escape.

What is fascinating is after this dark era, the country went on a growth miracle for 20 years of perpetual moderate growth. The key strategy employed was the construction of an international airport which was opened in October 1984 in order to facilitate a larger number of tourists. However, this encapsulated and symbolised the political nature of tourism development as a substantial portion of the capital (US$60 million) and technical assistance came from Cuba. USAID further financed and administered the completion of the international airport. Another policy strategy was the shift of the country's economic orientation from a mixed-economy approach to a market-based one facilitated by the USA (Grenade, 2015). More precisely, USAID financed the economic restructuring and free market deregulation policies led by USA's technocrats (Ferguson, 1990:114). Much USAID policy and finance was directed towards environmental and infrastructural improvements designed to attract foreign investment and tourism as well as encouraging private enterprises.

The mean growth rate in regime 3 of 104.4% is extremely high, but the transition probability of 0.39 is quite low and indicates that this phase is transitory. Consequently, the short average duration of 1.7 months is expected. This phase corresponds to the reorganization and restructuring phase, but the short duration indicates opportunities for regeneration have not been fully exploited. Moreover, this regime only occurred in the early to mid-eighties.

5.2. Comparative analysis of Barbados and Grenada

Table 3 shows that the estimation results for Barbados arrival growth rates are all statistically significant at the 1% level. The average growth rate in regime 1 is 5.3% with a transition probability of 0.93, indicating strong persistence. The average duration of this regime is 21.2 months, the longest of the three regimes. The longest period of this regime occurred between September 1992 and February 2001, which is 102 months or 8.5 years (refer to Figure 5 and Table 5). This period was interrupted by the 2001 global recession. Regime 1 represents a moderate growth regime and relates to the exploitation phase of the adaptive cycle model, which is predicted to have high resilience. However, Barbados tourist arrivals were knocked out of this regime during each global recession dating from the 1980/82 recession onwards.

In relative terms, Grenada's 9.3% average growth in the exploitative phase outperformed Barbados' 5.3% growth. It could be a reflection of Grenada's lesser stringent visa policies, which facilitates hassle-free tourist travel. These policies are demonstrated by its visa-free issuance to 133 nations, unlike Barbados, which allows only 113 nationalities through their border without a visa. Bangwayo-Skeete and Skeete (2017) provided a framework for eliminating visa requirements for some countries that will boost tourist arrivals without compromising safety and security. Worrell, Boamah, and Campbell (1996) attributed Barbados' sluggish tourism performance to low price competitiveness. The relative price of Barbados' tourism increased faster than its competitors; hence, the island lost its regional market share perpetually to Puerto Rico, Bahamas and Jamaica over the 1980s and 1990s (Howard, 2006 p.81; Worrell, Boamah, and Campbell, 1996). As for Grenada, its market share was rising faster, catching-up to Barbados' despite the two nations operating a fixed exchange for decades. Barbados dollar is pegged at US$2, and Grenada's Eastern Caribbean dollar is fixed at US$2.7. Thus, both countries have stable currencies.

Barbados' regime 2 mean growth rate is -5.7% with transition probability of 0.94. Hence, the negative growth regime 2 is as persistent as the moderate growth regime 1. On average, it lasts for 16.7 months, about five months less than regime 1. This regime represents the decline and release phase of the adaptive cycle model and has low resilience, given its persistence and protracted duration. In contrast, Grenada's decline phases are deeper, transitory, but considerably shorter. Barbados, on the other hand, struggles immensely with emerging from the decline regime. As previously stated, the phase coincided with all four global recessions during the period of analysis. It is important to note that while Grenada was not impacted by the 2008/09 recession, Barbados' adverse effects outlasted the duration of the global recession. While the world recession was active for 18 months, in Barbados it depressed stayover arrivals for 25 months. A similar story is told for every other global recession.

According to the adaptive cycle model, inference points to mismanagement of recessions, weak interconnectedness of the industry's stakeholders, and insufficient innovation. This mismanagement is also reflected in inconsistent marketing strategies, as evidenced by the changing composition of market shares every decade. Specifically, in the 1970s Canadian tourists predominately visited Barbados while in the 1980s USA tourists were dominant, and since the mid-1990s the United Kingdom held the greatest market share. Furthermore, Barbados has not effectively articulated why tourists should visit Barbados and, hence, are not able to accurately position the country in the global marketplace (Environmental Planning Group Inc and HLA Consultants, 2014). Most Caribbean nations are predicated on the "sun, sand and sea" motto. An additional unique marketing theme is essential in branding the island's image, which

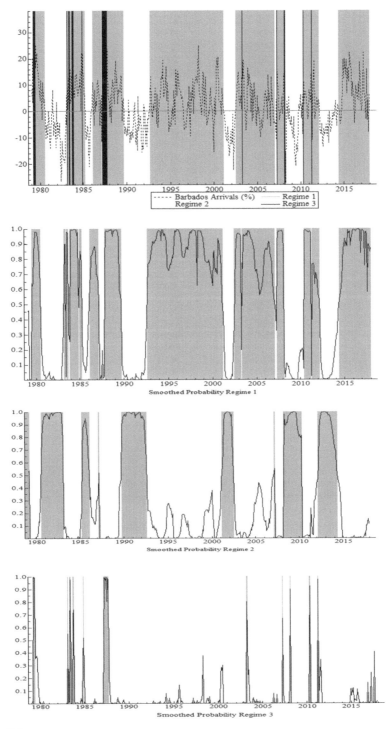

Notes:
- This is a graphical representation of the information in table 5.

Figure 5. Barbados' year-to-year monthly growth of tourist arrivals and probabilities smoothed.
Source: Authors

Table 5. Barbados' Regime classification and duration based on smooth probabilities.

Regime	Start Date: Year (month)	End Date: Year (month)	Duration in months	Average Probability
1 (moderate growth)	1979(7)	1980(7)	13	0.82
	1983(4)	1983(5)	2	0.90
	1983(12)	1984(11)	12	0.96
	1985(1)	1985(3)	3	0.79
	1986(3)	1987(2)	12	0.78
	1987(11)	1989(9)	23	0.92
	1992(9)	2001(2)	102	0.87
	2002(7)	2003(3)	9	0.90
	2003(5)	2007(1)	45	0.81
	2007(5)	2008(2)	10	0.96
	2010(6)	2011(3)	10	0.98
	2011(5)	2012(2)	10	0.68
	2014(6)	2017(12)	43	0.90
2 (decline)	1979(2)	1979(3)	2	0.53
	1980(8)	1983(2)	31	0.96
	1985(4)	1986(2)	11	0.79
	1987(3)	1987(3)	1	0.52
	1989(10)	1992(8)	35	0.95
	2001(3)	2002(6)	16	0.91
	2007(2)	2007(3)	2	0.54
	2008(4)	2010(4)	25	0.93
	2012(3)	2014(5)	27	0.88
3 (high growth)	1979(4)	1979(6)	3	1.00
	1983(3)	1983(3)	1	0.55
	1983(6)	1983(6)	1	0.98
	1983(10)	1983(11)	2	0.72
	1984(12)	1984(12)	1	0.52
	1987(4)	1987(10)	7	0.96
	2003(4)	2003(4)	1	0.80
	2007(4)	2007(4)	1	0.67
	2008(3)	2008(3)	1	0.90
	2010(5)	2010(5)	1	0.93
	2011(4)	2011(4)	1	0.98

Notes: • 1979(7) refers to July of year 1979, 1983(4) represents the month of April in 1983 and so forth.
• An average probability of 0.82 means there is 82 percentage chance (or probability) the tourism arrivals series remains in regime 1 of moderate growth during the 12 month duration spanning from July 1979 to July 1980.
Source: Authors.

captures the visitor's imagination and resonates with them post visitation. To lure visitors, other Caribbean nations have catchy themes. For Grenada its "Pure Grenada *The Spice of the Caribbean*", Turks and Caicos sells "Beautiful by Nature", Dominica it's "The Nature Island" and Guyana "The Amazon Adventure". These themes also stand out on the respective country's logo (refer to https://www.caribbeantravel.com/caribbean-islands).

Another plausible explanation for longer decline phases is the variation in operating costs. Barbados exhibits relatively high operational costs in terms of wages, interest rates, and cost of living, which impose severe financial hardship on hotel operators (Howard, 2006). A related issue is that the cost of vacationing in Barbados is high. Tourists require a higher budget travelling to Barbados than Grenada. This higher cost has implications during economic recessions where travellers prioritize cheaper destinations like Grenada. Thus, it is harder for Barbados to rebound quickly from recessions.

The fragile interconnectness among the industry's stakeholders is evidenced by lack of cohesiveness in governing the tourism sector (see Environmental Planning Group Inc and HLA Consultants, 2014). The Environmental Planning Group Inc and HLA Consultants (2014) in their Barbados Tourism Masterplan 2014–2023 further highlighted the absence of an integrated inter-sectoral planning and developmental framework reflecting a broader thematic filter through which all tourism is organized and delivered. This issue calls for new policy strategies necessary for a speedy recovery and greater resilience.

Barbados' regime 3 average growth rate is 23.1% with transition probability of 0.51, signifying a relatively transitory regime. Consequently, the average duration is a mere 1.8 months. The longest period of this regime was for seven months between April and October of 1987. In April 2007, the tourism growth series was in the high regime for one month only as a result of the country hosting the Cricket World Cup finals. This outcome is consistent with empirical literature finding no evidence of long-term benefits from hosting international sports events like the Olympics (Billings and Holladay, 2012). Akin to Grenada, this high growth regime 3 phase aligns with the reorganization phase in the adaptive cycle but the short average duration of fewer than 1.8 months and its transitory nature points to opportunities for transformation yet to be fully exploited in the tourism sector.

6. Conclusion

Tourism resilience is a trending topic, particularly in Small Island States given their vulnerability to extreme weather events, climate change, geopolitical events, and global recessions and their dependency on the tourism industry. Using a two-island case study, the Markov switching autoregressive model was utilized to examine the applicability of the adaptive cycle model, which proposes four non-sequential phases: reorganization; exploitation; consolidation and, decline. Each stage of the cycle is associated with varying degrees of resilience, connectedness, and capital accumulation or release.

The two-island tourism economies exhibited different resistance to shocks, with Grenada showing greater resilience than Barbados. Both nations have largely experienced the exploitation and decline phases of the adaptive cycle model. Nonetheless, Barbados' average tourist growth rate in the exploitation stage is considerably lower than in Grenada's. In addition, the exploitation stage in Grenada underwent the longest stretch of growth spanning 18 consecutive years (from 1986 to 2004) compared to Barbados' 8.5 continuous years (starting 1992 to 2001). Though Grenada's decline phases were fewer, shorter-lived and transitory, there were more disruptive. Nevertheless, the nation emerged out of these terrible disruptions quickly and more vibrant. Barbados, on the other hand, needs to review its strategies in dealing with the adverse effects of all global recessions. Of notable significance is Grenada's escape from the negative effects of 2008-2009 global economic crisis. This analysis suggests that Grenada's successful adaptation to adverse shocks and its growth strongly relied on adequate international, regional, and government support, macroeconomic restructuring, and political and social cohesion. It also emerged for Grenada that natural disasters are harder to absorb, which is understandable since the infrastructure is typically severely damaged. Hence, policymakers need improved coping mechanisms with regards to natural disasters, such as building more resilient structures.

Further evidence indicates that both nations experienced rare spikes of high growth rates, indicating untapped opportunities for the full reorganization phase of the adaptive cycle. This implies that the tourism industries in the respective countries still have room for innovation and regeneration for a sustained reorganization phase to occur. A lesson learnt is that the form of resilience differ depending on the type of shock and not the phase in the adaptive cycle. Another notable finding is that both islands have not undergone the consolidation stage of the adaptive cycle, which is characterized by low growth rates, revealing signs that the destinations have not yet matured.

This study suggests that the adaptive cycle model is useful in analysing the degree of resilience of the tourism sector in small island economies, in identifying shortcomings of the management of the sector, inadequate connectedness of stakeholders and the industry's potential for innovation despite the proclivity to be disrupted by external events. While the two nations provide stark contrast regarding their resilience capability, they show untapped opportunities for transformation and regeneration of their tourism industries. The established regimes provide benchmarks on the industry's performance and its position on the adaptive cycle. Hence, this information recommends policymakers of strategies that raise resilience especially strengthening management, stakeholder connectedness and raising innovation, thereby strengthening the tourism sector to enhance sustainable development. An overriding conclusion is that while the adaptive cycle is relevant in explaining urban and regional development, it is also a useful framework for delineating the development of highly tourism-dependent economies.

This research is limited to two-country case studies and their associated stress events of which some are country-specific. Given the specific shocks, it is imperative for future research to provide additional evidence on the application of Adaptive Cycle Model to various tourist destinations for a conclusive general operationalization of the theory.

Disclosure statement

No potential conflict of interest was reported by the author(s).

Acknowledgement

The authors express gratitude to Dr. Wendy Grenade for the insights provided on Grenada's historical developments and the literature she provided.

References

Alberts, A., & Baldacchino, G. (2017). Resilience and Tourism in Islands: Insights from the Caribbean. In R. W. Butler (Ed.), *Tourism and resilience* (pp. 150–162). CABI.

Bangwayo-Skeete, P. F., & Skeete, R. W. (2017). Who travels visa-free? Insights into tourist hassle-free travel. *Journal of Travel Research, 56*(3), 407–418.

Billings, S. B., & Holladay, J. S. (2012). Should cities go for the gold? The long-term impacts of hosting the Olympics. *Economic Inquiry, 50*(3), 754–772. doi:10.1111/j.1465-7295.2011.00373.x

Briguglio, L., Cordina, G., Farrugia, N., & Vella, S. (2009). Economic vulnerability and resilience: concepts and measurements. *Oxford Development Studies, 37*(3), 229–247. doi:10.1080/13600810903089893

Bristow, G., & Healy, A. (2014). Regional resilience: an agency perspective. *Regional Studies, 48*(5), 923–935. doi:10.1080/00343404.2013.854879

Cochrane, J. (2010). The sphere of tourism resilience. *Tourism Recreation Research, 35*(2), 173–185. doi:10.1080/02508281.2010.11081632

Davies, R. B. (1987). Hypothesis testing when a nuisance parameter is present only under the alternative. *Biometrika, 74*(1), 33–43.

Donovan, S. K., & Jackson, T. A. eds. (1994). *Caribbean geology: an introduction.* University of the West Indies Publishers' Association.

Donovan, S. K., & Harper, D. A. (2005). The geology of Barbados: a field guide. *Caribbean Journal of Earth Science, 38*, 21–33.

Environmental Planning Group Inc and HLA Consultants. (2014). Barbados Tourism Master Plan 2014 – 2023. Report I: The Master Plan. http://www.bhta.org/images/TMP/TMP-Report-I.pdf

Farrell, B. H., & Twining-Ward, L. (2004). Reconceptualizing tourism. *Annals of Tourism Research, 31*(2), 274–295. doi:10.1016/j.annals.2003.12.002

Ferguson, J. (1990). *Grenada: revolution in reverse.* Latin America Bureau.

Grenade, W. C. (2008). An unwelcome guest: unpacking the tourism and HIV/AIDS dilemma in the Caribbean: a case study of Grenada. In *New perspectives in Caribbean tourism* (pp. 200–230). Routledge.

Grenade, K. H. I. (2015). Grenada: Socioeconomic overview, 1960-2012. In W. C. Grenade, (Ed.). *The grenada revolution: Reflections and lessons* (pp. 37–55). University Press.

Grenade, W. C. (Ed.). (2015). *The Grenada Revolution: Reflections and lessons.* University Press.

Hall, C. M., Prayag, G., & Amore, A. (2018). *Tourism and resilience: Individual, organisational and destination perspectives.* Channel View Publications.

Hamilton, J. D. (1989). A new approach to the economic analysis of nonstationary time series and the business cycle. *Econometrica, 57*(2), 357–384. doi:10.2307/1912559

Hamzah, A., & Hampton, M. P. (2013). Resilience and non-linear change in island tourism. *Tourism Geographies, 15*(1), 43–67. doi:10.1080/14616688.2012.675582

Holling, C. S. (1973). Resilience and stability of ecological systems. *Annual Review of Ecology and Systematics, 4*(1), 1–23. doi:10.1146/annurev.es.04.110173.000245

Holling, C. S. (2001). Understanding the complexity of economic, ecological, and social systems. *Ecosystems, 4*(5), 390–405. doi:10.1007/s10021-001-0101-5

Holling, C. S., & Gunderson, L. H. (2002). Resilience and adaptive cycles. In *Panarchy: Understanding transformations in human and natural systems,* Island Press, 25–62.

Howard, M. (2006). *The economic development of Barbados.* University of West Indies Press.

Kates, R. W., & Clark, W. C. (1996). Environmental surprise: expecting the unexpected? *Environment: Science and Policy for Sustainable Development, 38*(2), 6–34. doi:10.1080/00139157.1996.9933458

Keefer, P., & Knack, S. (1997). Why don't poor countries catch up? A cross-national test of an institutional explanation. *Economic Inquiry, 35*(3), 590–602. doi:10.1111/j.1465-7295.1997.tb02035.x

Kim, C. J. (1994). Dynamic linear models with Markov-switching. *Journal of Econometrics, 60*(1–2), 1–22. doi:10.1016/0304-4076(94)90036-1

Kubickova, M., Kirimhan, D., & Li, H. (2019). The impact of crises on hotel rooms' demand in developing economies: The case of terrorist attacks of 9/11 and the global financial crisis of 2008. *Journal of Hospitality and Tourism Management, 38*, 27–38. doi:10.1016/j.jhtm.2018.10.002

Lanouar, C., & Goaied, M. (2019). Tourism, terrorism and political violence in Tunisia: Evidence from Markov-switching models. *Tourism Management, 70*, 404–418. doi:10.1016/j.tourman.2018.09.002

Leiper, N. (1979). The framework of tourism: Towards a definition of tourism, tourist, and the tourist industry. *Annals of Tourism Research, 6*(4), 390–407. doi:10.1016/0160-7383(79)90003-3

Leiper, N. (1990). Tourist attraction systems. *Annals of Tourism Research, 17*(3), 367–384. doi:10.1016/0160-7383(90)90004-B

Lepp, A. (2008). Attitudes towards initial tourism development in a community with no prior tourism experience: The case of Bigodi. *Journal of Sustainable Tourism, 16*(1), 5–22. doi:10.2167/jost630.0

Lew, A. A. (2014). Scale, change and resilience in community tourism planning. *Tourism Geographies*, *16*(1), 14–22. doi:10.1080/14616688.2013.864325

Lew, A. A. (2017). Modeling the resilience adaptive cycle. collaborative for sustainable tourism and resilient communities blog. (21 January). http://www.tourismcommunities.com/blog/modeling-the-resilience-adaptive-cycle.

Luthe, T., & Wyss, R. (2014). Assessing and planning resilience in tourism. *Tourism Management*, *44*, 161–163. doi:10.1016/j.tourman.2014.03.011

McDonald, J. R. (2009). Complexity science: an alternative world view for understanding sustainable tourism development. *Journal of Sustainable Tourism*, *17*(4), 455–471. doi:10.1080/09669580802495709

McGlade, J., Murray, R., Baldwin, J., Ridgway, K., & Winder, B. (2006). Industrial resilience and decline: A co-evolutionary framework. In *Complexity and co-Evolution: Continuity and Change in Socio-Economic Systems*, 147–176.

McKercher, B. (2005). Destinations as products? A reflection on butler's life cycle. *Tourism Recreation Research*, *30*(3), 97–102. doi:10.1080/02508281.2005.11081491

Moore, W., & Whitehall, P. (2005). The tourism area lifecycle and regime switching models. *Annals of Tourism Research*, *32*(1), 112–126. doi:10.1016/j.annals.2004.05.006

Pendall, R., Foster, K. A., Cowell, M., et al. (2008). *Resilience and regions: Building understanding of the metaphor*. Mimeo Institute of Urban and Regional Development, Cornell University.

Peterson, G. (2000). Political ecology and ecological resilience: An integration of human and ecological dynamics. *Ecological Economics*, *35*(3), 323–336. doi:10.1016/S0921-8009(00)00217-2

Ramlogan, R., & Metcalfe, J. S. (2006). Restless capitalism: a complexity perspective on modern capitalist economies. In *Complexity and co-Evolution: Continuity and Change in Socio-Economic Systems*, Edward Elgar Publishing Limited, 115–146.

Reliefweb. (2009). Grenada: Dealing with the aftermath of Hurricane Ivan. https://reliefweb.int/report/grenada/grenada-dealing-aftermath-hurricane-ivan

Ritchie, J. B., Amaya Molinar, C. M., & Frechtling, D. C. (2010). Impacts of the world recession and economic crisis on tourism: North America. *Journal of Travel Research*, *49*(1), 5–15. doi:10.1177/0047287509353193

Russell, R., & Faulkner, B. (1999). Movers and shakers: chaos makers in tourism development. *Tourism Management*, *20*(4), 411–423. doi:10.1016/S0261-5177(99)00014-X

Simmie, J., & Martin, R. (2010). The economic resilience of regions: towards an evolutionary approach. *Cambridge Journal of Regions, Economy and Society*, *3*(1), 27–43. doi:10.1093/cjres/rsp029

Walker, B., Holling, C. S., Carpenter, S. R., & Kinzig, A. (2004). Resilience, adaptability and transformability in social–ecological systems. *Ecology and Society*, *9*(2), 5. doi:10.5751/ES-00650-090205

Walker, B., & Salt, D. (2012). *Resilience thinking: Sustaining ecosystems and people in a changing world*. Island press.

Weaver, D., & Oppermann, M. (2000). *Tourism management*. John Wiley and Sons.

World Bank. (2018). International Economics Dept. Development Data Group. *World Development Indicators*. World Bank.

Worrell, D., Boamah, D., & Campbell, T. (1996). The price competitiveness of Barbados' exports. *Central Bank of Barbados Economic Review*, *23*(1), 12–32.

WTTC. (2018). World Travel and Tourism Council (2018). report.

Social-ecological resilience and community-based tourism in the commonwealth of Dominica

Kristin Weis (iD), Catherine Chambers and Patrick J. Holladay

ABSTRACT

Coastal zones and tropical islands are some of the most popular tourism destinations worldwide, and recent scholarship has explored the linkages between community-based tourism development and social-ecological resilience. Social-ecological resilience is the capacity of a social-ecological system to adapt to change from shocks or surprises, which also applies to the context of community-based tourism development. Data were collected on the island of the Commonwealth of Dominica. In the six coastal communities of Roseau, Portsmouth, Mero, Soufriere, Layou, and Scotts Head, resident perceptions of social-ecological resilience were examined through 40 semi-structured interviews using snowball sampling with community members who were self-employed in either the farming, fishing, or tourism industries, community leaders, or those who were involved in tourism-related efforts or policy at a mid- to senior-level. Interview transcripts were coded inductively for salient themes. Results indicate that community member access to the benefits of tourism are enabled by factors such as the island's tourism reputation and its interconnected primary industries (farming, fishing, and tourism). These emergent themes that hinder local residents' access to benefits from tourism, such as limited physical access to and within the island and grant dependency, have the potential to threaten resilience. Limited access influenced seasonal tourism, related income dynamics, and contributed to grant dependency and income diversification. Income was not viewed as a social-cultural cue. Understanding what does and does not support access to the benefits of tourism can help evaluate measures of social-ecological resilience for a tourism destination community. Evaluating measures of social-ecological resilience can help evaluate the success of related development policies and provide focus for future ones. Coastal areas with high measures of social-cultural resilience are less vulnerable and more able to adapt or transform to shocks or disturbances.

摘要

沿海地区和热带岛屿是世界上最受欢迎的旅游目的地之一，最近的学术研究探讨了基于社区的旅游发展和社会生态恢复力之间的联系。社会-生态恢复力是指社会-生态系统适应冲击或意外变化的能力，也适用于基于社区的旅游开发背景。本文的数据是在多米尼加共和国岛上收集的。本文采取滚雪球抽样方法对40个社区成员（包括农民、渔民、旅游从业者、社区领导以及从事旅游事业或政策制定的中高层人员）进行了半结构访谈，研究他们对社会生态恢复力的感知。对突出主题的访谈文本进行归纳编码。结果表明，社区成员获得旅游利益是由岛屿的旅游声誉和其相互关联的第一产业(农业、渔业和旅游业)等因素促成的。这些浮现出的主题有诸多阻碍了当地居民享受旅游业带来的好处（例如，进入岛屿和在岛上的实际机会有限，以及补助依赖），有可能威胁旅游业的恢复力。有限的准入影响了旅游的季节性和相关收入的动态变化，并影响补助依赖和收入多样化。收入并不是社会文化的标志。了解什么有利于、什么不利于获取旅游利益，有助于评估旅游目的地社区的社会-生态恢复力措施。社会-生态恢复力的评价指标有助于评价相关发展政策的成效，并为未来发展政策的制定提供依据。具有较高社会文化恢复能力的沿海地区较不容易受到冲击，更有能力适应或改变冲击或扰动。

Introduction

Coastal zones and tropical islands are some of the most popular tourism destinations worldwide, and recent scholarship explores the linkages between tourism development and social-ecological resilience. Social-ecological resilience is the capacity of a social-ecological system to adapt to change from shocks or surprises. Tourism is often linked with resilience and considered to be a tool for economic development and related incentives for environmental protection, which are both aspects of social-ecological resilience; however this link requires further study (Bec et al., 2016, p. 1). Tourism is commonly understood to be one of the most globally significant types of income and economic growth (Edgell, 2015; Hall & Page, 2014, p. 1). International tourism represented 9.8% of the global Gross Development Product (GDP) in 2014 (Edgell, 2015), and is growing at a rate of about 3.3% annually, with projections of international visitors to increase from 1.186 billion in 2015 to 1.8 billion by 2030 (UNWTO, 2016). GDP has been linked to resilience where sustainable tourism development programs have been used to diversify a country's economy and support GDP recovery in response to economic shocks, such as those caused by hurricanes or a primary industry's collapse (Holladay & Powell, 2013). Examples include Hurricane Dean's damage, estimated at roughly 20% of Dominica's GDP, and the Banana Crash, where the island's primary industry of banana exports collapsed (Holladay & Powell, 2013). Tourism growth depends on robust economic, social, cultural, and environmental dynamics (Edgell, 2015) and can support social-ecological resilience by enhancing the ability of individuals and communities to adjust to change and to mitigate their rigidity and related vulnerability to adapt (Carpenter & Brock, 2008; Folke, 2016; Gallopín, 2006; F. Miller et al., 2010; B. Walker et al., 2004). Such growth has also led to questions about the negative consequences for communities that are tourism destinations, such as the carrying capacity of their infrastructure, ecosystems, and general support and space required for a positive tourist experience (Archer et al., 2005). These are important considerations that can impact community member access to the benefits of tourism. Access to the benefits of tourism, such as economic diversity, can support resilience to environmental change, such as climate change and related shocks.

This research aimed to understand local perceptions of community-based tourism development and social-ecological resilience, specifically the governance, social, eco-logical, and economic aspects, in coastal communities in Dominica. Tourism in coastal zones and coastal communities is expanding rapidly as coastal areas have seen a glo-bal increase in population and recreation activity (Gillis, 2012; Hall & Page, 2014; Orams, 1999; Small & Nicholls, 2003). Dominica therefore served as a case study to understand aspects related to tourism development in coastal communities through the lens of social-ecological resilience theories. Specifically, the objectives of this research were to 1) explore the opportunities and barriers that impact community member access to the benefits of tourism, and 2) understand potential social-cultural shifts related to tourism development, where tourism was considered to be under-developed and a key component of current and future development. While tourism and tourism destination communities have been extensively researched, the dynamics between coastal community-based tourism and social-ecological resilience in Small Island Developing States (SIDS) warrants further analysis, as SIDS face unique vulner-abilities and challenges. Understanding community member perceptions about the impact of tourism on coastal communities can inform more effective strategies that promote healthy coastal communities and marine environments.

Literature review

This research employed a combination of concepts in order to best explore local per-ceptions of community-based tourism development and social-ecological resilience. Here, we first provide a short review of resilience theory and the primary concepts of social-ecological resilience that most relate to the research. Next, we specifically nar-row in on SIDS and tourism, providing a background for how these bodies of literature relate to resilience studies. Finally, we give contextual background on Dominica that provides the reader a deeper understanding of the results of the research.

Social-ecological resilience theory

Resilience has become a popular term in the international development sphere and is sometimes understood differently from its original theoretical framework (Gaillard, 2010). Different understandings of resilience can lead to different policy objectives or definitions of success, such as those for coastal communities (Holladay & Powell, 2016), and so it is necessary to clearly define and explore the theoretical foundations of resilience research. This need to address definition and theory is true of destination resilience, in the context of tourism and resilience, in that resilient destinations have a complex set of variables to contend with such as risk, vulnerability and opportunity (Holladay, 2018). Indeed, understanding of the cyclical and fragile nature of tourism systems is important to learning how change can be adapted for strength and growth within destination resilience (Holladay et al., 2018).

Modern resilience theory stems directly from ecological studies during the 1960s and 1970s, which first observed multiple basins of attraction in ecosystems (Folke, 2006; Folke et al., 2004; Holling, 1973; J. Walker & Cooper, 2011). The understanding of complex system dynamics—the complex dynamics of multiple basins of attraction—has also shifted perceptions of change, where it is something to be navigated rather than prevented (Folke, 2016). Resilience theory further expanded to account for the interdependent nature of social and ecological systems, as human actions were observed to directly impact the capacity of ecosystems to function (Folke, 2006). This broader lens frames *social-ecological resilience*, which focuses on a system's ability to reorganize across spatial and temporal domains, and to reorganize or transform in response to shocks or disturbances (Folke, 2006). In this current understanding of resilience, human behavior is emphasized as part of complex systems (Folke, 2006). Social-ecological resilience is an aspect of social-ecological systems (SES), in which human (societal) and natural (biophysical) subsystems interact with mutual reaction and interdependence (Folke et al., 2010; Gallopín, 2006).

The terms *resilience*, *sustainability*, *vulnerability*, and *adaptive capacity* have non-standardized definitions in different academic contexts, and so their meaning and relationship to each other can be unclear (Gallopín, 2006). In the context of this study and social-ecological resilience, they have the following definitions and relationships. Resilience is a system's ability to hold its function and structure despite exposure to disturbances (B. Walker & Salt, 2012). A system's resilience enables its sustainability, or its continued functionality despite disturbances (B. Walker et al., 2002). Disturbances are external stresses or threats to a system. A system's vulnerability is its lack of capacity to adapt, or its susceptibility to any negative impacts of disturbances related to environmental and social change (Adger, 2006). Adaptability is a component of resilience (Folke et al., 2010).

A system's capacity to adapt, or adaptive capacity, is its ability to mitigate negative impacts of a disturbance (Gallopín, 2006). This type of mitigation, for example, manifested in Utuado, Puerto Rico post-Hurricane Maria, wherein community self-organizing behaviors catalyzed farm rehabilitation and agritourism for socio-economic development (Holladay et al., 2019). Similarly, high levels of financial investment by BP Oil in positive messaging and marketing contributed to resort, lodging and coastal tourism resilience following the 2010 *Deepwater Horizon* oil spill (Holladay, 2014; Ritchie et al., 2013). Understanding a system's operational capability and its function when exposed to disturbances can aid efforts to strengthen its capacity to cope with change (Berkes et al., 2008).

Resilience thinking is the capacity of people and social aspects to adapt, transform, or minimize shocks to development pathways in response to uncertainty and change (Folke, 2016). Central to resilience thinking is the concept of persistence, which is achieved via adaptation to uncertainty and the unknowable, including complex social and ecological system dynamics with unpredictable variables, sudden and gradual changes, and surprising processes and outcomes (Berkes et al., 2008; Folke, 2016). The related idea of molding opportunity from change can be thought of as 'creative destruction' (Berkes et al., 2003, p. 18), where responding to change is a cyclical process of adaptation, transformation and/or reorganization. This type of change response is important for tourism destination resilience, in particular when considering threshold tipping points that could lead to regime shifts (Hall, 2018).

Transformability is the capacity of a SES to create new structures of stability (Folke et al., 2010). A new system emerges from one that is unsustainable due to social, political, economic, or ecological conditions (B. Walker et al., 2004). Within the scope of resilience in tourism communities, this transformation is at times thought of in terms of innovation in response to change and/or some degree of economic diversification (Cheer & Lew, 2018). The ability of a SES to transform is understood as requiring three phases relating to social-ecological change: preparation for change, response to disturbances via creative destruction, and enhancing dimensions of resilience within the transformed SES (Folke et al., 2010).

SIDS, community-based tourism development, and resilience

Small island developing states (SIDS) are physically remote, underdeveloped nations with limited land mass, natural resources, and socioeconomic development (Sharpley & Telfer, 2015; van der Velde et al., 2007). SIDS are beset by issues of limited access and are described as insular, vulnerable, and with limited capacities (Briguglio, 1995, 2003; Pelling & Uitto, 2001; Turvey, 2007). Characteristics such as limited land, resources, and socioeconomic development contribute to their economic, social, and environmental vulnerabilities; and, much of SIDS literature focuses on their limited adaptive capacity and disproportionate vulnerability to natural disasters and climate change (Briguglio, 1995, 2003; Pelling & Uitto, 2001).

The traditional economic focus in vulnerability assessments is sometimes considered to be limited in its ability accurately detect SIDS challenges and responses in the form of effective development policy (Campling & Rosalie, 2006; Turvey, 2007). Social components must also be understood in order to accurately interpret environmental and economic vulnerabilities, as was noted in a 2006 case study of the Seychelles (Campling & Rosalie, 2006). Further, established dependency narratives (in which SIDS are classified as highly dependent on foreign assistance) and the exclusive focus on SIDS vulnerabilities (rather than their strengths) is understood to be a deficient framework with which to develop SIDS domestic policies and responses to challenges (Scheyvens & Momsen, 2008).

Community-based tourism is commonly considered to be a poverty reduction strategy among international development actors (Scheyvens & Momsen, 2008b). Further, these authors argue that community-based tourism is only effective at reducing poverty when it is part of more holistic policies that incorporate social sustainability along with the traditional environmental and economic sustainability focus. This holism in community-based tourism development includes building social capital through participation, power sharing and collaboration (Ozaki, 2008). Indeed, these variables are some of the major tenets of community-based tourism resilience (Holladay & Powell, 2013). Resilience in community-based tourism may be predicated on the understanding that these community-based tourism systems are cyclical, that change is inevitable and adaptation by local stakeholders is important (Holladay et al., 2018). Sustainability and resilience in community-based tourism is strengthened by involving local stakeholders in the identification of assets (Holladay et al., 2018), by understanding local perceptions of community resilience dynamics (Powell et al., 2018) and including community residents in the tourism development planning process (Blackstock, 2005).

The Banana Crash

Dominica's pursuit of tourism is driven by a desire to replace its past boom-and-bust agriculture markets and avoid a repeat of its banana export market crash in the 1990s (Weis, 2018; Weis et al., 2019). The island's historically agricultural economy was heavily dependent on banana exports from the 1950s to the 1990s (Payne, 2008). Bananas were considered to be such a lucrative commodity that they were nicknamed 'green gold' and cited as a contributing factor to Dominica's 1978 independence from Great Britain and subsequent development (Payne, 2008). By the 1990s, bananas accounted for a fifth of Dominica's GDP; nearly half of its total exports (Payne, 2008); about two thirds of its agricultural exports (Slinger, 2002); and a third of Dominica's workforce, either directly or indirectly (Slinger, 2002). The collapse of Dominica's banana export market can be traced to its post-colonial relationship and the European Union's preferential treatment of Caribbean banana exports (Slinger, 2002). In 1993, this preferential trade relationship was successfully challenged in a 'banana trade war' by the United States and South American multinational corporations (Holladay & Powell, 2016). The subsequent World Trade Organization (WTO) ruling ended Dominica's 'green gold' era: From the 1980s to 2009, banana farmers declined by roughly 92% and, from 1993 to 2001, banana exports decreased by about two thirds in both tonnage and USD (Holladay & Powell, 2016).

Current poverty rates are linked to the legacy of Dominica's prior dependence on banana exports and the related WTO ruling (UNDP, 2016). As with other SIDS, Dominica has focused on tourism as a tool for development and as a buffer against future economic instabilities. The EU has aided Dominica's post-WTO ruling recovery and participation in the international economy: It is Dominica's primary grant patron and it has funded efforts to diversify the island's agriculture and alternative economic industries, such as funding programs to re-train former banana farmers and build the island's eco-tourism presence (UNDP, 2016). The EU has also funded the development of community tourism as part of the effort to help Dominica diversify its economy (Holladay & Powell, 2013).

The Nature Island

Within the Caribbean, the most prominent form of tourism is Sun, Sea, Sand (3S) tourism (Weaver, 1993). 3S tourism centers on recreational and leisure activities in the coastal zone, characterized by warm sunshine, sea, and sandy beaches (Mowforth & Munt, 2015; Orams, 1999; Sharpley & Telfer, 2015). Unlike other SIDS and Caribbean islands, Dominica lacks 3S-friendly sandy beaches and large-scale tourism and domestic infrastructure development is limited by inherently difficult movement on the island (Baker, 1994). Infrastructure is constrained by expensive, recurrent road and bridge development and repair due to the combination of mountainous terrain, heavy rains, and related flooding and erosion (Baker, 1994). As a result, the island has developed a niche tourism brand, referring to itself as the Nature Island.

Compared to other Caribbean islands, the tourism industry in Dominica is underdeveloped (Edgell & Swanson, 2013) and more than a quarter of Dominica's 70,000 residents are considered below the poverty line (Caribbean Development Bank, 2010). Consistent with characteristics of SIDS, it relies on tourism revenue for development and faces limited access issues and exposure to natural disasters (Holladay & Powell, 2016). While other Caribbean islands pursued extensive tourism development after World War II, Dominica's geographical challenges and lack of tourism-supporting infrastructure prevented it from similar developments that would decrease its agricultural dependency (Weaver, 1991). For example, Weaver (1991) argues that Dominica's insufficient lodging, port, and airfield access was a cyclical challenge that limited immediate tourism growth as well as the access and development that would support future tourism growth. Unlike its Caribbean neighbors, Dominica did not develop 3S tourism because it lacks 3S-style white sand beaches and access to the island is limited by Dominica's geographical location and topography (Holladay & Powell, 2013; Weaver, 1991). While there have been some efforts to develop pockets of beach tourism on the island's small, dark sand volcanic beaches, the island's frequently overcast and rainy weather further impedes 3S tourism growth (Weaver, 1991; Weis, 2018). As a result of being unable to effectively compete with 3S markets, Dominica developed a niche tourism model and established itself as the Nature Island of the Caribbean (Discover Dominica Authority, 2013a; M. M. Miller & Henthorne, 2007). This Nature Island brand serves as a competitive alternative to 3S tourism options in the region, and serves to attract international visitors to the island (M. M. Miller & Henthorne, 2007). Dominica has leveraged tourism as a key development tool for its population and its Nature Island tourism model appears to rely on unique features such as the island's distinct culture and volcanic activity (Edgell & Swanson, 2013). Dominica has received a large amount of investment from the European Commission to develop community-based tourism as a strategy for enhancing dimensions of resilience; however, an understanding of specifics related to social-ecological resilience remains undertheorized (Holladay & Powell, 2013). Dominica has a primarily coastal tourism model as most of its target tourist activities take place within or near the coastal zone (e.g. coastal walks, coastal community festivals, coastal restaurants)—although it also has some marine tourism activities (e.g. whale watching, snorkeling, scuba diving).

Methods

Study site

The Commonwealth of Dominica, a lush, mountainous SIDS in the Lesser Antilles region of the Caribbean, commonly uses tourism as a key development tool (Weis, 2018). It contains a unique environment, history, and culture, and its landscape is often characterized as both rich in essential resources and wild, untamed, or potentially volatile (Allen & Lines, 2001; Hypolite et al., 2002). There is ample freshwater (Allen & Lines, 2001), biodiversity (Hypolite et al., 2002), and small-scale fishing and agriculture that allows for a highly localized subsistence lifestyle (Peteru et al., 2010);

Table 1. Study site community description and criteria.

Community	Relative size	Primary industries
Roseau	Large (Capital)	Government, Tourism
Portsmouth	Large	Tourism, Fishing
Mero	Medium	Tourism
Soufriere	Medium	Tourism, Fishing
Layou	Small	Tourism, Fishing
Scotts Head	Small	Tourism, Fishing

Note. Relative size is based on public data of population estimates (small, about 200–1,000; medium, 1,000–2,000; large, more than 3,000).
Source: Authors.

however, there is also volcanic activity, steep terrain, exposure to hurricanes and large amounts of rainfall, and the subsequent damage caused to modern development, infrastructure, and agriculture (Baker, 1994). Dominica's location and topography are commonly linked to its history and culture, which is diverse with African, French, English, and indigenous influences. The majority of the population is of African descent (Caribbean Community (CARICOM) Secretariat, 2009) and the island is also home to the Kalinago, the last indigenous population in the Caribbean—also referred to as Caribs, the European name (Discover Dominica Authority, n.d.). Dominica's primary industries are commonly cited as agriculture and tourism (Payne, 2008; Weaver, 1991), and national and international perceptions view tourism as a more reliable industry that should replace agriculture as the island's primary revenue source (Holladay & Powell, 2016).

Study communities

This research focused on six coastal communities in Dominica and examined resident perceptions of social-ecological resilience through semi-structured interviews with community members who were self-employed in either the farming, fishing, or tourism industries, community leaders, or those who were involved in tourism-related efforts or policy at a mid- to senior-level. The objective was to explore trends *within* communities in Dominica, and not to thoroughly compare *between* communities or to deduce trends for the entire island. The selection criteria for including a community in this study required that 1) its geographic location fulfill the definition of a *coastal community*, defined for the purposes of this study as one that is located, at least in part, directly on the coast or beach; 2) that there is a balanced representation of diverse communities with tourism activity (i.e. size, location, urban and rural); 3) that all communities reside on the Caribbean Sea side of the island, for logistical reasons including time and budget; and, 4) that key informants were available to participate during the data collection phase.

The six communities selected were Roseau, Scotts Head, Soufriere, Layou, Mero, and Portsmouth—all coastal communities along the Caribbean Sea with tourism as one of their primary industries (Tables 1 and 2). Roseau, the largest community and capital of Dominica, is the administrative center for government and business affairs and is home to the island's primary cruise ship port. Portsmouth, the second largest community, is home to the secondary cruise ship port. Scotts Head and Layou are both fishing villages with underdeveloped tourism activity. Soufriere and Mero also

Table 2. Breakdown of interviews by primary industry.

Primary industry	N	%
Tourism	21	52.5
Government	14	35
Fishing	5	12.5

Source: Authors.

have fishing activity and neighbor Scotts Head and Layou, respectively, but they are comparatively larger with more tourism activity. Hurricane Maria occurred after the completion of this research; and, while all six communities in this study were affected, information about their sustained damage and subsequent recovery is limited beyond the score of this article.

Data collection

Collected data were qualitative in nature and therefore qualitative data analysis was employed. Data were collected using semi-structured interviews, which are defined as formal, scheduled interviews that generally follow a script and cover a range of topics (Bernard, 2005, p. 210). They are ideal for enabling the collection of 'reliable, comparative qualitative data' (Bernard, 2005, p.212) when the data collection is limited to a single interview per informant, such as in this study. The interviews all followed the same interview protocol, a unique script designed for this study, which focused on identifying factors that influenced community member access to the benefits of tourism and the effect of tourism on social and cultural dynamics. The interview protocol contained 13 questions relating to each of the four components of social-ecological resilience: governance, social, ecological, and economic aspects (Table 3). Within each study site community, the criteria for selecting key informants required that they represent five perspectives related to the island's primary industries of farming, fishing, and tourism: governance (e.g. government official or community leader), fishing (e.g. fisher), agriculture (e.g. farmer), experience-related tourism (e.g. tour operator), and hospitality (e.g. restaurant owner, hotel manager). While initially the criteria held more formal distinctions between industries, it was updated to accommodate the cultural norm that individuals often participated in multiple industries.

Across the six communities, a total of 40 individuals were interviewed to accommodate for the more nuanced variance among the industry categories. Interviews were conducted within the communities and averaged approximately 45 minutes. The number of interviews in each community were roughly proportionate to community size: eleven (28%) in Roseau, the largest community, capital, and administrative center of the island; eight (20%) in Portsmouth, the second-largest on the island and primary urban community for the northern region; seven (18%) in Soufriere, the capital of the island's southern-most parish, Saint Mark Parish, and three (8%) in Scotts Head, its neighboring fishing village at the southernmost tip of the island; four (10%) in Mero, a beachfront community between Roseau and Portsmouth, and seven (18%) in Layou, a nearby fishing village at the mouth of a river delta. The interviews were also roughly evenly distributed by gender, with 21 female key informants (52.5%) and 19 male key informants (47.5%). All key informants were members of the study site communities,

Table 3. Semi-structured interview questions.

	Question	Domain
1.	How are decisions made in the community? (Who makes decisions for the community?)	Governance
2.	Do you think you have the power to make decisions about issues that affect your community? (How much power or influence do you have?)	Governance
3.	How would you describe your community? What are the geographic boundaries?	Governance
4.	When there is a conflict in the community, how is it solved?	Social (Conflict)
5.	If you weren't going to do tourism, what would you do?	Social (Alternative Livelihoods)
6.	What's the difference between getting into agriculture and getting into fishing? What about between agriculture, fishing, and tourism?	Social (Alternative Livelihoods)
7.	What do you think the community should have in place to help with sustainable tourism development?	Social (Sustainability)
8.	Tell me about the current amount of tourism. Do you think there will be more or less? Do you want more or less?	Social (Sustainability)
9.	Do you see the potential for increased ecological impacts if there is an increase in tourism?	Ecological
10.	Do you see any negative aspects of this kind of tourism/an increase in tourism?	Ecological
11.	Is there any difference between people who work in tourism and people who don't?	Economic
12.	What is your community like now with this kind of tourism?	Economic
13.	What do locals think about tourism or tourists on the island? Or what do you think about tourism and tourists here?	Economic

Source: Authors.

and the majority identified as native Dominicans (82.5%), with the minority identifying as being born abroad (17.5%).

Data analysis

All interviews were conducted in-person, audio-recorded and followed the informed consent process. Audio recordings were transcribed and then transcript and field note data were coded inductively by hand to enable the study of informant responses and for understanding of the data to emerge. Inductive coding allowed for the exploration and discovery of larger themes in the data related to the larger questions of resilience and tourism (Bernard, 2005). Themes were identified by both their prominence in the interviews and their relevance to the research questions. Selected remarks were then categorized by the level of occurrence: a strong theme echoed by many or a smaller theme only mentioned by a few. Data reached saturation within the data analysis, where informants expressed similar and corresponding sentiments to the point that no new information was achieved through further coding (Fusch & Ness, 2015).

Results

Qualitative analysis of key informant interviews resulted in five major themes related to factors that both enabled and hindered community member access to the benefits and opportunities of tourism (Table 4). Aspects that enabled access emerged within the themes of Brand Authenticity and Tourism is Everybody's Business. Aspects that hindered access emerged within the themes of Limited Access, Seasonality, and the

Table 4. Summary of questions from interviews, emergent themes, and theme definitions.

Question	Themes	Definition
Ecological	Brand authenticity	Alignment between The Nature Island brand and tourist experiences
Governance	Tourism is everybody's business	The perception that tourism benefits all and that all should support tourism and positive tourist experiences
Economic	Limited access	Constrained benefits of potential tourism development and growth as a result of hindered visitor access to the island (e.g. geographic, infrastructure, financial, temporal)
Social	Seasonality	Fluctuating or cyclical industries and opportunities
Social	Hustle mindset	The pursuit of the most accessible, maximum income through short-term, varied opportunities

Source: Authors.

Hustle Mindset, respectively. Below, the major components related to the definition of the five major themes are outlined. Direct quotes from key informants are used to give context-specific results that highlight agreement, variation, or contrast among key informant perceptions.

Brand authenticity

Informants were sensitive to tourist perceptions of Dominica and the authenticity of the Nature Island brand. Both the formal Nature Island brand and informal word-of-mouth reputation were described as important for tourism to be successful and grow. The Nature Island brand was described as tailored for 'the modern traveler' who seeks destinations that are 'off the beaten path ... [and who will be] the first of their friends to hear about it and to go.' Informants explained that Dominica was such a place, and the Nature Island brand helped to attract tourists to the island. As one noted, 'there's an appeal [among tourists] to be the first. Dominica still has that. We're so unknown that we're actually ahead ... nobody knows about us ... and we're still untouched ... and I think that is a major opportunity.' The success of the Nature Island brand was dependent on the island's word-of-mouth reputation, as one explained, '[w]e bring Dominica to them, our waterfalls and everything, and they bring to us revenue and a good name if they enjoyed it, stayed.' If tourist experiences on the island matched expectations based on the Nature Island brand, then 'they [the tourists] will give us a good name and more tourists will come.' For some, the sensitivity to brand authenticity extended further, where 'the lifestyle of people must reflect what Dominica advertises'.

Tourism is everybody's business

The primary industries of farming, fishing, and tourism were described as 'all linked up.' Community members earned multiple incomes across multiple industries because 'in Dominica, it's hard to make money' and so one must 'make money when they [opportunities] come.' Tourism was seen as a lucrative option, as 'tourism money impacts the whole community' and 'if dollar is rolling, everything is rolling.' For example, some informants were both fishers and tour guides who would 'fish early ... and maybe drive later' in the day and then farm family plots on weekends. The ability to earn multiple incomes from varying sources was viewed positively, as *'everything goes into the same pot at the end of the day.'* Similarly, a *'day-to-day'* focus was valued as flexible income sources could be adjusted to sudden changes or trends (e.g. storm damage, declining fish populations, global economic crisis). Informants consistently stated that *'tourism is everybody's business'*, meaning that, as tourism impacted every-one, everyone should support tourism and tourists' positive experiences on the island.

Limited access

Visiting Dominica was described as logistically difficult and expensive to visit, where *'it takes a lot to come here [to Dominica].'* As one community member said, *'you have to want to come to Dominica.'* Limited ferry options, multiple flight connections, and fre-quently cancelled flights due to *'poor weather'* and *'inexperienced pilots'* were cited as some of the logistical challenges that limited access to the island. For example, one informant described the challenge of being restricted to indirect flights that connected through other Caribbean islands as *'why go [on] to Dominica when you already in the Caribbean?'* Limited access to the island primarily referred to the challenges in increas-ing the amount of stayover tourism. Cruise ship tourism was generally viewed as less desirable as it was *'more footsteps, less profit'*, although a minority of informants viewed any type of tourism as positive, where *'more is more.'* Logistics challenges and financial costs that *'capped'* stayover tourism numbers were viewed as a factor that hindered access to the benefits of tourism.

Seasonality

Farming, fishing, and tourism were all considered to be seasonal, meaning that income fluctuated with the time of year. Income from any one of source was described as unreliable, and so having multiple sources of income was preferred. Because tourism was viewed as the industry with the most promising income opportu-nities, informants consistently expressed a desire to *'make it more regular'* because *'a longer [tourism] season is more money.'* The tourism season in Dominica was about *'six months, from November to May'*, which was determined by the cruise ship season. A longer tourism season would be *'a good thing'* because *'everyone does better'* during the tourism season. The limited season of the tourism industry was viewed as a factor that hindered access to the benefits of tourism.

Hustle mindset

A focus on short-term income opportunities rather than longer-term business projects was described during the interviews as common among community members. This was referred to as a *'hustle mindset'* where *'it's not about the job, it's about the money'*. While a short-term focus enabled one to pursue the most profitable opportunity each day, it hindered access to the benefits of a longer-term focus, such as *'craft[ing] a pro-fession'* with more consistent revenue. The hustle mindset was also described as a *'passive mindset'* and linked to the island's legacy of slavery. Foreign investment was described as *'part of the problem'* regarding the hustle mindset, where *'people expect handouts'* due to a steady flow of development funding. These dynamics also surfaced in the interviews on an individual level, as informants described how some community members will not take initiative to improve tourism opportunities; rather, they will *'wait for you to do it and then try to ride the wave of your success.'*

Discussion

As previously stated, the purpose of this research was to explore theories behind social-ecological resilience in the context of community-based tourism development. The definition of the five major themes above creates baseline data for the communities studied that in turn helps with understanding of the opportunities and barriers for community members involved with tourism and with current and future tourism development. This in-depth understanding is important for enhancing the resilience of community-based tourism within Dominica. Here, we discuss the five themes in relation to each other, and to social-ecological resilience theories.

The first theme was Brand Authenticity. Dominica's Nature Island brand is a formal, tourism-specific marketing campaign, and such campaigns are documented as able to attract tourists to a destination (Anholt, 2010; Buhalis, 2000; Kotler & Gertner, 2002). Cultivating Dominica's reputation as a tourism destination was viewed as an opportunity to grow tourism rather than as a threat. The authenticity of the Nature Island brand was perceived to contribute to a continued positive reputation via word-of-mouth, where tourists would give Dominica *'a good name'* abroad should their experience in Dominica align with the curated niche identity and culture of the island. The expressed sensitivity to Dominica's word-of-mouth reputation as a tourism destination is consistent with modern trends: tourists often use online tools to 'search, organize, share, and annotate their travel stories and experiences' (Leung et al., 2013, p. 4).

Authenticity has a role in the economic resilience of tourism; tourist perceptions have been noted to impact the economic resilience of tourism destinations, with both positive and negative perceptions influencing the rise and decline of tourism activity at tourism destinations, respectively (Tyrrell & Johnston, 2008). While smaller destinations are potentially more vulnerable than larger destinations due to characteristics such as comparably less economic diversity, more dependence on trade, and more impacts from natural disasters (Holladay et al., 2019)—all characteristics consistent with SIDS such as Dominica—niche markets that preserve their unique identity in the face of globalization may, in fact, increase their economic resilience, such as those that adhere to specific historic preservation in Monterey, California, or diverse ethnic cultural preservation in Nepal (Tyrrell & Johnston, 2008).

The second theme was the refrain that Tourism is Everybody's Business, which illustrated a widely adopted lifestyle or loose code of conduct for individuals as members of the greater community of the island. 'Tourism is everybody's business' was originally an official slogan that encouraged behaviors among residents which supported positive tourist perceptions and related economic benefits (Discover Dominica Authority, 2013b; Government Information Service, 2012, 2015, 2016). The slogan appeared to have been adopted on an individual level—it was used as a reminder that the actions of each community member impacted tourist perceptions of Dominica and what tourists would tell others after they left the island.

The individual and personal internalization of this slogan can be considered to be part of a lifestyle identity, which is related to the sharing, collaborative process of community-based tourism (Okazaki, 2008). Such socially-endorsed behavior that is perceived, even if solely by the individual, to be generally supportive or beneficial to the collective group, can also be tied to measures of social and economic resilience (Holladay & Powell, 2016). Indeed, perceived benefits are critical for community-based tourism success (Lee, 2013) and lifestyle identity has been positively linked to the resilience of tourism enterprises (Biggs, 2011). The slogan was also used as a reminder that farming, fishing, and tourism were interconnected and that farming and fishing supported the success of tourism; the success of tourism as an industry enabled community members to access the benefits of tourism, which is salient to community-based tourism participation among locals (Hung et al., 2011).

The third theme was Limited Access to potential tourism-related revenue. Tourist access to the island was perceived to be constrained and this limited the amount of potential tourism revenue; however, access to existing tourist-related opportunities was viewed positively. Community members described their direct access to the benefits of tourism through tourism income opportunities (e.g. tour guide, hotel manager, restaurant owner) and indirect access through a wider range of opportunities connected to tourism. Their access was also enabled by their ability to earn multiple incomes from multiple sources, which was viewed as a buffer against instabilities similar to the Banana Crash; tourism was seen as a sector that helped diversify revenue sources. Collectively, multiple and diverse sources of income can indicate higher measures of the local tourism industry's economic resilience, where residents have equitable access to consistent and sustainable tourism-related incomes (Cochrane, 2010).

Access was expanded by the interconnection of the primary industries (farming, fishing, tourism), such as when fishers or farmers sold their catch to hotel restaurants. The benefits of tourism also included the diverse use of tourism-earned revenue. Tourism revenue was considered a major source of funding for development projects on the island, such as infrastructure and education. Foreign aid and investment in tourism-related infrastructure projects was also seen as an enabling factor, such as investment in the international airport and grants for community tourism projects. Dominica's niche Nature Island brand and corresponding authenticity for tourist experiences on the island was also linked to development funding, as the model was viewed as an attractive alternative to neighboring islands' 3S tourism models.

The fourth theme was Seasonality. This referred to the intermittent pattern of varying income sources, such as how the wider tourism season was determined by the approximately six-month cruise ship season. Seasonality limited access to the benefits of tourism, and an extended tourism season was desired to enable more access to tourism revenue and opportunities. Seasonality can also be linked to the Hustle Mindset theme and the more general approach of earning incomes from multiple sources. The practice of earning income from multiple sources can be a contributing factor to the perception of social equity between incomes. As the inflow of money mattered more than the type of income or industry in which it was earned, money appeared to be viewed as a tool for increasing quality of life, rather than a goal or reflection of social status.

Limited physical access to the island served as a bottleneck between the potential and actual amount of stayover tourism, which was more profitable and thus more desirable as compared to cruise tourism. Limited physical access within the island contributed to tourism hubs and concentrated tourism activity near key sites. This hindered access to the benefits of tourism for those outside of these areas. Limited infrastructure, such as domestic flights, ferries, roads, and bridges, hindered physical access between communities and increased the cost—time, money, effort—of visiting areas further from the concentrated tourism activity. These are persistent limitations, as similar challenges restricted the island's participation in the larger region's post-World War II tourism expansion (Weaver, 1991). Consistent with key informant desires for a longer tourism season, the extension of tourism seasons is known to reduce a destination's vulnerability and increase measures of its resilience (Heslinga et al., 2019).

The fifth theme was the Hustle Mindset, a short-term focus on flexible income opportunities. The phrase 'hustle mindset' was used to describe behavior that both hindered and enabled access to the benefits of tourism. When described as a more passive attitude, a lack of initiative, or a dependence on government programs, it hindered long-term potential for the wider community's access to the benefits of tourism. Conversely, when described as a flexibility to shift between fluctuating income opportunities, it enabled access to the most profitable or appealing opportunity on any given day. The more passive behavior appears to be consistent with grant dependency, while the active maintenance of diverse, short-term sources of income appears to be an adaptation to seasonality. Grants intended to improve recipient welfare and spur entrepreneurial activity have been linked to results contrary to their aims, such as with smallholder maize producers in South Africa and their reduced incentive to commercialize their yields (Sinyolo et al., 2017). Self-reliance may be due to lower levels of grant funding and thus the lack of dependence upon them (Clark et al., 2007; Holladay & Powell, 2016).

The hustle mindset appears to reflect in part the broader aims of economic diversity, and there was a clear tension between stability (long-term focus) and flexibility (short-term hustle mindset) in the interviews. Economic diversity has long been noted to reduce vulnerability to unpredictable tourism trends, including among Caribbean SIDS (Wilkinson, 1987). Increasing measures of social-ecological resilience also requires a balanced response to unexpected shocks, as observed in post-2004 tsunami Sri Lanka where short-term coastal protection policies led to long-term social, economic, and ecological vulnerabilities (Ingram et al., 2006). Grant dependency and the hustle mindset can be linked to the economic instability in the 1990s following the banana crash. After the banana crash, in which many Dominicans relied on a single source of revenue, the Dominican government sought to stabilize its economy through international assistance (Holladay, 2011). Tourism was identified as an industry that could be developed as a more stable alternative to the island's past volatile agricultural export markets. Dominica received International Monetary Fund (IMF) assistance and the EU provided two large grants to develop Dominica's tourism sector—the Ecotourism Development Program (ETDP) and the Tourism Sector Development

Program (TSDP), from 2003-2006 and 2008-2010, respectively (Holladay & Powell, 2016). There is a common assumption in community development finance that there is underdeveloped entrepreneurial potential in underprivileged communities (Affleck & Mellor, 2006, p. 305). The EU grants incorporated this assumption and aimed to develop entrepreneurial opportunities for coastal communities in Dominica.

Conclusion

This study aids in understanding community member access to the benefits and opportunities of community-based tourism and related social-cultural dynamics within the context of resilience theory. Community member perceptions were the focus of this study as theirs were most able to highlight local dynamics relating to tourism development in Dominica. Increasing components of social-ecological resilience may support the sustainability of the island's community-based tourism, one of its primary industries. Findings indicated that the increasing some measures of social-ecological resilience could support the sustainability of the island's community-based tourism. Extending the tourism season, increasing physical access to the island, aligning tourist experiences on the island with the Nature Island brand, and enhancing equitable access to tourism-related income opportunities would all support areas of social-ecological resilience.

The findings of this study overlap and indicate some positive measures of social-ecological resilience. Authenticity concerns about the Nature Island brand correspond with the mindful attitude to individually support tourism efforts, as tourism was understood to have a rippling effect beyond tourism-related activity. The active maintenance of an authentic Nature Island brand along with an individual sense of responsibility could lead to higher measures of ecological resilience. Authenticity, seasonality, and limited access concerns also intersect, where an authentic brand, more access to the island, and a longer tourism season could all contribute to higher measures of economic resilience. Limited access and seasonality have also contributed to an adaptive hustle mindset, where economic diversification and flexible opportunity is prioritized and social identity is not based on one's source(s) of income; this lifestyle can enhance higher measures of economic and social resilience.

This study can serve as a baseline for future observations, particularly in a post-Hurricane Maria context and as tourism development advances in Dominica. Future research recommendations are to observe the relationship between tourism and additional coastal communities, and to assess measures of resilience in more coastal communities engaged in tourism efforts. Exploring the effectiveness of tourism development policies in SIDS, particularly with regards to known trends such as limited access and grant dependency, would be particularly useful. Understanding which policies and factors enable access the benefits of tourism will aid communities in developing a more advantageous tourism sector. An understanding of related measures of resilience warrants more exploration.

While the findings can signal future areas of study, the data is specific to the study site communities in Dominica. The results of this study are not able to be generalized across scales or represent trends among the island's entire population; they are limited in their ability to explore perceptions in the study's six coastal communities of Roseau, Portsmouth, Mero, Soufriere, Layou, and Scotts Head. While data were gathered in these six defined areas, community boundaries often blurred or were interpreted differently by community members, and individuals often identified with multiple communities (e.g. ancestral, work, home). Therefore, understanding perceptions among community members within these communities was limited due to the lack of clear, universally defined community boundaries and identification criteria for an individual's primary community. The results of this study can be used to inform coastal management strategies in Dominica and related efforts increase social-ecological resilience and support the sustainability of its tourism development. Knowledge about how tourism is or is not benefitting community members in Dominica can be used to create more effective tourism strategies on the island, and potentially inform strategies for other SIDS with similar dynamics.

Disclosure statement

No potential conflict of interest was reported by the authors.

ORCID

Kristin Weis (iD) http://orcid.org/0000-0003-3909-4537

References

Adger, W. N. (2006). Vulnerability. *Global Environmental Change, 16*(3), 268–281. https://doi.org/ 10.1016/j.gloenvcha.2006.02.006

Affleck, A., & Mellor, M. (2006). Community development finance: A neo-market solution to social exclusion? *Journal of Social Policy, 35*(2), 303–319. https://doi.org/10.1017/S0047279405009542

Allen, B., & Lines, L. (2001). External economic pressures and park planning: A case study from Dominica. In D. Harmon (Ed.), *Crossing boundaries in park management* (pp. 332–335). Presented at the Proceedings of the 11th conference on research and resource management in parks and on public lands, Hancock. http://www.georgewright.org/57allen.pdf

Anholt, S. (2010). *Places: Identity, image and reputation.* Springer.

Archer, B., Cooper, C., & Ruhanen, L. (2005). The positive and negative impacts of tourism. In William F. Theobald, ed, *Global Tourism* (3rd ed), Butterworth-Heinemann, 2005 (pp 79–102).

Baker, P. L. (1994). *Centering the periphery: Chaos, order, and the ethnohistory of Dominica.* McGill-Queen's Press - MQUP.

Bec, A., McLennan, C., & Moyle, B. D. (2016). Community resilience to long-term tourism decline and rejuvenation: A literature review and conceptual model. *Current Issues in Tourism, 19*(5), 431–457. https://doi.org/10.1080/13683500.2015.1083538

Berkes, F., Colding, J., Folke, C. (2003). Navigating social ecological systems: Building resilience complexity and change. Retrieved August 29, 2017, from Cambridge University Press website: http://www.cambridge.org/us/academic/subjects/life-sciences/ecology-and-conservation/nav-igating-social-ecological-systems-building-resilience-complexity-and-change

Berkes, F., Colding, J., & Folke, C. (2008). *Navigating social-ecological systems: Building resilience for complexity and change.* Cambridge University Press.

Bernard, H. R. (2005). *Research methods in anthropology: Qualitative and quantitative approaches* (4th ed.). AltaMira Press.

Biggs, D. (2011). Understanding resilience in a vulnerable industry: The case of reef tourism in Australia. *Ecology and Society, 16*(1). https://doi.org/10.5751/ES-03948-160130

Blackstock, K. (2005). A critical look at community based tourism. *Community Development Journal, 40*(1), 39–49. https://doi.org/10.1093/cdj/bsi005

Briguglio, L. (1995). Small island developing states and their economic vulnerabilities. *World Development, 23*(9), 1615–1632. https://doi.org/10.1016/0305-750X(95)00065-K

Briguglio, L. (2003, September). *The Vulnerability Index and small island developing states: A review of conceptual and methodological issues.* Presented at the AIMS Regional Preparatory Meeting on the Ten Year Review of the Barbados Programme of Action, Praia, Cape Verde. https://www.um.edu.mt/__data/assets/pdf_file/0019/44137/vulnerability_paper_sep03.pdf

Buhalis, D. (2000). Marketing the competitive destination of the future. *Tourism Management, 21*(1), 97–116. https://doi.org/10.1016/S0261-5177(99)00095-3

Campling, L., & Rosalie, M. (2006). Sustaining social development in a small island developing state? The case of Seychelles. *Sustainable Development, 14*(2), 115–125. https://doi.org/10.1002/sd.298

Caribbean Community (CARICOM) Secretariat. (2009). *Dominica—Population and Housing Census 2001.* http://catalog.ihsn.org/index.php/catalog/4088

Caribbean Development Bank. (2010). Country poverty assessment—Dominica. 1, 196. Retrieved September 30, 2017 from https://catalog.ihsn.org/index.php/catalog/4295/download/56274.

Carpenter, S., & Brock, W. (2008). Adaptive capacity and traps. *Ecology and Society, 13*(2). https://doi.org/10.5751/ES-02716-130240

Cheer, J. M. & Lew, A. A. (2018). Understanding tourism resilience: Adapting to social, political, and economic change. In J. Cheer and A. A. Lew, editors. 2017. *Tourism, Resilience, and Sustainability: Adapting to Social, Political and Economic Change,* 3–17. London: Routledge.

Clark, D., Southern, R., & Beer, J. (2007). Rural governance, community empowerment and the new institutionalism: A case study of the Isle of Wight. *Journal of Rural Studies, 23*(2), 254–266. https://doi.org/10.1016/j.jrurstud.2006.10.004

Cochrane, J. (2010). The sphere of tourism resilience. *Tourism Recreation Research*, *35*(2), 173–185. https://doi.org/10.1080/02508281.2010.11081632

Discover Dominica Authority. (2013a). *Discover Dominica, the Nature Island*. Retrieved April 11, 2017, from http://dominica.dm/

Discover Dominica Authority. (2013b). *Tourism awareness month*. Retrieved September 30, 2017, from http://www.dominica.dm/index.php/events-calendar?sobi2Task=sobi2Details&catid=12&sobi2Id=81

Discover Dominica Authority. (n.d.). *Kalinago Territory*. Retrieved September 30, 2017, from http://kalinagoterritory.com/

Edgell, D. L. S. (2015). International sustainable tourism policy. *Brown Journal of World Affairs*, *22*, 25.

Edgell, D. L. S., & Swanson, J. (2013). *Tourism policy and planning: Yesterday, today, and tomorrow*. Routledge.

Folke, C. (2006). Resilience: The emergence of a perspective for social–ecological systems analyses. *Global Environmental Change*, *16*(3), 253–267. https://doi.org/10.1016/j.gloenvcha.2006.04.002

Folke, C. (2016, December). Resilience (Republished) *21*(4), 44. https://doi.org/10.5751/ES-09088-210444

Folke, C., Carpenter, S. R., Walker, B., Scheffer, M., Chapin, T., & Rockstrom, J. (2010). *Resilience thinking: Integrating resilience, adaptability and transformability*. https://www.treesearch.fs.fed.us/pubs/42598

Folke, C., Carpenter, S., Walker, B., Scheffer, M., Elmqvist, T., Gunderson, L., & Holling, C. S. (2004). Regime shifts, resilience, and biodiversity in ecosystem management. *Annual Review of Ecology, Evolution, and Systematics*, *35*(1), 557–581. https://doi.org/10.1146/annurev.ecolsys.35.021103.105711

Fusch, P. I., & Ness, L. R. (2015). Are we there yet? Data saturation in qualitative research. *The Qualitative Report*, *20*(9), 1408.

Gaillard, J. C. (2010). Vulnerability, capacity and resilience: Perspectives for climate and development policy. *Journal of International Development*, *22*(2), 218–232. https://doi.org/10.1002/jid.1675

Gallopín, G. C. (2006). Linkages between vulnerability, resilience, and adaptive capacity. *Global Environmental Change*, *16*(3), 293–303. https://doi.org/10.1016/j.gloenvcha.2006.02.004

Gillis, J. R. (2012). *The human shore: Seacoasts in history*. University of Chicago Press.

Government Information Service. (2012, May 1). *Government declares May tourism awareness month*. Retrieved October 21, 2017, from http://news.gov.dm/index.php/news/106-government-declares-may-as-tourism-awareness-month

Government Information Service. (2015, May 6). *DDA officially launches May as tourism awareness month*. Retrieved October 22, 2017, from http://news.gov.dm/index.php/news/2490-dda-officially-launches-may-as-tourism-awareness-month

Government Information Service. (2016, May 5). *Tourism awareness month for reflection and collaboration*. Retrieved October 22, 2017, from http://news.gov.dm/index.php/news/3602-tourism-awareness-month-for-reflection-and-collaboration

Hall, C. M., & Page, S. J. (2014). *The geography of tourism and recreation: Environment, place and space* (4th ed.). Routledge.

Heslinga, J. H., Hillebrand, H., & Emonts, T. (2019). How to improve innovation in sustainable tourism? Five lessons learned from the Austrian Alps. *Journal of Tourism Futures*, *5*(1), 35–42. https://doi.org/10.1108/JTF-09-2018-0054

Holladay, P., Dixon, A. W., Nguyen, M. C., Bao, L. N., Xu, S., & Price-Howard, K. (2018). Stakeholder perceptions of tourism assets and sustainable tourism development in Da Nang. *Enlightening Tourism. A Pathmaking Journal*, *8*(2), 74–98. https://doi.org/10.33776/et.v8i2.3357

Holladay, P. J. (2011). *An integrated approach to assessing the resilience and sustainability of community-based tourism development in the Commonwealth of Dominica—ProQuest*. Clemson University. https://search.proquest.com/openview/923452c1a5817470bfad7ef99a545fbc/1?pq-origsite=gscholar&cbl=18750&diss=y

Holladay, P. J. (2018). Destination resilience and sustainable tourism development. *Tourism Review International*, *22*(3), 251–261. https://doi.org/10.3727/154427218X15369305779029

Holladay, P. J., Mendez-Lazaro, P., Centeno, H. M., Rivera-Gutierrez, R., Adams, K., & Brundiers, K. (2019). Utuado, Puerto Rico and community resilience post-hurricane Maria: The case of Tetuan reborn. *Recreation, Parks, and Tourism in Public Health, 3*, 5–16.

Holladay, P. J., & Powell, R. B. (2013). Resident perceptions of social–ecological resilience and the sustainability of community-based tourism development in the Commonwealth of Dominica. *Journal of Sustainable Tourism, 21*(8), 1188–1211. https://doi.org/10.1080/09669582.2013. 776059

Holladay, P. J., & Powell, R. B. (2016). Social-ecological systems, stakeholders and sustainability: A qualitative inquiry into community-based tourism in the Commonwealth of Dominica. *Caribbean Studies, 44*(1–2), 3–28.

Holling, C. S. (1973). Resilience and stability of ecological systems. *Annual Review of Ecology and Systematics, 4*(1), 1–23. https://doi.org/10.1146/annurev.es.04.110173.000245

Hung, K., Sirakaya-Turk, E., & Ingram, L. J. (2011). Testing the efficacy of an integrative model for community participation. *Journal of Travel Research, 50*(3), 276–288. https://doi.org/10.1177/ 0047287510362781

Hypolite, E., Green, G. C., & Burley, J. (2002). Ecotourism: Its potential role in forest resource conservation in the Commonwealth of Dominica. *International Forestry Review, 4*(4), 298–306. https://doi.org/10.1505/ifor.4.4.298.40529

Ingram, J. C., Franco, G., Rio, C. R., & Khazai, B. (2006). Post-disaster recovery dilemmas: Challenges in balancing short-term and long-term needs for vulnerability reduction. *Environmental Science & Policy, 9*(7), 607–613.

Kotler, P., & Gertner, D. (2002). Country as brand, product, and beyond: A place marketing and brand management perspective. *Journal of Brand Management, 9*(4), 249–261. https://doi.org/ 10.1057/palgrave.bm.2540076

Lee, T. H. (2013). Influence analysis of community resident support for sustainable tourism development. *Tourism Management, 34*, 37–46. https://doi.org/10.1016/j.tourman.2012.03.007

Leung, D., Law, R., Hoof, H. v., & Buhalis, D. (2013). Social media in tourism and hospitality: A literature review. *Journal of Travel & Tourism Marketing, 30*(1–2), 3–22.

Miller, F., Osbahr, H., Boyd, E., Thomalla, F., Bharwani, S., Ziervogel, G., Walker, B., Birkmann, J., van der Leeuw, S., Rockström, J., Hinkel, J., Downing, T., Folke, C., & Nelson, D. (2010). Resilience and vulnerability: Complementary or conflicting concepts? *Ecology and Society, 15*(3). https://doi.org/10.5751/ES-03378-150311

Miller, M. M., & Henthorne, T. L. (2007). In search of competitive advantage in Caribbean tourism websites. *Journal of Travel & Tourism Marketing, 21*(2–3), 49–62.

Mowforth, M., & Munt, I. (2015). *Tourism and sustainability: Development, globalisation and new tourism in the Third World* (4th ed.). Routledge.

Okazaki, E. (2008). A community-based tourism model: Its conception and use. *Journal of Sustainable Tourism, 16*(5), 511–529. https://doi.org/10.1080/09669580802159594

Orams, M. (1999). *Marine tourism: Development, impacts and management.* Routledge.

Payne, A. (2008). After Bananas: The IMF and the politics of stabilisation and diversification in Dominica. *Bulletin of Latin American Research, 27*(3), 317–332. https://doi.org/10.1111/j.1470-9856.2008.00272.x

Pelling, M., & Uitto, J. I. (2001). Small island developing states: Natural disaster vulnerability and global change. *Global Environmental Change Part B: Environmental Hazards, 3*(2), 49–62. https://doi.org/10.1016/S1464-2867(01)00018-3

Peteru, S., Regan, S., & Klak, T. (2010). Local vibrancy in a globalizing world: Evidence from Dominica, Eastern Caribbean. *Focus on Geography, 53*(4), 125–133. https://doi.org/10.1111/j. 1949-8535.2010.00015.x

Powell, R. B., Green, T. F., Holladay, P. J., Krafte, K. E., Duda, M., Nguyen, M. T., Spencer, J. H., & Das, P. (2018). Examining community resilience to assist in sustainable tourism development planning in Dong Van Karst Plateau Geopark, Vietnam. *Tourism Planning & Development, 15*(4), 436–457.

Price-Howard, K. & Holladay, P. J. (2014). Resorts, resilience and retention ater the BP oil spill disaster of 2010, *Journal of Tourism Insights. 5*(1), Article 2. https://doi.org/10.9707/2328-0824.1044

Ritchie, J. et al. (2013). *Qualitative Research Practice: A Guide for Social Science Students and Researchers*.

Scheyvens, R., & Momsen, J. (2008). Tourism in small island states: From vulnerability to strengths. *Journal of Sustainable Tourism, 16*(5), 491–510. https://doi.org/10.1080/09669580802159586

Sharpley, R., & Telfer, D. J. (2015). Tourism and development: Concepts and issues. Channel View Publications.

Sinyolo, S., Mudhara, M., & Wale, E. (2017). The impact of social grant dependency on smallholder maize producers' market participation in South Africa: Application of the double-hurdle model. *South African Journal of Economic and Management Sciences, 20*(1), 1–10. https://doi.org/10.4102/sajems.v20i1.1474

Slinger, V. A. V. (2002). *Ecotourism in a small Caribbean island: Lessons learned for economic development and nature preservation* [Doctoral dissertation]. University of Florida. http://uf.catalog.fcla.edu/uf.jsp?st=UF029665854&ix=pm&l=0&V=D&pm=1

Small, C., & Nicholls, R. J. (2003). A global analysis of human settlement in coastal zones. *Journal of Coastal Research, 19*(3), 584–599.

Turvey, R. (2007). Vulnerability assessment of developing countries: The case of small-island developing states. *Development Policy Review, 25*(2), 243–264. https://doi.org/10.1111/j.1467-7679.2007.00368.x

Tyrrell, T. J., & Johnston, R. J. (2008). Tourism sustainability, resiliency and dynamics: Towards a more comprehensive perspective. *Tourism and Hospitality Research, 8*(1), 14–24. https://doi.org/10.1057/thr.2008.8

UNDP. (2016). *About The Commonwealth of Dominica*. Retrieved October 26, 2017, from UNDP in Barbados & the OECS website: http://www.bb.undp.org/content/barbados/en/home/countryinfo/the_commonwealth_of_dominica.html

UNWTO. (2016). *UNWTO tourism highlights* (p. 16). Retrieved from UNWTO website: http://mkt.unwto.org/publication/unwto-tourism-highlights-2016-edition

van der Velde, M., Green, S. R., Vanclooster, M., & Clothier, B. E. (2007). Sustainable development in small island developing states: Agricultural intensification, economic development, and freshwater resources management on the coral atoll of Tongatapu. *Ecological Economics, 61*(2–3), 456–468. https://doi.org/10.1016/j.ecolecon.2006.03.017

Walker, B., Carpenter, S. R., Anderies, J. M., Abel, N., Cumming, G., Janssen, M. A., Lebel, L., Norberg, J., Peterson, G. D., & Pritchard, R. (2002). Resilience management in social-ecological systems: A working hypothesis for a participatory approach. *Conservation Ecology, 6*(1). https://doi.org/10.5751/ES-00356-060114

Walker, B., Holling, C. S., Carpenter, S., & Kinzig, A. (2004). Resilience, adaptability and transformability in social–ecological systems. *Ecology and Society, 9*(2). https://doi.org/10.5751/ES-00650-090205

Walker, B., & Salt, D. (2012). *Resilience practice: Building capacity to absorb disturbance and maintain function*. Retrieved from https://islandpress.org/book/resilience-practice

Walker, J., & Cooper, M. (2011, May 9). *Genealogies of resilience: From systems ecology to the political economy of crisis adaptation*. Retrieved July 3, 2017, from http://journals.sagepub.com/doi/abs/10.1177/0967010611399616

Weaver, D. B. (1991). Alternative to mass tourism in Dominica. *Annals of Tourism Research, 18*(3), 414–432. https://doi.org/10.1016/0160-7383(91)90049-H

Weaver, D. B. (1993). Ecotourism in the small island Caribbean. *GeoJournal, 31*(4), 457–465.

Weis, K. (2018). *Social-ecological resilience and tourism in the coastal zone: A case study in Dominica* (327-343). University of Akureyri.

Weis, K., Chambers, C., & Holladay, P. (2019). Tourism in the coastal zone: Livelihoods and opportunity for youth in Dominica. In C. P. Heidcamp & J. Morrissey (Eds.), *Towards coastal resilience and sustainability*. Routledge.

Wilkinson, P. F. (1987). Tourism in small island nations: A fragile dependence. *Leisure Studies, 6*(2), 127–146. https://doi.org/10.1080/02614368700390111

Economic and social resilience accounts for the recovery of Ibiza's tourism sector

Joan Carles Cirer-Costa

ABSTRACT

Islands tend to offer almost everything needed to become a tourist destination, such as good weather, beaches and landscapes, but it also requires the provision of competitively priced transport services, lodging and entertainment. This supply is not possible without a competent business community and a social consensus able to cope with the downsides of tourism development for the local population. Both of these two elements were present in Ibiza in the nineteen-thirties, when the island became a key tourist destination. The growth of Ibiza's tourism sector was interrupted by the outbreak of the Spanish Civil War in 1936, followed by the Second World War and subsequently by several years of total isolation. The island's tourism began a robust revival in 1950 and rose to become one of the leading destinations for mass tourism in the nineteen-sixties. This extraordinary resilience was built on the recovery of previously accumulated physical, human and social capital and on the capacity of the local business community to reinvent their product and adapt it to new circumstances. Ascertaining the foundations of this resilience is the central aim of this study. Consequently, the following methodology and tools of economic history are used: demand analysis, identification of capital sources and professional skills, and origins of applied innovations. The study also employs the concept of attractors, which is borrowed from the field of evolutionary ecology.

摘要

岛屿往往提供成为旅游目的地所需的几乎所有东西，如良好的天气、海滩和景观，但它也需要提供价格有竞争力的交通服务、住宿和娱乐。如果没有一个有能力的商界和社会共识来应对旅游业发展给当地居民带来的负面影响，这种供应是不可能的。这两种元素在20世纪30年代都出现在伊比沙岛，当时该岛成为了一个重要的旅游目的地。伊比沙岛旅游业的发展因1936年西班牙内战的爆发而中断，接着是第二次世界大战，随后是数年的完全孤立。该岛的旅游业在1950年开始强劲复苏，并在20世纪60年代成为大众旅游的主要目的地之一。这种非凡的恢复力是建立在恢复以前积累的物质、人力和社会资本的基础上，建立在当地商界改造其产品并使其适应新形势的能力上。确定这种恢复力的基础是本研究的中心目标。因此，使用了以下经济史的方法和工具:需求分析、确定资本来源和专业技能以及应用创新的源泉。本研究还采用了引子的概念，引子是从进化生态学领域借用来的。

Introduction

Today on the island of Ibiza, tourism permeates everything. As an economic activity, it has become the only source of primary income and it affects every other aspect of island life either directly or indirectly, including politics, urban planning and education. Clearly, the current state of affairs has an evolutionary history, a dynamic that has gone through distinct phases before arriving at the current monopoly of tourism on island life. These pages will analyse the first two phases of this development process: its initial phase, which spans from 1930 to 1935, and, above all, the phase of resilience that extends from 1936 to 1958. In the first of these two phases, tourism sprang out of nowhere and in a very short time succeeded in becoming an essential element in the well-being of population. As we shall see, the process had strictly local roots and emerged as a consequence of an economy that was exceptionally open to international markets, not as a result of decisions taken elsewhere.

Subsequently, an analysis of the second phase will demonstrate that tourism on Ibiza was subjected to severe pressures that practically led to its permanent disappearance, but that the local population nevertheless strove to keep it alive. In times of extreme scarcity, Ibizans came to view tourism as their only possibility of progress, clinging to it and ensuring its survival. Through their involvement, the island population endowed tourism with its resilience, its capacity to overcome obstacles to its development.

The foundations of future tourism development: the accumulation of different types of capital in the context of an industrial district

The first distinctive feature of our object of study is that the research is conducted entirely within the specific geographical environment of an island. Geography affects every social and economic relationship on an island, especially if it is small (Karampela, Kizos, & Spilanis, 2014, p. 295). The island of Ibiza has an area of slightly greater than 500 km^2 and its population in 1930 was 28,500 inhabitants, who were almost exclusively engaged in the primary sector, specifically agriculture, fisheries and salt production, but who nonetheless enjoyed a considerable level of prosperity in the Spanish context of the time (Cirer-Costa, 2008, p. 113). The island's close proximity to mainland Spain facilitated maritime communications with the ports of Barcelona and Valencia, while the numerous foreign vessels that came for Ibiza's salt connected the island to the ports of Northern Europe.

Another core concept in the argument concerns the accumulation of different types of capital. In this respect, three types of capital are distinguished: physical, human and social. In the case of Ibiza, the physical capital has two facets: private physical capital, which consists almost entirely of hotel properties, and public physical capital, which includes key infrastructure like ports, highways and airports.

Human capital covers a set of skills and abilities that people develop over the course of a lifetime, especially in their earliest stages of life. In this regard, human capital accumulation can be viewed as having two forms: traditional and formal. In the former, the only means of transmission is experience, a mechanism that does not, in principle, foster innovation (Schultz, 1975, p. 832).

Formal schooling, by contrast, provides a set of cultural resources that enable an individual to face new situations (Schultz, 1975, p. 843). Such schooling extends from the simple learning of reading and writing, which enables the individual to read an instruction manual, for instance, to university studies like chemistry and engineering. It includes international business management, which covers tools like foreign exchange and ship dispatching, all basic skills needed to receive tourists, as well as branches of knowledge like architecture and engineering, which permitted the construction of hotels of European quality and infrastructure projects such as the airport and which made possible the use of modern means of transport.

In addition, the case of Ibiza features mixed types of knowledge frequently acquired informally by Ibizans who emigrated from the island and subsequently returned. The most important one was a knowledge of foreign languages, which was common among crew on seafaring vessels. However, other more diffuse examples include knowledge of foreigners' gastronomical tastes and their customs. All of these elements helped to shape a 'global mindset' that proved especially conducive to the introduction of tourism, a new industry that required the mobilisation of all the pre-existing resources and capabilities among the island's firms and the local society (Helfat & Lieberman, 2002, p. 276; Turunen & Nummela, 2016, p. 10).

If human capital has an essentially individual basis, social capital is collective and shared in nature. The definition that best fits the case in question and our objectives is the one put forward by Cohen & Prusak, who emphasise trust and civic commitment: 'Social capital consists of the stock of active connections among people; the trust, mutual understanding, and shared values and behaviours that bind the members of human networks and communities and make cooperative action possible' (Cohen & Prusak, 2001, p. 4). By introducing the term 'social capital', the analysis includes those human bonds that are present in the daily life of all members of a community, not only those among entrepreneurs (Hopp & Stephan, 2012, p. 920; North, 1991, p. 97). The development of social capital involves the predominance of civic and group cooperation over aggression (Staber, 2007, p. 506; Stephan & Uhlaner, 2010, p.1360). The individual's commitment to the community forms the basis for the joint competitiveness of the network or group and for the innovative capacity that it deploys (Fitjar, Gjelsvik, & Rodríguez, 2013, p. 502; Holmes, Miller, Hitt, & Salmador, 2013, p. 532).

This civic cooperation is an essential element for tourism to take hold in a new destination and overcome the difficulties that arise from the initial contact between a traditional society and new visitors. At first, the presence of tourists constituted a novelty that tended to be annoying or irritating for most residents; the behaviour of the newcomers inevitably clashed with local customs and readily invited aggressive reactions (Cole, 2006, p. 630; Malek & Costa, 2014, p. 293; Tolkach, King, & Pearlman, 2013, p. 29). By contrast, the economic benefits from the budding tourism industry were limited and only flowed to a few members of the business community: hoteliers, taxi drivers, restaurateurs, etc.

At this point, social capital became crucial as a moderating influence on any potential aggressiveness toward tourists triggered by the unequal distribution of burdens and benefits that resulted from their presence. In a society endowed with strong internal bonds, the perceived benefit of tourism to some members will mitigate the negative responses of members who receive no direct advantages. Most of the population will accept that the improvement in the common welfare is reason enough to be tolerant of visitors or even to get involved in tourism development as a factor in the progress of the community as a whole (Crnogaj, Rebernik, Hojnik, & Gomezelj, 2014, p. 386).

The accumulation of social capital finds its highest expression in the industrial district. This complex concept was introduced by A. Marshall, who noted that the intense productive specialisation of a given geographical space ultimately creates an environment in which the 'mysteries of the industry' become a matter of common knowledge, absorbed by the inhabitants from childhood (Marshall, 1920, p. 271). Within an industrial district, people develop the cultural, social and family bonds that typify the accumulation of social capital, strengthen economic connections and give those connections an extraordinary resilience when disturbances hit the markets where the district's firms operate (Becattini, 2004, p. 19; Markusen, 1996, p. 296; Ottati, 1991, p. 56; Sammarra & Biggiero, 2001, 77).

The robustness of an industrial district rests on its diversity and competitiveness, on its capacity to embrace a host of firms of different sizes that strive to limit internal conflict and predatory behaviour. As a consequence, the firms belonging to a district will, if possible, focus their competitiveness on external markets and test all the possibilities offered by those markets (Feldman, Francis, & Bercovitz, 2005, p. 133). The success of the district is based on its ability to distribute information at low cost, enabling its members to specialise, uncover new opportunities or correct past mistakes (Jones & Pitelis, 2015, p. 315; You & Wilkinson, 1994, p. 260).

In the case of a tourist destination, visitors demand a wide array of products and services that require the joint efforts of many providers. Different entrepreneurs will seek to offer differentiated products and services before entering into a conflict that may prove harmful for the community as a whole (Butler & Weidenfeld, 2012, p. 19; Jones & Spadafora, 2016, p. 40). This same diversity facilitates the development of the dynamic capabilities needed to identify any opportunities that may happen to emerge as the process of tourism development advances and to reconfigure any available resources as a function of the new demands arising from the growing number of visitors (Kindström, Kowalkowski, & Sandberg, 2013, p. 5; Teece, 2007, p. 1335).

Evolutionary dynamics and resilience

According to the ecological paradigm, the stability of any complex system is positively correlated to its diversity, that is, to its capacity to accommodate a large number of mutually complementary elements, whereby its diversity increases its ability to absorb external disturbances (Loreau et al., 2001, p. 806; McCann, 2000, p. 231; Yachi & Loreau, 1999, p. 1465).

However, a high level of diversity can only be achieved in relatively mature systems, because young systems, which occupy an empty space, tend to undergo recurrent and chaotic expansion and contraction (Gorman, 1991, p. 42; Margalef, 1986, p. 20). Over time, the different components in a system occupy specific niches, adapting mutually to one another and reaching maturity, achieving the dynamic stability that is typically represented in models through the figure of 'attractors' (Ives & Carpenter, 2007, p. 58). Attractors are stable, regular points of dynamic equilibrium around which systems oscillate when they absorb disturbances that do not exceed a given critical threshold. When a disturbance exceeds this threshold, however, the system's adaptive mechanisms are saturated and the system embarks on a new path, which could lead back to the starting point, toward a different attractor or toward collapse.

How a system evolves when it absorbs a major impact that exceeds its critical threshold will be determined by the resilience of the internal relationships that characterise it. If the system tends towards the degradation and collapse of internal bonds, it will show its vulnerability. However, if it survives and adapts, it will show its resilience, that is, its ability to resituate its elements to absorb the change (Bec, McLennan, & Moyle, 2015, p. 431). This resilience, understood as adaptability, can take three forms:

1. Engineering resilience consists of a system's ability to absorb a major disturbance and return to the same starting point without undergoing significant changes (Bergen, Bolton, & Fridley, 2001, p. 205; Lew, 2013, p. 15; Palmer, Filoso, & Fanelli, 2014).
2. Adaptive resilience is part of the ecological paradigm that proposes the existence of many relatively similar points of equilibrium, the previously mentioned attractors. In this case, the system absorbs a disturbance by moving from one point of equilibrium to another one that has different proportions of elements, where these differences configure a position that is better adapted to the new situation (Allen & Holling, 2010). Generally, this type of resilience involves the cyclical evolution of the system, maintaining its vital components but never returning to its starting point (Cochrane, 2010, p. 173; Dahles & Susilowati, 2015, p. 46).
3. Transformative resilience exists when the system absorbs an impact and is substantially transformed. This type 'addresses a system's capacity to transform the stability landscape and to create new system pathways when ecological, economic or social structures make the existing system untenable' (Folke, 2006; Keck & Sakdapolrak, 2013, p. 7; Walker, Holling, Carpenter, & Kinzig, 2004). In this case, the system loses some of its essential attributes and components and embarks on a new evolutionary path that is clearly distinct from its origins and will lead to a new point of equilibrium unrelated to the initially available ones.

Particular historical antecedents

The island of Ibiza has been integrated into the trade routes of the Western Mediterranean since the Middle Ages, as a consecuence to its salt production. From that time onwards, the limited productive possibilities of the island were directed at external markets, likely the best way to maximise the local population's income on a small island with very scarce resources (Bertram & Poirine, 2007, p. 365). With the Industrial Revolution, the possibilities of access to external markets multiplied and, starting in the mid-nineteenth century, the domination of salt declined and Ibiza began instead to export Mediterranean products, led by almonds and carob beans, to international markets.

The downside of Ibiza's international integration was its dependence on trade, given that the island increasingly produced less food than necessary for the survival of its population. The dangers of dependence became apparent during the First World War, a period that subjected Ibiza's community to extreme hardship. The island came through the ordeal with a demonstration of engineering resilience. Ten years after the outbreak of the conflict, the island's production system had practically returned to its position in 1914.

Despite its specialisation in tradable products, however, it must be noted that Ibiza's economy in the first third of the twentieth century did not show any of the typical signs of dependence beyond its dependence on foodstuffs. The island was able to build its own business and commercial foundations, and exports to international markets were administered, transported and financed by local entrepreneurs who, in turn, acquired foodstuffs on the continent to meet the population's subsistence needs. In the Spanish context, this commercial and export capability was uncommon in the period, but Ibiza shared it with its immediate geographical neighbours, the other Balearic Islands and the mainland region of Valencia (Pinilla & Ayuda, 2010, p. 249; Tirado, 1996, p. 66).

By the mid-nineteen-twenties, the island economy had already recovered and was gathering considerable speed: new crops were introduced, the fleet was mechanised, the first factories sprang up and a budding financial sector emerged, the city expanded and became electrified and the literacy rate doubled in only ten years (Cirer-Costa, 2008, p. 106). The island's society went through deep and rapid changes without any apparent fissures, an essential condition for innovators in search of the necessary social support.

Economic growth gave rise to a significant accumulation of physical capital that would form one of the foundations on which to sustain future tourism development. In those years, the port was enlarged, new roads were opened and urban expansion provided local builders with the know-how to construct high-quality buildings like the ones that would house future hotels. Human capital was also enhanced significantly with the development of skills that would later be especially valuable in the tourism environment. In the offices of Ibiza's exporters and shippers, people learnt to read and write in French and English, they took payments in foreign currency and they negotiated routinely with businesspeople from Northern Europe.

The entire island population became involved in the new commercial economy. Each year the port of Ibiza Town received dozens of foreign vessels whose crews engaged in ordinary interactions with the local population, which gradually became accustomed to the presence of outsiders in the streets and accepted the advantages of doing business with them.

Farmers, salt workers, mariners and merchants tended to specialise in specific products or activities, limiting internal competition and creating a structure of informal institutions based on mutual trust that encompassed the entire population and that circulated relevant, trustworthy information, an essential condition to maximise the mutual effectiveness of the system. In a very short time, Ibiza's export-oriented industrial district accumulated a substantial amount of social capital that would prove decisive for the future resilience of the tourism-based industrial district.

Figure 1. Ibiza Island.
Source: Author.

Another important factor in favour of tourism was the island's accessibility, which was a consequence of the density of maritime traffic generated by a dynamic export economy. Tourism to Ibiza was not hobbled by problems of accessibility, which proved to be determining factors in the isolation of many Mediterranean islands (Karampela et al., 2014, p. 295).

The arrival of tourism on the scene (1931–1934)

From the beginning of the twentieth century to 1930, Ibiza Town had only two hotel establishments in operation: *La Marina* and *El Comercio*, two small, low-quality inns geared to the few professionals that came to the island to sell their wares (Cirer-Costa, 2004, p. 133). In 1931, work began on the first tourist-oriented properties, which opened their doors in the year that followed. By 1933, a genuine hotel boom was underway: in January, the *Buenavista* opened in Santa Eulària and the *Portmany* and *Ses Savines* opened in Sant Antoni, followed shortly by the *Gran Hotel Ibiza*, the largest and most luxurious of all (Figure 1). Throughout the two subsequent years, hotel openings continued apace until there were a dozen luxury establishments (Cirer-Costa, 2004, 2014, p. 25). These hotels were all completely new properties of high quality, offering a European level of comfort that far exceeded the Spanish standards of the day.

In addition to the hotels noted above, a dozen other establishments of lower category focused on international tourism as well, along with a considerable number of travel agencies, bars, restaurants and firms conducting bus tours and boat trips (Cirer-Costa, 2004, p. 115). Within three short years from 1931 to 1934, the island built a new industrial district, this time revolving around tourism. Ibiza's economic system abandoned its initial equilibrium position focusing on export goods and moved toward a new attractor in which tourism played a fundamental role. Ibiza's tourism entrepreneurs acted as prototypical Schumpeterian innovators by creating new firms that offered hitherto unknown products: tourism services (Schumpeter, 1928, p. 377).

To understand the involvement of Ibizan society in tourism development, it is important to highlight four particularly significant elements:

First, unlike the First World War, the external disturbance of the Great Depression was not instantaneous. Economic agents had time to determine its scope and gauge risks before deciding on the response that they should give. For this reason, we can speak of tourism as a conscious, well-planned choice that was put into effect in 1931.

Second, we can see that no conflicts broke out between the business world and the community. The former led the change and the latter gave its unqualified support. Between the two groups, the divergence anticipated by some authors did not appear (Bec, Mclennan, & Moyle, 2015, p. 444; Cheer & Lew, 2018, 12). Nor at any point did the local newspapers let up in their reporting on the activities of tourism innovators who were celebrated as modern-day heroes for risking their own capital in an initiative that benefited the entire body of society. Initially, the strong public support for tourism in Ibiza was not articulated through the island's political representatives as Arnstein's ladder of participation proposes (1969, p. 218), but rather through diffuse institutional legitimacy: 'Legitimacy is a generalised perception or assumption that the actions of an entity are desirable, proper, or appropriate within some socially constructed system of norms, values, beliefs, and definitions' (Suchman, 1995, p. 574). This social support enabled Ibiza's tourism entrepreneurs to avoid resistance and gain access to resources whose ownership was diffuse or communal, such as beaches (Chabowski & Mena, 2017, p. 7). Important in this respect were the articles that spoke glowingly of tourism development in the Catholic weekly *Excelsior*, the Church's leading publication on the island. For instance, a piece published on 28 February 1932 announced the construction of a new hotel and remarked: 'We welcome the idea and would be very sorry not to see it accomplished in short order'.

Third, the innovative behaviour was led by people who were highly active and especially important members of the island community and who had enormous experience and sound financial backing. In Ibiza, tourism was not the extravagant venture of a handful of visionaries at the informal margins of the industrial district (Biggs, 2011, p. 4). Innovative hoteliers took on a leadership role that received the full consent of the rest of society (Cochrane, 2010, p. 178; Crossland & Hambrick, 2011, p. 801).

Lastly, the hotels that opened between 1932 and 1935 with a focus on international tourism reflected a wide range of offering. Some were urban and others were located at the beach. Some were large and luxurious, while others were small and economical. Their diversity shows that each new entrepreneur who went into business tried to find his own space according to his financial means and his entrepreneurial skills, but without entering into conflict with other already established counterparts. The industrial district shared information efficiently and tourism entrepreneurs used it rationally to build a diverse and attractive offering. The industrial district distributed information efficiently and tourism entrepreneurs used the information rationally to build a diverse and appealing offering, which demonstrates the capacity of an industrial district to become an incubator for new companies (Cavallo, Ghezzi, Colombelli, & Casali, 2018, p. 17).

First serious difficulties for tourism and the interruption of warfare

Just as tourism in Majorca and Ibiza was reaching its high point, the Balearic Islands faced an unexpected setback: the posting of General Francisco Franco as military commander of the archipelago. No sooner had he arrived in 1933 than he took note of the massive presence of foreign tourists along the coastline and deemed them a serious threat to the national defence. As a consequence, he inspired an extraordinarily burdensome piece of legislation aimed solely at the tourism sector in the Balearic Islands, which was, it should be recalled, the only region of Spain where tourism was flourishing at the time. In practice, the law's implementation meant that it would be impossible to build new hotels, already opened hotels would be put at risk of demolition and every tourist would be turned into a potential spy in need of close monitoring (Cirer-Costa, 2009, pp. 108–111; 2019b, p. 7).

The reaction of the islands' inhabitants, however, was overwhelming. On 9 March 1934, every business in the capital of Palma (Majorca) pulled down its shutters and an enormous protest poured through the city's streets. This showed the local population's strong support for the tourism industry, which according to the newspaper *Diario de Ibiza* 'is the main business of these islands' (Cirer-Costa, 2004, p. 166). Indeed, the discontent of the island's population was so stark and so widespread that local politicians were forced to backtrack in great haste to avoid being swept from office. Within a few months, a number of the new rules were repealed and the remainder were simply ignored or reduced to ineffectiveness.

In the interim, General Franco, who had put up a fierce defence of the anti-tourism rules, stepped down from his post in the islands. In light of the population's unconditional support for tourism, the new laws were not applied, but the future dictator had made it very clear to the society on the islands where he stood on international tourism.

In October 1934, Spain was shaken by severe revolutionary upheavals and the expansionism of Italian fascism cast a shadow of war over the Mediterranean, scaring off British tourism. In 1935, the number of visitors dropped sharply and the summer season of 1936 opened amid dire portents. On 18 July, General Franco launched a coup whose partial failure lit the match that started the Spanish Civil War.

Then, with the conflict barely finished, the Second World War kicked off and the complete shutdown of all tourism activity was prolonged until 1945. At the close of the global conflict, however, Spain's economic situation did not improve. Indeed, it worsened amid the Francoist regime's isolation by all the countries of Western Europe until 1950, when the French border was finally reopened.

For an economy like Ibiza's that was open to the world, the international isolation caused first by two wars and then by Europe's rejection of the Francoist regime was to have devastating effects. Indeed, the period from 1936 to 1949 is remembered in Ibiza as 'es anys de sa fam', or the years of hunger.

The survival and resurgence of tourism on Ibiza

Upon winning the Spanish Civil War, General Franco instituted a personal dictatorship that relied on the Catholic religion as a central pillar of its ideology. The doctrines and morals espoused by the Catholic Church were raised into mandatory rules of behaviour that had to be followed by all Spanish citizens and by all foreigners visiting the country and the rules were not at all permissive toward tourism. Throughout the nineteen-forties, entry was permitted only to individuals who were openly sympathetic to the regime and would submit to complete monitoring of their movements (Holguin, 2005, p. 1421).

The circumstances were not in the least conducive to the development of tourism in Spain. Nevertheless, the reopening of the French border in 1950 had entirely unexpected effects. Within a few months, the province of Girona was flooded by French visitors who were drawn to the beaches of the Costa Brava and the exceptionally low prices in Spain at the time (Cirer-Costa, 2016, p. 26. The surprising flood of tourists gave the Francoist regime a source of precious foreign currency and the survival instinct of the regime's top officials persuaded them to abandon their moral and patriotic scruples and accept a degree of permissiveness toward the incoming tourists (Carrasco, 2012, p. 112).

After Girona, the tourism boom soon spread to Majorca, which could be reached by new airlines that used surplus DC-3 planes from the Second World War (Cirer-Costa, 2016, p. 26). Air transport cut the average journey time to roughly 8-12 hours, bringing the Balearic Islands within reach of anyone who had only two weeks' holiday, an improvement that did not take long to affect the island of Ibiza as well, since it could be reached by boat from Palma (Majorca).

As a result of the new situation, Ibiza witnessed a second tourism boom between 1950 and 1955. By 1955, the number of tourists exceeded 14,000 and the number of available hotel beds stood at 2,000 (Figures 2–4). Among the visitors, the French were the most numerous (28%), followed by strong contingents of English and German visitors (19% and 15%, respectively). According to contemporary commentators in the media, if even more foreign tourists did not come to Ibiza, it was only because of the limited capacity of the rickety, ageing vessels that linked the island to the ports of Barcelona and Palma (Majorca), because the ships that did arrive throughout the summer were overflowing with passengers (Table 1).

At first, the tourists coming to the Balearic Islands were very similar socially to the tourists of the thirties. Indeed, many of them had been to Ibiza or Majorca in the thirties and sought to recapture the memory of their distant stay in the islands, a 'peaceful, natural and simple place' that would reconnect them to days gone by, as if the war had never happened (Moyà, 2015, p. 6). The presence of repeat tourists with a strong sentimental attachment was crucial to the rebound in tourism, because they were more willing to put up with the tiresome red tape at customs, the discomfort of a slow and hazardous boat journey and the poor quality of the accommodation.

Much like what was happening at the time in Girona and Majorca, the business grew very fast in Ibiza and it did not take long to accumulate profits that were immediately reinvested in upgrading and expanding establishments (Cirer-Costa, 2016, p. 28). Between 1953 and 1955, the growth in hotels was based on expanding and transforming existing properties, which further lowered the general quality a little. From 1955, however, it became possible to purchase materials off-island and construction

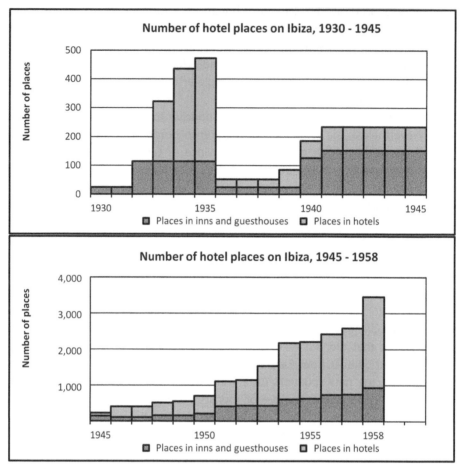

Figure 2. Estimated evolution of hotel rooms on Ibiza between 1930 and 1958. The top graph shows the growth of tourism in the early nineteen-thirties, the near-total shutdown during the Spanish civil war (1936–39) and the sector's survival phase, while the bottom graph highlights the exponential growth in hotel rooms between 1949 and 1958.
Source: Own elaboration.

began on finer establishments, though the high level of quality that had existed in 1935 was yet to be regained. A new period of unbridled growth centred around the Bay of Sant Antoni, which became home to two-thirds of all Ibiza's tourist accommodation and which once again saw new plans for hotels of international standing (Corke, 1956, p. 51).

Between 1955 and 1958, the growth in tourism was explosive and the business focus zeroed in on foreign customers at the medium to low end of the market. The earlier clientele of small and medium-sized businesspeople, senior civil servants and independent professionals gave way to a new batch of visitors dominated by mid-level civil servants and skilled workers, who were taking their first paid holidays.

With the upswing in the European economy came the expansion of a new middle class that could afford one to two weeks of holidaymaking abroad, while, at the same time, a taste for warm water beaches spread with extraordinary speed (National

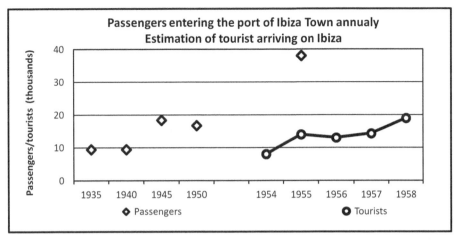

Figure 3. Annual number of passengers entering the port of Ibiza Town and an estimation of the number of tourists arriving on the island of Ibiza. The tourist figure refers to people staying in hotel establishments.
Source: Ramón (1964), Zornoza (1961a, 1961b).

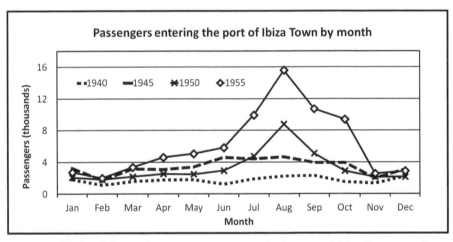

Figure 4. Monthly breakdown of passenger movements in the port of Ibiza Town over the period 1940–1955. The graph shows a sharp increase in summer seasonality, which began to occur in 1950 and was entirely caused by the rebound in tourism.
Source: Zornoza (1961b).

Recreation Association (NRA), 1934, p. 2). Both conditions offered a golden opportunity to all Mediterranean beach destinations, but they were not all able to respond to the new demand. More traditional spots, such as the French Riviera or Alassio in Italy, were unable to adapt to the low budgets of the new tourists and captured only a small share of the new market. By contrast, the Balearic Islands rapidly focused their tourism offering on visitors seeking sun and beach at budget prices (Grabacke, 2006, p. 3).

Another key factor in the popularisation of travel to the Mediterranean sun was the appearance of new types of intermediaries and transport companies. Travel agencies that were typically working class, such as the Workers Travel Association in the UK,

Table 1. Comparison of the evolution of hotel rooms in Ibiza and Spain.

	Ibiza		Spain		
	Rooms	Index	Rooms	Index	% Ibiza / Spain
1954	832	100	56,311	100	1.48
1955	872	105	57,786	103	1.51
1956	903	109	61,745	110	1.46
1957	987	119	61,745	110	1.60
1958	1,352	163	68,428	122	1.98
1959	1,699	204	72,076	128	2.36

Source: For Ibiza, own elaboration. For Spain, the Spanish National Statistics Institute (INE). Statistical Yearbook, 1955–1960.

began to offer package holidays to the Mediterranean in 1949 (Barton, 2005, p. 199) and chartered flights were launched by small independent airlines (Lyth & Dierikx, 1994, p. 103).

The island of Ibiza integrated itself definitively into the new tourism business with the opening of its airport in 1958, followed six years later by improvements and enlargements that made the airport international. The construction of the airport was the result of the tenacity of Ibizan society, who viewed it as a crucial infrastructure project for their development. As Ernesto Ramon, one of Ibiza's most important tourism professionals, explains in one of his books: 'In reality, the Administration could hardly undertake a public works project of these characteristics at the time without the collaboration of the population. And they did collaborate enormously … The local tourism promotion board [*Foment del Turisme*] started a subscription drive to raise money, but many individuals also gave in kind. They contributed gravel lorries, paid workers' wages, provided free transport to workers and more' (Ramon, 2001, p. 74).

Another aspect in which private initiative was needed to substitute for public initiative was in the construction of highways to connect the beaches to the poor network of existing roads. A textbook example is offered by the highway linking Sant Josep to Cala Tarida, which was built on the initiative of local entrepreneur Antonio Mari Viñas and used almost no public money even though it served hundreds of neighbours in addition to the new hotels (Castro, 2003, p. 224; Ramon, 1964, p. 4). Similarly, local initiative was important in tourism promotion, which was carried out by the local tourism board [*Foment del Turisme*], a strictly private association. The tourism board's campaigns were funded almost exclusively by hoteliers, but the design, management and organisation of the campaigns drew on the altruistic collaboration of 'many people who had nothing to do with tourism' (Juan & Valero, 2010, p. 1). This serves as a good example of the population's involvement in the development of tourism and of the extent of the tourism-based industrial district's reach within Ibizan society.

The spectacular rise of tourism in the nineteen-fifties was only made possible because of the recovery of the productive capacities and social consensus that had been developed in the thirties. Physical capital in the form of hotel premises was still available. Only one hotel, the *Isla Blanca*, had disappeared, having been converted into housing. The remaining properties, which survived to 1950 in fair condition, no longer had their furnishings and amenities, but they could be returned to service. The human capital survived too. In fifteen years, the people who had professional skills, such as a knowledge of languages, cooking or hotel management, did not disappear.

Lastly, the survival of the social consensus in support of tourism paved the way for initiatives such as the construction of new infrastructure projects indicated above in detail.

Exceptional witnesses of a rapidly evolving society

The preceding pages have frequently cited social capital as an essential element in understanding the creation and survival of tourism in Ibiza. Social capital is a particularly abstract and elusive concept, which can only be evaluated qualitatively. In order to show the local society's commitment to tourism in the case of Ibiza, this analysis can draw on the exceptional first-hand accounts of writers, both foreigners and Spaniards, who travelled to and lived in Ibiza during the period.

The foreign writers in question were fully integrated into the local community: they knew the Catalan language, lived in houses in the countryside in close contact with their neighbours, and had first-hand knowledge of their neighbours' way of thinking, their interests and hopes. By contrast, the Spanish authors first travelled to Ibiza as tourists, but their stay on the island made a deep impression on them and they became regular visitors, putting them in a position to witness the evolution of the island's tourism, which they described in detail in their essays and memoirs.

First and foremost is Borthen (2010, pp. 31–32), who visited Ibiza in the nineteen-thirties and returned twenty years later. Borthen, a Norwegian author, tells of the clash between the island's population and their bishop in the fifties. The bishop was a living example of the most conservative faction of Spanish Catholicism and, as such, viewed tourism as a source of unacceptable immorality and corruption. Surprisingly, the confrontation ended with the bishop's resignation under fierce pressure from parishioners who did not shy away from risking the reprisals of the Franco regime.

In 1954, the British writer Norman Lewis came to Ibiza. Already an acclaimed author who was very knowledgeable about Spain, Lewis had spent a number of summers on the Costa Brava in Catalonia before taking the decision to go to Ibiza to escape from the expansion of mass tourism along the Catalan coast (Evans, 2008, p. 397). As a result, he witnessed the arrival of the first tourists in Santa Eulària in the fifties, observing the expectations that were raised and the local population's permissive attitudes toward the customs of foreigners (Lewis, 1959, p. 404). The Madrid-based writer Josefina Aldecoa, who began to visit Ibiza in 1957, also remarked on the locals' permissive attitudes toward tourists and the sense of freedom that pervaded the island in the fifties: 'Ibiza. They say it's the most beautiful island in the Mediterranean. And that it doesn't seem like Spain. It's a free island …' (Aldecoa, 1986, p. 175). Using similar language, another Spanish author, Fernando Guillermo de Castro, wrote in 1956 that 'Ibiza was the physical embodiment of the joy of being alive' (Castro, 2003, p. 10).

The last account here comes from Alexis Brown, an English writer of tales who lived in Cala de San Vicent between 1961 and 1964, when tourism was already well-established in the Bay of Sant Antoni and in Santa Eulària, but not yet elsewhere on the island (Figure 1). At the time, the Cala de Sant Vicent did not have any overland connection to the rest of the island and the local inhabitants used small sailing craft to go in and out of their secluded valley and to haul their limited surplus to market.

Brown recounts the efforts of the local young people in such a remote spot to learn English and the envy that was aroused by anyone who emigrated to Sant Antoni to work in tourism. Perhaps the most striking aspect of this attitude is that it did not raise the hackles of their elders. As the English author writes: 'Many of the right-minded did not look with disapproval on the young people's flight from the countryside' (Brown, 2008, p. 107).

Ronald James Cooper captured this social conviction perfectly in the following characterisation: 'In complete contrast, the overwhelming majority of Ibizans (including —interestingly— the older generations of country-people) associate the past with economic "misery" and with sociocultural "backwardness" ["we were savages" and "we were backward"]; and they are actively (though not uncritically) assisting in the transformation of their own society which has been made possible by mass tourism' (Cooper, 2002, p. 27).

Discussion

On the preceding pages, it has been shown that tourism grew extremely fast on the island of Ibiza, but that this growth was only possible because of the existence of a particularly favourable economic substrate. Ibiza's economic foundations were rooted in the export of primary goods, which had the advantage of providing permanent contact with external markets. This contact facilitated the development of professional skills that would later prove highly useful when tourism appeared and there was a need to disseminate tolerance toward foreigners and their habits and customs . The island's outward-looking economy was able to grow almost without interruption during the fifty years in which Ibiza rose from a self-sufficiency marked by poverty to a strong economic position.

In this period, the chief agents were independent farmers, merchants and shipowners, but they were soon joined by ancillary businesses of all kinds, including shipbuilders, banks, translators and others, which together gave shape to an almost canonical Marshallian industrial district (Markusen, 1996, p. 294; Marshall, 1920, p. 271, Ottati, 1991, p. 54). The entirety of the productive system was located on a small island. In such a limited environment, it was inevitable that entrepreneurial skills would, as they matured, become intertwined with family ties, religious institutions and social entities and expand to embrace the entirety of the population (Brown, 2008; Cirer-Costa, 2004, 2008; Cooper, 2002; Ramon, 2001).

The island's limited size minimised the length of intermediation channels and entrepreneurs gained enormous social prominence or visibility that was positively associated with economic well-being (Hopp & Stephan, 2012, p. 921; Holmes et al., 2013, p. 533; Stephan & Uhlaner, 2010, p. 1358). Business initiative and entrepreneurial spirit drew favourable opinions that became widespread and they were not viewed as factors that would threaten social stability, but rather the contrary (Cole, 2006, p. 637; Crossland & Hambrick, 2011, p. 816). Economic well-being gave solidity to a social fabric that isolated predatory conduct, fostered mutual trust and facilitated the establishment of all sorts of implicit and informal contracts (Becattini, 2004, p. 19; Sammarra & Biggiero, 2001, p. 77).

In addition, this community extended its influence by thousands of kilometers, drawing on the contacts forged by merchants and sailors with the outside world as well as the return of emigrants. Given these factors, the island was on the receiving end of a constant flow of all sorts of information with which it was able to adapt to the changing conditions of international markets and fend off the stagnation that is the chief threat facing any compact industrial district.

By the start of the nineteen-thirties, Ibiza's economy had reached a high degree of maturity, so that the crisis of 1929 could be expected to cause a fall in the number of firms and a reduction in the complexity of the cluster (Staber, 2007, p. 510). However, adversity had the opposite effect. Rather than contracting, the cluster expanded, maintained all of its well-established components and added tourism as a basic economic activity. The island's productive ecosystem demonstrated its adaptive capacity, abandoned its current attractor and set off toward a new one that was more complex and larger in size (Allen & Holling, 2010, p. 6; Bec et al., 2015, p. 432; Ives & Carpenter, 2007, p. 58; Folke, 2006, p. 258).

Obviously, the introduction of tourism did not occur by chance. Rather, it was a totally unexpected effect of the Great Depression, which had prompted a drop in fares on long-distance ships that then made the costs of travel to the Mediterranean extraordinarily cheap (Cirer-Costa, 2014, 2019a). As a consequence, the island of Ibiza was presented with an unexpected opportunity and its entrepreneurs, who were well informed about what was happening in the outside world and well aware of their own possibilities and of the social support that they enjoyed, did not squander their chances (Crnogaj et al., 2014, p. 383).

The development of the tourism industry in Ibiza did not have any direct precedent that might serve as a guidepost for innovative entrepreneurs. At first, they acted in an empty space and some focused their businesses poorly and disappeared. However, through a rapid process of trial and error, all available market niches were filled by 1935 (Margalef, 1986, p. 20; McCann, 2000, p. 230). In only four years, Ibiza's tourism businesses had developed individually and established complex relationships that were horizontal (competitive), vertical (suppler-customer) and diagonal (supply of complementary goods and services) (Butler & Weidenfeld, 2012, p. 19).

With the outbreak of the Spanish civil war on 18 July 1936, tourism simply disappeared from the island. However, a number of small hotels and restaurants did succeed in surviving by cutting their supply and redirecting it toward the military garrison that had increased troop numbers at very short notice (Cirer-Costa, 2004, p. 172). This showed that in a diverse and complex system possessing a high degree of functional diversity, even especially dramatic shocks can give rise to the emergence of unexpected adaptive capacities that enable part of the system to survive (Loreau et al., 2001, p. 806).

The island's tourism-based industrial district survived almost intact after an interruption of fifteen years, this extreme resilience had economic components, but its social components were probably even more important, while the social components included a personal commitment to tourism among the entrepreneurs and professionals who had overseen its initial establishment and who now reclaimed their leadership role as quickly as possible (Cochrane, 2010, p. 178; Dahles & Susilowati, 2015, p.

42; Lew, 2013). It is also necessary to highlight emotional values like confidence to explain how in 1946, when the Spanish economy was mired in abject poverty, a group of eleven merchants and entrepreneurs, who have been mentioned earlier, risked their scarce capital on reopening the *Gran Hotel* (Cirer-Costa, 2004, p. 184).

The resilience of tourism on Ibiza can in no way be separated from its strictly local origins. Indeed, it was a prototypical 'bottom-up' process (Malek & Costa, 2014, p. 286; Tolkach et al., 2013, p. 2), which achieved a strong social consensus and not only attracted a good number of entrepreneurs and investors, but also drew on the participation of many of the island's inhabitants who did not benefit directly from tourism, but who nonetheless saw tourism as an element of progress that was spreading to the entirety of Ibiza's society.

As a result of all of these efforts, tourism on Ibiza began to recover quickly in 1950 and it did not take long to embark on a new phase of rapid growth. At the end of the fifties, the expectation was that the Ibiza cluster would level off and cease growth as it became institutionalised (Feldman et al., 2005, p. 136). If it did not reach a new point of dynamic equilibrium, that is, a stable new attractor, this was because the circumstances changed again and Ibiza's entrepreneurs were able once more to adapt to new conditions. The introduction of cheap charter flights and of package holidays sold by the major tour operators greatly increased the tourism demand and the island of Ibiza radically transformed its economy to set off toward a new attractor in which tourism held an absolute monopoly and practically no room remained for traditional production.

Conclusions

At the beginning of the nineteen-thirties, Ibiza could offer all of the features that were in demand by the new tourists of the period: good travel connections, a pleasant climate, beautiful landscapes, sandy beaches, etc. However, dozens of other Mediterranean islands shared the same characteristics. If Ibiza succeeded in attaining a leading position, it was because of the ability of its entrepreneurs to meet the potential demand with a sufficient supply of competitively priced transport services, lodging and entertainment.

Ibiza's rapid adaptation to demand requirements was made possible by the prior existence of a Marshallian industrial district focused on the export of Mediterranean products: salt, almonds, carob beans, fish, etc. This structure facilitated the rapid dissemination of information and sufficient local capital to build infrastructure and businesses able to meet visitors' demands. The presence of a strong local business community enabled Ibiza to develop as an integrated tourism destination and prevented it from becoming simply an enclave, a mere backdrop or scenery used by foreign investors to satisfy similarly foreign tourists.

For the emergence of an integrated destination to occur, the Ibiza example shows that an island society must provide an entrepreneurial class that has the necessary financial means and an ability to perceive the opportunity associated with the flourishing of tourism. This business community must be able to innovate to meet a totally unknown demand and to adapt to conditions that the very growth in tourism itself will cause to change quickly. In addition, the society must be tolerant of the unfamiliar behaviours of visitors and accept that the presence of tourists will distort local markets, harming a portion of the populace.

Once tourism activity succeeds in becoming established, it generates an accumulation of physical, human and social capital that forms the basis of tourism resilience, that is, of the sector's ability to survive in the face of external shocks. After a temporary downturn in the influx of tourists, it is no longer necessary to look again for the existence of an opportunity, which is now well known, nor is it necessary to create physical infrastructure or entrepreneurial and professional skills of a new kind, because the previously acquired ones are still present.

The Ibiza case analysed here is a prototypical example of an integrated destination that developed solely based on the island society's own resources. External capital was not needed and most of the necessary professional skills were also local in origin, having already been developed within the environment of an economy that was exceptionally open to international markets. Even the Spanish state played a role that proved more negative than positive both in the initial growth phase of the nineteen-thirties and in the later phase of resilience and rebuilding.

After the appearance and consolidation of tourism in the thirties, the island suffered an interruption of fifteen years. From 1950 onwards, however, the tourists began to flock back and the earlier local entrepreneurs returned the old hotel properties to their former splendour. When they had accumulated sufficient capital, they resumed investing in new hotels and infrastructure adapted to the market conditions that prevailed at the time. Engineering resilience gave way to adaptive resilience, which pushed the island's economy toward a new attractor in which tourism now played a stronger, more prominent role than traditional products.

However, it was not until the opening of the international airport, which took place subsequent to the timescale covered in this study, that tourism became a transformative whirlwind sweeping away all of the other economic sectors that remained on the island.

From 1960 onwards, mass tourism became dominant and, within a few short years, pushed aside the production of salt, agriculture and fishing.

Disclosure statement

No potential conflict of interest was reported by the authors.

References

Aldecoa, J. (1986). *Porque éramos jóvenes. [Because we were young]*. Barcelona: Seix Barral.
Allen, C. R., & Holling, C. S. (2010). *Novelty, adaptive capacity, and resilience*. Lincoln: Nebraska Cooperative Fish & Wildlife Research.
Arnstein, S. R. (1969). A ladder of citizen participation. *Journal of the American Institute of Planners, 35*(4), 216–224. doi:10.1080/01944366908977225
Barton, S. (2005). *Working-class organisations and popular tourism, 1840-1970*. Manchester: Manchester University Press.

Bec, A., McLennan, C. L., & Moyle, B. D. (2015). Community resilience to long-term tourism decline and rejuvenation: A literature review and conceptual model. *Current Issues in Tourism*, *19*(5), 431–457. doi:10.1080/13683500.2015.1083538

Becattini, G. (2004). *Industrial districts: New approach to industrial change.* Cheltenham: Edward Elgar Publishing Limited.

Bergen, S. D., Bolton, S. M., & Fridley, J. L. (2001). Design principles for ecological engineering. *Ecological Engineering, 18*(2), 201–210. doi:10.1016/S0925-8574(01)00078-7

Bertram, G., & Poirine, B. (2007). Island political economy. In G. Baldacchino (Ed.), *A world of islands* (pp. 325–377). Charlottetown: Institute of Island Studies.

Biggs, D. (2011). Understanding resilience in a vulnerable industry: The case of reef tourism in Australia. *Ecology and Society, 16*(1), 30–48. doi:10.5751/ES-03948-160130

Borthen, L. (2010). El camí a Sant Vicent. [The road to Sant Vicent]. In M. Davies (Ed.), *El Camí a Sant Vicent. Eivissa* (pp. 15–49). Eivissa: Barbary Press.

Brown, A. (2008). *A valley wide.* Eivissa: Barbary Press.

Butler, R., & Weidenfeld, A. (2012). Cooperation and competition during the resort lifecycle. *Tourism Recreation Research, 37*(1), 15–26. doi:10.1080/02508281.2012.11081684

Carrasco, J. A. (2012). The Marshall plan and the Spanish postwar economy: A welfare loss analysis. *The Economic History Review, 65*(1), 91–119.

Castro, F. G. (2003). *La isla perdida (Memoria de una época de Ibiza). [The Lost Island (Memoir of a time in Ibiza)].* Eivissa: Editorial Mediterrània.

Cavallo, A., Ghezzi, A., Colombelli, A., & Casali, G. L. (2018). Agglomeration dynamics of innovative start-ups in Italy beyond the industrial district era. *International Entrepreneurship and Management Journal.* 1–23. doi:10.1007/s11365-018-0521-8.

Chabowski, B. R., & Mena, J. A. (2017). A review of global competitiveness research: Past advances and future directions. *Journal of International Marketing, 25*(4), 1–24. doi:10.1509/jim.16.0053

Cheer, J. M., & Lew, A. A. (2018). Understanding tourism resilience. Adapting to social, political, and economic change. In J. M. Cheer & A. A. Lew (Eds.), *Tourism, resilience and sustainability* (pp. 1–18). Oxon: Routledge.

Cirer-Costa, J. C. (2004). *De la fonda a l'hotel. [From Inn to Hotel].* Palma de Mallorca: Documenta Balear.

Cirer-Costa, J. C. (2008). Capital humano y desarrollo económico, una compleja relación. [Human resources and economic development: A complex relationship]. *Estudios de Economía Aplicada, 26*(3), 89–114.

Cirer-Costa, J. C. (2009). Aproximación a la ideología económica del General Franco a través de una entrevista mantenida en 1934. [Approach to the economic ideology of General Franco through an interview held in 1934]. *Historia Actual Online, 18*, 105–115.

Cirer-Costa, J. C. (2014). Spain's new coastal destinations. 1883-1936: The mainstay of the development of tourism before the Second World War. *Annals of Tourism Research, 45*, 18–29. doi:10.1016/j.annals.2013.11.002

Cirer-Costa, J. C. (2016). Cinema and the automobile: Driving factors of new tourism models in the early years of the Golden Age. *Tourism Management Perspectives, 19*, 24–31. doi:10.1016/j.tmp.2016.04.005

Cirer-Costa, J. C. (2019a). Spain's tourism models in the first third of the twentieth century. *MPRA*, 91824, 1–43. doi:10.1016/j.tmp.2016.04.005

Cirer-Costa, J. C. (2019b). The crumbling of Francoist Spain's isolationism thanks to foreign currency brought by European tourists in the early years of the Golden Age. *MPRA*, 95578, 1–31.

Cochrane, J. (2010). The sphere of tourism resilience. *Tourism Recreation Research, 35*(2), 173–185. doi:10.1080/02508281.2010.11081632

Cohen, D., & Prusak, L. (2001). *In good company: How social capital makes organizations work.* Cambridge, MA: Harvard Business School Press.

Cole, S. (2006). Information and empowerment: The keys to achieving sustainable tourism. *Journal of Sustainable Tourism, 14*(6), 629–644. doi:10.2167/jost607.0

Cooper, R. J. (2002). Una anàlisi d'alguns aspectes de canvi social i adaptació al turisme a Eivissa. [An analysis of aspects of social change and adaptation to tourism in Ibiza]. *Estudis Sobre Turisme a Eivissa i Formentera, 3*, 15–36.

Corke, H. E. J. (1956). *A seaside project at San Antonio Abad, Ibiza* (Unpublished doctoral dissertation). University of Liverpool, Liverpool.

Crnogaj, K., Rebernik, M., Hojnik, B. B., & Gomezelj, D. O. (2014). Model of researching the sustainable entrepreneurship in the tourism sector. *Kybernetes, 43*(3/4), 377–393. doi:10.1108/K-07-2013-0155

Crossland, C., & Hambrick, D. C. (2011). Differences in managerial discretion across countries: How nation-level institutions affect the degree to which CEOs matter. *Strategic Management Journal, 32*(8), 797–819. doi:10.1002/smj.913

Dahles, H., & Susilowati, T. P. (2015). Business resilience in times of growth and crisis. *Annals of Tourism Research, 51*, 34–50. doi:10.1016/j.annals.2015.01.002

Evans, J. (2008). *Semi-invisible man: The life of Norman Lewis*. London: Jonathan Cape.

Feldman, M. P., Francis, J., & Bercovitz, J. (2005). Creating a cluster while building a firm: Entrepreneurs and the formation of industrial clusters. *Regional Studies, 39*(1), 129–141. doi:10.1080/0034340052000320888

Fitjar, R. D., Gjelsvik, M., & Rodríguez, A. (2013). The combined impact of managerial and relational capabilities on innovation in firms. *Entrepreneurship & Regional Development, 25*(5), 500–520. doi:10.1080/08985626.2013.798353

Folke, C. (2006). Resilience: The emergence of a perspective for social–ecological systems analyses. *Global Environmental Change, 16*(3), 253–267. doi:10.1016/j.gloenvcha.2006.04.002

Gorman, M. L. (1991). *Ecología insular. [Island ecology]*. Barcelona: Vedrà.

Grabacke, C. (2006). March). *Organised leisure for the working class-European: Popular travel and leisure organisations in the interwar period*. Economic History Annual Conference, Reading.

Helfat, C. E., & Lieberman, M. B. (2002). The birth of capabilities: Market entry and the importance of pre-history. *Industrial and Corporate Change, 11*(4), 725–760. doi:10.1093/icc/11.4.725

Holguin, S. (2005). National Spain invites you. *American Historical Review, 110*(5), 1399–1426.

Holmes, R. M., Miller, T., Hitt, M. A., & Salmador, M. P. (2013). The interrelationships among informal institutions, formal institutions, and inward foreign direct investment. *Journal of Management, 39*(2), 531–566. doi:10.1177/0149206310393503

Hopp, C., & Stephan, U. (2012). The influence of socio-cultural environments on the performance of nascent entrepreneurs: Community culture, motivation, self-efficacy and start-up success. *Entrepreneurship & Regional Development, 24*(9), 917–945. doi:10.1080/08985626.2012.742326

Ives, A. R., & Carpenter, S. R. (2007). Stability and diversity of ecosystems. *Science, 317*(5834), 58–62. doi:10.1126/science.1133258

Jones, G., & Pitelis, C. (2015). Entrepreneurial imagination and a demand and supply-side perspective on the MNE and cross-border organization. *Journal of International Management, 21*(4), 309–321. doi:10.1016/j.intman.2015.07.003

Jones, G., & Spadafora, A. (2016). *Entrepreneurs and the co-creation of ecotourism in Costa Rica*. Allston: Harvard Business School.

Juan, V., & Valero, V. (2010). *Vicente Juan Guasch. En primera persona. [Vicente Juan Guasch: In First Person]*. Eivissa: Diario de Ibiza.

Karampela, S., Kizos, T., & Spilanis, I. (2014). Accessibility of islands: Towards a new geography based on transportation modes and choices. *Island Studies Journal, 9*(2), 293–306.

Keck, M., & Sakdapolrak, P. (2013). What is social resilience? Lessons learned and ways forward. *Erdkunde, 67*(1), 5–19. doi:10.3112/erdkunde.2013.01.02

Kindström, D., Kowalkowski, C., & Sandberg, E. (2013). Enabling service innovation: A dynamic capabilities approach. *Journal of Business Research, 66*(8), 1063–1073. doi:10.1016/j.jbusres.2012.03.003

Lew, A. A. (2013). Scale, change and resilience in community tourism planning. *Tourism Geographies, 16*(1), 14–22. doi:10.1080/14616688.2013.864325

Lewis, N. (1959). *The changing sky: Travels of a novelist*. New York NY: Pantheon Books.

Loreau, M., Naeem, S., Inchausti, P., Bengtsson, J., Grime, J. P., Hector, A., ... Wardle, D. A. (2001). Biodiversity and ecosystem functioning: Current knowledge and future challenges. *Science, 294*(5543), 804–808. doi:10.1126/science.1064088

Lyth, P., & Dierikx, M. L. J. (1994). From privilege to popularity: The growth of leisure air travel since 1945. *The Journal of Transport History, 15*(2), 97–116. doi:10.1177/002252669401500202

Malek, A., & Costa, C. (2014). Integrating communities into tourism planning through social innovation. *Tourism Planning & Development, 12*(3), 281–299. doi:10.1080/21568316.2014.951125

Margalef, R. (1986). *Ecología. [Ecology]*. Barcelona: Planeta.

Markusen, A. (1996). Sticky places in slippery space: A typology of industrial districts. *Economic Geography, 72*(3), 293–313. doi:10.2307/144402

Marshall, A. (1920). *Principles of economics*. London: Macmillan.

McCann, K. S. (2000). The diversity-stability debate. *Nature, 405*(6783), 228–233. doi:10.1038/35012234

Moyà, E. (2015). Palma: The oscillating core of a suspended periphery. An imagologic approach to an island city and its discourse of pleasure. *Journal of Marine and Island Cultures, 4*(1), 1–9. doi:10.1016/j.imic.2015.06.001

National Recreation Association (NRA). (1934). *The leisure hours of 5,000 people*. New York NY: National Recreation Association.

North, D. C. (1991). Institutions. *Journal of Economic Perspectives, 5*(1), 97–112. doi:10.1257/jep.5.1.97

Ottati, G. (1991). The economic bases of diffuse industrialization. *International Studies of Management & Organization, 21*(1), 53–74. doi:10.1080/00208825.1991.11656549

Palmer, M. A., Filoso, S., & Fanelli, R. M. (2014). From ecosystems to ecosystem services: Stream restoration as ecological engineering. *Ecological Engineering, 65*, 62–70. doi:10.1016/j.ecoleng.2013.07.059

Pinilla, V., & Ayuda, M. I. (2010). Taking advantage of globalization? Spain and the building of the international market in Mediterranean horticultural products, 1850–1935. *European Review of Economic History, 14*(2), 239–274. doi:10.1017/S136149161000002X

Ramón, E. [Enrique] (1964). Ibiza, 1963. *Bocoin, 644*, 2–7.

Ramon, E. [Ernesto] (2001). *Història del turisme a Eivissa. [History of tourism in Ibiza]*. Eivissa: Genial Ediciones.

Sammarra, A., & Biggiero, L. (2001). Identity and identification in industrial districts. *Journal of Management and Governance, 5*(1), 61–82. doi:10.1023/A:1017937506664

Schultz, T. W. (1975). The value of the ability to deal with disequilibria. *Journal of Economic Literature, 13*(3), 827–846.

Schumpeter, J. A. (1928). The instability of capitalism. *The Economic Journal, 151*, 361–386. doi:10.2307/2224315

Staber, U. (2007). Contextualizing research on social capital in regional clusters. *International Journal of Urban and Regional Research, 31*(3), 505–521. doi:10.1111/j.1468-2427.2007.00742.x

Stephan, U., & Uhlaner, L. M. (2010). Performance-based vs socially supportive culture: A cross-national study of descriptive norms and entrepreneurship. *Journal of International Business Studies, 41*(8), 1347–1364. doi:10.1057/jibs.2010.14

Suchman, M. C. (1995). Managing legitimacy: Strategic and institutional approaches. *Academy of Management Review, 20*(3), 571–610. doi:10.5465/amr.1995.9508080331

Teece, D. J. (2007). Explicating dynamic capabilities: The nature and microfoundations of (sustainable) enterprise performance. *Strategic Management Journal, 28*(13), 1319–1350. doi:10.1002/smj.640

Tirado, D. A. (1996). Protección arancelaria y evolución de la economía española durante la Restauración: Un ensayo interpretativo. [Tariff protection and Spanish economic behaviour during the Restoration: An interpretative essay]. *Revista de Història Industrial, 9*, 53–81.

Tolkach, D., King, B., & Pearlman, M. (2013). An attribute-based approach to classifying community-based tourism networks. *Tourism Planning & Development, 10*(3), 319–337. doi:10.1080/21568316.2012.747985

Turunen, H., & Nummela, N. (2016). Internationalisation at home: The internationalisation of location-bound service SMEs. *Journal of International Entrepreneurship*, *15*(1), 36–54. doi:10.1007/s10843-016-0167-y

Walker, B., Holling, C. S., Carpenter, S. R., & Kinzig, A. (2004). Resilience, adaptability and transformability in social–ecological systems. *Ecology and Society*, *9*(2), 1–9. doi:10.5751/ES-00650-090205

Yachi, S., & Loreau, M. (1999). Biodiversity and ecosystem productivity in a fluctuating environment: The insurance hypothesis. *Proceedings of the National Academy of Sciences*, *96*(4), 1463–1468. doi:10.1073/pnas.96.4.1463

You, J. I., & Wilkinson, F. (1994). Competition and co-operation towards understanding industrial districts. *Review of Political Economy*, *6*(3), 259–278. doi:10.1080/09538259400000039

Zornoza, J. (1961a). El turismo en Ibiza y Formentera. [Tourism in Ibiza and Formentera]. *Bocoin*, *630*, 48–54.

Zornoza, J. (1961b). Las comunicaciones marítimas con Ibiza. [Ibiza's maritime connections]. *Bocoin*, *630*, 60–64.

Brexit – threat or opportunity? Resilience and tourism in Britain's Island Territories

Maria Amoamo

ABSTRACT

As a catalyst of both change and complexity, Brexit prompts a re-think on the common focus in island studies on boundaries, borders and dichotomies of core–periphery that unsettle/disrupt static tropes of island insularity and dependence. Framed within the relational turn in island studies, this paper conceptualises resilience as a 'new political reality' in the broader geopolitical context of Brexit and tourism-dependent island environments. The sheer complexity of Brexit processes and outcomes necessitate a different way of thinking about resilience as a post-liberal episteme that actively responds to complex life. Research findings show, rather than being a barrier to change complexity presents new opportunities for island tourism engagement and self-organising adaptivity. The implications of which reflect the growing enrolment of tourism in international and domestic relations through an understanding of tourism as a geopolitical practice in the broader discourses of nation building and territorialization. Brexit affects the United Kingdom's 14 Overseas Territories (OTs), most of which are islands, on a number of fronts including trade, security, access, mobility, identity and tourism. Methodology using primary and secondary literature, semi-structured interviews and ethnographic case study of Pitcairn Island advance the notion 'revisionary core–periphery' to positively foreground resilience as an active force and, in turn examine resilience actions that stem from preparedness (or not) in this relationship. Britain's OTs' in negotiating the Brexit machinery show an ability to transform diplomatic practices through rapid response and engagement that counters the limiting of dependency threatened by political decisions of their parent state. This creates a discursive shift from the mantra of small island vulnerability while the Pitcairn Island case study expands the idea of tourism as an agent of resilience through economic diversity and core–periphery realignment.

摘要

作为一种变化和复杂性的催化剂, 英国退欧促使人们重新思考岛屿研究的共同焦点:界线、边缘地区和核心-外围的二分法, 它们动摇或瓦解了岛屿孤立性和依赖性的静态比喻。 本文以岛屿研究的关系转向为框架, 在退欧和旅游依赖型岛屿环境的更广泛地缘政治背景下, 将弹性定义为一种"新的政治现实"。 英国退欧进程和结果的绝对复杂性, 要求我们以一种不同的方式, 将恢复力视为一种积极回应复杂生活的后自由主义认识论。 研究结果显示, 岛屿旅游参与和自组织适应能力不仅没有成为改变复杂性的障碍, 反而带来了新的机遇。其影响反映了旅游业在国际和国内关系中越来越多的参与, 因为人们认识到旅游业是在更广泛的国家建设和领土化的讨论中的一种地缘政治实践。英国脱欧影响了英国的14个海外领地(OTs), 其中大部分是岛屿, 包括贸易、安全、准入、流动性、身份和旅游等方面。使用一手和二手文献、半结构式访谈和皮特凯恩岛的民族志案例研究, 提出了"校正的核心-外围"的概念, 积极地把恢复力作为一种积极的力量, 并反过来检查恢复力行动是否源于这种关系中做好准备 (或不做准备) 。英国海外领地在英国退欧机制的谈判中表现出了通过快速反应和接触改变外交实践的能力, 这种快速反应和接触能够对抗受到母国政治决定威胁的依赖的限制。这使人们从小岛屿脆弱性的咒语中产生了一种散漫的转变, 而皮特凯恩岛的案例研究通过经济多样性和核心-外围重新组合, 扩展了旅游业作为恢复力指标的概念。

Introduction

Global uncertainty and the rise of the notion 'risk society' (Beck, 2009, p. 8) invariably align with the rise of resilience thinking and development of adaptive capacities to deal with both expected and unexpected change. In a globalized and interdependent world, all countries today face threats and dependencies none more so than small island states. This paper contributes theoretical and case study discourse on resilience thinking by examining the impact of home (core) country's political decisions on island states' development including tourism using the context of Brexit and British Overseas Territories (OTs). It reflects the growing enrolment of tourism in international and domestic relations through an understanding of tourism as a geopolitical practice (Mostafanezhad, 2018) in the broader discourses of nation building and territorialization. As a catalyst of both change and complexity, Brexit prompts a re-think on the common focus in island studies on boundaries, borders and dichotomies of core–periphery that unsettle/disrupt static tropes of island insularity, dependence and peripherality.

The key contours of Brexit's impact on the OTs has largely been ignored by politicians and the media and apart from Clegg (2016a, 2016b, 2017) little research exists on the topic. This study seeks to remedy that gap by examining core–periphery power dynamics and capability of small island states when tested by the politics of their parent state. Brexit will affect the United Kingdom's (UK) 14 Overseas Territories, most of which are islands. Several are highly vulnerable on a number of fronts including trade, security, access, mobility, and identity and tourism development. As the OTs juggle the dualism of opportunity and crises emerging through Brexit the mantra of small island vulnerability is reimagined as sites of reciprocal power projection reinforced by the quality of embedded and collective capacity for resilience. Framed within the 'relational turn' (Grydehoj, 2017; Pugh, 2016) in island studies the question posed is how preparedness resilience actions might be brought to bear on the degrees of dependency threatened by Brexit and through rapid response how might transformation of diplomatic practices (old and new diplomacy) between core and periphery operate within their own power in space? To address this question, resilience is contextualized in light of Pugh's (2017, p. 206) view of resilience as a 'new political reality' positioned in the broader geopolitical context of Brexit and its impact on the core–periphery relationship. Viewed in this light 'resilience' emerges as a post-liberal episteme that actively responds to complex life (Pugh, 2014, p. 313). Rather than being a barrier to change complexity presents new opportunities for engagement and self-organising adaptivity (Berkes, 2007).

New approaches to thinking about the core–periphery relation frame resilience as an active force in island cultures' dealing with threats or opportunities arising from changing political and socio-economic circumstances. Politically, this interweaves Lemke's (2001) concept of biopower and techniques concerning the exercise of political sovereignty. As a form of biopower resilience 'conditions' subjects to the inevitability of complex systems and uneven political, social and economic orders (Pugh, 2014, p. 316). A biopolitical response allows a measure of strategic reversal of core–periphery power relations to be recognised, for example, in the periphery's smart employment of territorial resources (off-shoring strategies) and (re)structuring of possible fields of collective action exhibited in OTs response to Brexit. Thus, the OTs emerge as state-like assemblages in a 'becoming together' of peripheral political subjectivities (McConnell & Dittmer, 2018, p. 140).

It is clear Brexit will affect the OTs on a number of fronts including tourism. As a dynamic tipping point, Brexit creates a new political reality that views small island states as multiplicities and relational forces rather than as static categories (McConnell & Dittmer, 2018). In order to counter a long-standing core–periphery narrative that frames subnational-island jurisdictions (SNIJs) within the context of persistent external dependency (Weaver, 2017), I posit the notion *revisionary core–periphery* to examine *resilience actions* that stem from degrees of preparedness in this relationship. Philosophically this new perspective is under-pinned by the quality of 'embedded' resilience; that is, the idea that preparation is an inherent trait of island culture(s) capability. This in turn raises another question: are peripheral communities endowed with special abilities/resilience actions stemming from long experience of their remote location and self-reliance. From here, the paper discusses literature on vulnerability, resilience and small island tourism followed by a profile of the UKOTs and study methodology. Negotiating Brexit reveals 'revisionary core–periphery' power relations that emerge through OTs' singular and collective responsiveness in resilience actions. A case study of OT Pitcairn Island is presented that expands the idea of tourism as an agent of resilience through economic diversity and core–periphery realignment that together will in large part determine the island community's future.

Tourism and small island states: the mantra of vulnerability and resilience

Tourism literature has consistently emphasized the increasing importance and impact of the visitor industry in small islands (Bojanic & Lo, 2016; Pratt, 2015). Research examining socio-cultural, political and environmental issues faced by small island states has drawn attention to sustainability and resilience (Butler, 2017; Graci & Dodds, 2010), while conceptual analyses include issues of cultural realignment (MacLeod, 2013), and competitiveness and quality of life (Modica & Uysal, 2016). Thinking pieces on islands in the Anthropocene (Chandler & Pugh, 2018) and archipelago (Hayward, 2012; Pugh, 2013) reflect a spatial turn in thinking whereas the 'relational turn' in island geographies/studies counters older tropes of island insularity, dependency and peripherality that reductively conceptualize islands 'in isolation' (Grydehoj & Hayward, 2014). Such views emphasize islands as mobile, multiple and interconnected relational forms beyond singularity (Hau'ofa, 2008). While some authors (Hay, 2006) have criticized this approach as negating a sense of 'islandness' and loss of distinctiveness, others (Pugh, 2016, p. 1053) contend it actually foregrounds distinctiveness and gives greater appreciation of the individuality of island culture. A point echoed by Glissant (1997) that island life is the product of a *relational rootedness*; relationality is its very condition. In understanding islands as relational spaces of interconnection and potentiality, islands provide new resources for knowledge of how to better govern complex systems (Chandler & Pugh, 2018, p. 2). This counters the 'trap' of traditional resilience discourse that overshadows endogenous forces of creativity, flows, fluidities, relations and movements.

Weaver (2017, p. 19) deems small islands, out of both necessity and endowment, to be impressive sites of resilience and innovation ... within contexts of optimal autonomy and retained cultural and environmental distinctiveness. Notwithstanding small islands are exemplars of resilience paradigms for international policy-making and academic research, the mantra of small island vulnerability still exists. Thus, residents of small island developing states (SIDS) become the unwitting captives of a 'deficit discourse' (Philpot, Gray, & Stead, 2015, p. 33) that can work to constrain rather than emancipate collective agency. Likewise, Western paradigms of resilience reductively type SIDS in terms of their vulnerabilities to disasters; imposing an external international development agenda at odds with more progressive but older ideals of island national independence (Pugh, 2016).

While vulnerability and insecurity are now inevitable parts of complex ecological systems and uneven political, social and economic orders (Reid, 2012), the capabilities of small island economies to deal with 'small events writ large' can and do counter such views. Here, 'bottom-up' strategic flexibility versus 'top-down' vulnerability in the performance of small island economies is based on (island) actors' ability to practice 'change-management' (Baldacchino, 2011, p. 238, 243–244). Living and coping with change results in 'rapid response capability' (Bertram & Poirine, 2007, p. 333) at multiple levels and is both a default/reactive and strategic/proactive disposition to opportunity. Other authors attribute the good performance of some small island states to 'nurtured economic resilience' not because of but in spite of small size (Briguglio, Cordina, Vella, & Vigilance, 2010, p. 22). Coupled with the resourcefulness of jurisdictional powers many islands have deployed the tools of governance to practise 'agency in place' crafting niches in turbulent markets (Vodden, Gibson, & Baldacchino, 2015, p. 27). The openness of small economies to international trade can also be a source of strength rather than a weakness by creating the need to strive for competitiveness in regional and international markets (Alesina & Spolaore, 2003). The transition of economies such as Caribbean islands St Lucia and Cayman Islands are a case in point – transitioning from plantation economies to highly successful tourism destinations and/or offshore financial centres. Perhaps in a need to respond to the legacies of colonialism, these islands exhibit the trope of metamorphosis (Pugh, 2013) showing how island communities/societies transfigure/transform inheritances and reject the idea of static form.

There are several approaches to resilience and tourism thinking with the intrinsic element of 'change' being a defining characteristic (Lew, 2018, p. 368). Definitions are often characterised as 'fast' change events (disaster or crisis) and other slower change processes. Changes in political relations can affect tourism and occur at the regional, national or sub-national levels including radical changes that can cause tourists to fear for their safety and avoid a country (Jenkins, 2012). While the vulnerability of tourism to political change is evident, tourism also has the capacity to recover quickly from political disturbances such as political coups. For example, the Fiji tourism industry has been resilient and the effects of coup though serious, have been relatively short-term (Harrison & Pratt, 2010). More critically, rather than seeing resilience as a quality, a paradigm or a theory, some scholars understand the term as inherently dynamic and complex and not always a desirable feature of social, political or economic life (Bourbeau, 2015). This draws attention to how resilience frameworks support rather than challenge an understanding of life and culture as merely being about adapting and adjusting to relational complexities, rather than more earnestly transforming them (Chandler, 2014). Conceptually, community resilience has moved from a focus on the capacity to 'bounce back' to an original state toward a more proactive 'human agency' focussed approach within a context of constant (rather than episodic) change (Skerrat, 2013, p. 36). Thus, it is about the ability to parry adverse events, to prepare, to bear them, to recover and to adapt in an increasingly better and opportunistic way. In this view, the resilience cycle rather than the event becomes paramount for better crisis management.

SNIJs and the 'new political reality'

For many island jurisdictions, the colonial experience (past and present) has trapped them in a Western and metropolitan-oriented conceptualisation of small island state identity (Baldacchino, 2018, p. 221). Relevant to the core–periphery theme of this paper, the focus of research is on islands characterized as subnational (or non-sovereign) island jurisdictions. These non-state entities enjoy varying levels of autonomy and self-determination that are yet (or likely to be) independent and which in diverse ways challenge, disrupt or reconfigure the relationship between sovereignty and territory (McConnell, 2009, p. 1904). As such, boundaries between autonomy and sovereignty are fluid notwithstanding the asymmetry of political and economic dependence between core and periphery. In understanding Pugh's view of resilience as a 'new political reality' several SNIJs exercise 'creative political economy with a wily and adroit commercialisation of imaginative resources' (Baldacchino, 2014, p. 1) with the ability to tap into and attract exogenous revenue from tourism, remittances, circular migration and foreign aid. Political affiliation with a larger and richer patron brings (military) security, law and order, and bestows regulatory legitimacy in sectors such as offshore finance and banking. Connectivity provides two-way benefits in areas of tourism enabling both the metropole's tourists to visit and boost island economy and freedom of movement for islanders to the metropole for education and employment (Baldacchino, 2010, p. 189).

Small islands and SNIJs have also shown their collective mettle on the global stage through actions of paradiplomacy – or the capacity to engage with the outside world through varying patterns of communication and representation (Bartmann, 2006). Examples of para-diplomatic structures are the Organization of Eastern Caribbean States (OECS) with its own diplomatic missions in Ottawa and Brussels and CARICOM involving UKOT associate members Anguilla, Bermuda, British Virgin Islands (BVI), Cayman Islands, and Turks and Caicos Islands. At 17 percent, SNIJs constitute a notable voting bloc within the UN General Assembly and assert their voice through entities like the 44-member Alliance of Small and Island States (AOSIS) on global issues like climate change. Island groupings like the Overseas Countries and Territories (OCTs) demonstrate optimal endogenous policy formulation and implementation via a successful 'international political economy' (Armstrong & Read, 1998, p. 13) in their association with the EU. The purpose of this association is to promote the economic and social development of the OCTs and to establish close economic relations between them and the Community as a whole (EU International Cooperation & Development 2016). OCT status determines access to both the EU market and EU development funding (EDF), preferential trading rights and the right to free movement of OCT workers (Clegg, 2017).

The development of new categories of peripherality and research on places 'peripheral' like rural, island and remote regions seek to challenge the limitations of the core–periphery dichotomy. In so doing the importance of local actions and practices, thus 'culture' – inherited/embedded/creative/innovative are an integral part of regional development and tool for ensuring a region's sustainability. A resilient community, organisation or destination requires strong inter-connectivity (Hall, Prayag, & Amore, 2018, p. 155) and importantly, actor engagement requires the development of trust and working together towards common goals. Brexit has caused a disruptive factor in OTs' development life cycle particularly concerning EU funding that builds tourism growth. However, re-energised pathways of political pursuits such as Brexit reflect a relational turn in which survival strategies usurp reductive paradigms of resilience and vulnerability. In sum, it could be argued the core–periphery relationship and the political and economic asymmetric dependence of SNIJs are not so much 'failures of decolonization' (Aldrich, 2000, p. 174) but represent resilience as the 'new political reality' (Pugh, 2017) of contemporary island polities and globalization.

The British Overseas Territories

The UKOTs are generally described as unusual political entities in a state-dominated geopolitical landscape (Harmer, 2018, p. 2). The territories are neither fully integrated into the political community of the UK (their populations cannot vote in UK general elections) nor are they entirely separate (e.g. they have the right to British citizenship and right of abode in the UK) (Harmer, Gaskarth, & Gibb, 2015, p. 512). The British Parliament is empowered to legislate for the territories – an authority that defines

Table 1. The UK Overseas Territories.

Territory	Location	Area (sq. km)	Population	Key industries
Anguilla	Caribbean	96	13,500 (2006 est.)	Tourism, construction, financial services
Bermuda	North Atlantic	53	64,000 (2007 est.)	Financial services, tourism
British Antarctic Territory	Antarctica	1,710,000	0	
British Indian Ocean Territory	Indian Ocean	60	0	
British Virgin Islands	Caribbean	153	27,000 (2005)	Financial services, tourism
Cayman Islands	Caribbean	259	56,092 (2013)	Financial services, tourism
Falkland Islands	South Atlantic	12,173	2,955 (2006 census)	Fisheries, agriculture, tourism
Gibraltar[a]	Europe	6	28,800 (2005 est.)	
Montserrat	Caribbean	102	4655 (2006 est.)	Construction, tourism, agriculture
Pltcairn Islands	Pacific Ocean	5	49 (2014)	Subsistence fishing, stamp sales, horticulture, tourism
St Helena Ascension & Tristan da Cunha	East Atlantic	122 88 98	4255 (2008 est.) 880 (est.) 300 (est.)	Tourism, coffee, stamp sales, fishing, agriculture
South Georgia & South Sandwich Islands	South Atlantic	3903	0	
Turks and Caicos Islands	Caribbean	430	32,000 (2006 census)	Tourism, construction, financial services

Sources: (Clegg, 2016b; https://en.wikipedia.org/wiki/British_Overseas_Territories; https://www.worldatlas.com/articles/british-overseas-territories-by-area.html).
[a]Crown colony.

them as non-sovereign. Legally, the OTs are administered by their various constitutions including councils and governments, holding varying degrees of delegated power.

The 14 territories (Table 1) comprise some 250,000 people and are geographically, economically, environmentally and culturally diverse. The populated territories' main industries are tourism, financial services, and fisheries and agriculture with the majority of territories relying heavily on one or two economic sectors. The financial services industry is one of the main contributors to the economies of Bermuda, the Cayman Islands, BVI and Gibraltar. Tourism is a significant part of the economy for Caribbean islands Anguilla, Montserrat and Turks and Caicos Islands and remote Pitcairn in the Pacific, while agriculture and fishing are significant sectors for the Falkland Islands, St Helena and Tristan da Cunha. The Territories have vital interests in continuing to develop traditional economic sectors but recognize the importance of continuing to diversify their economies. Several OTs such as Montserrat, Anguilla, St Helena and Pitcairn Islands are not economically self-sufficient and depend on British aid.

The temporal nature of UK/OT relations is a colonial one and suffice to say far from a homogenous phenomenon. The political reality of administering such a geographically distant and culturally diverse group of territories has resulted in fundamental structural problems due to size, scale and locale while issues of erasure exist by virtue of the imbalance of power and the scrutiny of processes of social negotiation between core and periphery (Amoamo, 2013). That said, over the past two decades, the UK's economic, political and social oversight of the territories has increased with emphasis on the territories to be as economically independent as possible and where possible, with evidence of responsible governance and management to have more control over their jurisdictions. The shift in relational responsibilities was solidified in two White Papers: *'Partnerships for Progress and Prosperity'* (1999) and *'Security, Success and Sustainability'* (2012) advocating a 'shared post-colonial relationship' (Clegg, 2015, p. 34) with a series of new institutional arrangements. These included the formation of a dedicated OT Department, the appointment of a minister for the territories and the establishment of a new political forum, the Joint Ministerial Council (JMC)[1] enabling OTs' elected representatives to have direct input into decision-making with UK central government (Clegg, 2015). As such, devolution of power (to some extent) to the territories was seen as a means of promoting more resilient, entrepreneurial economies in the OTs while relieving the UK somewhat of potential financial liabilities.

However, recent research highlights a degree of uncertainty, tension and ambiguity still exists regarding the extent of UK Parliament's remit in respect of the territories. In recent years, the OTs have come to prominence as 'spaces of concern' in UK public debate. Unfavourable examples include BVI and Anguilla's implication in hosting companies mentioned in the 'Panama Papers' (BBC News, 2016), the challenges of air access to remote St Helena (Harmer, 2018, p. 2) and the 2004 Pitcairn sexual abuse trials. Empire and identity aside, a reworking of the core–periphery state assemblage is evident in the dynamism of political change and 'becoming together' that is the new political reality of the OTs. As diplomatic actors several distinct formations or multiplicities emerge being either political subordinate (periphery) to the UK (core) or as independent diplomatic actors with revisionary core–periphery capacity. The current catalyst for rapid change in this regard is Brexit. Following sections discuss the OTs' response and transformation from liminal/peripheral political subjectivities to one of *communitas* (McConnell, 2017) or shared equality through enforced engagement with the core.

Methodology

The approach of this study is qualitative using primary and secondary literature, semi-structured interviews and ethnography. In-depth ethnographic experience has enabled the author to develop a comprehensive knowledge of Pitcairn both historical and contemporary and build enduring relationships with the island community. The combination of these methods provides the basis for examining the dynamic environment of Brexit via emerging academic literature and that of the media. A useful framework has been built through access to a number of public documents, particularly UK Parliament transcripts, reports, and related evidence pertaining to Brexit negotiations. Face-to-face interviews and email correspondence with Pitcairn's Brexit representative, tourism co-ordinator and other community members support the methodology to present a case study of Pitcairn as a resilient tourism destination. The conceptual approach is informed by extant tourism literature relating to small island development and the growing plethora of new tourism scholarship on resilience thinking within tourism studies. As one of the 'Grand Challenges' facing the world (Coles, 2018, p. 925) Brexit is a topic that expands resilience thinking into new empirical and theoretical terrains while broadening the scope of its contextual application within the discipline.

Brexit means Brexit: revisioning core–periphery relations

Several related material and ideational forces point to the acrimonious referendum result of 23 June 2016 and subsequent Prime Minister Teresa May's declaration 'Brexit means Brexit' (Crace, 2016). These include the economic and cultural divisions and dislocations of globalization, cross-border labour flows, systematic failings of public policy and corporate governance, and powerful conceptions of Britain's standing and role in the world to name a few (Blagden, 2017, p. 14). The UK's decision to leave the EU (delayed exit from 30 March to 31 October 2019) has created a ripple affect across the world affecting small states and SNIJs in Europe and beyond. The growing impacts and risks of an impending Brexit is now clear on a number of fronts. For example, on Britain's withdrawal from the EU the special regime that regulates the Association of OCTs will no long apply to UKOTs (EU, 2018).

Conversely, following Brexit the broader geopolitical context (economic policy-making, trade, security) of shifting power balances within the EU may present opportunities for smaller member states including the OTs. Brexit has forced the OTs closer together as a collective entity and as a consequence the territories realise they must be more proactive in mitigating potential new vulnerabilities (Clegg, 2016a). It is useful to take Oliver's (2016) suggestion that for the OTs, Brexit be conceptualised not as an event but as a process - one of *resilient action*. As will be shown by exercising their agency, the OTs become a site of reciprocal power projection through collective efficacy and political partnerships. This in turn shows a re-visioning of traditional core–periphery dualities.

Arguably, the complex at times conflict-ridden core–periphery relationship between the UK and OTs has in the latter nurtured and built domestic capacity for mitigating and dealing with external threats and managing change. Therefore, understanding resilience as a *process* offers a point of entry to discuss the notion 'revisionary core–periphery' through *resilient actions*. Actions and interactions underpin the emergence of collective capacity for resilience and response (Morgeson & Hofmann, 1999, p. 154). In this, response exhibits a correlation between vulnerability and its adaptive capacity with system characteristics including diversity, efficiency, adaptability and cohesion (Fiksel, 2003). Not all of these characteristics are uniform across the OTs but they reveal elements of multiple forms and behaviours, flexibility to change in response to new pressures and existence of unifying relationships and linkages between actors. This section aims to re-imagine the OTs as sites of reciprocal power projection reinforced by the quality of collective capacity for resilience.

Negotiating Brexit: resilient action and the UKOTs

I believe the Overseas Territories can be instrumental in helping the UK achieve its vision of becoming a "Global Britain" (O. Smith, BVI Premier, 2017).

In an increasingly geopolitical world, the emergence of new diplomatic actors on the international stage is challenging the idea of diplomacy as the special preserve of the state (Dittmer & McConnell, 2016). Using the conceptual lenses of liminality and assemblage, McConnell and Dittmer (2018, p. 140) argue diplomatic encounters operating in 'power spaces' produce new potentials for political change that is both dynamic and contingent. Turning attention to the oft-overlooked diplomatic articulations of the UKOTs, these authors contend such entities can take on several distinct formations and relations that rework the state assemblage as 'becoming together' in ways that are productive of multiple political subjectivities. In terms of Brexit and geo-politics, this supports the notion of SNIJs as part of complex and cross cutting systems of regional and global interaction (Baldacchino, 2010, p. 10). A point that also aligns with the *relational* turn in island studies that regards islands as 'inextricably interwoven into complex, multifaceted and shifting arrays of relations and assemblages' (Pugh, 2016, p. 1041). A 'revisionary core–periphery' perspective sheds insight into the nature and dynamics of political subjectivity, practice and discourse – including the processes by which geopolitical categories and actors are produced and the spatiality and temporality of geopolitical becoming, belonging and recognition (McConnell, 2017, p. 150).

In the period leading up to the 2016 Referendum, several MPs raised concerns regarding the lack of representation of OTs in the Brexit process and potential risk to their position of strength as funding recipients of EDF. A claim that was supported by an interviewee who attended subsequent Brexit meetings, stating they (OTs) were virtually 'ignored' during the first year of Brexit negotiations (personal communication); a point also reiterated by Tristan da Cunha's representative:

> the risk that the OTs will simply be forgotten or side-lined as too complicated, too distant, and in some cases too small, for British politicians to be devoting significant share of mind to (Megaw, 2017).

However, since 2017 a process of strengthened engagement is evident in the creation of the UK-Overseas Territories Joint Ministerial Council on European Negotiations (JMS-OT EN) and subsequent meetings held in February and July 2017 in addition to the annual November JMC forum. In this, the OTs appear to have strong support from the Parliamentary Under Secretary of State, Robin Walker on their priorities and interests with assurances the Committee will continue to work closely with the leaders of the OTs. This process contrasts past JMC meetings whereby 'the agenda was ultimately set by the FCO and that some representatives from the UKOTs did not feel they were equal participants' (The Environmental Audit Committee, 2014). Moreover, the rhetoric of a Government White Paper, *The Future Relationship between the United Kingdom and the European Union* (July 2018) recognizes the significant and mutually beneficial economic ties between the economies of OT and EU members. The paper states the UK will be seeking specific arrangements for the Crown Dependencies, Gibraltar and the other OTs as part of the 'British family' (Select Committee on the EU, 2018, p. 26).

In July 2017, the House of Lords (HOL) EU Select Committee heard evidence from representatives of the OTs to discuss the impact of Brexit upon their Territories (HOL, 2017). Subsequently, the HOL committee called on Brexit secretary David Davis to ensure the territories are 'properly taken into account' during negotiations because 'they seem awfully small from the centre, these issues are terribly important to the territories concerned' (Lord Jay Ewelme, Select Committee on the EU, 2018, p. 27). We could construe this statement as centre-periphery adjustment with UK authorities showing more awareness of the OTs inclusion in the 'British family'. A number of key issues and risks were raised at the meeting by the OTs (Table 2) including: access to EU funding; trade; tourism; bilateral and regional aid disbursements, financial services;

Table 2. Brexit and key concerns of the UKOTs.

Key concern	UKOT territory
EU Funding	*"the support from the EU from EDF funding accounted for some 36% of our capital budget in 2016 ... this is critical"* (**Anguilla**)
	"We have hundreds of evacuees still on the island after 18 years who are waiting for permanent hurricane-resistant homes. EDF funding has helped us to build up to 100 homes". (**Montserrat**)
	"Capital aid from the EU has allowed significant improvements to the island, including cliff stabilisation, wharf widening, customs and freight terminals, and rebuilding of roads". (**St Helena**)
Trade	*"Our ability to import lobster to the EU tariff-free is extremely valuable"* (**Tristan da Cunha**)
	"We produce wool and meat as export crops. Currently, wool has no quota or tariff attached wherever it is sold. Our meat is slaughtered to EU standards ... post-Brexit tariffs or taxes could apply" (**Falkland Islands**)
Financial services	*"Funds of EDF 11 are assisting us in making our destination a bit more attractive and attracting foreign direct investment. That is important with a small population"*. (**Turks and Caicos**)
	*"Financial services are very significant to the economy of the **BVI** ... with Brexit, we have to be sure that the (supportive role) of the British Government will continue"*.
Freedom of movement	*"We are an isolated island. Our nearest neighbour is French Polynesia. The southernmost part of that is 300 nautical miles away at Mangareva. It is not an international port. By agreement with our friends in French Polynesia and France, we use that as an international port. Will we still be allowed to do so? If not, we have serious problems in terms of our increasing isolation"*. (**Pitcairn Island**)
	40% of **Gibraltar's** entire workforce crosses daily from Spain, while the vast majority of tourists arrive through the frontier. A 'harder' border would have a damaging impact on Gibraltar's economy (Bishop & Clegg, 2018).
Relations with other OCTs	*"The border relationship of **Anguilla** with Two EU member states is critical to our development ... because of its relatively small population of 15,000 compared to a population of 100,000 in French and Dutch St Martin, Anguilla's people were reliant on their neighbours for many social services"*.
	"We have a population of 5,000 and therefore we cannot attract the specialist care that is needed. Oftentimes it is urgent medical care that has to be evacuated to Guadeloupe or neighbouring islands". (**Montserrat**) *"We use the hospital in Tahiti for our people to get surgery"*. (**Pitcairn Island**)
Tourism	*"we benefit from the EU's horizontal programmes, particularly when it comes to biodiversity ... we have a project going on in the most tourist-oriented part of the island, where the beach and reef has been damaged by run-off"*. (**BVI**)
	*"(**Montserrat**) is seeking to use the current EDF tranche to develop a port to enhance our tourism industry"*.
	"in its primary industry of tourism, 90% of visitors to Anguilla used St Martin as a hub ... Many (Anguillans) go to St Martin to work in education, in the hotel sector, in construction and other areas of work". (**Anguilla**)

Source: (Bishop & Clegg, 2018; House of Lords, 2017).

freedom of movement; relations with EU and neighbouring territories. Of these, EU bilateral funding for the UKOTs is a primary concern with the current 11th EDF (2014-2020) funding tranche totaling €76.8 million contributing to areas like economic capacity building and climate change adaptation and mitigation as well as sustainable energy development. The OTs have also benefited from access to EU trade and information all of which has major indirect effects on the environment while cohesive arrangements with neighbouring OCTs is important for islands like Anguilla, Pitcairn and Montserrat who lack core social resources such as medical facilities.

Destinations such as Bermuda, Caymans, Turks and Caicos and BVI are some of the most penetrated small island tourism economies (SITE) in the Caribbean. These islands exhibit very capital-intensive facilities and high levels of promotional spending, man-made attractions, and cruise and excursionist traffic. As a result, these mature resort areas suffer the negative externalities of over-growth including rising environmental damage (Berry, 2006). The OTs face a number of challenges in supporting positive environmental action given their small size and economies of scale. UK support is limited with The Darwin Plus initiative being the only source of funding available to the OTs, while the EU has been a source of considerable funds in terms of resources, technical advice (particularly in the renewable energy sector) and infrastructure development. Of note, a regional envelope for the Caribbean OCTs under EDF11 foresees €40 million for sustainable energy and marine biodiversity cooperation (Clegg, 2016a, p. 547) while Gibraltar has benefited from EU funds to support business growth and encourage enterprise in areas of light industry, ecotourism, medical and health services as well as micro-renewable energy projects.

Another example is the OCTA Innovation project with a budget of €5 million for technical assistance and pilot projects aimed to meet the challenge 'Innovation for sustainable islands' growth' (von Gesseneck & Zieroth, 2017) – a project especially beneficial to islands like Pitcairn, St Helena and Montserrat in receipt of Official Development Assistance as defined by the OECD. Sharing experience of diversification amongst OTs is encouraged by the UK, as is the move towards developing alternative energy sources. As a centre of excellence in volcanology Montserrat is exploring the development of geothermal energy to reduce dependence on imported fossil (Foreign & Commonwealth Office, 2012) with The Montserrat Energy Policy 2016–2030 and target of 100% renewable energy generation by 2020 (Richter, 2018). Likewise, research into alternative energy based on Biodiesel is the focus of Bermuda's Institute of Ocean Sciences research with the potential to broaden the island's economy while 10th EDF funding is supporting St Helena's conversion of biodegradable waste into biogas and renewable energy (St Helena Government, 2017, p. 2). The UK Government have since guaranteed OTs will continue to receive funding over a project's lifetime if they successfully bid in EU-funded programmes (Her Majesty's Government [HMG], 2018). That said skepticism remains over the lost advantages accrued via links to the EU and the OTs involvement in the final deal (Clegg, 2018).

Brexit: potential opportunities for overseas territories

For small islands states like those in the Pacific and Caribbean regionalism is a necessary imperative for development. As a collective, the Caribbean UKOTs are part of the

15 nation Caribbean Community CARICOM and its associated Body CARIFORUM whose main objective is to promote economic integration and cooperation among its members and to coordinate foreign policy (Hornbeck, 2008). The pursuit of regional integration in the Caribbean region predates independence and has not always been successful.[2] Critics have expressed doubts over delivery of development outcomes from such models based on trade liberalisation and for CARICOM's top-down agenda adopting mandates unmatched by implementation capacity (Warner & Anatol, 2014). Furthermore, from a postcolonial stance DeLoughrey (2001) points to U.S. involvement in the region as a contributory factor that fracture Caribbean regionalism.

Geopolitically, Brexit affects the Caribbean region in that the EU is CARIFORUM's second largest trading partner after the USA. Brexit may, in the short to medium-term impact Caribbean tourism in that a potentially weaker UK economy may create greater caution around consumer spending. That said the Caribbean UKOTs recognize certain opportunities arising from Brexit. As a catalyst for regionalism, Brexit has encouraged a recommitment and adjustment of CARICOM despite its own past fissures and cohesion challenges (Lewis, 2016). Indeed, the impetus of such a grouping of small island states was to seek, through regional solidarity a way to boost their economies and mitigate their weak political influence in the global arena. In this, Humphrey (2016) argues the Caribbean should see the post-Brexit environment as an opportunity on a number of fronts. One, as a stimulus for rethinking Caribbean regionalism; two, to bring a new orientation to its longstanding relationship with the UK; three, explore new development paradigms including possibilities for strategic alliances with other centres of influence (e.g. with organisations such as the Community of Latin American and Caribbean States (CELAC)); and four, develop new trade arrangements with the UK. The Organisation of Eastern Caribbean States (OECS) to which Montserrat, BVI and Anguilla belong is one promising model of governance and policy; often identified as an exemplar of small island state regional integration and cooperation (Warner & Anatol, 2014).

What is more, Brexit presents an opportunity to enhance the existing Economic Partnership Agreement (EPA) between CARIFORUM and the EU through dialogue on specific EPA-related concerns. The numerical strength of CARIFORUM makes the region a highly valued partner (Humphrey, 2016, p. vi). Stoll-Davey (2017, p. 16) also proposes the UK-OCTs may be 'assets' of the EU post-Brexit stating the 'UK-OCTS are relatively prosperous and currently received very little 'hard' development aid from the EU or the UK' but rather offer 'soft' benefits to both. She believes opportunities lie in geostrategic advantages such as the remarkable biodiversity and wealth of UK-OCTs' marine ecosystems; locations for experimentation to combat the effects of climate change; as scientific portals for their geographical areas; strengthening regional integration and cooperation (especially in the Caribbean region); and enhanced trade through upgrade and alignment of UK-OCTs' legislation with EU standards. Existing programmes like TEFRA in the Falklands and the Blue Iguana Recovery Programme in Cayman Islands benefit UKOTs eco-tourism development with emphasis on conservation of nature and habitats.

Fast change response is imminent. The OTs realise they must be proactive in mitigating potential new vulnerabilities – especially through linkages with other OCTs and external groupings like NGOs. Regional connectivity and broadening participation aligns with principles of resilience in tourism communities and contexts in that key opportunities for resilience building both sustain and support the well-being of people in a rapidly changing world (Cheer & Lew, 2018). Pitcairn already has assurance from the French Polynesian Vice President that, as its neighbour, French Polynesia 'will not turn their back on their friends from Pitcairn because of Brexit and that regional co-operation will continue'. Moreover, there 'was huge support for the UKOTs from our friends from France, The Netherlands and Denmark and their respective OTs' (personal communication).

In sum, though short-term uncertainty exists for all OTs post Brexit there is opportunity individually and collectively, to take responsibility for their affairs and to develop and implement long-term strategies for the transformative growth and development of their economies. In this, a new development paradigm provides a shift in SNIJ development philosophy from dependence to 'true self-determination' (Humphrey, 2016, p. 10). In the following Pitcairn Island case study, dependence on the UK will be inevitable. However, the island communities self-determined tourism development plan exhibits an ability to deal with situational change and maintain at least the existing steady state of the remote community. As such, Pitcairn may present an example of community resilience defined as 'a process linking a set of networked adaptive capacities to a positive trajectory of functioning and adaptation in constituent populations after a disturbance' (Norris, Stevens, Pfefferbaum, Wyche, & Pfefferbaum, 2008, p. 127).

Case study: Pitcairn Island

Pitcairn is the UKs last remaining OT in the Pacific and one of the most isolated jurisdictions in the world. The island is located halfway between its administrative headquarters in New Zealand and Chile, and 2170 km to the southeast of its nearest neighbour Tahiti. There are four islands comprising Henderson, Ducie and Oeno with Pitcairn being the only inhabited one with a population of about 50 people and land area of only 4.7 square kilometres (sq. km) (Figure 1). The Pitcairn Islands boast an EEZ area of over 800,000 sq. km designated as a Marine Protected Area (MPA) and UNESCO world heritage site (Henderson Island) housing a number of endemic plants and birds. Famously linked to the settlement of *Bounty* mutineers who, together with their Tahitian companions settled the island in 1790 Pitcairn's history has a romantic cachet that has persisted for over two hundred years, recounted in a plethora of media that has also helped develop a tourism image based on the island's unique heritage. The islanders speak 'Pitkern,' a mixed language of 18th-century English dialect infused with Tahitian elements and an identity manifest in a sense of exclusivity as *Bounty* descendants.

Reliance on the sea for both trade and sustenance has led to the development of a livelihood system that copes under difficult circumstances, based on local knowledge, adaptation and the ability to combine new strategies or external knowledge into the community over time. Resilience is evident in the social capital of the community and characteristics of the temporal dynamics of a human-in-ecosystem perspective that

Figure 1. Pitcairn Island.
(Source. www.visitpitcairn.pn)

has led to 'adaptive capacity and opportunity' (Davidson-Hunt & Berkes, 2003, p. 76). In this, Pitcairn society has progressed through cyclic transformations due to deep changes that generate cycles of growth, collapse, reorganisation, renewal and re-establishment (Holling, 2003).

Pitcairn economic development

Like many small Pacific islands, Pitcairn has suffered outmigration[3] and a declining population. The current demographic is ageing (with a dependency ratio[4] projected to be 86% in 2020) hence, severe capacity issues challenge the island and lack of financial services (DFID, 2017). Pitcairn has no airfield and is accessible only by ship, with a charter supply/passenger vessel currently making four round-trips a year from New Zealand. In short, Pitcairn is essentially a nano-economy based on a subsistence/barter economy of fish, apiculture and agriculture, and shared labour supplemented by the sale of handicraft to passing cruise ship and yacht tourists. Today, the resident population is mostly self-employed with wages paid to members who participate in local government activities and communal work. Predictions that 'this is the last generation of Pitcairners' has been rife since the mid twentieth century (Government of Pitcairn Islands [GPI], 2013). Key challenges for Pitcairn include diversifying economic activities, re-population, environmental management and accessibility. The current situation is summarised in a SWOT table (Table 3). The islanders have prioritised tourism development as the most promising avenue of island revenue; an economic pathway supported by the UK Government who realise tourism as the key and only driver to help

Table 3. SWOT analysis Pitcairn Island.

Strengths	Opportunities
• Unique historical brand 'Bounty' • Natural environment • HMG commitment to sustain and support Pitcairn • Improved infrastructure • Development of private sector • Regional support (French Polynesia)	• development of cruise tourism • market for exports of honey and fresh produce • major repopulation drive • diversify private sector economy • Develop eco walks for Henderson Island • Astro-tourism
Weaknesses	**Threats**
• isolation and access • ageing population • lack of new immigrants • high aid dependency • need for ongoing workforce training	• lack of affordable shipping service • changing economic circumstances and induced uncertainty of Brexit • ageing population • environmental issues (climate change; waste management; soil erosion)
Funding sources for Pitcairn (government)	Funding sources for Pitcairn (non-government)
1. HMG 2. European Union (EU) 3. Secretariat of the Pacific Community (SPC) 4. Income derived from the island and traditional sources (e.g. philately, cruise passenger landing fees and internet domain registration)	1. Royal Society for the Protection of Birds (RSPB) 2. Darwin Plus 3. PEW Environmental Group 4. Joint Nature Conservation Committee (JNCC)

reduce dependence on budgetary aid. Pitcairn's ecology, remoteness and historic interest contribute to a unique tourism offering, while the development of cruise tourism, special interest and ecotourism present future opportunities for the island community.

Island resilience: core–periphery relations

In terms of revisionary core–periphery relations Pitcairn's major impediment stems from the contemporary notoriety of 'Operation Unique' (OU) – the U.K. investigation of historical sexual abuse against women and young girls and subsequent trials (in 2004) and imprisonment of island men. The court case became a battle over the island's way of life and spurred much academic writing about Britain's oversight and neglect of its last Pacific colony and subsequent imperial domination (Oliver, 2009). Indeed, many Pitcairners feared evacuation of the island as a result. That said Pitcairners realise the need for cultural realignment relies on intentional agency and objectives combined with more local and specific image building and reinvention with a view to 'change something to a different position or state' (MacLeod, 2013, p. 77). In conceptualising resilience, risk mitigation and adaptation are intrinsic because risks concern the possibility of future occurrences (Beck, 2009, p. 9). In recent years, through collaborative work between HMG and Pitcairn Islands Council (PIC) Pitcairn is now among the leaders of the UKOTs in terms of child safeguarding with A Child Wellbeing Charter operational on the island (Pitcairn Island Tourism Department, 2015, p. 15).

Since 2004, the jurisdictional capacity of Pitcairn has improved due to UK efforts to re-structure the island's political and socio-economic systems via a combination of autochthonous and exogenous processes aimed at developing a self-sufficient local economic model and positive steps towards self-determined development (DFID, 2017). This includes its own sustainable development policy the 2014–2018 Strategic

Development Plan (SDP); an overarching plan providing strategic direction to policy objectives. If Pitcairn is to create a viable future for its small and ageing population local, regional and global positionality will need a revisionary approach. This entails re-branding of destination image tarnished by OU leading to a new customer perception and tourist gaze (Urry, 1990); demonstrating 'strategic flexibility' based on (island) actors' ability to practice 'change-management' (Baldacchino, 2011, p. 243). Arguably, OU has resulted in coping with change results in 'rapid response capability' (Bertram & Poirine, 2007, p. 333) at multiple levels. Herein, a certain 'nurtured economic resilience' (Briguglio et al., 2010, p. 22) founded on adaptive capacity and opportunity instill a preparedness to plan for the island's future and outcome of Brexit.

Pitcairn tourism development

In a competitive global tourism industry, small remote islands (thus offering small-scale tourism) capitalize on diversifying rapidly into various niches, preserving authenticity, avoiding commodification and having local control over infrastructure. Pitcairn fits this characterisation on a micro scale with current plans to progress a renewable energy project, increased tourist visitation, regional collaboration with neighbours Tahiti, and proposed astro-tourism. Current tourism activity on Pitcairn is restricted to three forms: day visitors via cruise ships, individual travellers who travel on official business via HMG's supply ship, private yachts and charter/expedition groups. Tourism is currently supply constraint by dual capacity; (1) supply ship manifest arrivals show around 70–80 passenger arrivals per annum due to limited berths, and (2) limited on-island accommodation (Solomon & Burnett, 2014). However, growth of cruise tourism (from six in 2011 to 16 in 2014) plus a new supply shipping vessel, the *MV Bravo Supporter* in 2019 providing increased passenger capacity and schedules will improve the situation.

Of the various lifecycle stages, Pitcairn has now surpassed the first stage (i.e. exploration) of Butler's (1980) TALC model and in the past five years has progressed to the second stage of involvement wherein locals respond to an increase in visitors and develop facilities and products toward a projection of growth. As a result almost all Pitcairn households offer accommodation on either a home-stay, private self-contained or self-catering basis. There are also plans to develop a Pitcairn Island Eco Tourism Lodge over the next five years to provide more contemporary accommodation options for short-term visitors (Pitcairn Islands Tourism Department, 2015, p. 10). EU funding in excess of €6 million has contributed to projects including improvement to Bounty Bay harbour; the construction of an alternative landing site at Tedside (western side of the island) for cruise landings; and tourism facilities including a new cultural centre, museum, proposed passenger ship to shore vessel and specialized passenger-land transport vehicles. Currently, Pitcairn is on the cusp of Butler's (1980) third development stage whereby the main tourist market is well defined but requires further diversification. While this stage often sees local involvement and control decrease, Pitcairn's limited human resources offset this. Butler's TALC model correlates with a destination's sustainability but also raises the risk of Quality of Life (QOL); the impact of tourism on the destination's residents and tourists connected by the destination they share

(Beardsley, 2016, p. 93). While far from the fourth stage of consolidation and subsequent (yet unknown) stages of stagnation/decline/rejuvenation there is a risk Pitcairn residents will over time experience increased levels of carrying capacity and associated feelings of resentment of tourism-related facilities. Personal communication with some residents already alludes to a certain reluctance in changing their 'way of life' for tourists.

The aim of Pitcairn's Sustainable Tourism Development Master Plan (STDMP) 2015–2019 is to encourage a spirit of local 'ownership'. The STDMP is premised on establishing a careful balance between environmental, economic and socio-cultural characteristics of the islands; one that ensures Pitcairn's niche tourism industry is built with care, whilst enriching both the tourism experience and wellbeing of the community through reduction of dependency. Importantly, lessons learned from previous tourism development plans have resulted in a review and clarification on what type of tourism Pitcairn should realistically sustain. In keeping with STDMP strategies of 'blue and green,' Pitcairn is currently exploring the niche product of astro-tourism. The latter not only capitalises on the island's unique points of difference but also highlights the ability of enterprising peripheral communities to identify and commodify notions of the periphery itself.

Astro tourism – proposed dark sky sanctuary for Pitcairn

> Pitcairn has amazing dark skyscapes. In line with our commitment to protecting our environment, we aim to curate a world-class night sky-viewing experience on Pitcairn. Being such a pristine and remote island, our natural amphitheatre will provide an ideal location for intrepid astro visitors (The Pitcairn Miscellany January, 2018a, p. 8).

Astro tourism (AT) is a rapidly growing industry and in recent years heralded as an industry leader among sustainably minded travellers and travel companies. Based on the special interest of tourists in sky-related activities and classified as a subcategory of nature-based tourism, AT is highly reliant on physical attributes of the place (Collison & Poe, 2013). From a tourism studies perspective, AT is a new medium in conceptualising tourism destination image by combining destination earth features as well as sky features (Soleimani, Bruwer, Gross, & Lee, 2018). The International Dark-Sky Association (IDA) Dark Sky Places program offers five types of designations; the most common being Dark Sky Preserves (DSP) and Dark Sky Reserves (DSR) where the majority of an area has no light pollution (Rodrigues, Rodrigues, & Peroff, 2015). According to the IDA, light pollution (or 'sky glow') has a number of negative effects including disruption of ecosystems and adverse health effect on communities. The majority of new DSR are in the USA and Canada, notwithstanding countries such as Portugal, Scotland and New Zealand are pursuing the establishment of such reserves.

A Dark Sky Sanctuary (DSS) differs from a DSP or DSR in that it is typically situated in a very remote location with few (if any) nearby threats to the quality of its dark night skies and whose conservation state is most fragile. Ten Certified IDA International Dark Sky Sanctuaries exist in diverse geographic locations of USA, Chile, South Africa, Australia and New Zealand with Pitcairn being the latest addition (in April 2019) and world's first island group to gain the designation. The IDA classify such locations as having exceptional or distinguished quality of starry nights and a nocturnal environment that is protected for its scientific, natural, or educational value, its cultural heritage and/or public enjoyment (IDA 2018). For Pitcairn, the designation of Mata ke ti Rangi – or Eyes to the Sky International DSS was a natural progression following that of the MPA. Moreover, according to the representative of Pitcairn Islands Tourism it holds cultural and heritage significance: 'We're a maritime community and Pitcairn has always been since the early Polynesian days and right through to the *Bounty* mutineers making their way here. So, it's an important component, the stars and the skies, for us' (Round, 2019).

The addition of AT for Pitcairn offers a low impact yet potentially high yielding niche product for the local community. In early 2018, Pitcairn invited an expert in the field to visit the island and assess both the suitability of the island for AT as it relates to the training of night-sky guides, location scouting, and light metering, and to begin to train local residents. The assessment revealed Pitcairn had very low light pollution levels around the island, meeting the main criteria due to its geographical isolation and zero light emissions after 10 pm. IDA Director of Conservation believed Pitcairn had an excellent chance of becoming the next DSS in the world stating, 'It will be a valid application given the islands' isolation and quality of the night skies. They just have to make the world aware of this great resource' (The Pitcairn Miscellany, 2018b, p. 3). To capitalise on the IDA application and create awareness of Pitcairn's unique tourism offering Pitcairn Islands Tourism also launched an exclusive tour to celebrate the total solar eclipse that passed over the Pitcairn Islands in July 2019 (BTN News, 2018). The 18 night/19-day tour started at NZ$16,250 and visited the UNESCO site Henderson Island, and Oeno Island to view the eclipse as well as a four-day stay on Pitcairn. With the new passenger supply ship *MV Bravo Supporter* commencing in 2019 Pitcairn's Tourism Co-ordinator stated, 'Pitcairn is looking to open up new markets and the solar eclipse presents us with a unique opportunity to showcase The Pitcairn Islands like never before' (BTN News, 2018).

Like other OTs, Brexit has introduced a high level of uncertainty for Pitcairn's future development with the primary concern being whether current UK budget support will increase to compensate for loss of EU funds. That said, Pitcairn continues to exhibit characteristics of resilience in terms of adapting to disturbances and change, collapse and recovery to their original state, through varying rates (rapid/slow) of response. In this, the received fixity of core–periphery relationships requires a 'revisionary' approach, harnessing creative, innovative and strategic local/global positioning through bottom-up energies, resources and achievements (Vodden et al., 2015). For Pitcairn, the crafting of this choice is pivotal not only for tourism but for the community's future livelihood on the island.

Conclusion

This paper presents a new approach to resilience thinking of dependent island environments that are predominantly tourism destinations by focusing on resilience as a 'new political reality' in the broader geopolitical context and complexity of Brexit. It has shown SNIJs exhibit an embedded capacity of resilience associated with bio-political responses to shifting techniques of governmentality that give rise to both risk and opportunity pertaining to their liminal position in the international system. Under post-liberal resilience frameworks complexity presents new opportunities, thus resilience emerges as a bio-political response to the contemporary idea of complex life. This directly relates to Brexit with an emphasis on UKOTs' *active* response (immediate and potential) within the complexity of international intervention.

The notion 'revisionary core–periphery' positively foregrounds resilience as an *active force* of island cultures ability to deal with threats or opportunities arising from changing political and socio-economic circumstances. In turn, *resilience actions* stem from preparedness (or not) in this relationship. This represents a discursive shift from the mantra of SNIJ vulnerability to one that engages with the 'reality' of complex life in a positive sense; one that empowers and enables island people to adapt to the conditions of their lives via *active response* (Pugh, 2017, p. 209). Transformation of diplomatic practices between core and periphery have been shown to operate within their own power in space evident in the realignment of core–periphery relations between the UK and the OTs inasmuch Brexit has enlarged the bio-political imaginary of the UK beyond the territorial border of the state (Harmer, 2018). For example, in negotiating with the Brexit machinery UKOTs have shown through various meetings with the EU Select Committee an ability to transform diplomatic practices through rapid response and engagement that seek to improve the limiting of dependency threatened by their parent state.

The UKOTs have, through change-management in response to White Papers strengthened their ties with the UK – moving from constrained autonomy to one of self-determination and collective (in)dependence (Amoamo, 2018). Rather than governance around certain goals (e.g. security, development) this 'new political reality' of resilience suggests that goals cannot be imposed upon complex relational systems. Development of joint core–periphery strategies is addressing politically driven situational change to maintain at least the existing steady state of remote island communities while addressing the impacts of Brexit. While Brexit raises concerns for all OTs in terms of on-going financial support, potentially exciting opportunities exist to strengthen partnerships between the UK, UKOTs, and Crown Dependencies especially in trade, finance and tourism development as well as opportunities for regional collaboration and new development paradigms particularly for the Caribbean islands. Opportunism also underpins the way forward for OTs with the chance to debate a new status that advances the process of self-reliance and self-determination with the EU (Jessop, 2016). Resilience thus emerges as a dominant response and opportunity for engagement associated with wider forms of contemporary bio-power (Pugh, 2017, p. 210).

In conclusion, I revisit the question are peripheral communities endowed with special abilities stemming from remoteness and self-reliance. As a heuristic device, we could argue the concept 'islandness' as the embedded need to adapt, adjust and become resilient to survive in often, remote and resource-constrained islands environments. For some, the nature of islandness lies in 'vigilant cooperation' (Putz, 1984, p. 26) that stems from island life as rigidly communal and reliant on each other. For others, it is the very condition of relationality itself (Glissant, 1997). Examples of reliance and willingness to help each other are evident in examples of UKOT collaboration and resilient action; cultivating a sense of identity and fellowship that rework notions of power and agency; postcolonialism and sovereignty. The resilience of small island tourism economies depends on embracing the inherent disruption of tourism, the paradox of sustainability, and the complexity of islandness (Peterson, Harrill, & Dipietro, 2017, p. 416).

Notes

1. The JMC is an annual forum involving UK Ministers and UKOTs Governments and first convened in 2012.
2. The short-lived West Indies Federation promoted by the British authorities did not withstand the pressure of divergent interests and lacked strong popular support (Warner & Anatol, 2014, p. 187).
3. Pitcairn has a diaspora of approximately 400, based in New Zealand and Norfolk Island
4. Dependency ratio is under 18 and over 65 years compared to the productive population.

Disclosure statement

No potential conflict of interest was reported by the author.

References

Aldrich, R. (2000). The decolonisation of the Pacific Islands. *Itinerario, 24*(3–4), 173–191. doi:10.1017/S0165115300014558

Alesina, A., & Spolaore, D. (2003). *The size of nations*. Cambridge, MA: MIT Press.

Amoamo, M. (2013). Empire and erasure: A case study of Pitcairn Island. *Island Studies Journal, 8*(2), 233–254.

Amoamo, M. (2018). More thoughts on core-periphery and tourism: Brexit and the UK Overseas Territories. *Tourism Recreation Research, 43*(3), 289–304. doi:10.1080/02508281.2018.1455015

Armstrong, H. W., & Read, R. (1998). *The international political economy of micro-states: An overview*. Paper presented at the 5th Islands of the World Conference, Mauritius, University of Mauritius.

Baldacchino, G. (2010). *Island enclaves: Offshoring strategies, creative governance, and subnational island jurisdictions*. Montreal and Kingston: McGill-Queen's University Press.

Baldacchino, G. (2011). Surfers of the ocean waves: Change management, intersectoral migration and the economic development of small island states. *Asia Pacific Viewpoint, 52*(3), 236–246. doi:10.1111/j.1467-8373.2011.01456.x

Baldacchino, G. (2014). Small island states: Vulnerable, resilient, doggedly perseverant or cleverly opportunistic? Etudes caribeennes, pp. 1–18.   Retrieved from https://etudescaribeennes.revues.org/6984 doi:10.4000/etudescaribeennes.6984

Baldacchino, G. (2018). Seizing history: Development and non-climate change in Small Island Developing States. *International Journal of Climate Change Strategies and Management, 10*(2), 217–228. doi:10.1108/IJCCSM-02-2017-0037

Bartmann, B. (2006). In or out: Sub-national island jurisdictions and the antechamber of paradiplomacy. *The Round Table, 95*(386), 541–560. doi:10.1080/00358530600929974

BBC News. (2016, April 5). Panama papers Q&A: British overseas territories and Crown dependencies. Retrieved from http://www.bbc.com/news/uk-35969481

Beardsley, M. (2016). Quality of life, the tourism area life cycle and sustainability. In P. Modica & M. Uysal (Eds.), *Sustainable island tourism competitiveness and quality of life* (pp. 93–105). Oxfordshire, UK: CABI.

Beck, U. (2009). *World at risk*. Cambridge: Polity.

Berkes, F. (2007). Understanding uncertainty and reducing vulnerability: Lessons from resilience thinking. *Natural Hazards, 41*(2), 283–295. doi:10.1007/s11069-006-9036-7

Berry, T. (2006). The predictive potential of the TALC model. In R. W. Butler (Ed.), *The tourism area life cycle* (Vol. 2, pp. 254–279). Clevedon: Channel View Publications.

Bertram, G., & Poirine, B. (2007). Island political economy. In G. Baldacchino (Ed.), *A world of islands: An island studies reader* (pp. 323–378). Charlottetown: Institute of Island Studies, Luqa and Malta Agenda Academic.

Bishop, M. L., & Clegg, P. (2018). Brexit: Challenges and Opportunities for Small Countries and Territories. *The Round Table, 107*(3), 329–339

Blagden, D. (2017). Britain and the world after Brexit. *International Politics, 54*(1), 1–25. doi:10.1057/s41311-017-0015-2

Bojanic, D. C., & Lo, M. (2016). A comparison of the moderating effect of tourism reliance on the economic development for islands and other countries. *Tourism Management, 53*, 207–214. doi:10.1016/j.tourman.2015.10.006

Bourbeau, P. (2015). Resilience and international politics: Premises, debates, agenda. *International Studies Review, 17*, 374–395. doi:10.1111/misr.12226

Briguglio, L., Cordina, G., Vella, S., & Vigilance, C. (Eds.) (2010). *Profiling vulnerability and resilience: A manual for small states*. London: Commonwealth Secretariat.

BTN News. (2018). Pitcairn Islands to mark solar eclipse with exclusive tour. Retrieved from http://impactpub.com.au/micebtn/85-news/btn-news/23240-pitcairn-islands-to-mark-solar-eclipse-with-exclusive-tour

Butler, R. (1980). The concept of a tourist area cycle of evolution: Implications for management of resources. *The Canadian Geographer, 24*(1), 5–12. doi:10.1111/j.1541-0064.1980.tb00970.x

Butler, R. (Ed.). (2017). *Tourism and resilience*. Wallingford, UK: CABI.

Chandler, D. (2014). *Resilience: The governance of complexity*. Abingdon, UK: Routledge.

Chandler, D., & Pugh, J. (2018). Islands of relationality and resilience: The shifting stakes of the Anthropocene. *Area* (Special Section), 1–8. doi:10.1111/area.12459

Cheer, J. M., & Lew, A. A. (Eds.). (2018). *Tourism, resilience and sustainability adapting to social, political and economic change*. Oxon, UK: Routledge.

Clegg, P. (2015). Non-self-governing territories of the Caribbean and debates over autonomy. In J. West (Ed.), *South America, Central America and the Caribbean* (pp. 33–39). Abingdon: Routledge.

Clegg, P. (2016a). Brexit and the Overseas Territories: Repercussions for the periphery. *The Round Table, 105*(5), 543–555. doi:10.1080/00358533.2016.1229420

Clegg, P. (2016b). *The United Kingdom Overseas Territories and the European Union: Benefits and prospects*. London: UKOTA. Retrieved from www.ukota.org/manage/wp … /UKOTA-Final-Report-on-Benefits-of-EU-to-UKOTs.pdf

Clegg, P. (2017). UK Overseas Territories and Brexit. *E-International Relations*. Retrieved from http://www.e-ir.info/2017/03/07/uk-overseas-territories-and-brexit/

Clegg, P. (2018). The United Kingdom and its overseas territories: No longer a 'benevolent patron'? *Small States and Territories, 1*(2), 149–168.

Coles, T. (2018). Tourism geographies at 20: Notes from a 'small island'. *Tourism Geographies, 20*(5), 923–925. doi:10.1080/14616688.2018.1486879

Collison, F., & Poe, K. (2013). "Astronomical tourism": The astronomy and dark skyprogram at Bryce Canyon National Park. *Tourism Management Perspectives, 7*, 1–15. doi:10.1016/j.tmp.2013.01.002

Crace, J. (2016). So Brexit means Brexit means Brexit. Is that it? *The Guardian.* Retrieved from https://www.theguardian.com/politics/2016/sep/05/so-brexit-means-brexit-means-brexit-is-that-it

Davidson-Hunt, I., & Berkes, F. (2003). Nature and society through the lens of resilience: Toward a human-in-ecosystem perspective. In F. Berkes, J. Colding, & C. Folke (Eds.), *Navigating social-ecological systems building resilience for complexity and change* (pp. 53–81). Cambridge: Cambridge University Press.

DeLoughrey, E. M. (2001). Pitfalls of Caribbean regionalism, colonial roots, and migratory routes. *Journal of Caribbean Literatures, 3*(1), 35–55.

Department for International Development (DFID). (2017). *Business case Pitcairn financial aid settlement 2017-18,* London. Retrieved from https://devtracker,dfid.gov.uk/countries/PN/projects

Dittmer, J., & McConnell, F. (2016). *Diplomatic cultures and international politics: Translations, spaces and alternatives.* Abingdon: Routledge.

European Commission. (2018). Communication from the Commission to the European Parliament, The European Council, The Council, The European Central Bank, The European Economic and Social Committee, The Committee of the Regions and The European Investment Bank [press release]. Retrieved from http://europa.eu/rapid/press-release_IP-18-4545_en.htm

European Commission International Cooperation and Development. (2016). OCT-EU association. Retrieved from https://ec.europa.eu/europeaid/regions/overseas-countries-and-territories-octs/oct-eu-association_en

Fiksel, J. (2003). Designing resilient, sustainable systems. *Environmental Science & Technology, 37*(23), 5330–5339. doi:10.1021/es0344819

Foreign & Commonwealth Office. (2012). *The overseas territories: Security, success and sustainability.* London: UK Government. Retrieved from www.fco.gov.uk

Glissant, E. (1997). *Poetics of relation.* Ann Arbor, MI: University of Michigan Press.

Government of Pitcairn Islands. (2013). *Pitcairn Islands Strategic Development Plan 2014–2018.* Pitcairn: Government of Pitcairn Islands. Retrieved from http://www.government.pn/policies/SDP%202014-2018%20-%20Amended%2011-05-2016.pdf

Graci, S., & Dodds, R. (2010). *Sustainable tourism in island destinations.* London: Earthscan.

Grydehoj, A. (2017). A future of island studies. *Island Studies Journal, 12*(1), 3–16.

Grydehoj, A., & Hayward, P. (2014). Social and economic effects of spatial distribution in island communities: Comparing the Isles of Scilly and Isle of Wight, UK. *Journal of Marine and Island Cultures, 3,* 9–19. doi:10.1016/j.imic.2014.03.002

Hall, C. M., Prayag, G., & Amore, A. (2018). *Tourism and resilience individual, organisational and destination perspectives.* Bristol, UK: Channel View Publications.

Harmer, N. (2018). Spaces of concern: Parliamentary discourse on Britain's Overseas Territories. *The Geographical Journal, 184*(4), 384–397. doi:10.1111/geoj.12273

Harmer, N., Gaskarth, J., & Gibb, R. (2015). Distant relations: Identity and materiality in Elite discourse on Britain's Overseas Territories. *Global Society, 29*(4), 510–529. doi:10.1080/13600826.2015.1012487

Harrison, D., & Pratt, S. (2010). Political change and tourism: Political coups in Fiji. In R. Butler & W. Suntikul (Eds.), *Tourism and political change* (pp. 160–174). Oxford, UK: Goodfellow Publishers.

Hau'ofa, E. (2008). *We are the ocean.* Honolulu, Hawaii: University of Hawai'i Press.

Hay, P. (2006). A phenomenology of islands. *Island Studies Journal, 1*(1), 19–42.

Hayward, P. (2012). Aquapelagos and aquapelagic assemblages. *Shima: The International Journal of Research into Island Cultures, 6,* 1–11. doi:10.21463/shima.12.2.03

Her Majesty's Government. (2018). *White paper: The future relationship between the United Kingdom and The European Union* (CM 9593). London: HMG. Retrieved from www.gov.uk/government/publications

Holling, C. S. (2003). Foreword: The backloop to sustainability. In F. Berkes, J. Colding, & C. Folke (Eds.), *Navigating social-ecological systems* (pp. xv–xxi). Cambridge: Cambridge University Press.

Hornbeck, J. F. (2008). *CARICOM: Challenges and opportunities for Caribbean economic integration* (Order Code RL34308). Washington, USA: Congressional Research Service. Retrieved from http://fpc.state.gov/documents/organization/102655.pdf

House of Lords. (2017). *Select committee on the European Union uncorrected oral evidence: Brexit: Overseas Territories*. London: UK Government.

Humphrey, E. (2016). *How will BREXIT affect the Caribbean? Overview and indicative recommendations*. The Netherlands: European Centre for Development Policy Management. Retrieved from www.ecdpm.org

Jenkins, C. L. (2012). Tourism and political change. *Journal of Policy Research in Tourism, Leisure and Events*, 4(3), 382–383. doi:10.1080/19407963.2011.613231

Jessop, D. (2016, March 13). Brexit and UK Overseas Territories – An opportunity for new thinking. The Gleaner. Retrieved from http://images.jamaica-gleaner.com/article/business/20160313/david-jessop-brexit-and-uk-overseas-territories-opportunity-new-thinking

Lemke, T. (2001). The Birth of Bio-Politics - Michel Foucault's Lecture at the College de France on Neo-Liberal Governmentality. *Economy and Society*, 30(2), 190–207.

Lew, A. A. (2018). Grasping for resilience. *Tourism Geographies*, 20(2), 367–369.

Lewis, P. (2016). The repercussions of Brexit for CARICOM's cohesion. *The Round Table*, 105(5), 531–542. doi:10.1080/00358533.2016.1231311

MacLeod, D. (2013). Cultural realignment, islands and the influence of tourism. *Shima: The International Journal of Research into Island Cultures*, 7(2), 74–91.

McConnell, F. (2009). Governments-in-exile: Statehood statelessness and the reconfiguration of territory and sovereignty. *Geography Compass*, 3(5), 1902–1919. doi:10.1111/j.1749-8198.2009.00274.x

McConnell, F. (2017). Liminal geopolitics: The subjectivity and spatiality of diplomacy at the margins. *Transactions of the Institute of British Geographers*, 42, 139–152. doi:10.1111/tran.12156

McConnell, F., & Dittmer, J. (2018). Liminality and the diplomacy of the British Overseas Territories: An assemblage approach. *Environment and Planning D: Society and Space*, 36(1), 139–158. doi:10.1177/0263775817733479

Megaw, N. (2017). Overseas territories warn of 'catastrophic' post-Brexit funding loss and Falklands risk. *The Financial Times*. Retrieved from www.ft.com/content/6ce603d6-0ec4-3bc0-a7ca-0d893ele69ac

Modica, P., & Uysal, M. (Eds.). (2016). *Sustainable island tourism: Competitiveness and quality of life*. Wallingford, UK: CABI.

Morgeson, F. P., & Hofmann, D. A. (1999). The structure and function of collective constructs: Implications for multilevel research and theory development. *The Academy of Management Review*, 24(2), 249–265. doi:10.2307/259081

Mostafanezhad, M. (2018). The geopolitical turn in tourism geographies. *Tourism Geographies*, 20(2), 343–346. doi:10.1080/14616688.2018.1434820

Norris, F. H., Stevens, S. P., Pfefferbaum, B., Wyche, K. F., & Pfefferbaum, R. L. (2008). Community resilience as a metaphor, theory, set of capacities, and strategy for disaster readiness. *American Journal of Community Psychology*, 41(1–2), 127–150. doi:10.1007/s10464-007-9156-6

Oliver, D. (Ed.) (2009). *Justice, legality, and the rule of law lessons from the Pitcairn prosecutions*. Oxford: Oxford University Press.

Oliver, T. (2016). The world after Brexit: From British referendum to global agenda. *International Politics*, 53(6), 689–707. doi:10.1057/s41311-016-0012-x

Peterson, R., Harrill, R., & Dipietro, R. B. (2017). Sustainability and resilience in Caribbean tourism economies: A critical inquiry. *Tourism Analysis*, 22(3), 407–419. doi:10.3727/108354217X14955605216131

Philpot, D., Gray, T. S., & Stead, S. M. (2015). Seychelles, a vulnerable or resilient SIDS? A local perspective. *Island Studies Journal*, 10(1), 31–48.

Pitcairn Island Tourism Department. (2015). *Sustainable tourism development master plan 2015-2019*. Pitcairn Islands: Pitcairn Island Government.

Pratt, S. (2015). The economic impact of tourism in SIDS. *Annals of Tourism Research, 52*, 148–160. doi:10.1016/j.annals.2015.03.005

Pugh, J. (2013). Island movements: Thinking with the Archipelago. *Island Studies Journal, 8*(1), 9–24. doi:10.24043/isj.48

Pugh, J. (2014). Resilience, complexity and post-liberalism. *Area, 46*(3), 313–319. doi:10.1111/area. 12118

Pugh, J. (2016). The relational turn in island geographies: Bringing together island, sea and ship relations and the case of the landship. *Social & Cultural Geography, 17*(8), 1040–1059. doi:10. 1080/14649365.2016.1147064

Pugh, J. (2017). Resilience as new political reality. In R. Butler (Ed.), *Tourism and resilience* (pp. 206–214). Wallingford, Oxfordshire, UK: CABI.

Pugh, J. (2018). Relationality and island studies in the Antrhopocene. *Island Studies Journal, 13*(2), 93–110. doi:10.24043/isj.48

Putz, G. (1984). On islanders. *Island Journal, 1*, 26–29.

Reid, J. (2012). The disastrous and politically debased subject of resilience. *Development Dialogue, 58*, 67–81.

Richter, A. (2018). Montserrat to recommence work on third well of geothermal project. *Think Geoenergy*. Retrieved from http://www.thinkgeoenergy.com/montserrat-to-recommence-work-on-third-well-of-geothermal-project/

Rodrigues, A. L., Rodrigues, A., & Peroff, D. M. (2015). The sky and sustainable tourism development: A case study of a Dark Sky Reserve Implementation in Alqueva. *International Journal of Tourism Research, 17*(3), 292–302. doi:10.1002/jtr.1987

Round, S. (2019). Eclipse and Dark Sky status mean stars collide for Pitcairn. Retrieved from https://www.rnz.co.nz/international/pacific-news/393481/eclipse-and-dark-sky-status-mean-stars-collide-for-pitcairn

Select Committee on the European Union. (2018). *Uncorrected oral evidence: Scrutiny of the Brexit negotiations*. London: UK Parliament House of Commons. Retrieved from https://www.parliament.uk/business/committees/committees-a-z/lords-select/eu-select-committee-/inquiries/parliament-2017/scrutiny-of-brexit-negotiations/scrutiny-of-brexit-negotiations-publications/

Skerrat, S. (2013). Enhancing the analysis of rural community resilience: Evidence from community land ownership. *Journal of Rural Studies, 31*, 36–46.

Smith, O. (2017). The Overseas Territories can help achieve a 'Global Britain' – But we must secure our relationship with the EU. Retrieved from https://brexitcentral.com/overseas-territories-can-help-achieve-global-britain-must-secure-relationship-eu/

Soleimani, S., Bruwer, J., Gross, M. J., & Lee, R. (2018). Astro-tourism conceptualisation as special-interest tourism (SIT) field: A phenomonological approach. *Current Issues in Tourism, 22*(18), 2299-2314. doi:10.1080/13683500.2018.1444021

Solomon, R., & Burnett, K. (2014). *Pitcairn Island economic review*. Wellington, New Zealand: Solomon Leonard.

St Helena Government. (2017). *Written evidence on Brexit to the House of Lords European Union Committee*. London: UK Parliament EU Select Committee. Retrieved from http://data.parliament. uk/writtenevidence/committeeevidence.svc/evidencedocument/european-union-committee/brexit-overseas-territories/written/69296.pdf

Stoll-Davey, C. (2017). *After Brexit: The legal relationship of the UK-OCTs with the EU*. London: Institute of Advanced Legal Studies, School of Advanced Study, University of London.

The Environmental Audit Committee. (2014). *Sustainability in the UK Overseas Territories: Government response to the Committee's Tenth Report of Session 2013–14 Eighth Special Report of Session 2013–14*. London: UK Parliament Commons Select Committee. Retrieved from https://publications.parliament.uk/pa/cm201314/cmselect/cmenvaud/1167/1167.pdf

The Pitcairn Miscellany. (2018a). Pitcairn Island continues to progress its vision to become accredited as a Dark Sky Sanctuary. *The Pitcairn Miscellany, 61*(6), 1–9.

The Pitcairn Miscellany. (2018b). Pitcairn Tourism and its South Pacific Island Partners Join Forces at Seatrade Cruise Global 2018. *The Pitcairn Miscellany*, *61*(3), 1–10.

Urry, J. (1990). *The Tourist Gaze: Leisure and travel in contemporary societies*. London: Sage Publications.

Vodden, K., Gibson, R., & Baldacchino, G. (2015). *Place peripheral: Place-based development in rural, island and remote regions*. Retrieved from https://www.researchgate.net/publication/280024278_Place_Peripheral_Place-Based_Development_in_Rural_Island_and_Remote_Regions/citations

von Gesseneck, M. J., & Zieroth, G. H. (2017). *Renewable energy feasibility study Pitcairn Island*. Retrieved from http://octa-innovation.eu/category/leslie-jaques/

Warner, R., & Anatol, M. (2014). Caribbean integration – Lessons for the Pacific? *Asia & the Pacific Policy Studies*, *2*(1), 183–196. doi:10.1002/app5.65

Weaver, D. B. (2017). Core–periphery relationships and the sustainability paradox of small island tourism. *Tourism Recreation Research*, *42*(1), 11–21. doi:10.1080/02508281.2016.1228559

Immigrant entrepreneur knowledge in the tourism industry of island destinations

Pedro Calero-Lemes and Desiderio Juan García-Almeida

ABSTRACT

The economy of many islands is heavily based on tourism. In mature tourism islands, the tourism sector acts as a magnet for immigrant workforce that help resolve some human resource problems. Due to some blockades in the local job market and/or the opportunities they identify based on their knowledge, many immigrants set up new ventures in the tourism industry. Immigrants' new ventures could increase destination supply in the sector, providing innovation and differentiation that avoid and delay the decline stage. In the island context, the creation of immigrant businesses is affected by a relative isolation and lack of easy connections with continental territories, which suggest the existence of interesting dynamics in the acquisition and use of knowledge. Immigrants' life experiences and relationships in the home and host countries contribute to their knowledge construction to set up and manage their new businesses on islands. A survey on immigrant restaurant entrepreneurs in the tourism industry on the three Eastern Canary Islands was conducted. Results show the high relevance of knowledge obtained from experience, and the low importance of knowledge from institutions and written material; moreover, education in the home country is more relevant than education in the host country; in addition, networks and Internet also provide some entrepreneurial knowledge. The existence of two groups of immigrant entrepreneurs on islands with different knowledge characteristics is also shown.

摘要

许多岛屿的经济严重依赖于旅游业。在成熟的旅游岛屿, 旅游部门就像一块磁石, 吸引移民劳动力, 帮助解决一些人力资源问题。由于当地就业市场的一些封锁和/或他们根据自己的知识找到的机会, 许多移民在旅游业建立了新的企业。移民的新企业可以增加该行业的目的地供给, 提供创新和差异化, 避免和推迟岛屿旅游的衰退阶段。在岛屿方面, 移民企业的建立受到相对孤立和与大陆地区缺乏多方联系的影响, 这表明在获取和使用知识方面存在着令人感兴趣的动力机制。移民在母国和东道国的生活经历和关系有助于他们在岛上建立和管理新企业的知识建设。对加那利群岛东部三岛旅游业中的移民餐馆经营者进行了一项调查。结果表明,经验知识较为重要, 制度知识和书面材料知识的重要性较低;此外, 母国的教育比东道国的教育更重要;此外, 网络和互联网也提供了 一些创业知识。同时也显示出根据知识特征可以划分出两个不同 的岛上外来企业家群体。

Introduction

In the new global economy, tourism has been one of the few activities in which many islands are competitive across the world. The development of tourism in open and globalised economies such as islands has generated many job and business opportunities. This has resulted in the attraction of immigrants to a growing tourism sector, which is becoming an increasingly important topic and even a concern for island destinations. At the same time, when tourist destinations reach maturity stages, they must implement resilient actions such as innovation and adaptation to the changing market in order to rejuvenate the destination.

The concept of mature destination tends to integrate ideas from the product life cycle in the marketing literature and the tourist area lifecycle model presented by Butler (1980). According to Butler's approach (2012), a mature island destination is an insular area that has been developed for some time and needs rejuvenation to avoid decline. In that sense, this kind of island destinations faces problems in attracting new markets effectively. Most mature destinations have an existing image that targets specific market segments, but action is required to transform that image and reposition the destination in the market (Butler, 2012). An important part of these actions can be taken by immigrant entrepreneurs.

Immigrant entrepreneurship relates to the self-employment efforts of individuals who migrate to a different country and engage in ownership of businesses (Chaganti et al., 2008). Skandalis and Ghazzawi (2014, p. 97) outline that 'immigrant entrepreneurship can inject new dynamism into an economy and be a very important tool for the future of economic development'. Immigrants are exposed to different types and sources of knowledge in various geographical contexts, which can be valuable in new business creation. The increase in entrepreneurial activity by immigrants has highlighted resources they have constructed that residents of an island destination do not have, including knowledge acquired in their home country and in the host country. Immigrant entrepreneurs could therefore be in a position to increase destination supply and provide innovation and differentiation, which are relevant aspects to increase the destination performance and competitiveness.

There is a growing body of literature that recognises the importance of immigration and entrepreneurial orientation focussing on the different resources that immigrants possess (Altinay & Altinay, 2006; Basu & Altinay, 2002), even entrepreneurship and knowledge (West & Noel, 2009). There has also been academic interest in the relationship between knowledge and tourism (McLeod, 2014). Research on knowledge regarding immigrant entrepreneurs has been more limited and mainly related to highly skilled immigrants (Saxenian, 2002). There is an evident lack of academic literature on the knowledge of immigrant entrepreneurs in the tourism industry, especially in the case of island destinations. Recently, researchers have shown increased interest in the role of immigrants and entrepreneurship on islands (Baldacchino, 2010), even on the importance of knowledge (Burnett & Danson, 2017). However, no research has been found that analyses the impact of knowledge in the entrepreneurial process of immigrants on islands.

This work attempts to describe immigrant entrepreneurs' sources and origin of knowledge based on the needs to start, operate and manage their new tourism firms in island destinations. In order to address the knowledge sources, aspects such as education, experience, networks, institutions, Internet and other written material (books, journals, etc.) are analysed. In terms of education, experience and networks, it is also interesting to distinguish the origin of this knowledge (i.e. home country versus host country). Furthermore, the combination of their knowledge sources and origins allows us to identify knowledge profiles of immigrant entrepreneurs on islands. The paper directly addresses two topics of interest for this special issue: island tourism migration and island tourism networks, enterprises and organisations.

Following this introduction, a theoretical framework to address the relevant topics of the work is presented in two sections: the first one deals with immigrant entrepreneurship in island destinations, and the second one analyses the knowledge immigrants possess for creating new firms. We then describe the empirical research method used followed by a presentation of the results. The paper concludes with a discussion of the findings and main conclusions.

Immigrant entrepreneurship in island tourist destinations

Tourism has been a desired activity of many island destinations. Isolation and lack of road and rail transportation links with other territories have prevented islands from developing manufacturing industries that can compete in global markets. Internationally competitive service industries are far easier to develop on islands, as long as valuable resources are available for exploitation and development. Tourism is one of the service sectors where islands can successfully compete, as the services satisfy a specific demand and are contingent on the availability of extraordinary resources. In fact, many islands are tourist destinations (Sharpley, 2012).

Tourism has relevant impacts on the islands' residents and resources. Tourism activities can have three types of positive and negative impacts in three different domains: economic, sociocultural and environmental (García-Almeida, 2011). All in all, the tourism industry has become a source of wealth and employment for islands, but there have also been negative reactions from the islanders, such as overtourism or xenophobia against the arrival of foreign tourists or immigrants (Baldacchino, 2010). One of the challenges that islands face is migration, and it deeply impacts the tourism industry. The relevance of labour migration to the tourism industry workforce is well documented (Baum, 2007). In this sense, the current consequences of migratory waves make islands interesting settings for researching the impacts of migration (King, 2009).

Many islands attract significant volumes of tourists (Sharpley, 2012). Islands have been considered 'idyllic tourism destinations for centuries' (Carlsen & Butler, 2011). Though the exact nature of the appeal of visiting islands is hard to explain, it seems there are psychological, geographical, economic, climatic, sensual and convenience reason for it (Butler, 2002). Many islands with significant economic sectors enjoy high average incomes and advanced level of socio-economic development (Sharpley, 2012). In highly developed islands where tourism is an important economic activity, or when islands with significant tourism activities achieve a higher level of development, many jobs in the tourism industry seem to be unattractive to locals (García-Almeida & Hormiga, 2017). Moreover, the lack of a large local population in many cases can mean a general lack of expertise to accommodate the international tourist (Butler, 2002). Thus, the tourism industry on islands can suffer from a shortage of human resources in certain activities. Aitken and Hall (2000) state that the growing competitiveness of destinations and businesses mean that foreign skills are a necessity.

Islands have traditionally been places with a long history of emigration. However, mature island destinations tend to be a host society for immigrants working in a labour-intensive tourism sector; the opposite can be said of islands in the early stages of their life cycle, where emigrants leave in search of opportunities (McElroy & Hamma, 2010). The development of tourism and other industries has managed to stop emigration from islands and many of them have become magnets for immigrants in search of new opportunities (Gössling & Schulz, 2005), particularly as the development stage progresses (Butler, 1980). Globalisation, combined with the better conditions for mobility, have been causes for the statistical increase of tourism and migration year after year (Illés & Michalkó, 2008), resulting in an increase in inbound tourism and immigration, in the case of island destinations. In this respect, many immigrants are very satisfied with working in a sector that offer jobs and higher salaries than those on offer in their home countries, or allows for living in an island atmosphere. In that sense, some jobs in the tourism sector require a low level of knowledge (Divisekera & Nguyen, 2018), and are an excellent entry point for immigrants who are unfamiliar with the island institutions and local knowledge. However, many immigrants may encounter social integration difficulties, and they cannot use professional qualifications obtained in the home country due to the host islands' academic recognition system. These frustrations can often lead them to perceive entrepreneurship as an interesting career move in the tourism industry.

The increase in tourism demand is accompanied by an increase in the number of activities on offer. Considering the low barriers of entry and cost of some services too, the effect is that new business opportunities are generated (Othman & Rosli, 2011). This has been a catalysing factor for the increase in the flow of immigrants seeking to improve their standard of living (Sahin et al., 2009) and set up new ventures. The tourism industry provides immigrants not only with income-generating jobs but also allows them to acquire valuable knowledge through work experience (Janta et al., 2011) or the opportunity to use their prior knowledge in their own business. In this way, some immigrants use this acquired knowledge to identify opportunities and become entrepreneurs in restaurants, cafeterias, etc. For Chaganti et al. (2008), immigrant entrepreneurship refers to the self-employment efforts of individuals who migrate to a different country and become involved in business ownership. In the tourism sector, Biddulph (2017) found that local landowners largely retained their properties during early stage of tourism expansion but business ownership in the sector was dominated by outsiders.

Mature tourism destinations must engage in resilient actions such as innovation and adaptation to the changing market in order to rejuvenate the destination (Hamzah & Hampton, 2013). Immigrant entrepreneurs are an important part of island destinations and can contribute to these actions. Collins and Shin (2014) empirically found that the immigrant restaurant entrepreneurs in their sample are innovative and are always looking to improve their business, and to take advantage of better opportunities. Moreover, tourists in island destinations tend to perceive that immigrants exert a positive influence on the innovation and creation of new things to offer in the tourism industry, and on the existence of a diverse supply in tourism services (García-Almeida & Hormiga, 2017).

Human capital is a significant factor to generate service innovation in tourism (Divisekera & Nguyen, 2018), and, among other things, the innovative capacity in the tourism industry relies on knowledge and competence (Rønningen, 2010). On this basis, immigrant entrepreneurs in the tourism sector are likely to be in a position to innovate and/or unleash and foster innovation in their new ventures. This innovation is highly necessary when island destinations, especially those targeting sun, sand and sea tourism, are in the consolidation/stagnation stage in their life cycle (Butler, 1980). Innovation provides differentiation from traditional activities and/or diversification of tourism products and experiences. These aspects postpone and even cancel the decline stage, as they generate dynamism and avoid inertia (Butler, 2009).

Entrepreneurs need knowledge to create their businesses and to generate and exploit innovation in the tourism sector. Immigrant entrepreneurs who decide to create new ventures on islands may have a competitive advantage due to the specific nature of the knowledge they have been constructing. In fact, migrants tend to have a higher level of entrepreneurship and a global orientation due to the experience of the migration process and their cross-cultural experience (Vandor & Franke, 2016). Some of the explanations for the entrepreneurial tendency of certain immigrant communities are the so-called ethnic resources such as cheap labour, co-ethnic customers, networks, access to cheap finance, but knowledge must also be outlined (Robb & Fairlie, 2009). This knowledge, obtained from different sources and origins, could provide immigrants on islands with a competitive edge compared to the relative isolation that locals have experienced.

Knowledge for creating new firms: types, geographical origin and sources

Knowledge and entrepreneurship have been widely discussed in the academic literature. According to Leonard and Sensiper (1998, p. 113), knowledge can be defined as 'information that is relevant, actionable, and based at least partially on experience'. For Koohang and Paliszkiewicz (2013), knowledge develops over time, and through experience that includes what one assimilates from instructional courses, books, mentors and/or informal learning. In order to understand knowledge construction and dynamics of immigrant entrepreneurship on islands, aspects such as the knowledge to create new ventures, the geographical origin of knowledge, and knowledge sources need to be addressed.

Knowledge to create new firms

Availability of knowledge resources in the tourism sector is becoming both increasingly important and necessary for operating a business in changing environments, which changes the use of the types and sources of knowledge (McLeod, 2014). This also applies to entrepreneurs in the tourism industry, who need knowledge on how to start a business, how to manage it and how to operate in the tourism sector. For West and Noel (2009), the three relevant types of procedural knowledge that entrepreneurs require are knowledge about the industry, about the business approach adopted, and about creating and building new ventures. A differential knowledge base by the entrepreneur helps to mitigate the uncertainty of creating a company and positively affects the decision to run it (De Clercq & Arenius, 2006). The construction of knowledge to create new firms on islands is highly challenging for immigrants. This is due to the general assumption that immigrants experience the liability of foreignness to a certain degree, and that mobility to take full advantage of network connections is hindered.

The concept of business knowledge includes the capacity to find and obtain resources, and at the same time, know how to exploit them in a business (Alvarez & Busenitz, 2001). Entrepreneurs with a prior knowledge base have the capability to evaluate the new venture and acquire the necessary resources (Zhang et al., 2010). Key aspects where entrepreneurs use their knowledge are managing information about demand, using technology, organising available resources, and understanding and interacting with the market and suppliers (Baptista et al., 2014). Once the company is created, its growth and positive performance are fundamentally based on business knowledge in all those dimensions. This emphasises the role of the entrepreneur's skills, functional knowledge, trust and training (Omerzel & Antončič, 2008), since specific knowledge in areas such as marketing, finance and strategic planning clearly contribute to performance (Ganotakis, 2012).

Geographical origin of knowledge

From a geographical point of view, immigrants acquire relevant information regarding firm creation and management in different knowledge contexts (Agarwal & Shah, 2014). Geographical mobility means that the immigrant entrepreneur has got relevant information obtained from having lived in different countries and cultures, in which s/he has acquired the knowledge and skills necessary to search for the information s/he is looking for (Okonta & Pandya, 2007). In fact, immigrants bring with them the knowledge acquired in their country of origin, acting as diffusers in the host country. But they are also capable of acquiring knowledge in the new geographical context, making entrepreneurship easier (Li et al., 2018). The migratory process itself and the return trips to the country of origin allow for the accumulation of knowledge that also fosters entrepreneurship, although not always in a profitable way (Frederiksen et al., 2016). Immigrants bring from their country of origin information and knowledge about consumers' preferences, new processes and strategies, which will allow them to create and manage businesses in the host country (Sequeira et al., 2009). This knowledge was acquired in their country of origin through different sources and will be used to detect business opportunities, but also improves the idea with new knowledge in the host country (Aliaga-Isla & Rialp, 2012).

Islands, which are characterised by varying degrees of geographical isolation and connectivity, present several particularities beyond general assumptions of host territories. This is especially acute in the case of small islands states. These particularities are discussed next, in the presentation of knowledge sources.

Sources of knowledge

New firms need useful knowledge to effectively perform and grow, which they acquire from different sources (West & Noel, 2009). These rely on external sources of knowledge to exploit strategic opportunities (Foss et al., 2013). Five main sources can be used to discuss the main inputs in the process of immigrant entrepreneurs' knowledge construction for starting and managing new ventures in the tourism industry (Calero-Lemes et al., 2010). These sources pose specific challenges on islands due to their characteristics.

Education

Higher education institutions and other educational centres, such as vocational training centres, are sources of relevant knowledge to be directly used/applied to management and entrepreneurship in the tourism sector. For some authors (e.g. Rueda-Armengot & Peris-Ortiz 2012) formal education is related to success and growth. Under this perspective, a well-trained workforce recognises the value of knowledge, and the previously unexploited opportunities and ideas that lead to innovation (Divisekera & Nguyen, 2018). However, some authors argue that education, in general, is not a determining factor in the growth of a company (Altinay & Altinay, 2006), or for detecting business opportunities (Aliaga-Isla, 2014). Some academic literature suggests that completing higher education will have less effect than simply completing secondary education (De Clercq & Arenius, 2006). In fact, technical education is not a clear success factor when facing entrepreneurial activities, unless it is complemented with managerial training/experience, which will improve performance (Ganotakis, 2012). Others do see academic education as a relevant factor in some aspects, such as a way to compensate for the lack of experience in inexperienced entrepreneurs to detect innovative opportunities (Ucbasaran et al., 2009).

A paramount aspect of education is that it allows for acquiring new knowledge (Ployhart & Moliterno, 2011), and it is particularly relevant to start-ups in dynamic environments that require innovation to survive or effectively compete. Some islands provide high-quality university education in tourism and entrepreneurship, as some higher education rankings endorse, but educational supply tends to be more limited due to the mobility options available in continental territories. In addition, immigrants may have attended university in the home countries, and their short-term priorities and difficulties prevent them for studying in the universities of the host island.

Experience

Prior experience in non-managerial and managerial jobs, in or out the tourism industry, can offer the opportunity to construct relevant knowledge to start a new venture in the sector. Most of the literature on entrepreneurship states that experience plays a more important role than education when it comes to detecting opportunities (Aliaga-Isla, 2014). There is some controversy that previous experience in business setup improves the expected performance of entrepreneurs, in line with Cassar (2014) who finds no relationship between the two variables, whilst others find that skills acquired in previous experience benefit the companies created thereafter (Zhang, 2011).

Many immigrants specifically choose to work in restaurants to acquire the knowledge and skills necessary for starting their own business later (Collins & Shin, 2014). Immigrants with more experience in the host country tend to have a greater propensity for entrepreneurship, as they have easier access to the resources needed to start a business (Li, 2001). Many islands have internationally recognised attractions, and they have built a sound hospitality infrastructure for providing services to the tourist. Islands whose tourism industry is at consolidated stages of the life cycle offer an excellent setting for immigrants to gain experience, and who will later create a new venture in the sector. Nevertheless, even in islands with an incipient tourism sector and which offer limited possibilities for providing labour experience, immigrants can acquire practical knowledge working at home before emigrating and may find unexploited opportunities in the low level of tourism development on those islands.

Networks

The academic literature on entrepreneurship tends to emphasise the role of interaction with other people in the creation and success of new ventures. Entrepreneurs need the appropriate resources to develop their activity, and a good part of them are obtained through other people and institutions (Venkataraman, 1997). According to Hayter (2013) the academic literature tends to recognise the importance of networks for entrepreneurial success.

In the case of immigrants, networks, agents and institutions are fundamental in entrepreneurship, since they are highly dependent on local contacts and acquiring sufficient knowledge about the host society and to identify business opportunities (Katila & Wahlbeck, 2012). The literature on immigrant entrepreneur networks tends to emphasise networks developed in the host country, whether they involve communities of the same nationality, from third countries, or whether they are mostly locals. Nevertheless, with the development of information and communication technologies and the affordability of travel, networks in the home country can still have a major impact on these entrepreneurs. The strong ties of immigrant communities traditionally provided the so-called ethnic resources, such as ethnical market, labour and finance, but also knowledge as a vital resource for empowerment (Assudani 2009). However, such strong links may restrict the development of such enterprises at later stages (Deakins et al., 2007). Therefore, other networks outside their community must be taken into account. If the entrepreneur possesses significant prior knowledge, s/he can avoid excessive dependence on links with fellow nationals and forge links out of the immigrant community (Sequeira & Rasheed, 2006). On islands, the fellow national immigrant community tends to be smaller due to isolation with a likely trend to avoid the ethnic market, with one major exception: that the immigrant's country is also a major tourism market for the island. Local networks on the island are also an important source of knowledge since they can provide the immigrant with valuable specific knowledge about the island and its dynamics.

Institutions

Research on the impact of institutions on entrepreneurship has been highly productive, and they can sometimes be a relevant source of knowledge. Carlsson (2002) distinguishes four groups of institutional factors: the science base and mechanisms of technology transfer; the density of networks and the role of business support services and companies in related industries; the entrepreneurial climate, especially the availability of finance; and the policy environment and other infrastructure. Some of these institutions facilitate access to relevant knowledge that accelerates the business setup process, to learn about business development opportunities, and also to improve future business development (Capelleras et al., 2010). In addition, these institutions can mediate in the search for non-redundant knowledge, which will allow immigrant entrepreneurs to develop new projects (Assudani 2009). Immigrant entrepreneurs could build larger networks with weaker links, such as joining professional associations or organisations that allow them to create weak links (Sequeira & Rasheed, 2006) giving them access to new knowledge. Generally, the institutional context of the host country is not adequately understood by all immigrants (Lassmann & Busch, 2015). In situations where institutions are weaker and poorly perceived, social ties are stronger (Estrin et al., 2013). The level of development of the institutions on islands varies considerably. As the tourist industry of an island enters the consolidation stage in its life cycle, there will probably be a wide range of local institutions willing to provide knowledge and help to potential and current immigrant entrepreneurs. These institutions can be of a public nature (e.g. public administration dealing with entrepreneurship or public destination management organisations), of a private nature (e.g. banks, consultants, or even private professional associations of the tourism sector), or mixed (e.g. chambers of commerce or some destination management organisations). The perception of immigrants as outsider competitors who are depriving locals of income can be a major barrier to obtaining knowledge from such entities.

Internet and other codified sources

Information and communication technologies facilitate networking and create new links with like-minded people outside of the local setting (Chen & Wellman, 2009). Immigrant entrepreneurs use these technologies to build networks which enable them to put their diverse knowledge and skills into practice (Qureshi & York, 2008). Moreover, Internet repositories provide relevant codified knowledge that entrepreneurs can utilise, as well as books, specialised magazines, and newspapers which also analyse industrial issues, products, production technologies and industrial and market trends. Advances in information and communication technologies (ICTs) have reduced the distance and barriers to economic interaction with the rest of the world due to geographical separation, as in the case of islands (Agrawal et al., 2006; Baldacchino, 2018). In addition, the use of the Internet has a positive effect on the ethnic diversity of key business networks (Chen & Wellman, 2009).

A review of the literature in this section has laid the foundations for studying immigrant entrepreneurship on island destinations from a knowledge perspective, but it has also shed light about the gaps and challenges that research in this area faces, especially regarding knowledge sources and origins. These gaps are even more acute to understand the knowledge dynamics that characterise immigrant entrepreneurs on tourism islands.

Methodology

In order to meet the objective of this work from an empirical perspective, a survey was conducted among immigrant entrepreneurs who had opened restaurants in tourism areas of the three Eastern Canary Islands (Gran Canaria, Lanzarote, and Fuerteventura). The restaurant sector was chosen because it has the highest number of immigrant entrepreneurs in the tourism industry within these three islands, based on data about tourism firm creation held by the Government of the Canary Islands. This quantitative relevance is probably due to the relative lack of entry barriers.

The Canary Islands have become Europe's leading peripheral coastal destinations after the accelerated growth in tourism over recent decades, mainly because of their good climate and natural attractions. In the case of the Eastern Canary Islands, tourism development has led to a significant increase in population. In 2017 and according to the Canarian Institute of Statistics (ISTAC), the three islands had a population of 1,100,480, of which 16.4% were foreigners. The three islands jointly received 10,124,675 tourists during 2017. The number of restaurants and other food and beverage outlets on Gran Canaria in 2017 was 5,093, in Lanzarote there were 2,863, and Fuerteventura had 1,764. Between 2007 and 2015, 32% of new restaurant requests were submitted by immigrants.

The target population were immigrant entrepreneurs who were running a business with less than 10 years of existence. Defining the population was a difficult task. One of the problems was the lack of an updated database of immigrant entrepreneurs. The list of individuals in the population was based on data held by Canarian public institutions. A refining process was carried out based on the companies that were in operation, by using two specific actions: the analysis of tourism websites on the Internet (such as TripAdvisor and Google), observation at street level by the survey team as indicated in the fieldwork description, and referrals by other immigrant entrepreneurs. The final population comprised of approximately 3,110 food and beverage firms.

The questionnaire was prepared in English and Spanish. The basic scale used to measure the entrepreneur's knowledge constructed through education, experience, networks, institutions, Internet and other codified sources consisted of three items which were built on two works. On the one hand, West and Noel (2009) declare three types of knowledge considered to be important at start-up: (1) about the industry in which the venture competes; (2) about the type of business approach adopted; and (3) about creating, building, and harvesting new ventures. On the other hand, Chandler (1996) uses task environment knowledge and skills/abilities as the two dimensions of business similarity to study the entrepreneur's knowledge, skills, and abilities. In this work we use the terms 'knowledge' and 'skills' as a basis for addressing the entrepreneur's knowledge, since the word 'knowledge' tends to be observed as the content perspective of knowledge, and 'skills' encompasses a procedural one. Thus, survey respondents were asked about knowledge and skills in three areas: (1) business creation, (2) general management and (3) the sector, for each knowledge source. All the items were evaluated on a Likert scale ranging from 1 ('strongly disagree') to 7 ('strongly agree'). Due to relevant variations between the country of origin and the host country, the scales for education, experience and networks were duplicated to collect data from these two geographical areas. Additional information such as age, gender, propensity to return (sojourning) and number of employees was also collected. The questionnaire was pretested with three immigrant entrepreneurs, and some adaptations were performed after it.

During the fieldwork, participants were addressed by intentional, convenience and snowball sampling. The questionnaire was self-administered at the entrepreneur's business in the presence of a research assistant to help to clarify any questions. Three teams were established for data collection; one on each island. Participants were initially contacted directly at the address of the restaurant included in the original database, or found in the Internet or in the polling process. The data collection process was very complex due to the special characteristics of the population. The final sample comprised of 108 valid questionnaires and the margin of error is 7.78 at a confidence level of 0.90.

Regarding the characteristics of the sample, 62.2% of the respondents are male. The most common age range was between 41 and 50 years old (48.1%), followed by those between 31 and 40 years old (25%). In terms of the level of education completed, most respondents have completed secondary education in high school/college or vocational training (47.7%); 25.3% of the respondents have a university degree. Most immigrant entrepreneurs in the sample come from European countries (42.6%) followed by those who come from Latin America (32.4%) and Asia (21.3%). The average number of years that these entrepreneurs have lived in Spain is 12.15, and the average number of employees in the firms is 3.65.

The general goal of the empirical approach of this work deals with the description of several knowledge and knowledge-related characteristics of migrant entrepreneurs on islands. Data were analysed using IBM SPSS Statistics 26 software. Cronbach alphas, frequencies, percentages, medians, means and standard deviations, along with a cluster analysis were computed.

Results

The first set of analyses to meet the objective of this study examines immigrant entrepreneurs' knowledge sources and origin based on the knowledge needs to start, operate and manage their new tourism firms in island destinations. All Cronbach alphas are higher than 0.90. Table 1 displays data about the immigrant's education in relation to entrepreneurship, both in the home and host countries. Only two knowledge aspects (the one for setting up and implementing the business, and the one for operating in the tourism industry) barely exceed the average value of 4.

The analysis of experience (Table 2) reveals the high impact that this knowledge source has on immigrant entrepreneurship in island destinations. All average values for the knowledge types and geographical origins of the experience are higher than 4. The knowledge obtained through experience in the host country is quantitatively superior to that obtained in the host country, particularly in relation to knowledge for operating in the tourism industry (4.77 compared to 4.19) and for setting up a new venture (4.73 compared to 4.11). In general, more than 40% of the immigrants outlined the high relevance of experience in the host area on their entrepreneurship knowledge. It is also worth noting the relatively high values of experience in the home country, which are higher than 4.0 and also higher than those previously given for education.

Data on knowledge obtained via networks are shown in Table 3. None of the average values for the different knowledge types and origins is higher than 4, although one third of the immigrants in the sample outline the high relevance of home country networks in providing knowledge to start the new business. The knowledge obtained to set up and manage the business is higher in home country networks; conversely, the knowledge and skills for operating in the tourism industry obtained in host country networks is higher than that of home country networks.

The results from Internet, books, professional publications, and other written material, and institutions as sources for constructing knowledge are displayed in Table 4. Less than 20% of the individuals in the sample recognise Internet as a very relevant source to create and manage the new business. Similarly, most of the respondents state that books and other written material do not play a significant role in constructing knowledge to set up and manage a new tourism firm on islands. In this respect, average knowledge values are lower than 3, surpassed by only one knowledge type (knowledge and skills for the setup and implementation of the business).

The data collected do not seem to point to institutions as a relevant source for immigrant entrepreneurs on islands. Thus, immigrants tend to allocate a lower level of relevance to the role of institutions such as public administrations, chambers of commerce, and banks as valuable knowledge-providing organisations. The highest value they assign in this category is 3.0 (knowledge and skills for the creation and implementation of the business).

Groups of immigrant entrepreneurs in island destinations (cluster analysis)

In order to discover the existence of groups of immigrant entrepreneurs on islands based on their knowledge sources and origins, a two-step cluster analysis of their knowledge sources and origins was conducted (Table 5). Two groups of immigrant entrepreneurs on islands were identified: one which comprises 40% of the combined cases of the cluster study, and the other comprising almost 60%. These two groups

Table 1. Immigrants' knowledge from education in home and host country.

Type of knowledge	Education in home country						Education in host country					
	Mdn.	x̄	St. Dev.	Low %	Med %	High%	Mdn.	x̄	St. Dev.	Low%	Med%	High%
Knowledge and skills for the creation and impl. of the business	4.00	4.02	2.23	32.7	36.6	30.7	4.00	3.68	2.24	38.7	34.0	27.4
Knowledge and skills to manage the business	4.00	3.89	2.24	35.6	34.6	29.7	4.00	3.64	2.22	36.8	38.7	24.5
Knowledge and skills to operate in the tourism sector	4.00	4.00	2.34	36.0	30.0	34.0	4.00	3.88	2.34	37.4	29.8	33.7
Cronbach Alpha					0.936						0.950	

Source: Authors.
x̄: Mean; Mdn: Median.

Table 2. Immigrants' knowledge from experience in home and host country.

Type of knowledge	Experience in home country						Experience in host country					
	Mdn.	x̄	St. Dev.	Low %	Med %	High%	Mdn.	x̄	St. Dev.	Low%	Med%	High%
Knowledge and skills for the creation and impl. of the business	4.00	4.11	2.36	35.9	27.2	35.0	5.00	4.73	2.21	21.9	34.3	43.8
Knowledge and skills to manage the business	4.00	4.17	2.26	35.0	31.0	34.0	5.00	4.56	2.23	24.5	34.8	40.6
Knowledge and skills to operate in the tourism sector	4.00	4.19	2.28	29.4	35.2	35.3	5.00	4.77	2.17	21.9	30.5	47.6
Cronbach Alpha				0.946						0.916		

Source: Authors.

Table 3. Immigrants' knowledge from networks in home and host country.

Type of knowledge	Network in home country						Network in host country					
	Mdn.	x̄	St. Dev.	Low %	Med %	High%	Mdn.	x̄	St. Dev.	Low%	Med%	High%
Knowledge and skills for the creation and impl. of the business	3.50	3.85	2.36	35.2	31.4	33.3	4.00	3.74	2.01	30.5	46.3	23.2
Knowledge and skills to manage the business	4.00	3.83	2.22	33.4	38.9	27.8	4.00	3.79	2.01	30.6	45.4	24.1
Knowledge and skills to operate in the tourism sector	3.00	3.63	2.32	41.7	31.5	26.8	4.00	3.81	2.10	35.2	39.9	25.0
Cronbach Alpha			0.916						0.936			

Source: Authors.

Table 4. Immigrants' knowledge from Internet, books and written material, and institutions.

Type of Knowledge	Internet					Books and written materials					Institutions				
	Mdn.	x̄ (St. Dev)	Low %	Med %	High%	Mdn.	x̄ (St. Dev.)	Low%	Med%	High%	Mdn.	x̄ (St. Dev.)	Low %	Med %	High%
Kn. to create b.	3.00	3.55 (2.03)	34.6	45.7	19.6	2.00	3.03 (1.94)	52.4	33.3	14.3	3.00	3.00 (2.01)	49.1	33.3	17.6
Kn. to manage b.	3.00	3.51 (2.04)	36.2	43.9	19.6	2.00	2.91 (1.93)	57.8	27.5	14.7	2.00	2.82 (2.03)	53.7	29.6	16.7
Kn. to operate in tourism s.	4.00	3.68 (2.1)	33.6	42.0	24.3	2.00	2.90 (1.97)	54.9	28.8	16.3	2.00	2.86 (1.96)	50.9	34.2	14.8
Cronbach Alpha	0.925					0.969					0.946				

Source: Authors.

Table 5. Cluster distribution and knowledge sources by group.

Knowledge source	Group 1 [Integrated knowledgeable immigr. entrepreneurs]		Group 2 [Immigr. entrepreneurs in foreign communities]	
	Mean	Standard dev.	Mean	Standard dev.
Education in home country	4.676	2.181	3.097	2.029
Education in host country	5.874	1.233	2.661	1.623
Experience in home country	5.622	1.694	4.018	2.030
Experience in host country	6.171	0.951	2.830	1.666
Networks in home country	3.135	2.199	4.036	2.015
Networks in host country	3.955	1.988	3.321	1.750
Internet	4.351	1.934	3.006	1.764
Books and other written material	4.099	2.024	2.079	1.305
Institutions	3.559	2.077	2.346	1.498
Cluster distribution	*N*	*% of the combined cases*	*% of the total cases*	
Group 1	37	40.2%	34.3%	
Group 2	55	59.8%	50.9%	
Combined	92	100.0%	85.2%	
Excluded cases	16	–	14.8%	
Total	108	–	100,0%	

Source: Authors.

can be described by the different patterns of knowledge sources and origins used in the two-step cluster analysis.

The members in Group 1 have higher knowledge from all the sources and origins, with the exception of the knowledge obtained from networks in the home country. The latter is the knowledge characteristic that best describes the members of Group 2. Members in Group 1 highly value the knowledge sources of the host country, with distinctly higher scores in experience and education in the host country; they also value networks outside their community and consider the internet important. On the other hand, immigrants in Group 2 value less all sources in general, with those related to their country of origin being the most valued. Based on the detailed values of knowledge sources and origins, members of Group 1 could be labelled 'integrated knowledgeable immigrant entrepreneurs', and members of Group 2 could be considered 'immigrant entrepreneurs in foreign communities'. The higher level of knowledge from almost all the sources and the relevance of the host country for those sources have been decisive for the label of individuals in Group 1. In addition, the finding associated with the higher value of constructed knowledge from fellow nationals from the home country observed in the members of Group 2 has highlighted the dependence of these entrepreneurs on their home-country community.

Further descriptive analyses have been conducted in order to shed more light on the profiles of immigrant entrepreneurs included in the two groups, respectively. The *integrated knowledgeable immigrant entrepreneurs* (Group 1) are younger, speak the local language (i.e. Spanish) better, and tend to avoid going back to their home country even when they have spent less time in the host area. The *immigrant entrepreneurs in foreign communities* are on average two years older and express a higher level of desire to return to their home country. In relation to the tourism business that they have set up on the islands, they appear to have done so by necessity (and not by opportunity) to a higher degree than the *integrated knowledgeable immigrant entrepreneurs*, and their firms tend to be larger and with more employees from their home country.

In terms of gender, both groups are mostly male. However, the proportion of women is higher in the *integrated knowledgeable immigrant entrepreneurs* than in the *immigrant entrepreneurs in foreign communities* (42.9% and 35.3%, respectively). In terms of country of origin, the two groups show similar proportions: in Group 1 those migrating from other countries in the European Union are 45.9% and in Group 2 they are 45.5%.

Discussion

The findings of this work help to understand the role of knowledge in the immigrant entrepreneurial process in the tourism sector of islands. Any discussion about immigrant entrepreneurs is incomplete without recognising the role played by human capital (Sequeira & Rasheed, 2006). Immigrants turn to different sources and areas to construct the knowledge they need to start new firms in the tourism sector in islands.

The analysis of the knowledge sources has started with the role of education in immigrant entrepreneurship in the tourism sector of islands. However, it seems that education is not a very relevant knowledge source for setting up and managing new firms in this context, as many immigrants do not observe education as a major source of knowledge for entrepreneurship on the island. In fact, Ganotakis (2012) warns of the lack of positive impact of technical education without managerial experience or training. Immigrants tend to learn about tourism entrepreneurship via formal education in their home country. The relevance of education in the host country is lower, hence suggesting that immigrants do not have the ability, motivation or time/opportunities to access the educational system in the host islands for entrepreneurship purposes.

Experience is the main knowledge source for creating new ventures in the island tourism sector, as it is by far the most relevant source of the five addressed in this work. Corroborating the general significance found in the academic literature (e.g. Aliaga-Isla, 2014), immigrants seem to construct much of their knowledge from prior work experience. Results for the host country reveal that the island tourism sector can provide valuable local experience, especially for the setup, implementation and operation of new businesses in the industry. By having previously worked in the tourism sector, immigrants develop knowledge that prepares them not only for their jobs, but also for future entrepreneurship, as Collins and Shin (2014) suggest. Understanding tourists' needs and demands, and the complex system of interactions in the tourism sector, definitely helps to identify opportunities and manage new ventures. Experience in other industries also fosters the ability to manage firms and take risks, facilitates information on setting up a new venture, and even provides tips on approaching the tourism sector with new 'out of the box' ideas. The maturity of the tourism industry on islands propels the transfer and generation of knowledge, and immigrants can capitalise on it. Regarding the geographical comparison, it seems that immigrant entrepreneurs on islands tend to learn more from experience in the host countries than in their home areas.

Immigrant entrepreneurs on islands also construct knowledge from their interactions with other individuals, but the relevant role that networks play in entrepreneurship (e.g.

Sequeira & Rasheed, 2006) does not seem to be confirmed in this work. Knowledge from networks is not as high as that gained from experience or from education in the home country. The geographical characteristics of islands probably make it more diffi-cult for the entrepreneur to take advantage of their contacts, compared to wider contin-ental territories with a bigger critical mass of fellow nationals. Moreover, immigrants tend to learn more about setting up and managing a business in their home country, and they use networks in the host countries, especially on host islands, to acquire know-ledge on the particularities of the local tourism context. Another remark in this line is provided by Estrin et al., (2013) who draw a similar conclusion after observing that entrepreneurs have weaker social ties in territories where institutions are posi-tively perceived.

The two last categories of knowledge sources are the institutions and Internet and codified sources. Institutions such as public administrations, chambers of commerce and banks are the weakest knowledge source for immigrant entrepreneurs in the island tourism sector. The only noteworthy value in this trend in the data collected, is their role as information providers for creating and setting up the new venture, even though that role is exceeded by all other knowledge sources. Due to the classical assumption that these institutions encourage entrepreneurship and assign many resources to assist and foster entrepreneurship (e.g. Dana, 2000), this could be consid-ered a major failure in terms of their performance towards the immigrant collective on islands. One explanation could be the lack of language skills and cultural knowledge of staff in these organisations. Another potential reason lies in the very nature of the migration process, meaning that some of these entrepreneurs mistrust them due to irregular access to the country/island. Regarding Internet and other codified, written material, immigrants do not seem to prioritise them as very useful sources for setting up and managing new tourism firms on islands. This hinders the possibility of exploit-ing an area where islands could compete equally, considering the development and lack of physical barriers that ICTs imply. However, the distribution system possibly dis-courages the use of books and some publications since publishing houses restrict their diffusion on islands and the transport of goods takes longer to reach more isolated island territories.

Sequeira and Rasheed (2006) indicate that immigrants arrive in their host countries with differing levels of human capital, reinforcing the idea contained in the academic literature about the existence of different groups of immigrants regarding their know-ledge (unqualified immigrant workforce versus highly qualified immigrants that con-tribute to the loss of talent in their home countries). This study has also found the existence of two clearly different types of immigrant entrepreneurs on islands destina-tions: the *integrated knowledgeable immigrant entrepreneurs* and the *immigrant entre-preneurs in foreign communities*. The first type of immigrants tends to be younger and more embedded in local networks, and they take advantage of local education and experience in order to start up their new ventures. The *immigrant entrepreneurs in for-eign communities* have spent more time in the host country but they have a lower level of Spanish. These entrepreneurs have a higher propensity to return to their home countries and they have mainly constructed their knowledge for tourism entre-preneurship and management on the island from networks with individuals and experience from the home country. In addition, while the firms created by *integrated knowledgeable immigrant entrepreneurs* are smaller, they tend to have been created driven by opportunity, thus leaving room for a higher level of innovation and novelty in the tourism sector of the host islands. Moreover, there has been a change in recent years with the arrival of immigrants who are more willing to construct their knowledge from sources in their host area and from the Internet, written material and local institutions.

Conclusions

This work has described the main features of immigrant entrepreneurs' sources and origin of knowledge based on the needs to start, operate and manage their new tourism firms in island destinations. This description provides some interesting academic and practical implications, which represent several contributions that add to knowledge about immigrant entrepreneurship on islands. Firstly, the existence of some knowledge sources that are more relevant than others to face entrepreneurship in the immigrant community on islands has been highlighted. Secondly, the relevance of the two geographical scopes where knowledge by immigrants is constructed differs based on the knowledge source and even the specific learned aspect. A third relevant finding of this study reveals the existence of two groups or profiles of immigrant entrepreneurs based on their knowledge construction patterns.

The results of this work also enable to make several recommendations to public administrations and destination management organisations on islands. Firstly, islands should foster educational systems that provide entrepreneurship training for immigrants. While the immigrants' level of education appears to be not so relevant in terms of immigrant entrepreneurship from the data collected, this may be due to the lack of specific managerial training, in line with Ganotakis (2012). Management courses targeting new entrepreneurs from the island's main immigrant groups working in the tourism sector could be offered at university or vocational level. Moreover, another interesting measure to foster the transfer of knowledge could be the creation of associations of entrepreneurs with immigrant background, or sections in the chambers of commerce of islands that initiate networking programmes for the exchange of potential foreign entrepreneurs' entrepreneurial experiences. In this vein, services of public administrations and organisations that have an interest in local entrepreneurship on islands should also be guided to assist the main immigrant population collectives on the island.

This work has several limitations. The empirical study was conducted in the restaurant industry; while this subsector is highly relevant in the tourism industry and it is arguably the main subsector for immigrant entrepreneurship in island destinations, care should be taken when generalising the results for the global tourism industry. Moreover, the findings are based on a limited number of respondents due to the complex fieldwork and likely misunderstanding about the potential use of the information gathered; this limitation can affect the exact level of the quantitative values for each knowledge input, but the trend in the hierarchy of the knowledge sources is expected to remain in similar terms following the identified patterns. In addition, the data have been collected through a questionnaire. In this regard, a qualitative approach could complement the results of this study. Finally, it would be interesting to see the results of any future analyses of immigrant entrepreneurship in other islands (for example in the Caribbean and Southern Europe) in order to compare the results of this study with the situation in other important small island destinations.

Disclosure statement

No potential conflict of interest was reported by the authors.

References

Agrawal, A., Cockburn, I., & McHale, J. (2006). Gone but not forgotten: Knowledge flows, labor mobility, and enduring social relationships. *Journal of Economic Geography, 6*(5), 571–591. https://doi.org/10.1093/jeg/lbl016

Agarwal, R., & Shah, S. K. (2014). Knowledge sources of entrepreneurship: Firm formation by academic, user and employee innovators. *Research Policy, 43*(7), 1109–1133. https://doi.org/10.1016/j.respol.2014.04.012

Aitken, C., & Hall, C. M. (2000). Migrant and foreign skills and their relevance to the tourism industry. *Tourism Geographies, 2*(1), 66–86. https://doi.org/10.1080/146166800363457

Aliaga-Isla, R. (2014). A Percepção de Oportunidades de Negócios por Imigrantes na Espanha: O impacto do capital humano geral e específico. *Revista Brasileira de Gestão de Negócios, 16*(52), 416–433.

Aliaga-Isla, R., & Rialp, A. (2012). How do information and experience play a role in the discovery of entrepreneurial opportunities? The case of Latin-American immigrants in Barcelona. *Latin American Business Review, 13*(1), 59–80. https://doi.org/10.1080/10978526.2012.675866

Altinay, L., & Altinay, E. (2006). Determinants of ethnic minority entrepreneurial growth in the catering sector. *The Service Industries Journal, 26*(2), 203–221. https://doi.org/10.1080/02642060500369354

Alvarez, S. A., & Busenitz, L. W. (2001). The entrepreneurship of resource-based theory. *Journal of Management, 27*(6), 755–775. https://doi.org/10.1177/014920630102700609

Assudani, R. H. (2009). Ethnic entrepreneurship: The distinct role of ties. *Journal of Small Business & Entrepreneurship, 22*(2), 197–205. https://doi.org/10.1080/08276331.2009.10593450

Baldacchino, G. (2010). Island brands and 'the Island' as a brand: Insights from immigrant entrepreneurs on Prince Edward Island. *International Journal of Entrepreneurship and Small Business, 9*(4), 378–393. https://doi.org/10.1504/IJESB.2010.032400

Baldacchino, G. (2018). Connectivity, mobility and island life: Parallel narratives from Malta and Lesvos. *Symposia Melitensia, 14*, 7–17.

Baptista, R., Karaöz, M., & Mendonça, J. (2014). The impact of human capital on the early success of necessity versus opportunity-based entrepreneurs. *Small Business Economics, 42*(4), 831–847. https://doi.org/10.1007/s11187-013-9502-z

Basu, A., & Altinay, E. (2002). The interaction between culture and entrepreneurship in London's immigrant businesses. *International Small Business Journal: Researching Entrepreneurship, 20*(4), 371–393. https://doi.org/10.1177/0266242602204001

Baum, T. (2007). Human resources in tourism: Still waiting for change. *Tourism Management, 28*(6), 1383–1399. https://doi.org/10.1016/j.tourman.2007.04.005

Biddulph, R. (2017). Tourist territorialisation and geographies of opportunity at the edges of mass destinations. *Tourism Geographies, 19*(1), 27–43. https://doi.org/10.1080/14616688.2016.1217920

Burnett, K. A., & Danson, M. (2017). Enterprise and entrepreneurship on islands and remote rural environments. *The International Journal of Entrepreneurship and Innovation, 18*(1), 25–35. https://doi.org/10.1177/1465750316686237

Butler, R. W. (1980). The concept of a tourist area cycle of evolution: Implications for management of resources. *The Canadian Geographer/Le Géographe Canadien, 24*(1), 5–12. https://doi.org/10.1111/j.1541-0064.1980.tb00970.x

Butler, R. W. (2002). Tourism development in small islands: Past influences and future directions. In D. G. Lockhart, D. Drakakis-Smith, & J. Schembri (Eds.), *The development process in small island states* (pp. 71–91). Routledge.

Butler, R. (2009). Tourism in the future: Cycles, waves or wheels? *Futures, 41*(6), 346–352. https://doi.org/10.1016/j.futures.2008.11.002

Butler, R. (2012). Mature tourist destinations: Can we recapture and retain the magic? In J. F. V. Rebollo & I. R. Sánchez (Eds.), *Renovación y reestructuración de destinos turísticos en áreas costeras* (pp. 19–36). Universitat de València.

Calero-Lemes, P., García-Almeida, D. J., & Hormiga, E. (2010). The role of knowledge in the immigrant entrepreneurial process. *International Journal of Business Administration, 1*(1), 68–79.

Capelleras, J. L., Greene, F. J., Kantis, H., & Rabetino, R. (2010). Venture creation speed and subsequent growth: Evidence from South America. *Journal of Small Business Management, 48*(3), 302–324. https://doi.org/10.1111/j.1540-627X.2010.00296.x

Carlsen, J., & Butler, R. (2011). Introducing sustainable perspectives of island tourism. In J. Carlsen & R. Butler (Eds.), *Island tourism sustainable perspectives* (pp 1–8). CABI.

Carlsson, B. (2002). Institutions, entrepreneurship, and growth: Biomedicine and polymers in Sweden and Ohio. *Small Business Economics, 19*(2), 105–121. https://doi.org/10.1023/A:1016235022728

Cassar, G. (2014). Industry and startup experience on entrepreneur forecast performance in new firms. *Journal of Business Venturing, 29*(1), 137–151. https://doi.org/10.1016/j.jbusvent.2012.10.002

Chaganti, R. R. S., Watts, A. D., Chaganti, R., & Zimmerman-Treichel, M. (2008). Ethnic-immigrants in founding teams: Effects on prospector strategy and performance in new Internet ventures. *Journal of Business Venturing, 23*(1), 113–139. https://doi.org/10.1016/j.jbusvent.2006.07.004

Chandler, G. N. (1996). Business similarity as a moderator of the relationship between pre-ownership experience and venture performance. *Entrepreneurship Theory and Practice, 20*(3), 51–65. https://doi.org/10.1177/104225879602000304

Chen, W., & Wellman, B. (2009). Net and jet: The Internet use, travel and social networks of Chinese Canadian entrepreneurs. *Information, Communication & Society, 12*(4), 525–547. https://doi.org/10.1080/13691180902858080

Collins, J., & Shin, J. (2014). Korean immigrant entrepreneurs in the Sydney restaurant industry. *Labour and Management in Development Journal, 15*, 1–25.

Dana, L. P. (2000). Creating entrepreneurs in India. *Journal of Small Business Management, 38*(1), 86–91.

De Clercq, D., & Arenius, P. (2006). The role of knowledge in business start-up activity. *International Small Business Journal: Researching Entrepreneurship, 24*(4), 339–358. https://doi.org/10.1177/0266242606065507

Deakins, D., Ishaq, M., Smallbone, D., Whittam, G., & Wyper, J. (2007). Ethnic minority businesses in Scotland and the role of social capital. *International Small Business Journal: Researching Entrepreneurship, 25*(3), 307–326. https://doi.org/10.1177/0266242607076530

Divisekera, S., & Nguyen, V. K. (2018). Determinants of innovation in tourism evidence from Australia. *Tourism Management, 67*, 157–167. https://doi.org/10.1016/j.tourman.2018.01.010

Estrin, S., Korosteleva, J., & Mickiewicz, T. (2013). Which institutions encourage entrepreneurial growth aspirations? *Journal of Business Venturing, 28*(4), 564–580. https://doi.org/10.1016/j.jbusvent.2012.05.001

Foss, N. J., Lyngsie, J., & Zahra, S. A. (2013). The role of external knowledge sources and organizational design in the process of opportunity exploitation. *Strategic Management Journal, 34*(12), 1453–1471. https://doi.org/10.1002/smj.2135

Frederiksen, L., Wennberg, K., & Balachandran, C. (2016). Mobility and entrepreneurship: Evaluating the scope of knowledge–based theories of entrepreneurship. *Entrepreneurship Theory and Practice, 40*(2), 359–380. https://doi.org/10.1111/etap.12223

Ganotakis, P. (2012). Founders' human capital and the performance of UK new technology based firms. *Small Business Economics, 39*(2), 495–515. https://doi.org/10.1007/s11187-010-9309-0

García-Almeida, D. J. (2011). *Dirección de empresas turísticas*. Universidad de Las Palmas de Gran Canaria.

García-Almeida, D. J., & Hormiga, E. (2017). Immigration and the competitiveness of an island tourism destination: A knowledge-based reputation analysis of Lanzarote. *Island Studies Journal, 12*(1), 207–222. https://doi.org/10.24043/isj.13

Gössling, S., & Schulz, U. (2005). Tourism-related migration in Zanzibar, Tanzania. *Tourism Geographies, 7*(1), 43–62. https://doi.org/10.1080/1461668042000324058

Hamzah, A., & Hampton, M. P. (2013). Resilience and non-linear change in island tourism. *Tourism Geographies, 15*(1), 43–67. https://doi.org/10.1080/14616688.2012.675582

Hayter, C. S. (2013). Conceptualizing knowledge-based entrepreneurship networks: Perspectives from the literature. *Small Business Economics, 41*(4), 899–911. https://doi.org/10.1007/s11187-013-9512-x

Illés, S., & Michalkó, G. (2008). Relationships between international tourism and migration in Hungary: Tourism flows and foreign property ownership. *Tourism Geographies, 10*(1), 98–118. https://doi.org/10.1080/14616680701825271

Janta, H., Brown, L., Lugosi, P., & Ladkin, A. (2011). Migrant relationships and tourism employment. *Annals of Tourism Research, 38*(4), 1322–1343. https://doi.org/10.1016/j.annals.2011.03.004

Katila, S., & Wahlbeck, Ö. (2012). The role of (transnational) social capital in the start-up processes of immigrant businesses: The case of Chinese and Turkish restaurant businesses in Finland. *International Small Business Journal: Researching Entrepreneurship, 30*(3), 294–309. https://doi.org/10.1177/0266242610383789

King, R. (2009). Geography, islands and migration in an Era of global mobility. *Island Studies Journal, 4*(1), 53–84.

Koohang, A., & Paliszkiewicz, J. (2013). Knowledge construction in e-learning: An empirical validation of an active learning model. *Journal of Computer Information Systems, 53*(3), 109–114. https://doi.org/10.1080/08874417.2013.11645637

Lassmann, A., & Busch, C. (2015). Revisiting native and immigrant entrepreneurial activity. *Small Business Economics, 45*(4), 841–873. https://doi.org/10.1007/s11187-015-9665-x

Leonard, D., & Sensiper, S. (1998). The role of tacit knowledge in group innovation. *California Management Review, 40*(3), 112–132. https://doi.org/10.2307/41165946

Li, C., Isidor, R., Dau, L. A., & Kabst, R. (2018). The more the merrier? Immigrant share and entrepreneurial activities. *Entrepreneurship Theory and Practice, 42*(5), 698–733. https://doi.org/10.1177/1042258718795344

Li, P. S. (2001). Immigrants' propensity to self-employment: Evidence from Canada. *International Migration Review, 35*(4), 1106–1128. https://doi.org/10.1111/j.1747-7379.2001.tb00054.x

McElroy, J. L., & Hamma, P. E. (2010). SITEs revisited: Socioeconomic and demographic contours of small island tourist economies. *Asia Pacific Viewpoint*, *51*(1), 36–46. https://doi.org/10.1111/j.1467-8373.2010.01412.x

McLeod, M. (2014). Analysing inter-business knowledge sharing in the tourism sector. In M. McLeod & R. Vaughan (Eds.), *Knowledge networks and tourism* (pp. 157–171). Routledge.

Okonta, P., & Pandya, K. V. (2007). Entrepreneurial potentials of African-Caribbeans in the United Kingdom. *Journal of Small Business and Enterprise Development*, *14*(4), 702–718. https://doi.org/10.1108/14626000710832785

Omerzel, D. G., & Antončič, B. (2008). Critical entrepreneur knowledge dimensions for the SME performance. *Industrial Management & Data Systems*, *108*(9), 1182–1199. https://doi.org/10.1108/02635570810914883

Othman, P., & Rosli, M. M. (2011). The impact of tourism on small business performance: Empirical evidence from Malaysian islands. *International Journal of Business and Social Science*, *2*(1), 11–21.

Ployhart, R. E., & Moliterno, T. P. (2011). Emergence of the human capital resource: A multilevel model. *Academy of Management Review*, *36*(1), 127–150. https://doi.org/10.5465/amr.2009.0318

Qureshi, S., York, A. S. (2008). Information technology adoption by small businesses in minority and ethnic communities. In *Proceedings of the 41st Annual Hawaii International Conference on System Sciences (HICSS 2008)* (pp. 447–447). IEEE.

Robb, A. M., & Fairlie, R. W. (2009). Determinants of business success: An examination of Asian-owned businesses in the USA. *Journal of Population Economics*, *22*(4), 827–858. https://doi.org/10.1007/s00148-008-0193-8

Rønningen, M. (2010). Innovative processes in a nature-based tourism case: The role of a tour-operator as the driver of innovation. *Scandinavian Journal of Hospitality and Tourism*, *10*(3), 190–206. https://doi.org/10.1080/15022250.2010.491255

Rueda-Armengot, C., & Peris-Ortiz, M. (2012). The emigrant entrepreneur: A theoretical framework and empirical approximation. *International Entrepreneurship and Management Journal*, *8*(1), 99–118. https://doi.org/10.1007/s11365-010-0164-x

Sahin, M., Nijkamp, P., & Rietdijk, M. (2009). Cultural diversity and urban innovativeness: Personal and business characteristics of urban migrant entrepreneurs. *Innovation: The European Journal of Social Science Research*, *22*(3), 251–281. https://doi.org/10.1080/13511610903354364

Saxenian, A. (2002). Silicon Valley's new immigrant high-growth entrepreneurs. *Economic Development Quarterly*, *16*(1), 20–31. https://doi.org/10.1177/0891242402016001003

Sequeira, J. M., Carr, J. C., & Rasheed, A. A. (2009). Transnational entrepreneurship: Determinants of firm type and owner attributions of success. *Entrepreneurship Theory and Practice*, *33*(5), 1023–1044. https://doi.org/10.1111/j.1540-6520.2009.00333.x

Sequeira, J. M., & Rasheed, A. A. (2006). Start-up and growth of immigrant small businesses: The impact of social and human capital. *Journal of Developmental Entrepreneurship*, *11*(04), 357–375. https://doi.org/10.1142/S1084946706000490

Sharpley, R. (2012). Island tourism or tourism on islands? *Tourism Recreation Research*, *37*(2), 167–172. https://doi.org/10.1080/02508281.2012.11081701

Skandalis, K. S., & Ghazzawi, I. A. (2014). Immigration and entrepreneurship in Greece: Factors influencing and shaping entrepreneurship establishments by immigrants. *International Journal of Entrepreneurship*, *18*, 77–141.

Ucbasaran, D., Westhead, P., & Wright, M. (2009). The extent and nature of opportunity identification by experienced entrepreneurs. *Journal of Business Venturing*, *24*(2), 99–115. https://doi.org/10.1016/j.jbusvent.2008.01.008

Vandor, P., Franke, N. (2016). See Paris and … found a business? The impact of cross-cultural experience on opportunity recognition capabilities. *Journal of Business Venturing*, *31*(4), 388–407. https://doi.org/10.1016/j.jbusvent.2016.03.003

Venkataraman, S. (1997). The distinctive domain of entrepreneurship research. *Advances in Entrepreneurship, Firm Emergence and Growth*, *3*(1), 119–138.

West, G. P., III, & Noel, T. W. (2009). The impact of knowledge resources on new venture per-formance. *Journal of Small Business Management*, *47*(1), 1–22. https://doi.org/10.1111/j.1540-627X.2008.00259.x

Zhang, J. (2011). The advantage of experienced start-up founders in venture capital acquisition: Evidence from serial entrepreneurs. *Small Business Economics*, *36*(2), 187–208. https://doi.org/10.1007/s11187-009-9216-4

Zhang, J., Soh, P. H., & Wong, P. K. (2010). Entrepreneurial resource acquisition through indirect ties: Compensatory effects of prior knowledge. *Journal of Management*, *36*(2), 511–536. https://doi.org/10.1177/0149206308329963

Cultivating the Chinese market through destination loyalty: enhancing resilience in the Maldives

David Weaver, Chuanzhong Tang, Laura Lawton and Yang Liu

ABSTRACT

Market diversification, one critical means by which tourism-dependent small island states can maintain sector resilience and destination life cycle stability, requires understanding of the destination loyalty of strategic new inbound markets such as China. An online survey of 1260 Chinese adults with previous travel experience to the Maldives identified positive proclivities with respect to revisitation and recommendation intentions as well as agreement that Chinese visitors were well catered for. Sample diversity, however, was demonstrated by cluster analysis, which revealed dominant 'highly loyal' (31.2%) and 'loyal' (37.1%) segments along with specialized clusters ambivalent about the catering (14.3%) or the revisitation intent (17.4%). Loyalty was strongly associated with older, married and higher income visitors who were aware that the Maldives is an Islamic country and who included the capital city of Male in their itinerary. Such information is invaluable for assisting target marketing and product development strategies, but situates in a context of bilateral asymmetry in which the Chinese government can destabilize small island tourism through decisions that curtail visitation by otherwise loyal residents.

摘要：对于依赖于旅游业的小型岛屿型国家来说，市场多元化是其保证旅游弹性以及目的地生命周期稳定性的重要途径。这就要求这些小型岛屿旅游目的地深入的理解其战略性质的新入境旅游市场，比如中国，的目的地忠诚度。本研究通过网络问卷的方式，调查了1260名曾经前往马尔代夫旅游的中国成年游客，深入剖析了其对马尔代夫的积极倾向，包括重游意愿，推荐意向以及旅游需求满足程度等。通过层次聚类的方法对多元化样本进行分析后，"高度忠诚"（31.2%）以及"忠诚"（37.1%）的细分聚类占有主导地位。另外两个细分聚类，对旅游需求满足程度（14.3%）以及重游意愿（17.4%）方面呈现出特别的矛盾心态。研究发现，对马尔代夫忠诚度较高的中国游客往往年纪稍长，已婚，同时拥有较高的收入。他们知道马尔代夫是一个伊斯兰国家，并且在他们游览的行程中往往包括首都马累。这些研究结果对于开拓目标市场以及制定旅游产品开发策略异常保贵。但是，在双边不对称的背景下，中国政府亦可以通过政策性的限制，影响其居民的访问意愿，从而影响小型岛屿国家旅游业的稳定性。

Introduction

The tsunami of outbound Chinese tourists, widely touted as one of the most significant international tourism developments of the early twenty-first century, is now delivering substantial numbers of new visitors to 'pleasure periphery' island-states. For the latter, this dispersal of Chinese travellers beyond traditional East Asian destinations is a welcome development given their dependency on tourism, and parallel – but increasingly precarious in light of exogenous shocks such as the 2007 Global Financial Crisis – dependency on mature origin regions such as Europe (Song & Lin, 2010). Such market diversification, accordingly, not only sustains local economic growth but can more broadly contribute to the stability of affected small island tourism systems by curtailing sector stagnation and decline, as per the 'resilience' paradigm. These benefits, however, may be similarly precarious over the longer term in the absence of knowledge about the new inbound markets, and in particular the extent to which their visits result in positive personal dispositions toward the destination. This research therefore uses a segmentation approach from survey results to identify the prevalence and variation of destination loyalty among Chinese adults who have already visited the Maldives, a hyper-dependent high-end archipelagic destination where Chinese visitors have expanded tenfold from 3% of all inbound arrivals in 2005 (Carlsen & Hughes, 2008) to 30% in 2015 (UNWTO, 2017a). Despite this growth and the potential of inbound Chinese tourists to contribute to destination life cycle stability through the market diversification it confers, the loyalty of Chinese visitors to the Maldives as a destination has never been systematically identified or differentiated. 'Destination loyalty' herein is expressed conatively through revisit intention and proclivity to recommend the destination to others, and attitudinally through an innovative culturally-specific service quality variable. Following a literature review of the constituent knowledge domains and an outline of the methodology, factors associated with the revealed loyalty are identified, and implications both theoretical and strategic are discussed along with associated limitations of the research.

Literature review

Destination loyalty

Destination loyalty is a relatively recent derivative of the much older idea of customer loyalty, and as such remains a matter of 'intense academic debate' as to definition and appropriate measurement (Wu, 2016, p. 2214). Knowledge derived from the parent concept has limited utility in this regard due to what Su, Hsu, and Swanson (2017) describe as the unique experiential context of tourist destinations. Distinguishing factors that contribute to a highly complex subject of investigation include product heterogeneity (each destination is unique), continuous product change, the numerous sub-experiences (e.g. seeing attractions, eating, travelling, sleeping) that a destination visit entails, and internal complexity, wherein assessments of 'destination' loyalty are more likely to implicate only some of the attendant qualities and locations, and only some of the aforementioned sub-experiences. In the tourism literature, the dual intentions to revisit the place and recommend it to others are commonly regarded as the core attributes of destination loyalty (Chen & Gursoy, 2001; Chen & Tsai, 2007; Hughes, 1991; Kim & Brown, 2012; Lee, Jeon, & Kim, 2011; Oppermann, 2000; Prayag & Ryan, 2012; Sönmez & Graefe, 1998; Su, Hsu, & Swanson, 2017; Yoon & Uysal, 2005).

Such 'conative' loyalty bears directly on tourism life cycle stability, as it is widely regarded as the best predictor of future behaviour and is thus a critical parameter of competitive advantage that enables the attraction and retention of target markets (Gursoy, Chen, & Chi, 2014; Kozak, 2001; Sun, Chi, & Xu, 2013). Also, loyal customers tend to be less pervious to price variations (Krishnamurthi & Papatla, 2003) and require lower marketing costs to retain compared with attracting first-time visitors (Reichheld, Markety, & Hopton, 2000). One arena of debate, however, is the relative merit of each aspect of conative loyalty. Chen and Gursoy (2001), for example, use only recommendation proclivity, since actual or intended repeat visitation may disguise spurious and hence unstable expressions of loyalty associated with affordability, family member preference or other factors. Moreover, long-haul destination visits in particular tend to entail high monetary and time risks, and hence are infrequent experiences repeated after long time intervals and often no more than once (Bianchi & Pike, 2011). The destination in such instances does not achieve short-term or enduring market gain despite the expressed intentions. In contrast, recommendations are normally very low risk actions, often carried out soon after or even during a visit, which can have a widespread positive influence through social media dissemination (Harris & Prideaux, 2017). Potential tourists considering a particular destination can mitigate the associated purchase risks by heeding recommendations from those who are trusted because of their prior direct experience with that destination (Qu, Kim, & Im, 2011; Tussyadiah, Park, & Fesenmaier, 2011).

Beyond revisits and recommendations, additional factors are positioned variably as parameters of cognitive/affective loyalty or, at least as commonly, antecedents to conative loyalty (Weaver & Lawton, 2011). Overall visit satisfaction is the most common of these variables, with numerous empirical studies demonstrating its high correlation with intentions to revisit and recommend (Chi & Qu, 2008; Sui & Baloglu, 2003; Wu, 2016; Yoon & Uysal, 2005). Others contend for a more tenuous association (Oliver, 1999), as for example in situations where novelty-seeking is an important motivation; here the visitor can be genuinely 'satisfied' but nevertheless seeks out new destinations for future travel. Also germane is evidence that evaluations of satisfaction are culturally mediated, with members of collectivist cultures typically displaying mid-level responses and acquiescence bias to save face and avoid uncertainty (Smith, 2004). A further limitation of overall satisfaction is that it does not on its own reveal which sub-experiences had the most positive influence. The potential spuriousness of overall satisfaction indicates the complexity of this and other cognitive/affective antecedents (Su, Hsu, & Swanson, 2017), many of which have been incorporated with mixed results into the empirical research. These variables include place attachment (Gursoy, Chen, & Chi, 2014; Weaver & Lawton, 2011; Xu & Zhang, 2016; Yuksel, Yuksel, & Bilim, 2010), destination image (Chen & Phou, 2013; Chi & Qu, 2008; Zhang et al., 2014), motivation (Yoon & Uysal, 2005), destination familiarity and perceived value (Sun, Chi, & Xu, 2013), service quality (Gursoy, Chen, & Chi, 2014; Lee, Graefe, & Burns, 2007; Su, Hsu, & Swanson, 2017) and travel experiences (Gursoy, Chen, & Chi, 2014; Kim & Brown, 2012).

Chinese outbound tourism

China is by far the leading country in outbound tourists and affiliated destination revenue, with departures increasing from 10 million in 2004 to 135 million in 2016. In that year, expenditures of US$261 billion were achieved (UNWTO, 2017b). The major underlying factors of growing discretionary income and time are augmented in China by the increased psychological and social positioning of leisure travel as a life necessity and major parameter of life quality and personal well-being (Chen, Lehto, & Cai, 2013). Although domestic trips and the proximate semi-autonomous 'international' destinations of Hong Kong and Macau still account for most Chinese tourism, rapid increases in longer distance travel – albeit from a small numeric base – reflect the country's transition from what Burton (1995) describes as an industrialising phase of travel diffusion to an industrialised pattern. Approved Destination Status (ADS), a government strategy since 1983 to permit outbound package tours to so-designated countries, can be regarded as both a facilitator and consequence of growing consumer demand for longer-haul international tourism (Arita et al., 2011).

Aspirations to understand, attract and retain a share of this burgeoning market have spawned numerous segmentation studies, including contentions from a generational perspective of a youth-oriented '2nd wave' of Chinese tourists during the early 2000s (Arlt, 2013) and a subsequent '3rd wave' dominated by middle-aged elites (Bao, Jin, & Weaver, 2018). More directly germane from a destination perspective is differentiation by motivation and, explicitly or implicitly, the place attributes that fulfil the latter. Empirical research by Kim, Guo, and Agrusa (2005) identified safety, beautiful scenery, well-equipped tourism facilities, novel cultural/historical resources and good weather as the five most important destination attributes of potential Chinese outbound tourists, while a later study by Sparks and Pan (2009) revealed natural beauty, quality infrastructure, autonomy, inspirational places and social self-enhancement. A combined motivation/attribute approach yielded the three overlapping segments of entertainment and adventure seekers (i.e. fun, stimulation, seeing and doing), life-seeing experience/culture explorers (new and unique social and cultural experiences) and relaxation/knowledge seekers (rest, relaxation, inner harmony) (Li, Meng, Uysal, & Mihalik, 2013).

Several studies have endeavoured to associate these patterns with traditional Chinese and broader East Asian cultural traits (e.g. Fu, Lehto, & Cai, 2012; Mok & Defranco, 2000), as well as combinations of traditional and contemporary influences (Pearce, Wu, & Osmond, 2013). The latter perspective is reflected in the 'updated' approach of Hsu and Huang (2016), who take modern values into account to reflect the profound social, cultural and economic changes experienced by China since the introduction of the reform era in the 1980s. Important contemporary terminal (or end result) values of convenience, indulgence, leisure/relaxation, liberation, self-interest and ostentation evoke broader constructs of individualism, hedonism and materialism wherein pleasure-seeking and living in the moment are key priorities. Major instrumental values (means of achieving these results) include the modern virtues of horizon broadening and traditional ones of knowledge, education, and stability/security. While Hsu and Huang (2016) remark further that the modern values are most salient among younger Chinese, Sun and Wang (2010) contend that Chinese people born since 1955 tend to share modern values such as individualism and self-development. Beyond knowledge-seeking, traditional values are perhaps less apparent in the leisure travel area given its recency as a mass phenomenon, but includes the probable influence of communalism, conformity and maintenance of social harmony on proclivities to visit a place when friends, family members, travel agents or other reference groups say that it is a good place to visit (Hsu, Kang, & Lam, 2006; Sparks & Pan, 2009). Electronic word-of-mouth (eWOM), through social media and blogs and using personal smart phones (Kantar Media, 2017), is an increasingly important vehicle through which such recommendations are disseminated (Kasabov, 2016).

The latter tendencies indicate for destinations the positive marketing implications of Chinese tourist intentions to recommend destinations to others. However, targeted studies of Chinese destination loyalty patterns are rare (Sun, Chi, & Xu, 2013; Tse, 2015), and scant understanding of this phenomenon remains (Su, Hsu, & Swanson, 2017). Nevertheless, the few studies that have been conducted, focusing on domestic destinations (Su, Hsu, & Swanson, 2017; Sun, Chi, & Xu, 2013; Xu & Zheng, 2016), the short-haul international destination of South Korea (Chiu, Zeng, & Cheng, 2016; Lee, Jeon, & Kim, 2011) and the long-haul destination of Australia (Mao and Zhang, 2014) all indicate a correlation between satisfaction and loyalty, and varying positive antecedents to satisfaction such as place attachment, image, motivation, familiarity and perceived value. The results, all based on structural equation modelling, generally accord with the overall literature but provide no clear indications of distinctive mainland Chinese destination loyalty patterns. This is an important shortcoming in the literature given growing evidence that the massive outbound Chinese market is an increasingly diverse entity (Chow & Murphy, 2007).

Small islands

Weaver (2018, p. 118) distinguishes small warm-weather islands as the 'little giants of tourism', with the 50 small island states and dependencies that report arrival data to the UNWTO accounting for just 0.36% of global population in 2015, but 4.2% of international overnight tourist arrivals and 54.8% of excursionists arriving on cruises originating in foreign ports. For the 26 that also supply economic data, the average contribution to GDP from inbound tourism revenue was 20.8%. Although often more difficult to quantify, this insularity effect is enlarged when tourism-intensive subnational entities such as Cozumel (Mexico), Hawaii (USA), Jeju (South Korea), Okinawa (Japan), Phuket (Thailand), Hainan (China), Lakshadweep (India), Crete (Greece) and Majorca (Spain) are included. Fundamentally underlying this performance is that insularity not only offers but amplifies projections and expectations of idyllic sea, sand and sun experiences, with place names such as Bali and Tahiti evoking more strongly than mainland coastal locations imaginaries of the remote, exotic, escapist and paradisiacal (Lockhart & Drakakis-Smith, 1997; Mountz, 2015). Yet, whether those images are warranted or not, small island success in attracting leisure tourists has been widely problematized as an ambivalent consequence of a syndrome entailing otherwise severe resource constraints, apparent paucity of viable economic alternatives, enduring dependency on historical 'core' countries, and susceptibility to severe economic disruption and stagnation or decline dynamics as per the destination life cycle if those dominant markets collapse. This syndrome has been effectively captured in the enduring idea of a pan-global 'pleasure periphery' (Turner & Ash, 1975).

A more recent counter-narrative, however, contends that small islands by necessity are also arenas of innovation and resilience wherein residents routinely seize opportunities to compensate for these shortcomings (Alberts & Baldacchino, 2017; Baldacchino, 2005; Weaver, 2017). What Baldacchino (2010, p. 189) describes as 'fairly sophisticated ways to exploit the opportunities of contemporary rampant globalization' variably includes offshore finance, passport sales, migrant detention centres, issuance of superfluous stamps and coins to collectors, online gaming and pornography sites, and 'dollar diplomacy'. A constructive reinterpretation of tourism within this counter-narrative situates the small island not merely as a disadvantaged geographic or pleasure periphery but simultaneously as an *experiential core* inherently well positioned to compete in the international tourism marketplace (Weaver, 2013). Assertive efforts since the late 1990s to woo mainland Chinese tourists, accordingly, are a complementary innovation intended to enhance sector resilience through strategic market diversification. This is reflected in patterns of travel facilitation – of the 26 countries that provided visa-free access to holders of mainland Chinese passports in 2018, 14 are small island states. Of the 31 small island countries in total, another nine offer a visa upon arrival, while only eight require a visa in advance.

Even though such efforts now have a history of almost 30 years for some small island states, these entities as a collective are just beginning to experience the outbound Chinese tsunami. The South Pacific, the Caribbean's rival as the largest concentration of independent tropical small island states (e.g. Fiji and Tonga) and their dependent counterparts (e.g. French Polynesia and Cook Islands), received in 2016 just 0.14% of Chinese outbound tourists, who nevertheless accounted for a significant 7.2% of inbound arrivals in the region (Cheer et al., 2018). Small absolute visitation base levels in some destinations mean that a relatively small increase in intake from a particular market can equate to a major increase in that market's relative share, with, for example, mainland China accounting for almost one-half (47.0%) of international arrivals in the tiny state of Palau in 2016. A more modest 6.2% share was claimed by larger Fiji, but that compares with just 0.8% seven years earlier in 2009. In tandem with the dominant foreign imaginaries, the main Chinese niche segments in Fiji are honeymoon, luxury and diving (Vada-Pareti, 2015). More generally, tropical island tours were identified by a sample of Chinese outbound tour operators as an important niche market, targeting not just countries such as Fiji but dependencies such as Guam, Tahiti and Bali, and sub-national entities such as Hawaii, Phuket and Langkawi (Xu & Wang, 2014).

The only identified study of destination loyalty among Chinese visitors to islands is the aforementioned work of Sun, Chi, and Xu (2013), who found that destination image, familiarity and perceived value influenced satisfaction, which influenced loyalty. Caution, however, should be exercised in extrapolations of these outcomes to the Maldives and similar destinations, since they pertain to Hainan, a short-haul domestic Chinese destination with accordant high repeat visit proclivities and emphasis on lower-end tourist experiences in high density urban settings such as Sanya. Other island-focused studies, all applying SEM to samples of international inbound arrivals as a whole, yielded similarly conventional loyalty antecedent outcomes in Mauritius (Prayag & Ryan, 2012; Ramseook-Munhurrun, Seebaluck, & Naidoo, 2015) and Northern Cyprus (Yoon & Uysal, 2005). Little in this literature, accordingly, suggests unique insular parameters of such relationships or in particular any knowledge pertaining to Chinese visitors to small islands, tropical or otherwise.

Resilience and tourism

Resilience provides a suitable framework for investigating the cultivation of new inbound markets in small-island and other tourist destinations. As elaborated elsewhere in this special issue, 'resilience' captures the essential idea of an affected entity having sufficient capacity to survive and even thrive, through appropriate adaptations, in an environment of seemingly permanent uncertainty and constant change (Magis, 2010). According to Lew (2014), the resilience paradigm therefore differs from the sustainability paradigm in its emphasis on adaptability over mitigation or prevention. Holling (2001), in contrast, regards the two paradigms as complementary. Though more through compelling and enduring macro-level push and pull factors than any concerted multilateral strategy or policy, contemporary global tourism has demonstrated remarkable long-term resilience, recording just relatively minor and temporary declines in overall international stayover numbers since 1950 as a result of major political (e.g. 9/11) or economic (GFC) crises (Weaver & Lawton, 2014). However, as the scale of inquiry reduces to individual destinations, significant and longer-term fluctuations resulting from these or local circumstances are more apparent along with more pronounced volatility in localized destination life cycles, and the issue of resilience subsequently becomes more compelling.

Holling's (2001) idea of panarchy, or combined set of hierarchies and adaptive cycles, provides a heuristic for analysing resilience at this scale. Hierarchy from above ('remembering') implicates long-held policy by small island authorities to prioritize leisure tourism development, therefore facilitating continuity and stability over a slower, larger time cycle. Concurrently, hierarchical impulse from below ('revolt') accounts for the strategic cultivation of new markets such as China as per positively disruptive learning and innovation during an embedded faster and smaller cycle. This occurs when small islands or other destinations are situated in the accumulation phase of the adaptive cycle, that is, when the serious risk factor of 'accumulated' over-dependency on mature markets necessitates restructuring to avoid system collapse. In the context of Butler, (1980), this starts to become a risk in the post-late development stage as critical carrying capacities are approached and more negative market reactions emerge. Factors that determine whether the restructuring will be successful and give rise to a renewal phase include wealth, which is having sufficient resources (i.e. sea, sand sun, marketing budgets, etc. to attract the new markets) and internal controllability (i.e. stakeholders within the destination having the capacity to control its own destiny), as well as adaptive capacity to leverage these advantages to successfully attract those markets. Destination loyalty locates within the panarchy framework as a critical indirect indicator of the extent to which this adaptive capacity is salient, as it captures collective intentions to revisit and recommend that propel continuing patronage from the new inbound market country.

The Maldives

A 298 km^2 Indian Ocean archipelagic state of 1192 coralline islands, the Maldives epitomizes the idyllic sea, sand and sun destination. Traditionally reliant on fishing, trade and overseas labour, tourism development began in the early 1970s and expanded rapidly to 42,000 in 1980, 600,000 in 2004 (Carlsen & Hughes, 2008), 1.2 million by 2014 almost 1.5 million in 2018, or approximately three arrivals for every resident. Yearly arrivals to 2014 as depicted in Figure 1 indicate the 'development' stage of the tourism area life cycle (Butler, 1980), notwithstanding temporary depressive effects from the Indian Ocean tsunami (2004) and the global financial crisis (2009).

The conservative Muslim population resides on just 188 of the constituent islands, and is insulated from the direct effects of tourism by a longstanding policy of confining most leisure visitors to luxury resorts on uninhabited islands (on a one resort per island basis) where contact with residents is restricted to resort employees. Leases for 99 years are available to foreign or domestic developers from the government, which retains ownership over all islands. This can be seen as another innovation 'from below' to prevent the accumulation of negative socio-cultural impacts that can induce stagnation in the destination life cycle. Of 32,000 beds in 2015, 75% were provided by remote island facilities, 109 of which were occupied by resorts and another 112 under development as of 2015, leaving over 800 available for future development (Shakeela & Weaver, 2016). The remaining inventory consists of hotels and guesthouses in the capital of Male and other inhabited islands, which serve to disperse the direct economic benefits of the sector to local communities as per further short cycle innovation.

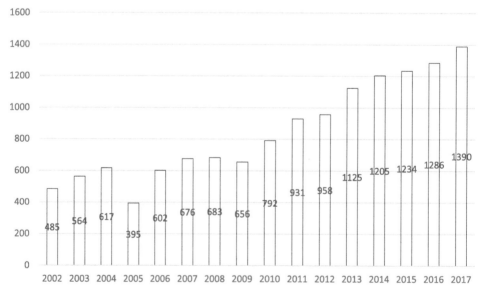

Figure 1. The Maldives: international arrivals 2002–2017. Source: Ministry of Tourism (2007–2018).

Following these parallel resort and 'alternative' paths (Shakeela & Weaver, 2016), tourism now makes a 27% direct contribution to GDP and a 70% total impact (i.e. direct, indirect and induced) (WTTC), indicating status as a 'hyper-destination' and suggesting that engagement with tourism resilience is tantamount in the foreseeable future to engaging with the overall economic resilience of the archipelago. Regardless of this dependency, local residents, even in remote and more conservative communities, appear supportive of tourism though with attendant reservations over the potential exposure of residents to alcohol and 'inappropriate' clothing. Environmental problems such as the destruction of coral reefs to construct 'overwater' accommodation units, and restrictions to traditional fishing grounds due to the establishment of exclusive-use water zones around resort enclaves are also evident. In part this support relates to appreciation for the lack of economic alternatives, but also to social exchange initiatives that shield residents from the perceived 'evils' of hedonistic tourism and thereby demonstrate informal modes of cultural and social resilience (Shakeela & Weaver, 2012, 2016, 2018). This equation of support, however, may erode if continued development exacerbates these noted social and environmental issues through a lack of their prioritization in attendant tourism planning.

This apparent bottom-up resilience is paralleled by compelling evidence of top-down sector resilience. The policy of strategically opening new uninhabited islands for luxury resort and approving households for guesthouse development, for example, reflects a concerted and to date successful attempt by government to facilitate economic resilience by avoiding under- or over-capacity in the crucial accommodation sector. Regarding responsiveness to crisis situations, international arrivals in the wake of the locally destructive 2004 Indian Ocean tsunami recovered to 70% of pre-disaster levels within just three months as a result of proactive strategies from government and industry (Carlsen & Hughes, 2008). Beyond strategic accommodation policy and effective responses to unexpected natural disasters, sector resilience is also evident in longstanding strategic attempts led by the Ministry of Tourism to attract outbound Chinese tourists in large part as a response to stagnation in traditional European markets such as the UK and Italy (Figure 2). In 2003, the Maldives became the second small island state after Malta to obtain ADS (Arita et al., 2011), and arrivals increased accordingly from 7000 in 2001 to 20,000 in 2004 (Carlsen & Hughes, 2008). Notably, the 119,000 Chinese arrivals in 2010 represented a doubling of the previous year, which substantially mitigated the otherwise negative market effect of the Global Financial Crisis (Kumar, 2012). China has held the status as the Maldives' most important country of visitor origin since 2009 (Shakeela & Weaver, 2016) and now consistently provides over 360,000 visitors per year, although numbers have decreased somewhat since 2014 (Figure 2). Based on core products such as snorkeling/scuba diving, honeymoons and family holidays the Maldives is solidly positioned among Chinese outbound leisure travellers, especially from the more prosperous coastal provinces, as a highly attractive and aspirational destination (Kozak, Kim, & Chon, 2017), including for independent travellers and young singles and families (Xiang, 2013).

Such penetration is but one aspect of the close cooperation that has been cultivated between China and the Maldives since the early 1980s, which for the latter has

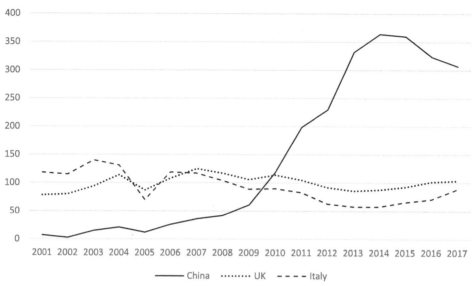

Figure 2. Maldives arrivals by selected country, 2002–2017. Source: Ministry of Tourism (2007–2018).

been motivated not only for reasons of market diversification but also from a desire, based on parallel adaptive cycles, to balance the geopolitical influence of neighbouring India (Fernando, 2010). Reciprocally, Kumar (2012) regards the countertrending 2010 intake as a deliberate exercise in 'economic diplomacy' by China to attract gratitude and further deepen the bilateral relationship in the interests of its own geostrategic objectives. As of early 2019, the status of the Maldives as impressively 'China-ready' was evidenced by direct flights from the major Chinese cities of Beijing, Guangzhou, Kunming, Shanghai and Chengdu as offered by Beijing Capital Airlines, China Southern Airlines, China Eastern Airlines and Sichuan Airlines (author search of air ticket search engine). Other evidence includes China Union Pay's availability at 95% of the country's ATMs, and negotiations underway with several Chinese companies to lease islands for enclave resort development (Kumar, 2016) that could specialize in the Chinese market. Many existing resorts offer full service in Chinese as well as Chinese food, though similar provision in Male or other inhabited islands remained limited as of 2019. Such high-level tourism-related machinations, however, are only relevant if consumers want to visit or recommend the target destination, and it is in this context that the destination loyalty of Chinese visitors to the Maldives is a strategically important subject of investigation, though one that has received scant attention, and apparently none at all from a segmentation perspective.

Methodology

This research identifies the destination loyalty of Chinese adults who have already visited the Maldives. The focus on the Maldives is merited because of the archipelago's hyper-dependency on tourism, the rapid emergence of China as its most important inbound tourist market and the absence of knowledge about this critical market's loyalty parameters. As the number of qualifying individuals (based on cumulative arrival statistics from that destination) is far below 1% of the Chinese population, a survey to a random sample of consumers would not efficiently yield the critical mass suitable for statistical analysis. Instead, a well-established (since 2005) and highly reputable China-based online marketing company was commissioned to provide 100 and 1200 valid returns (pilot and main survey respectively) from its database or 'panel' of 2.6 million adult Chinese consumers. This confines the outreach to the target country and yields diversity of response with regard to participants, year and season of visit. Biased responses, by comparison, can result from specific events or weather conditions, and from the presence of over- or under-represented segments (e.g. more family groups), that might occur during a time-constrained exit survey (e.g. during school holidays). Procedurally, the company emailed a solicitation to everyone in the database on 24 January 2018, providing an online questionnaire link for the convenience of those qualified and inclined to participate. Completed e-surveys were then submitted and accepted after screening for validity, in return for a small payment from the company, until the requested quota was reached. The request for 1200 responses was based on the desire to obtain a sample large enough to better represent the target population, achieve a robust case-to-item ratio and derive the greatest possible substantive segmentation diversity.

The two core behavioural loyalty items of repeat visit intention ('I will go to the Maldives again in the future') and recommendation intention ('I will recommend the Maldives as an attractive destination to other Chinese people') (Chen & Gursoy, 2001; Chen & Tsai, 2007; Hughes, 1991; Kim & Brown, 2012; Lee, Jeon, & Kim, 2011; Oppermann, 2000; Prayag & Ryan, 2012; Sönmez & Graefe, 1998; Su, Hsu, & Swanson, 2017; Yoon & Uysal, 2005) were used for clustering along with one attitudinal loyalty item. Parsimony with the latter was exercised since attitudes tend to be antecedal and complex. Overall visit satisfaction, though relatively simple, was initially considered despite potential cultural bias but rejected after the pilot study revealed strongly consistent high satisfaction, rendering this item unsuitable for sample differentiation. In contrast, the statement 'I believe that the Maldives caters to the needs of Chinese tourists very well', fulfillment of preferences being a dimension of satisfaction not found in the previous destination loyalty literature, avoids an explicit value judgement and perhaps for that reason did attract sufficient response diversity. Its subsequent inclusion in the clustering exercise was based also on its status as a service quality assessment that is culturally specific, extrapolated by each respondent to the target nationality, and amenable to management action based on details requested in the subsequent open-ended question, the content of which was content analysed using standard coding procedures to identify prominent themes. Because repeat travel to long-haul destinations is characterized by infrequency and long intervals between trips as well as greater uncertainty as to these time frames (Bianchi & Pike, 2011), no time stipulation was included in the revisitation item. All three statements were assessed on Likert-type scales ranging from 1 ('strongly disagree') to 5 ('strong agree').

Diversity of human behaviour, including participation in tourism, necessitates consumer segmentation as a foundational practice in marketing research, the intention being to obtain an optimal compromise between population generalization and customization (Li et al., 2013). Given the exploratory nature of the research, hierarchical cluster analysis using Ward's method with squared Euclidean distance was used to segment the sample on the basis of the above three loyalty items, since this is appropriate when there is no prior knowledge of the 'correct' cluster number. Also, this method maximizes the similarities and differences within and between the clusters respectively (Fredline, 2012; Hennig et al., 2015). Statistical tests such as comparison-of-means or chi-squared were then used as warranted to identify significant differences between the cluster based on relevant independent variables. The questionnaire itself, incorporating minor refinements from the pilot study, was composed in English, translated into Chinese, and then back-translated into English by author team members fluent in both languages to maximize cross-lingual fidelity.

Limitations

Limitations that qualify the reliability and validity of the findings include the assignment of equal weight to the three clustering variables, even though it is likely that they contribute unequally in importance to the broader 'loyalty' construct. Revisitation and recommendation intentions, moreover, are just that and do not necessarily presage future behaviour, while the sample may not represent Chinese visiting adults to Maldives as a whole, but just those motivated to join a marketing panel. Another issue is the potential role of 'face' in generating positive assessments of negative experiences so it does not appear as if the respondent made a bad destination choice (Kwek & Lee, 2015). Finally, while not a limitation as such, it may be that the potential Chinese visitor market to the Maldives and similar destinations is massive enough to render recommendations and repeat visits as unnecessary to ensure a robust ongoing intake.

Results

After almost four weeks of solicitation (18 February 2018), 1260 valid surveys were returned. The 60 extra responses were received after the company notified the authors that the budgeted amount allowed for additional responses. Overall findings of a high package component (70.0%), small group composition (44.5% and 23.0% in a group of two or three, respectively; 2.8% solo), residency in a coastal province (74.1%), recent visitation (12.4% before 2013; 71.0% in 2015 or more recently) and youthful age structure (92.0% younger than 40) indicate the sample to represent the target population, although only the latter variable was subsequently significant in differentiating the clusters. Gender (56.8% female) and province of residence were also insignificant at the 95% confidence level. All positive overall were the three clustering items of recommendation intention (4.22), revisit intention (4.04) and agreement that Chinese visitors were well catered for (3.92) (Table 1). Revisitation and recommendation, according to the open-ended comments, were based mainly on the quality of the marine environment, peace and tranquility, and effective catering to Chinese market needs and preferences.

A four-cluster solution was accepted based on cluster size, level of differentiation and interpretive logic. *Highly loyal* visitors (31.2%) score strongly on all three

Table 1. Cluster outcomes and differentiation by significant variables.

Variable	Overall (n = 1260)	1. Highly loyal n = 393 (31.2%)	2. Loyal n = 468 (37.1%)	3. Cater-ambivalent n = 180 (14.3%)	4. Revisit-ambivalent n = 219 (17.4%)
Cluster items[a]					
Caters to Chinese	3.92	**4.48**	4.01	<u>2.83</u>	3.64
Revisitation	4.04	**4.88**	3.97	<u>3.69</u>	2.95
Recommendation	4.22	**4.70**	4.19	4.08	<u>3.53</u>
Age ($\chi^2 = 48.9$, $p < 0.006$)					
% 18–25	18.4	14.5	17.9	20.6	24.7
% 26–30	33.6	35.6	33.5	33.9	29.7
% 31–35	27.5	29.8	26.7	26.1	26.0
% 36–40	12.5	13.5	13.9	10.6	9.6
% >40	8.0	6.7	7.9	9.0	10.1
Monthly household income ($\chi^2 = 52.3$, $p < 0.001$)					
% <10,000 RMB	10.0	6.9	9.0	13.9	14.6
% 10,001–14,999 RMB	22.3	18.8	22.0	24.4	27.4
% 15,000–19,999 RMB	25.3	22.9	25.2	28.9	26.9
% 20,000–24,999 RMB	17.2	18.6	19.9	11.7	13.7
% 25,000–29,999 RMB	9.9	10.7	11.3	9.4	5.9
% 30,000–34,999 RMB	5.2	7.9	5.1	2.2	2.7
% 35,000+ RMB	10.1	14.2	7.5	9.4	8.7
Marital status ($\chi^2 = 36.0$, $p < 0.001$)					
% single	25.8	18.1	26.9	32.2	32.0
% married	68.9	77.9	69.2	60.0	59.4
Children in household ($\chi^2 = 36.8$, $p < 0.001$)					
None	39.4	32.6	37.8	47.2	48.4
1	46.2	52.9	48.9	36.1	36.5
2	10.2	11.5	9.8	10.6	8.7
Employment status ($\chi^2 = 26.5$, $p < 0.009$)					
% full-time	88.3	91.1	88.9	89.4	80.8
% student	5.9	4.6	4.5	7.2	10.0
Awareness that Maldives is Muslim ($\chi^2 = 39.9$, $p < 0.001$)					
Yes	69.4	79.6	69.2	55.6	63.0
Travel to capital of Male ($\chi^2 = 14.5$, $p < 0.002$)					
Yes	52.5	60.3	49.8	47.2	48.4

aBolded and underlined means, respectively, are significantly higher and lower than other clusters at $p < .001$.

dimensions, and significantly more so than the other clusters, while *loyal* visitors (37.1%) – the normative segment – display moderately positive scores. Representative open-ended responses from members of these clusters indicated the Maldives' success in catering to the needs of Chinese visitors with regard to accommodation quality, transport, local hospitality, local and Chinese food, service quality, access to China, communication and scenery: 'the tourist facilities were adequate and the local people showed strong hospitality to Chinese tourists', 'the accommodation and transportation were very convenient in Maldives and there were a lot of delicious local snacks', 'the hotel provided high quality of service to Chinese tourists and we could enjoy a very relaxed vocation in Maldives', 'the Maldives are not far away from China and can be reached very easily', 'there were many Chinese staff in the hotel and I did not suffer any communication barriers', 'I could at least have some Chinese food in Maldives, which catered my needs well' and 'the scenery in Maldives is so beautiful, I don't need any extra service'.

Otherwise weakly positive *responsive-ambivalent* visitors (14.3%) are not sure if Chinese visitors are well catered for, while *revisit-ambivalent* visitors (17.4%) only weakly support the catering and recommendation statements while being unsure about their revisit intentions. Negative comments from these clusters were far more infrequent and isolated, but tended to implicate service deficiencies and incompatible price points: 'the service provided to Chinese tourists was not perfect', 'the price level in Maldives was unacceptable for Chinese tourists', 'the food did not cater the taste of Chinese tourists', 'there was no warm drinking water and no kettle in the hotel room', 'the credit card was not widely accepted and I did not have enough cash to enjoy more leisure activities' and 'there were no shopping areas and the leisure and recreation activities were limited'. Younger visitors were more likely to be ambivalent, as were lower-income respondents, singles, those without children, students, those less aware that the Maldives is a Muslim country, and those who did not include the capital city of Male in their itinerary.

Discussion

In tandem with the broader literature, studies of Chinese loyalty to tourist destinations, including small warm weather islands (Sun, Chi, & Xu, 2013), conventionally employ SEM to demonstrate correlations between overall satisfaction and behavioural loyalty as well as between a variety of other antecedents and satisfaction. Using the Maldives as a small island-state focus, this study uses cluster analysis to build on such results by dividing this population into distinct segments, since tourist behaviour and attitudes are not uniform. Overall outcomes indicate that the Maldives have been effective in spawning a visitor loyalty effect in which those who have experienced the destination are willing to recommend it to others and to revisit, and agree that Chinese visitors are well catered for; expectations of an idyllic tropical island destination, accordingly, are largely met, while theoretical expectations of positive inter-variable correlation also seem likely. That recommendation intent is higher than revisit intent is unsurprising, since the former entails low risk and many Chinese consumers regard this kind of destination as an aspirational and reliably satisfying luxury experience and/or most suitable for a 'one-off' rite of passage such as a honeymoon. Just slightly less positive assessments of culturally-specific catering satisfaction denote the Maldives moreover as largely successful in delivering idyllic experiences 'with Chinese characteristics'.

The segmentation exercise, however, more insightfully engages the market resilience implications. Indicated is a loyalty spectrum anchored on one pole by a relatively small group of ambivalent and probable one-visit visitors constrained respectively by income and/or life event fulfilment (e.g. honeymoon). Lack of pre-trip information or induction may also have created unrealistic expectations for this minority of surveyed visitors about the availability of Chinese food, credit card services and shopping opportunities in some resorts and on inhabited islands. Occupying the other pole and constituting a much larger cohort are somewhat older and wealthier ('high value') visitors who, tellingly, tend to be more knowledgeable about the Maldives based on awareness of its Muslim identity and inclusion of the non-resort capital city of Male in their itinerary. It is widely assumed that the tropical small island destination experience is epitomized by the remote 'unspoiled' island, and this is indeed provided by the enclave resorts; however, the vernacular cultural landscape of the inhabited islands, with its associated imperfections and risks, seems to serve as a complementary component that creates a richer experience and enhanced loyalty outcome. This result may reflect broader findings, evident for example in cruising (Jones, 2011), that identify both relaxation and stimulation as important (though not necessarily concurrent) motivations within the same leisure visit, the former being satisfied more by exposure to culture, and the latter more by exposure to nature. Small islands such as the Maldives, therefore, need to provide isolation as well as cultural and social exposure to meet both motivations. Reciprocal education and awareness programs, however, are also recommended to ensure that residents and Chinese visitors both find such interactions to be satisfying, since even one well-publicized negative incident such as a terrorist attack or less extreme anti-tourist incident can significantly affect market sentiments and intentions, at least in the short term (Shakeela & Weaver, 2012). Especially given recent stabilization in Chinese inbound numbers, the expansion of Chinese language, culture and food provision in Male and other inhabited islands is also warranted.

Whether or not the Maldives and other small tropical island-states can therefore enhance their resilience and avoid life cycle stagnation or decline through market diversification and the establishment of enduring loyalty among strategic new markets, several peculiarities of the resultant bilateral relationships give pause as to what can be realistically attained. Small island-states have shown initiative and innovation in cultivating the new Chinese market, but such efforts are not risk-free given the Chinese government's tendencies to harness outbound tourism as a form of diplomacy (Tse, 2013). While clearly benefiting the small island economy, China itself also benefits not just through the satisfaction of new consumer demands and enhanced quality of life, but from successfully projecting its soft power into geopolitically strategic regions (Lanteigne, 2012). Strong bilateral relations with small islands, attained at minimal cost, can therefore help to secure vital trade routes (with for example 30% of China's international sea trade moving through the Indian Ocean close to the Maldives (Khurana, 2008)), gain preferential access to fishing and other resources within disproportionately large Exclusive Economic Zones, and win diplomatic support in international forums such as the United Nations. In the case of the Maldives, continuing integration into China's sphere of influence is evidenced by the formalization of a free trade agreement in 2017 and a concurrent memorandum of understanding to bring the Maldives into the Maritime Silk Road (MSR) component of China's Belt and Road initiative. According to CIIS (2016), Maldives as of 2016 was already considered part of the MSR, which proclaimed the ambition of achieving full connectivity with China through Chinese investment in local infrastructure.

Growing dependence on China, moving beyond opportunistic flirtations intended in some cases to reignite broader Western interest in former small island colonies (Henderson & Reilly, 2003), can be costly however if perceived circumstances compel China to exert 'harder' power projections. This was demonstrated in 2018 when the Chinese government 'punished' Palau for continuing to recognize Taiwan by withdrawing permission for its nationals (almost one-half of the total intake) to visit there, causing a major crisis for the local tourism industry at minimal concurrent cost to China. Assumptions about freedom of movement that underpin conventional understandings of destination loyalty and its benefits must therefore be qualified when China is implicated as a major country of visitor origin. In a panarchical context, this equates with unstable internal controllability, one of the three critical factors for attaining and maintaining resilience (Holling, 2001). As stated succinctly by Han and Cheer (2018, p. 166), 'Chinese outbound tourism is partly influenced by market forces, [but] it is still ultimately under the control of the state and this maintains a situation where outbound visitation can be somewhat unpredictable and prone to wider bilateral political contexts'. Accordingly, new bottom-up short-term cycle dynamics may be merited to cultivate yet newer markets, ensuring that the Chinese share of inbound tourism does not reach a critical mass capable of inducing an economic crisis should China choose to exercise a Palau-like hard power decision.

A strong candidate for such strategic cultivation is India, with its spatial proximity, traditionally strong bilateral cooperation, large market and robust outbound tourism growth which in the context of Burton's (1995) model situates the country in a similar stage as China in the early 2000s. In 2017, India with 61,931 arrivals was the fifth largest origin country (Ministry of Tourism, 2018). From an Indian perspective, the desire to prevent an even deeper entrenchment of Chinese interests in the Maldives may incentivize its cooperation in such cultivation. For the Maldives, a strategy of maintaining a robust flow of Chinese visitors, but not being reliant upon this market, would be consistent with its prior pattern of actions to maintain its resilience. A final discussion point concerns the relevance of these findings and speculations to similar tourism-intensive but subnational island entities such as Hawaii and Okinawa. There is good reason to suppose that the loyalty findings derived from independent island-states such as the Maldives would pertain similarly, but supply-side dynamics indicate structural constraints that inhibit locally derived options for resilience innovation. Specifically, local authorities do not have 'gateway' powers to decide who can and cannot visit, they have limited authority to negotiate tourism-related initiatives with other countries, and uncontrolled flows of domestic tourists can compensate for disruptions in foreign traffic.

Conclusion

Investigations of destination loyalty in bilateral contexts involving large countries of visitor origin and small island states, or the 'mighty and the micro' (Henderson & Reilly, 2003, p. 94), are inherently asymmetrical, so that the potential decisions of governments representing the former to restrict the access of its citizens to the latter can almost instantly appear to obliterate years of effort to cultivate collective destination loyalty among those consumers, while concurrently inducing sudden and serious disruption to the destination life cycle and local economy. Yet, that effort could still be rewarded if the loyalty remains dormant and is manifested once again in revisitations and recommendations if and when such government decisions are rescinded. The investigation of consumer intentions in the context of such scenarios would be an innovative topic for follow-up research. This focused research provides a foundation for future investigations into the Chinese tourist engagement with the Maldives, as for example through expanded participant characteristics such as travel frequency and psychographic profile, the role of key opinion leaders (KOLs) in stimulating consumer interest in the archipelago, and pre-trip booking and on-site activity patterns including the use of social media. For the two conative variables, future research can investigate the speculative time frames for intended revisitation, and the means (e.g. WOM or eWOM) and timing (e.g. during or after trip) for recommending the Maldives to other Chinese.

Disclosure statement

No potential conflict of interest was reported by the authors.

References

Alberts, A., & Baldacchino, G. (2017). Resilience and tourism in islands: Insight from the Caribbean. In R. Butler (Ed.), *Tourism and resilience* (pp. 150–162). Wallingford, UK: CABI.

Arita, S., Edmonds, C., La Croix, S., & Mak, J. (2011). Impact of approved destination status on Chinese travel abroad: An econometric analysis. *Tourism Economics, 17*(5), 983–996. doi: 10.5367/te.2011.0076

Arlt, W. (2013). The second wave of Chinese outbound tourism. *Tourism Planning & Development, 10*, 126–133. doi:10.1080/21568316.2013.800350

Baldacchino, G. (2005). Islands – Objects of representation. *Geografiska Annaler, 87B*, 247–251. doi:10.1111/j.0435-3684.2005.00196.x

Baldacchino, G. (2010). 'Upside down decolonization' in subnational island jurisdictions: Questioning the 'post' in postcolonialism. *Space and Culture, 13*(2), 188–202. doi:10.1177/1206331209360865

Bao, J., Jin, X., & Weaver, D. (2018). Profiling the elite middle-age Chinese outbound travellers: A 3rd wave? *Current Issues in Tourism*, doi:10.1080/13683500.2018.1449817

Bianchi, C., & Pike, S. (2011). Antecedents of destination brand loyalty for a long-haul market: Australia's destination loyalty among Chilean travellers. *Journal of Travel & Tourism Marketing, 28*, 736–750. doi:10.1080/10548408.2011.611742

Burton, R. (1995). *Travel geography* (2nd ed.). London: Longman.

Butler, R. W. (1980). The concept of a tourist area cycle of evolution: Implications for management of resources. *Canadian Geographer, 24*(1), 5–12. doi:10.1111/j.1541-0064.1980.tb00970.x

Carlsen, J., & Hughes, M. (2008). Tourism market recovery in the Maldives after the 2004 Indian Ocean tsunami. *Journal of Travel & Tourism Marketing, 23*, 139–149. doi:10.1300/J073v23n02_11

Cheer, J., Pratt, S., Tolkach, D., Bailey, A., & Movono, A. (2018). Tourism in Pacific island countries: A status quo round-up. *Asia and the Pacific Policy Studies*, 1–20. doi:10.1002/app5.250

Chen, C., & Phou, S. (2013). A closer look at destination: Image, personality, relationship and loyalty. *Tourism Management, 36*, 269–278. doi:10.1016/j.tourman.2012.11.015

Chen, C., & Tsai, D. (2007). How do destination image and evaluative factors affect behavioural intentions? *Tourism Management, 28*(4), 1115–1122. doi:10.1016/j.tourman.2006.07.007

Chen, J., & Gursoy, D. (2001). An investigation of tourists' destination loyalty and preferences. *International Journal of Contemporary Hospitality Management, 13*(2), 79–85. doi:10.1108/09596110110381870

Chen, Y., Lehto, X., & Cai, L. (2013). Vacation and well-being: A study of Chinese tourists. *Annals of Tourism Research, 42*, 284–310. doi:10.1016/j.annals.2013.02.003

Chi, C., & Qu, H. (2008). Examining the structural relationships of destination image, tourist satisfaction and destination loyalty: An integrated approach. *Tourism Management, 29*(4), 624–636. doi:10.1016/j.tourman.2007.06.007

Chiu, W., Zeng, S., & Cheng, P. (2016). The influence of destination image and tourist satisfaction on tourist loyalty: A case study of Chinese tourists in Korea. *International Journal of Culture, Tourism and Hospitality Research, 10*(2), 223–234. doi:10.1108/IJCTHR-07-2015-0080

Chow, I., & Murphy, P. (2007). Travel activity preferences of Chinese outbound tourists for overseas destinations. *Journal of Hospitality & Leisure Marketing, 16*, 61–80. doi:10.1080/10507050802096885

CIIS (China Institute of International Studies). (2016). The Belt and Road initiative and its impact on Asia-Europe connectivity. Retrieved from http://www.ciis.org.cn/english/2016-07/21/content_8911184.htm

Fernando, S. (2010). China's relations with Sri Lanka and the Maldives: Models of good relations among big and small countries. *China Report, 46*(3), 285–297. doi:10.1177/000944551104600309

Fredline, E. (2012). Cluster analysis. In L. Dwyer, A. Gill and N. Seetaram (Eds.), *Handbook of research methods in tourism: Quantitative and qualitative approaches* (pp. 212–226). Cheltenham, UK: Edward Elgar.

Fu, X., Lehto, X., & Cai, L. (2012). Culture-based interpretation of vacation consumption. *Journal of China Tourism Research, 8*(3), 320–333. doi:10.1080/19388160.2012.704250

Gursoy, D., Chen, J., & Chi, C. (2014). Theoretical examination of destination loyalty formation. *International Journal of Contemporary Hospitality Management, 26*(5), 809–827. doi:10.1108/IJCHM-12-2013-0539

Han, X., & Cheer, J. (2018). Chinese tourist mobilities and destination resilience: Regional tourism perspectives. *Asian Journal of Tourism Research, 3*, 159–187.

Harris, A., & Prideaux, B. (2017). The potential for eWOM to affect consumer behaviour in tourism. In S. Dixit (Ed.), *Routledge handbook of consumer behavior for hospitality and tourism* (pp. 366–376). London: Routledge.

Henderson, J., & Reilly, B. (2003). Dragon in paradise: China's rising star in Oceania. *The National Interest, 72*, 94–105.

Hennig, C., Meila, F., Murtagh, F., & Rocci, R. (Eds.). (2015). *Handbook of cluster analysis.* Boca Raton: Chapman and Hall.

Holling, C. (2001). Understanding the complexity of economic, ecological, and social systems. *Ecosystems, 4*(5), 390–405. doi:10.1007/s10021-001-0101-5

Hsu, C., & Huang, S. (2016). Reconfiguring Chinese cultural values and their tourism implications. *Tourism Management, 54*, 230–242. doi:10.1016/j.tourman.2015.11.011

Hsu, C., Kang, S., & Lam, T. (2006). Reference group influences among Chinese travellers. *Journal of Travel Research, 44*(4), 474–485. doi:10.1177/0047287505282951

Hughes, K. (1991). Tourist satisfaction: A guided cultural tour in north Queensland. *Australian Psychologist, 26*(3), 166–171. doi:10.1080/00050069108257243

Jones, R. (2011). Motivations to cruise: An itinerary and cruise experience study. *Journal of Hospitality and Tourism Management, 18*(1), 30–40. doi:10.1375/jhtm.18.1.30

Kantar Media. (2017). China social media impact 2017. Retrieved from http://www.sohu.com/a/155100212_644778

Kasabov, E. (2016). Unknown, surprising, and economically significant: The realities of electronic word of mouth in Chinese social networking sites. *Journal of Business Research, 69*(2), 642–652. doi:10.1016/j.jbusres.2015.08.036

Khurana, G. (2008). China's 'string of pearls' in the Indian Ocean and its security implications. *Strategic Analysis, 32*(1), 1–39. doi:10.1080/09700160801886314

Kim, A., & Brown, G. (2012). Understanding the relationships between perceived travel experiences, overall satisfaction, and destination loyalty. *Anatolia, 23*(3), 328–347. doi:10.1080/13032917.2012.696272

Kim, S., Guo, Y., & Agrusa, J. (2005). Preference and positioning analyses of overseas destinations by Mainland Chinese outbound pleasure tourists. *Journal of Travel Research, 44*(2), 212–220. doi:10.1177/0047287505278979

Kozak, M. (2001). Repeaters' behavior at two distinct destinations. *Annals of Tourism Research, 28*(3), 784–807. doi:10.1016/S0160-7383(00)00078-5

Kozak, M., Kim, S., & Chon, K. (2017). Competitiveness of overseas pleasure destinations: A comparison study based on choice sets. *International Journal of Tourism Research*, *19*(5), 569–583. doi:10.1002/jtr.2130

Krishnamurthi, L., & Papatla, P. (2003). Accounting for heterogeneity and dynamics in the loyalty-price sensitivity relationship. *Journal of Retailing*, *79*(2), 121–135. doi:10.1016/S0022-4359(03)00010-1

Kumar, A. (2012). Chinese engagement with the Maldives: Impact on security environment in the Indian Ocean region. *Strategic Analysis*, *36*(2), 276–289. doi:10.1080/09700161.2012.646504

Kumar, S. (2016). China's footprints in Maldives: Concern for India? *Artha Journal of Social Science*, *15*(4), 15–29.

Kwek, A., & Lee, Y.-S. (2015). How "face" matters: Chinese corporate tourists in Australia. *Journal of Travel and Tourism Marketing*, *32*(1–2), 120–140. doi:10.1080/10548408.2014.986016

Lanteigne, M. (2012). Water dragon? China, power shifts and soft balancing in the South Pacific. *Political Science*, *64*(1), 21–38. doi:10.1177/0032318712447732

Lee, J., Graefe, A., & Burns, R. (2007). Examining the antecedents of destination loyalty in a forest setting. *Leisure Sciences*, *29*(5), 463–481. doi:10.1080/01490400701544634

Lee, S., Jeon, S., & Kim, D. (2011). The impact of tour quality and tourist satisfaction on tourist loyalty: The case of Chinese tourists in Korea. *Tourism Management*, *32*(5), 1115–1124. doi:10.1016/j.tourman.2010.09.016

Lew, A. (2014). Scale, change and resilience in community tourism planning. *Tourism Geographies*, *16*(1), 14–22. doi:10.1080/14616688.2013.864325

Li, X., Meng, F., Uysal, M., & Mihalik, B. (2013). Understanding China's long-haul outbound travel market: An overlapped segmentation approach. *Journal of Business Research*, *66*(6), 786–793. doi:10.1016/j.jbusres.2011.09.019

Lockhart, D., & Drakakis-Smith, D. (Eds.). (1997). *Island tourism: Trends and prospects*. London: Pinter.

Magis, K. (2010). Community resilience: An indicator of social sustainability. *Society and Natural Resources*, *23*(5), 401–416. doi:10.1080/08941920903305674

Mao, Y. I. M., & Zhang, H. Q. (2014). Structural relationships among destination preference, satisfaction and loyalty in Chinese tourists to Australia. *International Journal of Tourism Research*, *16*(2), 201–208.

Ministry of Tourism. (2007–2018). Tourism yearbooks. Retrieved from https://www.tourism.gov.mv/

Mok, C., & Defranco, A. (2000). Chinese cultural values: Their implications for travel and tourism marketing. *Journal of Travel & Tourism Marketing*, *8*(2), 99–114. doi:10.1300/J073v08n02_07

Mountz, A. (2015). Political geography II: Islands and archipelagos. *Progress in Human Geography*, *39*(5), 636–646. doi:10.1177/0309132514560958

Oliver, R. (1999). Whence consumer loyalty? *Journal of Marketing*, *63*(4_suppl1), 33–44. doi:10.2307/1252099

Oppermann, M. (2000). Tourism destination loyalty. *Journal of Travel Research*, *39*(1), 78–84. doi:10.1177/004728750003900110

Pearce, P., Wu, M., & Osmond, A. (2013). Puzzles in understanding Chinese tourist behaviour: Towards a triple-C gaze. *Tourism Recreation Research*, *38*(2), 145–157. doi:10.1080/02508281.2013.11081741

Prayag, G., & Ryan, C. (2012). Antecedents of tourists' loyalty to Mauritius: The role and influence of destination image, place attachment, personal involvement, and satisfaction. *Journal of Travel Research*, *51*(3), 342–356. doi:10.1177/0047287511410321

Qu, H., Kim, L., & Im, H. (2011). A model of destination branding: Integrating the concepts of the branding and destination image. *Tourism Management*, *32*(3), 465–476. doi:10.1016/j.tourman.2010.03.014

Ramseook-Munhurrun, P., Seebaluck, V., & Naidoo, P. (2015). Examining the structural relationships of destination image, perceived value, tourist satisfaction and loyalty: Case of Mauritius. *Procedia – Social and Behavioral Sciences*, *175*, 252–259. doi:10.1016/j.sbspro.2015.01.1198

Reichheld, F., Markety, R., & Hopton, C. (2000). The loyalty effect – The relationship between loyalty and profits. *European Business Journal, 12*, 134–139.

Shakeela, A., & Weaver, D. (2012). Resident reactions to a tourism incident: Mapping a Maldivian Emoscape. *Annals of Tourism Research, 39*(3), 1337–1358. doi:10.1016/j.annals.2012.01.007

Shakeela, A., & Weaver, D. (2016). The Maldives: Parallel paths of conventional and alternative tourism. In Hall, C.M., & Page. S. (Eds.), *Routledge handbook on tourism in Asia* (pp. 285–294). London: Routledge.

Shakeela, A., & Weaver, D. (2018). "Managed evils" of hedonistic tourism in the Maldives. *Annals of Tourism Research, 71*, 13–24. doi:10.1016/j.annals.2018.04.003

Smith, P. (2004). Acquiescent response bias as an aspect of cultural communication style. *Journal of Cross-Cultural Psychology, 35*(1), 50–61. doi:10.1177/0022022103260380

Song, H., & Lin, S. (2010). Impacts of the financial and economic crisis on tourism in Asia. *Journal of Travel Research, 49*(1), 16–30. doi:10.1177/0047287509353190

Sönmez, S., & Graefe, A. (1998). Determining future travel behavior from past travel experience and perceptions of risk and safety. *Journal of Travel Research, 37*(2), 171–177. doi:10.1177/004728759803700209

Sparks, B., & Pan, G. (2009). Chinese outbound tourists: Understanding their attitudes, constraints and use of information sources. *Tourism Management, 30*(4), 483–494. doi:10.1016/j.tourman.2008.10.014

Su, L., Hsu, M., & Swanson, S. (2017). The effect of tourist relationship perception on destination loyalty at a World Heritage Site in China: The mediating role of overall destination satisfaction and trust. *Journal of Hospitality & Tourism Research, 41*, 180–210. doi:10.1177/1096348014525630

Sui, J., & Baloglu, S. (2003). The role of emotional commitment in relationship marketing: an empirical investigation of loyalty models for casinos. *Journal of Hospitality & Tourism Research, 27*, 470–489. doi:10.1177/10963480030274006

Sun, J., & Wang, X. (2010). Value differences between generations in China: A study of Shanghai. *Journal of Youth Studies, 13*(1), 65–81. doi:10.1080/13676260903173462

Sun, X., Chi, C., & Xu, H. (2013). Developing destination loyalty: The case of Hainan Island. *Annals of Tourism Research, 43*, 547–577. doi:10.1016/j.annals.2013.04.006

Tse, T. (2013). Chinese outbound tourism as a form of diplomacy. *Tourism Planning & Development, 10*, 149–158. doi:10.1080/21568316.2013.783738

Tse, T. (2015). A review of Chinese outbound tourism research and the way forward. *Journal of China Tourism Research, 11*(1), 1–18. doi:10.1080/19388160.2014.984798

Turner, L., & Ash, J. (1975). *The Golden Hordes: International tourism and the pleasure periphery.* London: Constable.

Tussyadiah, I. P., Park, S., & Fesenmaier, D. R. (2011). Assessing the effectiveness of consumer narratives for destination marketing. *Journal of Hospitality & Tourism Research, 35*, 64–78. doi:10.1177/1096348010384594

UNWTO. (2017a). Penetrating the Chinese outbound tourism market – successful practices and solutions. Retrieved from https://www.e-unwto.org/doi/pdf/10.18111/9789284418992

UNWTO. (2017b). *UNWTO tourism highlights 2017 edition.* Madrid: UNWTO.

Vada-Pareti, S. (2015). The Chinese are coming – Is Fiji ready? A study of Chinese tourists to Fiji. *Journal of Pacific Studies, 35*, 145–167.

Weaver, D. (2013). Moving in from the margins: Experiential consumption and the pleasure core. *Tourism Recreation Research, 38*, 81–85.

Weaver, D. (2017). Core-periphery relationships and the sustainability paradox of small island tourism. *Tourism Recreation Research, 42*(1), 11–21. doi:10.1080/02508281.2016.1228559

Weaver, D. (2018). Creative periphery syndrome? Opportunities for sustainable tourism innovation in Timor-Leste, an early stage destination. *Tourism Recreation Research, 43*(1), 118–128. doi:10.1080/02508281.2017.1397838

Weaver, D., & Lawton, L. (2011). Visitor loyalty at a private South Carolina protected area. *Journal of Travel Research, 50*(3), 335–346. doi:10.1177/0047287510362920

Weaver, D., & Lawton, L. (2014). Tourism management (2nd ed.). Milton, Qld: Wiley.

Wu, C. (2016). Destination loyalty modeling of the global tourism. *Journal of Business Research*, *69*(6), 2213–2219. doi:10.1016/j.jbusres.2015.12.032

Xiang, Y. (2013). The characteristics of independent Chinese outbound tourists. *Tourism Planning & Development*, *10*, 134–148. doi:10.1080/21568316.2013.783740

Xu, F., & Wang, S. (2014). China's outbound tourism – Emerging trends and features in the second decade of the 21st century. *Perspectives in Asian Leisure and Tourism*, *2*. Article 2.

Xu, Z., & Zhang, J. (2016). Antecedents and consequences of place attachment: A comparison of Chinese and Western urban tourists in Hangzhou, China. *Journal of Destination Marketing & Management*, *5*, 86–96. doi:10.1016/j.jdmm.2015.11.003

Yoon, Y., & Uysal, M. (2005). An examination of the effects of motivation and satisfaction on destination loyalty: A structural model. *Tourism Management*, *26*(1), 45–56. doi:10.1016/j.tourman.2003.08.016

Yuksel, A., Yuksel, F., & Bilim, Y. (2010). Destination attachment: Effects on customer satisfaction and cognitive, affective and conative loyalty. *Tourism Management*, *31*(2), 274–284. doi:10.1016/j.tourman.2009.03.007

Zhang, H., Fu, X., Cai, L., & Lu, L. (2014). Destination image and tourist loyalty: A meta-analysis. *Tourism Management*, *40*, 213–223. doi:10.1016/j.tourman.2013.06.006

Tourists really do behave responsibly toward the environment in Camiguin Province, Philippines

Mary Stephanie E. King-Chan (iD), Robert Charles G. Capistrano(iD) and Emma Lina F. Lopez (iD)

ABSTRACT

Camiguin Province is the second smallest island province in the Philippines. Its environment is essential relative to other typical island destinations for its ecological diversity, numerous marine protected areas and wildlife endemicity and for harboring an ASEAN Heritage Park. The expansion of tourism on the island attracts a great number of tourists, thereby increasing the scope for potential forms of behavior as well as the range of potential environmental impact. This study focuses on understanding Camiguin tourists' environmentally responsible behavior (ERB), particularly its determinants, namely, environmental attitude, knowledge and value, as well as the role of local stakeholders in influencing such behavior on an island tourism destination. Using a convergent mixed method approach, the study used survey samples comprising 303 tourists and 22 qualitative in-depth interviews of local stakeholders. Descriptive analysis showed that tourists have positive self-perceived environmental attitude, knowledge and value as well as ERB. Correlation analysis revealed that tourists' environmental attitude, knowledge and value have significant effect on tourists' ERB, with environmental attitude having the highest coefficient. Meanwhile, interviews with local stakeholders showed that tourists behave favorably toward the island's environment and played a significant role in influencing tourists' ERB. The study's contribution to the existing literature provides a novel approach to examining ERB from the perspectives of the tourists and the different stakeholders on the island. Ultimately, the study's findings have implications in developing strategies toward creating a favorable impact on the island's environment.

摘要

卡米圭因省是菲律宾倒数第二小的岛屿省份。它的环境相对于其他典型的岛屿目的地来说是至关重要的, 因为它的生态多样性, 拥有众多的海洋保护区和具有地方特色的野生动物, 以及拥有一个东盟遗产公园。该岛旅游业的扩大吸引了大量游客, 从而扩大了潜在行为形式的范围以及潜在环境影响的范围。本研究的重点是了解卡米吉因游客的环境责任行为(ERB), 特别是其决定因素, 即环境态度、知识和价值, 以及当地利益相关者在影响海岛旅游目的地这种行为中的作用。本研究采用集聚的混合方法, 采集了由303名游客组成的调查样本和22位当地利益相关者的定性深度访谈。描述性分析表明, 游客对环境的自我感知态度、知识和价值以及环境责任行为都是积极的。相关分析显示, 游客的环境态度、知识和价值对游客的环境责任行为有显著影响, 其中环境态度的系数最高。与此同时, 对当地利益相关者的访谈表明, 游客对岛上的环境表现良好, 对游客的环境责任行为有重要影响。本研究对现有文献的贡献提供了一种从游客和岛上不同利益相关者的角度来研究环境责任行为的新方法。最终, 这项研究的结果对于制定对该岛环境产生有利影响的策略具有一定的意义。

Introduction

In many island destinations, tourism development has desired impacts, but it also produces undesired consequences. In particular, tourism development could have a negative impact on many islands due to anthropogenic pressures, such as increasing demand for accommodation, amenities and transportation to meet the needs of the growing number of tourists (Carlsen & Butler, 2011; Eagles, 2014). Likewise, uncontrolled visitor activities on island destinations can degrade the natural environment (Graci, 2013). If not properly managed, tourism could be considered a threat to the environment and to biodiversity. Hence, tourism activities on island destinations should be managed comprehensively and should help shape tourists' environmentally responsible behavior (ERB).

Sustainable tourism or ecotourism on islands, such as providing environmental education for tourists, community building, and nature conservation to achieve environmental benefits, has been well recognized as an important tool for tourism development in addressing environmental issues (Bagadion & Del Fierro-Juan, 2013). Sustainable tourism development can be achieved with the destination stakeholders' support and involvement. Likewise, issues like employing a top-down approach in decision-making and not reflecting public interest can be avoided when involving stakeholders (Byrd, 2007). These concepts require the present work to understand and identify the role of stakeholders in tourists' ERB toward island tourism sustainability.

In the Philippines, ecotourism is one of the major subsectors of tourism given its concentration on ecological and biodiversity composition. However, studies related to ERB remain scant despite the country being an ecotourism destination and a global biodiversity hotspot. Camiguin Province (Figure 1), with a total population of 88,478 (PSA, 2016) and a total land area of 29,187 hectares (Camiguin Provincial Tourism Office or CPTO, 2015), is the second smallest island province in the Philippines. It is considered as a top ecotourism destination in Region 10. The island is listed as an important biodiversity area (Mallari et al., 2001) for its distinctive features, including 14 volcanoes, four endemic faunas, marine protected areas, and Mt. Timpoong-Hibok-Hibok Natural Monument, which was declared as an Association of Southeast Asia Nations (ASEAN) Heritage Park.

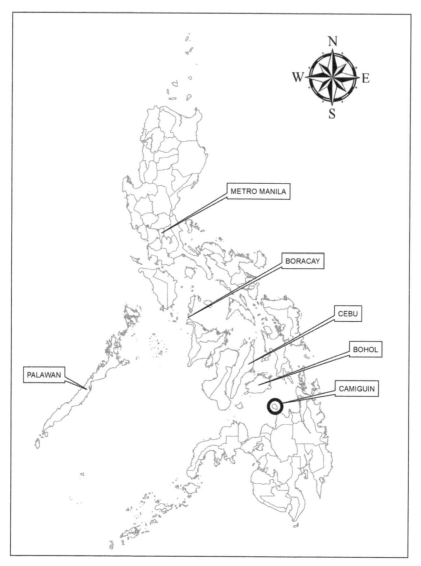

Figure 1. Location of Camiguin Island relative to other major island tourism destinations in the Philippines.

From 2013 to 2016, tourist arrivals consistently increased from 442,218 to 663,495, with 98% of the annual total number of arrivals being dominated by domestic tourists. However, in 2017, tourist arrivals decreased by 11.17% due to terrorism threats in Bohol Province, which is close to the island (CPTO, 2018). Nevertheless, the destination management organization on the island emphasized in their marketing efforts that Camiguin remains safe, with the absence of crime and accounts of terrorism threats, in order to recover tourist arrivals for the coming years (CPTO, 2018). With regard to seasonality, tourism is at its peak in the summer months of April and May and also on October for its annual celebration of Lanzones Festival (*Lancium sp.*). The province recorded an increase in gross income of PhP 6.7 million (approximately US$1,25,000) in 2015, compared to only PhP 5.3 million (approximately US$99,000) in 2014, which was accumulated from tourist facilities managed by the government (PIA, 2015). Tourism in Camiguin is considered as one of the dominant contributors to the local economy next to agriculture.(CPTO

The increasing number of arrivals on the island is predicted to continue. However, increasing visitor arrivals, along with other tourism-induced activities, could put more pressure on an island's limited resources if not managed well (Hall, 2010). The current literature about Camiguin focuses mainly on the biodiversity composition of marine and terrestrial environments and the potential extraction of natural resources (Heaney & Tabaranza, 2006). From a tourism management perspective, this study examines the island's tourism situation that may take a toll on the environment. It also investigates how key stakeholders will address tourism demand and conflict. Therefore, examining ERB, an important indicator of environmental sustainability (Berenguer et al., 2005), is necessary to minimize the negative impact on the destination.

This study aims to explore ERB that focuses on its determinants and the role of local stakeholders in influencing tourist behavior in Camiguin as an island destination. Specifically, the study seeks to examine tourists' self-reported ERB, the factors that influence such behavior and the perspectives and roles of destination stakeholders on tourists' ERB. The study contributes to the extant literature by providing a novel approach to examining ERB from the tourists' perspective and other key stakeholders of Camiguin. The findings provide baseline data in managing tourist impact as well as program and policy formulation toward islands' environmental sustainability.

Literature review

Island tourism – The Philippines

Island destinations remain important attractions due to their distinctive image of paradise. However, small islands are also vulnerable to environmental degradation caused by natural and anthropogenic pressures brought about by tourism (Hidayah et al., 2016). Beyond the economic benefits, such as increased revenue, employment, expansion in businesses and improvement in residents' quality of life, tourism poses a threat to the environment (Graci, 2013). Hall (2010) noted that islands are very susceptible to the impact of tourism on the environment, biodiversity conservation and waste disposal than any other destination. Hence, the tourism industry should maintain balance between the use of natural resources and economic gain. Small islands should be managed comprehensively with sustainable tourism as the most reliable long-term strategy (Graci, 2013; Hidayah et al., 2016). The major aim of sustainable tourism is to identify how the tourism industry can be developed and maintained viably at a destination without adversely contributing to environmental impact and preserve subsequently the destination's resources for present and future generations of residents and tourists (Dolnicar et al., 2008).

The Philippines has strengthened its commitment toward sustainable tourism as evident from the national government's action on the closure of the world-renowned tourist destination, Boracay Island. The island's shutdown to tourist traffic from April to

October 2018 was caused by poor management and tourism control as reflected in the increasing number of tourist arrivals and proliferation of private tourism establishments adjacent to sand beaches. These have resulted in numerous health and environmental problems like seawater and groundwater contamination, coral cover decline and land degradation (Cruz & Legaspi, 2019). Being a globally important biodiversity area (Catibog-Sinha & Heaney, 2006); driving tourism toward sustainability, especially in all island destinations is essential.

In Camiguin, local government units (LGUs) are committed toward environmental sustainability on the island, as shown by the implementation of various environmental policies. The *'Clean and Beautiful Camiguin'* campaign is the province's main environmental campaign program that aims to protect and preserve the island's environment while boosting local economy through tourism (CPTO, 2018). Under this program, local environmental policies were implemented, such as *solid waste management, no smoking policy* and the *no segregation, no collection policy*, in all tourist attractions. Moreover, site-specific policies are implemented in the two islets of Camiguin, such as the *no taking of white sand* on White Island and on Mantigue Island Nature Park and the *Plastic Free Mambajao* on the island's capital town (CPTO, 2018). These site-specific policies were found to be favorable ways to manage and regulate tourist behavior. Recently, the local government of Camiguin announced that prior steps were undertaken to regulate the entry of tourists by establishing the island's carrying capacity in order to sustain its environment (Jerusalem, 2020). Earlier studies on small islands show that they are very susceptible to visitors' impact that can significantly degrade the quality of the environment and place them more at risk compared to any other destination (Hall, 2010). This study contributes further in examining tourists' ERB, especially in the context of island destinations' fragility to degradation.

Environmentally responsible behavior (ERB)

Lee et al. (2013) meta-analyzed studies of ERB to understand the terminologies and provide a conclusive definition of ERB for tourism. Pro-environmental behavior (Kollmuss & Agyeman, 2002), environmental significant behavior (Stern, 2000) and sustainable behavior (Meijers & Stapel, 2011) are emerging terms that have been used in relation to ERB. The term ERB is defined here as 'the characteristics of tourists who strive to reduce environmental impacts, contribute to environmental conservation efforts, and do not disturb the ecosystem of a destination during tourism activities' (Lee et al., 2013).

A body of research aimed to assess and understand tourists' ERB and determine factors that may influence individuals to be conscious and eventually initiate positive behavior toward the environment (Dolnicar & Leisch, 2008; Han et al., 2016; Mobley et al., 2010; Puhakka, 2011; Zhang et al., 2013). For instance, Budeanu (2007) found that tourists are becoming more aware of the importance of protecting the environment and more involved in practicing environmentally friendly behavior during holidays. Puhakka (2011) concluded that ERB results when tourists acknowledge that their actions have a direct impact on the environment and they have to conform to regulations in the area. These findings suggest that tourists show serious concern for the environment and support conservation efforts during their stay in a destination.

However, other studies show contrasting results, saying that tourists don't always tend to behave responsibly while on vacation and that they have minimal concern toward the environment (Becken, 2004; Budeanu, 2007; Dolnicar & Leisch, 2008; Fairweather et al., 2005). Tourists feel more obligated to be in an environmentally friendly manner at home than on vacation (Dolnicar & Leisch, 2008) since they perceive that changing their travel behavior would affect their travel motivation for escape and relaxation (Becken, 2004). Moreover, tourists exhibit an unwillingness to pay for the environmental preservation of a destination, as only a few would purchase local products, choose eco-friendly transportation or behave conscientiously toward the hosts (Budeanu, 2007).

These conflicting results suggest the need to investigate the tourists' ERB, particularly on island destinations where degradation of the environment is likely to happen. Economic and environmental sustainability may be achieved more effectively if individuals behave responsibly toward the environment (Han et al., 2016).

Although most reviewed literature that examined tourists' ERB used quantitative approach (Cheng & Wu, 2015; Chiu et al., 2014; Kil et al., 2014; Lee & Jan, 2015; Zhang et al., 2013), understanding tourists' ERB using qualitative approach remains imperative. Lee (2013) found that previous studies used self-reported measures to assess tourists' ERB. This method may pose limitations due to the social desirability concept wherein participants may become biased with self-perceived behavior toward socially acceptable results. To the best of the authors' knowledge, no report has been found so far on using the observation of participants to evaluate tourists' ERB, specifically on an island tourism destination. To demonstrate the potential of these approaches and their suitability for application, this current study employed convergent mixed methods: survey approach for tourists' self-perceived behavior and interviews for observations of tourism stakeholders on tourists' ERB while at the destination. Any difference between self-reported and actual behavior in the context of tourism is worth examining.

ERB through the lenses of the theory of planned behavior and stakeholder theory

Tourists and their behavior connote differences that are influenced by several factors associated with the destination and the travellers (Dolnicar & Leisch, 2008). A number of studies have focused on factors influencing ERB, including psychological factors, such as place attachment and commitment (Lee, 2011), personal factors (Tabernero & Hernandez, 2011), outdoor recreation motive (Kil et al., 2014), perceptions and beliefs (Ramchurjee & Suresha, 2015), general and site-specific ERB (Lee et al., 2013) and destination image and value perception (Chiu et al., 2014). These factors were found to be important antecedents to ERB.

The present study utilizes two theories, the theory of planned behavior and the stakeholder theory, to understand ERB. These two provide a conceptual basis for examining the phenomenon and for understanding the complexities related to ERB from the perspectives of both the local stakeholders and the tourists. Several studies have applied the theory of planned behavior (TPB) as a basis to investigate an individual's sustainable behavior in tourism context, linking attitudes and behavior (Han & Kim, 2010; Paswan et al., 2017). Kaiser et al. (1999) promoted TPB as a theoretical framework to assess one's general ecological behavior and proposed three environmental attitude concepts of environmental knowledge and value and ecological intention behavior. Authors found a strong association of environmental knowledge and attitude toward ecological intention behavior, which in turn predicted general ecological behavior. This unified concept of attitude is further adopted in the present study to examine tourists' self-perceived behavior while on an island destination.

Kaiser et al. (1999) discussed two types of environmental attitude: attitude toward the natural environment and attitude toward ecological behavior. The present study used attitude toward the environment. In applying the latter, environmental knowledge and value are distinct from attitude (proposed by Rosenberg & Hovland, 1960, cited in Kaiser et al., 1999). Moreover, Milfont and Duckitt (2010) referred to environmental attitude as an individual's way of thinking or feeling relating to facts and issues of the natural environment, which are considered good or bad. Significant studies used attitude toward ecological behavior and found a notable effect of environmental attitude toward tourists' ERB in tourism destinations (Kil et al., 2014; Perkins & Brown, 2012; Wynveen et al., 2014). These studies revealed that an individual's positive attitude toward a particular behavior strengthens his or her intention to have such positive behavior. However, the relationship between environmental attitude and ERB is rarely examined in the context of island tourism (Kaiser et al., 1999).

Environmental knowledge allows individuals to have concerning facts and issues on environmental sustainability and increases their ability to understand and evaluate its impact on society and the environment (Wiernik et al., 2013). Early research found that environmental knowledge has direct influence on tourists' environmental behavior inclination (Qiuyin et al., 2009; Wurzinger & Johansson, 2006). Mobley et al. (2010) argued that tourists who are knowledgeable and concerned about the welfare of the environment will most likely exhibit ERB. This claim contradicts the result of the study conducted in one of the tourism destinations in China that knowledge has no effect on tourists' ERB (Zhang et al., 2013). Hence, further study should be undertaken. Furthermore, few studies have examined environmental knowledge as a direct predictor of ERB because of the central role knowledge plays in many theoretical models of attitude-behavior relations as a component of environmental attitude (Cheng & Wu, 2015). Despite this finding, knowledge is argued to be an operand and should be considered in establishing environmental concern (Nilsson & Küller, 2000).

Environmental value is defined as an individual's orientation on the environment and environmental problems, as well as assessment on phenomena based on cost and benefits to the ecosystem (Chiu et al., 2014; Wiernik et al., 2013). Schultz et al. (2005) found that value can only partially predict an individual's environmental concern. However, recent studies revealed that environmental value is a direct determinant and increases tourists' ERB (Lee & Jan, 2015; Zhang et al., 2013). These suggest the need to examine environmental value as a direct determinant of tourists' ERB.

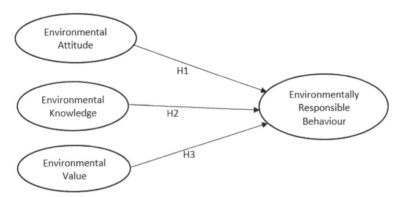

Figure 2. Conceptual Framework of Tourists' Environmentally Responsible Behaviour (Source: Authors; adapted from Kaiser et al. (1999) and made reference from other literature).

The aforementioned investigations indicated that most attention has focused on the indirect operand of variables toward ERB. Thus, the present study considers the direct effect of three factors, namely, environmental attitude, knowledge and value, on tourists' ERB (Figure 2). The study identifies the dependence of ERB and examines which among the determinants have a relationship on tourists' ERB on an island destination. However, the current work excludes the indirect effect of environmental knowledge and value as a component of attitude towards ecological behavior and the mediating effect of behavioral intention. To guide the study further, the following are the research hypotheses: (H_1) Environmental attitude has no significant effect on tourists' ERB; (H_2) Environmental knowledge has no significant effect on tourists' ERB; and (H_3) Environmental value has no significant effect on tourists' ERB.

The stakeholder concept uses an ethical management approach that considers the interest and involvement of stakeholders affected by the organizations' actions and outcomes instead of solely focusing on economic gain (Miles, 2012). Researchers have applied this theory in tourism context by identifying the roles of stakeholders in sustainable tourism development (Byrd, 2007), the importance of local stakeholders' inclusion (Peric et al., 2014), model application (Saftic et al., 2011) and advance community participation (Khazaei et al., 2015). The authors argued that the stakeholder approach is important in achieving sustainability in the tourism industry. Another author also claimed that the stakeholders' engagement has a strong positive impact on a restaurant's commitment in promoting environmental sustainability (Jang et al., 2017). Therefore, incorporating the stakeholder approach is important in studying destinations in relation to sustainability. This notion has motivated the present study.

Stakeholder may be defined as any group of people, organized or unorganized, who share a common interest or stake in a particular issue or system (Lyon et al., 2017). The succeeding discussion is the summary of stakeholder classification for an ecotourism destination by Drumm and Moore (2002), which was further adopted in this study. First, the government plays an important role in the planning, development and management of a tourism destination (Young & Dhanda, 2012). Mutana and Mukwada (2017) suggested that the local municipality has the overall responsibility for environmental management, but close association with other stakeholders is crucial. Second, non-government organizations (NGOs) in tourism are groups of individuals who share mutual interests, provide links among various interested individuals in the tourism industry and subscribe to certain principles or code of ethics based on the current trends in the industry (Drumm & Moore, 2002). Meanwhile, environmental NGOs are those that are centered on environment conservation and development and extend technical or financial assistance or directly manage a site (Young & Dhanda, 2012). Third, communities are groups of people sharing the same residence in the same geographical location with multiple perspectives. They are the original inhabitants, a core stakeholder group of a tourist destination (Marzo-Navarro et al., 2015). Their involvement in tourism planning is important for the success of the ecotourism destination (Drumm & Moore, 2002). This group often has mixed emotions and attitudes toward tourism development in the area. Some are welcoming of the concept while others are not. Lastly, the private sector or tourism private enterprise is a group of individuals who are involved in businesses (e.g., tour operators and travel agencies; airline and cruise ship employees; accommodation sector; etc.) that provide direct and indirect products and services to tourists. For the present study, the recruitment of stakeholders for interview is based on the aforementioned stakeholder groups.

Stakeholder collaboration is essential in managing and controlling tourism on small islands toward sustainability (Graci, 2013). Canavan (2017) listed negative consequences of dysfunctional collaboration between stakeholders, including a lack of shared vision for local tourism and a high level of mistrust between stakeholders, resulting in conflict, wasted resources, lost enthusiasm and a lack of strategic direction. Stakeholder participation in the decision-making process is essential for sustainable tourism on island destinations, as stakeholders play a wide variety of roles that may sometimes have competing aims and objectives. Aside from mapping stakeholder groups, their influences can also be mapped, which is an important tool to identify the varying degrees of stakeholder influence over decision-making or issues (Lyon et al., 2017) that may directly or indirectly impact tourism planning and development. Tourist behavior has an impact on these stakeholders, and conversely, stakeholders can influence how tourists behave while at the host destination. Opinions and interests may emerge differently among stakeholder groups (Marzo-Navarro et al., 2015). Hence, the influence of stakeholders on one another should be outlined and apprehended. However, tourism literature on stakeholders' influencing role on tourists' ERB on island destinations remains scarce, as most studies on this topic are tourist-centered. Therefore, the stakeholder theory was also applied in the current study to determine how stakeholders can influence tourists to behave favorably toward the environment, particularly on island destinations.

Methodology

This study used convergent mixed methods research design wherein different but complementary quantitative and qualitative data were collected on the same research topic (Creswell & Clark, 2007) to investigate holistically the tourists' ERB in Camiguin Province. A mixed methods research allows the complexity of human phenomenon to be obtained and responds to the interests and needs of diverse stakeholders involved in the research. Consequently, it offers greater possibilities than a single method approach in responding to decision makers' agenda and interest of other legitimate stakeholders (Doyle et al., 2009). The quantitative aspect of the study involved conducting a survey among tourists, while the qualitative section involved community stakeholders in Camiguin Island. In this case, a holistic approach in understanding the phenomenon involved examining ERB from tourists' perspectives and determining how community stakeholders influence tourists' behavior toward the island's environment.

Data gathering was conducted from April to June 2018, which is the peak season of tourism activities in Camiguin. Due to the rigor of data gathering, the authors trained two research assistants who entered into a confidentiality agreement to conduct the survey. Interviews were also conducted by the authors themselves. The succeeding sections provide in-depth discussion on the two approaches used in this current work.

For the quantitative approach, a survey questionnaire was used to examine tourists' self-reported behavior. The questionnaire design made references to environmental attitude (Dunlap et al., 2000; Kil et al., 2014), environmental knowledge (Cheng & Wu, 2015), environmental value (Lee & Jan, 2015; Zhang et al., 2013) and ERB (Lee & Jan, 2015). Subsequently, revisions were made to fit the present study. The questionnaire, written in English and accompanied by a Filipino translation, was self-explanatory. Each item measured the tourists' level of agreement with a five-point Likert scale, where 5 is highest (strongly agree) and 1 is lowest (strongly disagree). The instrument was further validated by other Filipino experts working in the field of tourism studies. A pilot survey was conducted to examine the reliability of the constructs using Cronbach's α, and only measurements under environmental value fell short of the rule of thumb for acceptability of alpha coefficient 0.7, as recommended by Hair et al. (2010). Additional measured items were adapted from Lee and Jan (2015). Using convenience sampling, 303 out of 322 questionnaires were completed and determined useful. Sample for foreign visitors was over-represented with 9.2% while domestic is 90.8% – noting that annual visitor arrivals in Camiguin were dominated by 98% domestic tourists (CPTO (Camiguin Provincial Tourism Office), 2018). Questionnaires were distributed at the Camiguin Domestic Airport – Departure Area and in major tourist spots on the island to recruit more participants for the survey. To quantify the relationships among latent constructs, correlation analysis was employed to analyze the level of closeness between variables. This demonstrates whether two phenomena are related in direction and size of change of development (Nunkoo & Ramkissoon, 2012).

The qualitative approach was facilitated using semi-structured interviews among local stakeholders to elicit their perception on tourists' ERB and identify their role in influencing tourists to behave in such way. A set of open-ended questions was prepared separately for each stakeholder group. These questions focused on the stakeholders' observations and perceived roles in influencing tourists' ERB. Probing questions followed afterward. Interview questions were translated to the local dialect Visayan-Cebuano, as this is widely spoken in the province, as requested by participants. Stakeholders were identified based on prior interview with the Camiguin Provincial Tourism Office, which is the regulatory body for local tourism. Using purposive sampling, the study interviewed 22 local stakeholders comprising 2 local government unit (LGU) representatives whose concern is on tourism, 2 NGO-tourism associations and environmental NGO, 3 private tourism enterprises and 15 local residents living near tourist sites. An interview consent form, which asks for their voluntary participation and states the study's purpose and benefit, confidentiality and mode of interviewing, was presented to the interviewees to ensure ethical standards. The interviewees were contacted through email, social media, or phone calls for appointment prior to the interview. Face-to-face double interview was conducted between two LGU representatives of Camiguin while the rest were individually interviewed.

Most interviews were conducted using the local dialect, as this was preferred by the interviewees. The interviews were recorded and transcribed for analysis. Before analysis, the responses were shared to participants to ensure that the interview was contextualized in their local language. Thereafter, the transcriptions were manually analyzed using content analysis based on the uncomplicated, simple and objective form of analyzing data (Bengtsson, 2016). The study also described and examined the characteristics of the content and underlying concepts within the communication. The analysis involved: (1) preparation – transcribed interviews were examined through several readings by first author (a native of Camiguin island); (2) organizing – categories or themes were created by first author and other members of the research team to analyze the existence of concepts that occurred in transcribed interviews and to determine the possibility of finding themes based on the frequency of their occurrence; and (3) reporting – the results were presented through categories or themes to answer the objectives of this work. Interviews conducted in Visayan-Cebuano were translated into English only during the reporting phase to present consistently and form the basis of results.

Results

Tourists' self-perceived ERB

The profile of surveyed participants showed that they were mostly female tourists (62.1%), aged between 25–34 (37.3%), dominantly single (52.9%) and over half had tertiary school qualification (60.1%) as highest level of education attained. Majority are domestic tourists (90.8%) and visited the island for recreation and vacation (57.1%), organized their island trip by themselves (69.3%), usually stayed from 2 to 4 days (42.0%) or more than a week (42.5%) and had a travel budget ranging from PhP 1,000 to 3,999 (27.7%) and more than PhP 10,000 (33.0%).

Tourists' responses from measured items of environmental attitude, knowledge, value and ERB are presented in Table 1. To examine further the instrument's reliability, Cronbach's alpha was calculated. Results show that reliability coefficients of each latent construct (EA = 0.86; EK = 0.87; EV = 0.72; ERB = 0.85) exceeded the 0.7 acceptable level of reliability (Hair et al., 2010). Overall, these results suggest that the instrument had good internal consistency. Thus, observed variables reflected and measured variables of interest.

Based on mean value obtained for environmental attitude, results showed that most participants strongly agreed on each statement under this construct. Participants

Table 1. Tourists' response on measured environmental items (Source: Authors).

Measured items	Mean	STD
Environmental Attitude (EA) = 0.86		
Plants and animals have as much right as humans to exist.	4.44	0.72
When humans interfere with nature it often produces disastrous consequences.	4.44	0.71
Balance of nature is very delicate and easily upset.	4.41	0.68
Despite our special abilities, humans are still subject to the laws of nature.	4.39	0.69
Humans were not meant to rule over the rest of nature.	4.32	0.87
Humans will eventually learn enough about how nature works to be able to control it.	4.32	0.75
The earth is like a spaceship with very limited room and resources.	4.23	0.95
Humans have no right to modify the natural environment to suit their needs.	4.22	0.99
We are approaching the limit of the number of people the earth can support.	4.21	0.90
Environmental Knowledge (EK) = 0.87		
I know that for the next generation, we should protect the natural resources of islands.	4.53	0.63
I know that the maintenance of ecological balance will enhance the sustainable development of islands.	4.41	0.68
I know that excessive ocean recreational activities will damage oceanic environments of islands.	4.41	0.74
I know that extensive development of natural resources will consume the islands.	4.39	0.72
I know that maintenance of diversity of species on islands will balance the ecology.	4.38	0.72
Environmental Value (EV) = 0.72		
The island's environment is worthy to be protected.	4.77	0.50
We should live with respect among other earth's species.	4.68	0.58
We should unite with nature.	4.68	0.54
Nature has sufficient balancing capability to eliminate the impact of modernization and industrialization.	4.11	0.90
Humans are entitled to change natural environment to meet their own need.	3.65	1.21
My concern of environmental problems is for the interest of my family and myself, not the society and others.	3.57	1.34
Environmentally Responsible Behavior = 0.85		
After a picnic, I leave the place as clean as it was originally.	4.70	0.56
I voluntarily stop visiting a favorite spot if it needed to recover from environmental damage.	4.51	0.75
I do not intend to disturb any creature and vegetation.	4.51	0.70
I understand residents' lifestyles.	4.48	0.68
I try to convince companions to adopt positive behaviors in the natural environments.	4.09	0.99
I buy environmentally friendly products.	4.04	0.88
I read reports, advertising, and books related to the environments of the destination.	4.01	0.97
I make a special effort to buy fruits and vegetables from locals.	3.98	0.90
I buy products packaged in containers that either can be reused or recycled or are made of recycled materials.	3.84	0.96
I share money or time to support an environmental organization.	3.73	1.04

expressed strong agreement that plants and animals have the same right to exist as humans do ($\mu = 4.44$) and human interference with nature will often result in disastrous consequences ($\mu = 4.44$). Likewise, participants expressed their strong agreement on measured items for environmental knowledge. They strongly agreed that protecting the island's resources is for the benefit of future generations ($\mu = 4.53$) and maintaining balance of ecology will support the island's sustainability ($\mu = 4.41$). Regarding environmental value, participants strongly agreed that the island's environment is worthy to be protected ($\mu = 4.77$), to live in harmony with other species ($\mu = 4.68$) and unite with nature ($\mu = 4.68$). The participants agreed that concern for environmental problems is for the interest of their family and themselves ($\mu = 3.57$), which

Table 2. Correlation (Pearson) (Source: Authors).

Conceptual Path	Correlation Coefficient (r)	p value	N	Result
EA ERB	0.434**	.001	303	**Reject**
EK ERB	0.408**	.001	303	**Reject**
EV ERB	0.420**	.001	303	**Reject**

Correlation is significant at **0.01 level.

ranked lowest for environmental value. Based on self-reported ERB, tourists behaved accordingly while at the destination. Tourists showed strong agreement that they left the place clean after their picnic ($\mu = 4.70$), they voluntarily stopped visiting a degraded spot for it to recover ($\mu = 4.51$) and did not intend to disturb any fauna and flora ($\mu = 4.51$). These three responses were the highest in rank based on mean values. In terms of effort and financial aspect, participants agreed that they donate money or give time to support an environmental organization ($\mu = 3.73$), which is the lowest mean value for ERB. Overall, EK ($\mu = 4.42$) had the highest overall mean value among the main variables.

A Pearson product-moment correlation coefficient was computed to examine the strength of association between independent variables, EA, EK and EV, and dependent variable, ERB. As depicted in Table 2 correlation analysis, a moderate, positive correlation existed among three hypothesized paths, EA and ERB ($r = 0.43$, $p < .001$), EK and ERB ($r = 0.41$, $p < .001$) and EV and ERB ($r = 0.42$, $p < .001$). Further, the correlation among hypothesized paths was significant at 0.01 level. Thus, the three hypotheses were rejected.

Stakeholder perspectives on tourists' behavior in Camiguin island

Succeeding results emphasized the stakeholders' perception of tourists' behavior during their stay on the island and their role in influencing tourists' ERB. To compare data on tourists' self-reported and actual behavior, the stakeholders' perceptions were solicited to validate the tourists' responses to the quantitative survey. Questions centered on: 'How do the tourists behave toward the natural environment and to the people of Camiguin Province as an island tourism destination?' and 'Why do you think tourists behave positively or negatively?' Probing questions followed.

The findings from interviews with local stakeholders encompassing their perspectives on tourists' ERB reflect that tourists were conscious and friendly in interacting with the natural environment and host community, respectively. Interviewed participants justified the actual behavior of tourists while at the destination. Meanwhile, local stakeholders perceived that tourists exhibit positive ERB due to two external factors: the natural setting of the island and environmental policies being implemented on the island. Local stakeholders viewed tourists as appreciative and aware of the natural setting of Camiguin, as environmental policies were observed based on the awareness and adaptability of tourists.

Majority stated that tourists behaved positively toward the environment. According to a Camiguin Provincial Tourism Office (CPTO) representative, no account has been recorded concerning tourist misbehavior. If there had been any negligence, these were only minor and were settled promptly. Other stakeholders supported this claim, saying tourists were mindful of their actions toward the island's environment:

> Our tour guides never had reports about tourists' misbehavior during day-tour on the island. *Stakeholder 6*

Locals found most tourists friendly and showed interest to interact with the host population:

> They initiated conversation with us, and even though I am not fluent in speaking English or *Tagalog* [Philippine language], still they managed to understand me. *Resident 5*

Despite differences, majority of the locals welcomed tourists to the island. Moreover, local stakeholders believed that Camiguin is endowed with a rich natural environment and has well-defined environmental policies. Thus, tourists would most likely exhibit positive behavior toward the environment of this island destination. Tourists are expected to be compliant with the local government's rules and regulations, especially those concerning the preservation of the island's natural environment. Hence, they are encouraged to cooperate toward this endeavor and are prohibited from doing what could possibly harm or contribute to the deterioration of the site. Any behavior contrary to the government's policies on preserving the environment in its natural state shall therefore constitute poor behavior:

> Here in Camiguin, we put much effort in protecting our island that is why environmental policies are strictly implemented to guide these tourists to be mindful of their behavior. *Stakeholder 1*

The preceding discussion depicts external factors that emerged to which stakeholders attributed tourists' positive behavior toward the environment.

Local stakeholders claimed that most tourists come to the island because of its unique topographies and that they are appreciative of the natural environment. Similarly, stakeholders affirmed that most tourists are aware of environmental degradation brought about by overuse of natural resources for tourism.

> Most of my guests would tell me that we should take care of our island to avoid what had happened to other island destinations, like Boracay. *Stakeholder 7*

Stakeholders perceived that tourists develop concern regarding issues related to environment. They shared their thoughts about the protection and preservation of the island to avoid another 'Boracay-like' issue. Boracay, a world-renowned island destination, was placed on a six-month closure period from tourism activities for rehabilitation and restoration, as it suffered from major environmental degradation due to lax implementation and monitoring of local ordinances on marine conservation, garbage and sanitation, zoning and construction.

All local stakeholders conveyed that environmental policies implemented on Camiguin island have influenced tourists to behave favorably toward the environment. Tourists are aware and are supportive of the local policies related to the natural environment and are compliant to such policies on the island.

> Most tourists appreciated what the island is doing for the protection and conservation of the environment [...] some groups come for benchmarking for the best practices on environmental programs in the island. *Stakeholder 3*

Significantly, stakeholders asserted that tourists leave the area clean, claiming this behavior may be due to the 'Leave No Trace Policy.' Tourists used non-plastic bags in buying goods and souvenirs since the 'Plastic Free Policy' is strictly implemented. Hence, tourists showed support and initiated adaptive behavior while on the island.

Stakeholders said few tourists expressed their plight about the Plastic Free Policy and emphasized the importance of letting tourists understand why the policies were in place.

> A few complained about the inconvenience of buying goods wrapped in papers, but eventually understood the ordinance. *Stakeholder 3*

These findings suggest that environmental policies on the island influenced tourists' behavior positively. Most tourists behaved appropriately once they were well-oriented and guided.

Role of stakeholders in tourists' ERB

Local stakeholders were asked regarding their role in influencing tourists to behave positively toward the environment. The main question focused on this. The succeeding section provides results from interviews with stakeholder groups vis-à-vis their role in island tourism.

Local government unit (LGU): vision setters

The LGUs have a clear vision for the island to drive tourism towards sustainability:

> The present administration advocates for environmental sustainability for the benefit of the future generations. *Stakeholder 1*

These agencies acknowledged the fact that tourists are enticed to visit the island because of its natural features. This gave them a motivation to strongly advocate for the protection of the island's natural resources.

> The main agenda of the government is to protect the island because this is our asset to boost the tourism industry. *Stakeholder 2*

As policy makers, LGUs perceived that protecting and preserving the environment of the island will continue the progress and contribution of the tourism industry to the island's local economy. As a legislative body, lawmakers formulated various ordinances and policies for the protection of the island's environment. Among these are *Solid Waste Management, No Smoking Policy* and *Leave No Trace Policy*, which are implemented in all tourism sites and establishments, and the *Plastic-Free Campaign*, which is implemented in the capital town. For instance, the *Leave No Trace Policy* mandates that all visitors should be responsible in disposing their own wastes and cleaning their area before leaving the site. The *Plastic-Free Policy* is an ordinance that bans the use of plastic bags in business establishments located in the capital town. LGUs strongly believed that these policies would influence tourists to be more responsible with their behavior. LGUs strictly implemented site-specific policies that would fit the ecological composition of certain tourist spots on the island. On White Island (one of the islets having pure white sandbar), tourists are not allowed to take white sand regardless of quantity, as it takes years before an island is formed.

The LGUs' role on environmental sustainability was further intensified following environmental issues in other island tourism destinations in the Philippines. They perceived that the monitoring phase of implemented policies is important to achieve their purpose. This phase is considered as a challenge for them given that they must ensure that policies are strictly followed by the public.

> If there is an existing policy but lacks monitoring, it is therefore non-existent at all. Thus, monitoring is the key. *Stakeholder 2*

LGUs believe that they can influence tourist behavior by empowering the local people.

Non-Government Organizations: Awareness raising and education

Two NGOs on the island were interviewed. Both are non-profit organizations and related to the tourism industry and environment, respectively. The former is composed of accredited tour guide professionals for Camiguin Province, while the latter is a pool of experts, researchers, marine biologists, dive masters and specialists for coral reef restoration that aim to assist various areas or provinces for the rehabilitation and/or restoration of coral reefs and promote underwater tourism.

These NGOs are perceived to have significant contributions to the environmental sustainability of the island. They make use of their skills and expertise for the preservation of the natural environment.

> As a group of tour guides, our primary role is to orient and educate tourists about the island's practices concerning the environment. *Stakeholder 3*

Non-government organizations serve as partners of the tourism industry in educating and raising awareness among locals as well as tourists in Camiguin. Education is highly perceived to influence the tourist.

> For example, if touching the corals will not only sting them but also disturb the creatures, tourists would not intend to touch any of it. *Stakeholder 4*

These NGOs saw themselves as role models. They also had a direct interaction with the tourists.

> The most effective way is role modeling, like that of tour guides, bringing with them eco-bags, initiating waste disposal and the like. *Stakeholder 3*

Private tourism enterprises: Support for environmental policies

The following were interviewed: resort manager, travel agency manager and island tour/mountain guide representing the private tourism enterprise. This group supported the protection and preservation of the island's natural environment due to its significant value for their business. Hence, they also supported the government's initiative for environmental protection:

> We are after the environment of the island because this is what we market to our clients […] Thus, we support the environmental ordinances on the island. *Stakeholder 6*

However, the resort manager shared they are financially challenged due to the high cost of wastewater disposal. Albeit challenged, they still complied with proper waste treatment and disposal because they believed it is their moral obligation for environmental protection:

> We are very compliant on this matter as we are closely monitored by the LGUs. We do not just release our wastewater into the sea because we have learned from the case of Boracay. *Stakeholder 5*

Nonetheless, resorts added that they were very positive that LGUs already have ongoing plans for this situation. This group mentioned being role models to their guests to influence their guests' behavior. They also adopted environmental policies within the nature of their business.

> If I see a small candy wrapper, I pick it up and throw it in a proper garbage container. That simple gesture of caring for the environment is effective because tourists somehow follow my lead. *Stakeholder 7*

> In our rooms, we put trash bins labeled for waste disposal segregation and we put "love letters" [as signage] – like for them to be reminded of the energy and water saving tips. *Stakeholder 5*

Local community: Role model and stewards

Interviews were conducted on 15 local residents who had been living on the island for more than 20 years. Most of them lived near the tourist site. The residents have positive attitude toward welcoming tourists to the island. They were very willing to share the environment they have to others. However, they had high hopes that tourists would also respect and love the island especially in following environmental policies.

> They should also consider our place as their second home. *Resident 5*

> We have rules on the island that they must also follow. No exception. *Resident 8*

A few expressed difficulty in communicating with tourists who speak other dialects or foreign languages. Nonetheless, residents continued being hospitable and augment communication through hand signals.

The local residents also saw themselves as stewards as they protect the island's environment because it is their home. Furthermore, they believed that tourists would behave positively if the tourists would see how they take care of their island's environment:

> I think they will be responsible for their behaviors if they will see that the people here are disciplined. *Resident 4*

Residents showed positive attitude toward supporting environmental policies and programs on the island. Majority of the interviewed residents expressed their support to the government's initiatives for environmental protection by helping in overseeing tourists' behavior:

As a resident of this island, I felt morally obligated to be a good keeper, thus, I will be sensible to tourists' actions. *Resident 14*

Analysis and discussion

Tourists who answered the survey demonstrated very positive environmental attitude. Most of them recognized the fragility of the environment. Survey participants viewed that humans must understand how the natural environment works, as the law of nature is inescapable. The study's findings revealed that tourists were explicitly knowledgeable on environmental issues. Generally, they were aware of the impact of overdevelopment and overuse of resources to the island's environment. These results are consistent with previous findings in which tourists were generally aware of environmental problems and knew their actions have an impact on the environment (Budeanu, 2007; Puhakka, 2011) and tourists became more concerned with the destination's environment when they had more knowledge about environmental issues (Wurzinger & Johansson, 2006).

Tourists appreciated the value of the natural environment of an island. This factor is reflected from stakeholders' observation that the island's natural setting influenced tourists to behave positively toward the environment. This finding further supports Perkins and Brown (2012), who stated that tourists usually value the intrinsic significance of nature and consider their impact to the environment. Additionally, the findings indicated that most tourists were conscious about their behavior toward the environment. However, this contradicts Dolnicar and Leisch (2008), who claimed that tourists felt more morally obligated to behave in an environmentally friendly manner at home than on vacation. This study's findings suggest that tourists on an island destination will most likely exhibit ERB, as expressed by the interviewed stakeholders who said that no tourist misbehavior has been recorded so far. In addition, tourists were willing to share ample amount of money or time favorably for the environment. This is contrary to Budeanu (2007) and Zhang et al. (2013), who believe that tourists have a negative response on the willingness to spend time and money to improve environmental quality.

Correlation analysis revealed a positive coefficient considering the direct effect of three factors, namely, environmental attitude, knowledge and value to tourists' ERB as presumed by the present study. The coefficient for environmental attitude has the highest value which suggests that it influences ERB the most. This contradicts the result from another study by Lee and Jan (2015) where environmental value has the highest coefficient. Tourists' environmental attitude had a positive and significant effect on tourists' ERB, which was consistent with previous studies (Kil et al., 2014; Lee & Jan, 2015; Wynveen et al., 2014). A tourist with a positive attitude will most likely behave favorably toward the island's environment.

The study's findings indicated that tourists' environmental knowledge has a positive and significant effect on tourists' ERB, which contradicted Zhang et al. (2013) but supported Cheng and Wu (2015) and Qiuyin et al. (2009). Hence, when tourists have rich knowledge about an island's environmental sustainability, they are more likely to be concerned with environmental issues and perform ERB. This finding supported Mobley et al. (2010) and Wurzinger and Johansson (2006) who reported that tourists who are knowledgeable and concerned with the welfare of the environment will most likely exhibit ERB.

Additionally, research findings suggest that tourists' environmental value has a positive and significant effect on tourists' ERB, which further supports the existing studies (Lee & Jan, 2015; Perkins & Brown, 2012; Zhang et al., 2013). If tourists had a greater value for the environment, they would consider the impact of their behavior and become more responsible for their actions toward the environment.

Qualitative data on stakeholders' perception validated the responses from quantitative results on tourists' self-reported ERB. For instance, tourists reported that they left the picnic area as clean as it was originally, did not disturb any creature and vegetation and understood the local residents' lifestyle. These tourists' self-reported behavior was further confirmed by stakeholders, showing that most tourists behaved responsibly during their stay on the island. Most tourists were reported to be more conscious with their actions and friendly to the locals. Perhaps tourists who visited other island destinations, where the environment was visibly deteriorating, may have developed a sense of environmental concern and became emotionally affected by the disheartening situation.

Consequently, tourists' increased consciousness in dealing with the environment prompted them to be more responsible with their actions. Stakeholders perceived that tourists' behavior was influenced by external factors present on the island, such as the island's natural setting and environmental policies. The natural features of the island influenced tourists to be responsible for their actions, and its unique setting may have met or exceeded tourists' satisfaction and expectation, which subsequently increased their concern for the island's environment.

Tourists were also found to be supportive of and adaptive to the implemented environmental policies, which served to remind tourists to behave while at the destination. Although being non-residents of the island, tourists sometimes complained about things they had to do outside their usual routine and felt that this inconvenience would affect their overall stay on the island. But even with these inconveniences, tourists remained to be morally obligated to behave in an environmentally friendly manner while on vacation. This response showed that proper orientation and explanation will help tourists understand the benefits of their responsible actions.

This study provides an understanding of the role of each local stakeholder in influencing tourists' ERB (Figure 3). Mainly, the role of LGUs focused on developing policies, regulation (i.e., legislation, administration, enforcement) and facilitation (cooperation with other stakeholders). Although LGUs have indirect influence on tourists' ERB, their function as legislators can regulate tourist behavior. This finding further confirms previous studies stating that LGUs play an important role in planning and development and is overall responsible for environmental management (Mutana & Mukwada, 2017; Young & Dhanda, 2012). The present study further revealed that the government functioned as the vision setter to all key stakeholders on the island toward the sustainability of island tourism while maximizing its economic benefits.

The significant role of the NGOs is primarily on the environmental education aspect, given their knowledge and expertise. NGOs as educators can influence tourists on the

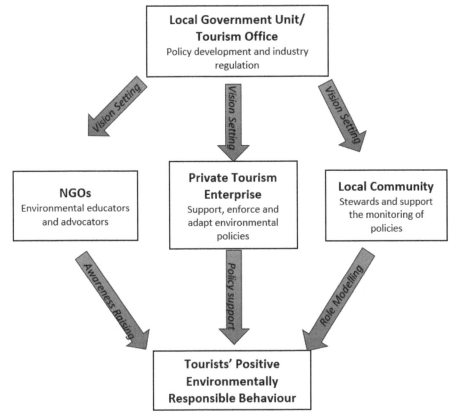

Figure 3. Role of Stakeholders on Tourists' Environmentally Responsible Behaviour (Source: Authors).

island by raising awareness on the impact of one's behavior toward the environment as well as informing them directly about the policies implemented. Private tourism entrepreneurs portrayed supportive roles in enforcing environmental policies set by the LGU and incorporating these policies within the nature of their businesses. Drumm and Moore (2002) added that this group plays an important role in encouraging tourists to adapt positive behavior and limit negative impact. The local community plays a supportive role as the model of good stewardship since they perceived that their actions and gestures are influential to how tourists feel, act or think. They also supported the government initiatives in protecting the natural environment of the island. Similarly, they are considered as the core stakeholder group of a tourist destination (Marzo-Navarro et al., 2015) as residents showed their commitment to help strengthen the vision toward the island's environmental protection by ensuring that everyone causes no harm to the environment.

Conclusion and recommendations

This study aimed at exploring tourists' ERB by primarily focusing on its determinants as well as identifying the role of stakeholders in influencing such behavior. Based on the study's findings, tourists in Camiguin have a positive attitude toward the environment, are highly educated on environmental sustainability concept and value the importance of the island's environment. This study shows that environmental knowledge is a direct predictor of ERB in which earlier studies tested it as a component of environmental attitude in many theoretical models of attitude-behavior relations. Therefore, the role of environmental knowledge should be an operand and its direct effect should be considered in influencing tourists' ERB.

Aside from predetermined factors, stakeholders attributed the responsible behavior of tourists to the island's image and local environmental policies. The emergence of two factors contributes to tourism literature, specifically as determinants of tourists' ERB. Moreover, each stakeholder group has significant roles in influencing tourists' ERB: LGUs as policy makers and vision setters; NGOs as support service, environmental advocators and educators; private sector as support and enforcer, as well as educators; and local community as stewards, role models/ambassadors and enforcers of environmental policies., These defined roles contribute to the sustainability of the island's environment and provide a foundation for the bottom-up approach in managing island tourism destinations given that scholarly literature on this subject remains unexplored. This finding is essential in enhancing and strengthening stakeholders' commitment toward environmental sustainability through their roles on tourists' ERB. Identifying the determinants of tourists' ERB can help tourism planners to formulate strategies for sustainable tourism. To achieve the goal of environmental sustainability in island tourism, local stakeholders' collaboration and partnerships are highly encouraged.

A novel approach of this research entails examining tourists' ERB from several perspectives. Previous literature mainly focuses on tourists or residents. A holistic approach of the study enabled understanding of the phenomenon from various perspectives. Hence, this study provided a broader picture of stakeholders' role in island tourism using the lenses of the theory of planned behavior and the stakeholder theory. Other island destinations may consider these in examining tourists' ERB and determining how community stakeholders influenced such behavior.

Tourism planners and other stakeholders involved in island tourism may consider these recommendations based on the study's findings: (1) destination managers may design and provide tourism activities that concentrate on the island's ecosystem and wildlife to enhance tourists' value-orientation; (2) guided tours or interpretive services may be highly valued and extensively offered to enhance visitors' awareness of and appreciation for the environment; and (3) destination managers may strengthen their site-specific guidelines in tourist attractions on the island to manage visits and create unified environmental codes of conduct. Furthermore, the study significantly contributes knowledge toward understanding ERB in the context of island tourism. While results showed that tourists have a positive ERB as affirmed by the island's stakeholders, future studies may examine tourists' ERB in different stages of the destination lifecycle (Butler, 2011). As the study was carried out in an emerging destination, results are not generalizable. Nevertheless, the study provided a cognitive schema of tourists' ERB that should be studied further in other island tourism destinations. Despite this study's contributions, findings presented herein are subject to limitations. First, a longitudinal study is recommended to examine the long-term ERB of tourists. Nonetheless, conducting the study during peak season enabled more responses to examine the tourists' ERB as many participants were involved in the study. Second, tourists were not asked if they were repeat visitors together with their point of origin that may have a predisposition with their natural environment. Studies may consider examining the effect of this type of tourist as motivation to visit island destinations and determine if being environment-friendly motivates tourists (whether local or foreign) to repeat their visit. Additionally, the present study looks into tourists' ERB as general; thus, future research should consider distinguishing domestic and foreign tourists' ERB for creating more specific policy and marketing strategies. Third, future studies may focus on other variables, such as the destination image and legislation aspects of an island, as stakeholders perceived that tourists' positive ERB are influenced by these factors. This perception may have an implication toward marketing and promoting island destinations. Finally, this study provided a foundation for literature on the role of stakeholders in influencing tourists' ERB. Future studies may be conducted among other entities, especially for tourism private enterprises, such as restaurants, accommodation and transportation services, among others. The perception of other entities for this group on influencing tourists' ERB must be solicited for further validation. Obtaining more samples for each stakeholder group is further recommended to provide a broader perspective of their role.

Acknowledgements

The lead author would like to express gratitude to the Commission on Higher Education (CHED) - Philippines for the support provided in the study. All authors are grateful to Rosalyn Sontillanosa for providing the map.

Disclosure statement

No potential conflict of interest was reported by the authors.

ORCID

Mary Stephanie E. King-Chan 🆔 http://orcid.org/0000-0001-9068-2874
Robert Charles G. Capistrano 🆔 http://orcid.org/0000-0002-6875-0700
Emma Lina F. Lopez 🆔 http://orcid.org/0000-0002-1834-2469

References

Bagadion, B., & Del Fierro-Juan, N. (2013). *Transforming protected areas into effective and sustainable ecotourism destinations: Lessons from the ground* (Working Paper 13-24). Asian Institute of Management.

Becken, S. (2004). How tourists and tourism experts perceive climate change and carbon-offsetting schemes. *Journal of Sustainable Tourism*, *12*(4), 332–345. https://doi.org/10.1080/09669580408667241

Bengtsson, M. (2016). How to plan and perform a qualitative study using content analysis. *Nursingplus Open*, *2*, 8–14. https://doi.org/10.1016/j.npls.2016.01.001

Berenguer, J., Corraliza, J. A., & Martín, R. (2005). Rural–urban differences in environmental concern, attitudes, and actions. *European Journal of Psychological Assessment*, *21*(2), 128–138. https://doi.org/10.1027/1015-5759.21.2.128

Budeanu, A. (2007). Sustainable tourist behavior – a discussion of opportunities for change. *International Journal of Consumer Studies*, *31*(5), 499–508. https://doi.org/10.1111/j.1470-6431.2007.00606.x

Butler, R. (2011). *Tourism area life cycle: Contemporary tourism reviews*. Goodfellow.

Byrd, E. T. (2007). Stakeholders in sustainable tourism development and their roles: Applying stakeholder theory to sustainable tourism development. *Tourism Review*, *62*(2), 6–13. https://doi.org/10.1108/16605370780000309

Canavan, B. (2017). Tourism stakeholder exclusion and conflict in small island. *Leisure Studies*, *36*(3), 1–422. https://doi.org/10.1080/02614367.2016.1141975

Carlsen, J., & Butler, R. (Eds.). (2011). *Island tourism: Towards a sustainable perspective*. CABI.

Catibog-Sinha, C., & Heaney, L. (2006). *Philippine biodiversity: Principles and practice*. Haribon Foundation.

Cheng, T., & Wu, H. (2015). How do environmental knowledge, environmental sensitivity, and place attachment affect environmentally responsible behavior? An integrated approach for sustainable island tourism. *Journal of Sustainable Tourism*, *23*(4), 557–576. https://doi.org/10.1080/09669582.2014.965177

Chiu, Y., Lee, W., & Chen, T. (2014). Environmentally responsible behavior in ecotourism: Antecedents and implications. *Tourism Management*, *40*, 321–329. https://doi.org/10.1016/j.tourman.2013.06.013

CPTO (Camiguin Provincial Tourism Office). (2018). *Report on the regional distribution of traveler – Camiguin Province*. personal communication.

CPTO (Camiguin Provincial Tourism Office). (2015). *Camiguin province data*.

Creswell, J., & Clark, V. L. P. (2007). *Designing and conducting mixed methods research*. SAGE.

Cruz, R., & Legaspi, G. F. (2019). Boracay beach closure: The role of the government and the private sector. In R. Dodds & R. Butler (Eds.), *Overtourism: Issues, realities and solution* (pp. 95–110). De Gruyter.

Dolnicar, S., Crouch, G. I., & Long, P. (2008). Environment-friendly tourists: What do we really know about them? *Journal of Sustainable Tourism*, *16*(2), 197–210. https://doi.org/10.2167/jost738.0

Dolnicar, S., & Leisch, R. (2008). An investigation of tourists' patterns of obligation to protect the environment. *Journal of Travel Research*, *46*(4), 381–391. https://doi.org/10.1177/0047287507308330

Doyle, L., Brady, A.-M., & Byrne, G. (2009). An overview of mixed methods research. *Journal of Research in Nursing, 14*(2), 175–185. https://doi.org/10.1177/1744987108093962

Drumm, A., & Moore, A. (2002). *Ecotourism development: A manual for conservation planners and managers. Volume 1: An introduction to ecotourism planning.* The Nature Conservancy.

Dunlap, R., Van Liere, K. D., Mertig, A. G., & Jones, R. E. (2000). New trends in measuring environmental attitudes: Measuring endorsement of the new ecological paradigm: A revised NEP scale. *Journal of Social Issues, 56*(3), 425–442. https://doi.org/10.1111/0022-4537.00176

Eagles, P. (2014). Research priorities in park tourism. *Journal of Sustainable Tourism, 22*(4), 528–549. https://doi.org/10.1080/09669582.2013.785554

Fairweather, J., Maslin, C., & Simmons, D. (2005). Environmental values and response to ecolabels among international visitors to New Zealand. *Journal of Sustainable Tourism, 13*(1), 82–98. https://doi.org/10.1080/17501220508668474

Graci, S. (2013). Collaboration and partnership development for sustainable tourism. *Tourism Geographies, 15*(1), 25–42. https://doi.org/10.1080/14616688.2012.675513

Hair, J., Black, W., Babin, B., & Anderson, R. (2010). *Multivariate data analysis.* Prentice Hall.

Hall, C. M. (2010). Island destinations: A natural laboratory for tourism: Introduction. *Asia Pacific Journal of Tourism Research, 15*(3), 245–249. https://doi.org/10.1080/10941665.2010.503613

Han, H., Jae, M., & Hwang, J. (2016). Cruise travelers' environmentally responsible decision-making: An integrative framework of goal-directed behavior and norm activation process. *International Journal of Hospitality Management, 53*, 94–105. https://doi.org/10.1016/j.ijhm.2015.12.005

Han, H., & Kim, Y. (2010). An investigation of green hotel customers' decision formation: Developing an extended model of the theory of planned behavior. *International Journal of Hospitality Management, 29*(4), 659–668. https://doi.org/10.1016/j.ijhm.2010.01.001

Heaney, L., & Tabaranza Jr, B. (2006). A new species of forest mouse, genus *Apomys* (Mammalia: Rodentia: Muridae) from Camiguin Island. *Philippines. Fieldiana Zoology, 106*, 14–27.

Hidayah, Z., Rosyid, D. M., & Armono, H. D. (2016). Planning for sustainable small island management: Case study of Gili Timur Island East Java Province Indonesia. *Procedia - Social and Behavioral Sciences, 227*, 785– 790. https://doi.org/10.1016/j.sbspro.2016.06.146

Jang, Y. J., Zheng, T., & Bosselman, R. (2017). Top managers' environmental values, leadership, and stakeholder engagement in promoting environmental sustainability in the restaurant industry. *International Journal of Hospitality Management, 63*, 101–111. https://doi.org/10.1016/j.ijhm.2017.03.005

Jerusalem, J. (2020, January 10). Camiguin eyes cap on tourist arrivals. *Inquirer.* https://www.google.com/amp/s/newsinfo.inquirer.net/1211098/camiguin-eyes-cap-on-tourist-arrivals/amp

Kaiser, F. G., Wölfing, S., & Fuhrer, U. (1999). Environmental attitude and ecological behaviour. *Journal of Environmental Psychology, 19*(1), 1–19. https://doi.org/10.1006/jevp.1998.0107

Khazaei, A., Elliot, S., & Joppe, M. (2015). An application of stakeholder theory to advance community participation in tourism planning: The case for engaging immigrants as fringe stakeholders. *Journal of Sustainable Tourism, 23*(7), 1049–1062. https://doi.org/10.1080/09669582.2015.1042481

Kil, M., Holland, S. M., & Stein, T. V. (2014). Structural relationships between environmental attitudes, recreation motivations, and environmentally responsible behaviors. *Journal of Outdoor Recreation and Tourism, 7-8*(8), 16–25. https://doi.org/10.1016/j.jort.2014.09.010

Kollmuss, A., & Agyeman, J. (2002). Mind the gap: Why do people act environmentally and what are the barriers to pro-environmental behavior? *Environmental Education Research, 8*(3), 239–260. https://doi.org/10.1080/13504620220145401

Lee, T. H. (2011). How recreation involvement, place attachment and conservation commitment affect environmentally responsible behavior. *Journal of Sustainable Tourism, 19*(7), 895–915. https://doi.org/10.1080/09669582.2011.570345

Lee, T. H. (2013). Environmentally responsible behavior of nature-based tourists: Related concepts, measurement, and research. *Journal of Tourism Hospitality, 2*(2), 1–2. https://doi.org/10.4172/2167-0269.1000e126

Lee, T. H., & Jan, F.-H. (2015). The influence of recreation experience and environmental attitude on the environmentally responsible behavior of community-based tourists in Taiwan. *Journal of Sustainable Tourism, 23*(7), 1063–1094. https://doi.org/10.1080/09669582.2015.1032298

Lee, T. H., Jan, F.-H., & Yang, C.-C. (2013). Conceptualizing and measuring environmentally responsible behavior from the perspective of community-based tourists. *Tourism Management, 36*, 454–468. https://doi.org/10.1016/j.tourman.2012.09.012

Lyon, A., Hunter-Jones, P., & Warnaby, G. (2017). Are we any closer to sustainable development? Listening to active stakeholder discourses of tourism development in the Waterberg Biosphere Reserve. Tourism Management, *61*, 234–247. https://doi.org/10.1016/j.tourman.2017.01.010

Mallari, N. A. D., Tabaranza Jr, B. R., & Crosby, M. J. (2001). *Key conservation sites in the Philippines: A Haribon Foundation & Birdlife International Directory of Important Bird Areas.* Bookmark.

Marzo-Navarro, M., Pedraja-Iglesias, M., & Vinzón, L. (2015). Sustainability indicators of rural tourism from the perspective of the residents. *Tourism Geographies, 17*(4), 586–602. https://doi.org/10.1080/14616688.2015.1062909

Meijers, M. H. C., & Stapel, D. A. (2011). Me tomorrow, the others later: How perspective fit increases sustainable behavior. *Journal of Environmental Psychology, 31*(1), 14–20. https://doi.org/10.1016/j.jenvp.2010.06.002

Miles, J. F. (2012). *Management and organization theories.* John Wiley & Sons.

Milfont, T. L., & Duckitt, J. (2010). The environmental attitudes inventory: A valid and reliable measure to assess the structure of environmental attitudes. *Journal of Environmental Psychology, 30*(1), 80–94. https://doi.org/10.1016/j.jenvp.2009.09.001

Mobley, C., Vagias, W. M., & DeWard, S. L. (2010). Exploring additional determinants of environmentally responsible behavior: The influence of environmental literature and environmental attitudes. *Environment and Behavior, 42*(4), 420–447. https://doi.org/10.1177/0013916508325002

Mutana, S., & Mukwada, G. (2017). An exploratory assessment of significant tourism sustainability indicators for a montane-based route in the Drakensberg Mountains. Sustainability, *9*(7), 1202. https://doi.org/10.3390/su9071202

Nilsson, M., & Küller, R. (2000). Travel behaviour and environmental concern. *Transportation Research Part D: Transport and Environment, 5*(3), 211–234. https://doi.org/10.1016/S1361-9209(99)00034-6 https://doi.org/10.1016/S1361-9209(99)00034-6

Nunkoo, R., & Ramkissoon, H. (2012). Structural equation modelling and regression analysis in tourism research. *Current Issues in Tourism, 15*(8), 777–802. https://doi.org/10.1080/13683500.2011.641947

Paswan, A., Guzman, F., & Lewin, J. (2017). Attitudinal determinants of environmentally sustainable behavior. *Journal of Consumer Marketing, 34*(5), 414–426. https://doi.org/10.1108/JCM-02-2016-1706

Peric, M., Drukin, J., & Lamot, I. (2014). Importance of stakeholder management in Tourism project: Case study of the Istra Inspirit project. In *Tourism and Hospitality Congress Proceedings: Trends in Tourism and Hospitality Industry* (pp. 273–286).

Perkins, H. E., & Brown, P. R. (2012). Environmental values and the so-called true ecotourist. *Journal of Travel Research, 51*(6), 793–803. https://doi.org/10.1177/0047287512451133

PIA, Philippine Information Agency. (2015, December 28). Domestic arrivals dominate Camiguin's tourism market. *Camiguin News Bulletin.* https://camiguinnews.wordpress.com/2015/12/30/domestic-arrivals-dominate-camiguins-tourism-market/

PSA (Philippines Statistic Authority). (2016). Region X Northern Mindanao: Total population by province, city municipality and barangay. *Census Population.* https://psa.gov.p/content/population-region-x-northern-mindanao-based-2015-census-population

Puhakka, R. (2011). Environmental concern and responsibility among nature tourists in Ounlanka PAN Park, Finland. *Scandinavian Journal of Hospitality and Tourism, 11*(1), 76–96. https://doi.org/10.1080/15022250.2011.532589

Qiuyin, Q., Zhang, J., Yang, Y., Shaojing, L., & Honglei, Z. (2009). On environmental attitudes and behavior intention of tourists in natural heritage site: A case study of. *Jiuzhaigou. Tourism Tribune, 24*(11), 41–46.

Ramchurjee, N., & Suresha, S. (2015). Are tourists' environmental behavior affected by their environmental perceptions and beliefs? *Journal of Environmental and Tourism Analyses, 3*(1), 26–44.

Rosenberg, M. J., & Hovland, C. I. (1960). Cognitive, affective, and behavioural components of attitudes. In M. J. Rosenberg, C. I. Hovland, W. J. McGuire, R. P. Ablson, & J. W. Brehm (Eds.), *Attitude organization and change* (pp. 1–14). Yale University Press.

Saftic, D., Tezak, A., & Luk, N. (2011, March). *Stakeholder approach in tourism management: Implication in Croatian tourism* [Paper Presentation]. 30th International Conference on Organizational Science Development, Portorož, Slovenia. http://bib.irb.hr/datoteka/507719. Stakeholder_approach_in_tourism_management.pdf

Schultz, P. W., Gouveia, V. V., Cameron, L. D., Tankha, G., Schmuck, P., & Franěk, M. (2005). Values and their relationship to environmental concern and conservation behavior. *Journal of Cross-Cultural Psychology, 36*(4), 457–475. https://doi.org/10.1177/0022022105275962

Stern, P. C. (2000). New environmental theories: Toward a coherent theory of environmentally significant behavior. *Journal of Social Issues, 56*(3), 407–424. https://doi.org/10.1111/0022-4537. 00175

Tabernero, C., & Hernandez, B. (2011). Self-efficacy and intrinsic motivation guiding environmental behavior. Environment and Behavior, *43*(5), 658–675. https://doi.org/10.1177/0013916510379759

Wiernik, B. M., Ones, D. S., & Dilchert, S. (2013). Age and environmental sustainability: A meta-analysis. *Journal of Managerial Psychology, 28*(7–8), 826–856. https://doi.org/10.1108/JMP-07-2013-0221

Wurzinger, S., & Johansson, M. (2006). Environmental concern and knowledge of ecotourism among three groups of Swedish tourists. *Journal of Travel Research, 45*(2), 217–226. https://doi.org/10.1177/0047287506291602

Wynveen, C. J., Kyle, G. T., & Sutton, S. G. (2014). Environmental worldview, place attachment, and awareness of environmental impacts in a marine environment. *Environment and Behavior, 46*(8), 993–1017. https://doi.org/10.1177/0013916513484325

Young, S., & Dhanda, K. (2012). *Sustainability: Essentials for business*. SAGE.

Zhang, M., Zhong, Z., & Gui, W. (2013). The empirical research on tourists' environmental attitude and environmental behavior – a case study of Shenzhen OCT East. *Journal of Hospitality & Tourism, 11*(2), 47–64.

Community meaning making for tourism sustainability on Madura Island, Indonesia

Tamara Young (iD), Dian Yulie Reindrawati, Patricia Johnson and Kevin Lyons

ABSTRACT

Resident perception orthodoxies have dominated host community research, undermining potentialities for human-centred sustainable tourism outcomes. Homogenised host gaze outcomes have been crafted from decades of surveys that largely overlook the perspectives of non-Western less-developed host communities, including residents of remote island locations. Indeed, despite the popularity of islands as destinations, little is known about residents' interpretations of tourismprior to the potential influx of tourists. Our study focuses on the meanings of tourism and variations of the host gaze that emerge from interviews with individual residents in a devout Islamic island community. The island of Madura, located off the coast of Java in Indonesia, has only recently been established and promoted as a tourist destination. A critical symbolic interactionist approach provides a method for exploring diverse meanings associated with tourism as they emerge in a particular social context, providing nuanced insights into meaning making that perception based analyses are unlikely to reveal. The findings of the qualitative analysis coalesce around five discursive themes: advancing enterprise, economic mobility, pilgrimage, moral decline, and commodification. Each of these discourses are dynamic and embed both positive and negative sentiments that challenge the notion of a homogenous host gaze. Rather, these discourses reflect the multiple gazes that emerge in the religio-cultural milieu that comprises Madura Island.

摘要

过去二十年来, 正统的学术文献一直主导着对居民感知的研究。被同质化了的东道主凝视的结果是根据几十年的调查精心设计的, 这些调查很大程度上忽视了非西方欠发达地区的东道主社区的视角, 包括偏远岛屿的社区居民。事实上, 尽管岛屿作为旅游目的地很受欢迎, 但在潜在的游客涌入之前, 人们对当地居民对旅游业的认识却知之甚少。我们的研究集中在旅游的意义和东道主社区凝视的变化, 这些变化来自于对一个虔诚的伊斯兰岛屿社区居民的访谈。位于印度尼西亚爪哇海岸外面的马都拉岛最近才被建设并宣传为旅游目的地。一个批判的符号交互作用方法提供了一种途径探索与旅游相关的各种意义, 因为它们出现在一个特定的社区环境中, 难以揭示基于知觉的分析结果。质性分析的结果凝聚为五个主题:企业发展、经济流动性、朝圣、道德沦丧和商品化。这些话语都是动态的, 并嵌入了积极和消极的情感, 挑战了同质化的东道主凝视的概念。相反, 这些论述反映了马都拉岛宗教文化环境中呈现出的多重凝视。

1. Introduction

Over the past two decades, research on resident perceptions of tourism have been pivotal to building consensus about how tourism impacts destination host communities
(Deery, Jago, & Fredline, 2012; Kim, Uysal, & Sirgy, 2013; Li, Ryan, & Cave, 2016; Nunkoo,
Smith, & Ramkissoon, 2013; Sharpley, 2014). This existing research has understandably
focused on established destinations where the impacts of tourism are acute (Nunkoo &
Gursoy, 2012; Nunkoo et al., 2013; Sharpley, 2014). However, Deery et al. (2012, p. 65) criti-
cise resident perception studies as being in 'a state of arrested development' neglecting
to address the heterogeneity of diverse host communities. Resident perceptions of tourism in diverse destination communities are either 'taken for granted or pushed aside as
unimportant' (Amuquandoh, 2010, p. 34) and there is a lack of published qualitative
research that elucidates how particular communities perceive and assign meaning to
tourism. The meanings behind resident perceptions towards tourism are often easily dis-
missed as outliers in the etic approaches that have dominated resident perception studies to date (Amuquandoh, 2010; Deery et al., 2012).

This article aligns with the growing body of research on the host gaze (Moufakkir &
Reisinger, 2013). Host gaze studies are positioned by Moufakkir (2011, pp. 77-78) as those
concerned with the construction, development, reinforcement and consequences of the
gaze: 'the host gaze starts where perceptions surveys stop'. Like the tourist gaze (Urry &
Larsen, 2011), the host gaze is recognised as being socially and culturally organised and
is 'subject to change with changing economic, demographic, social, political, cultural and
other social phenomena' (Moufakkir & Reisinger, 2013, p. xi). Host gaze studies are effective in capturing the nuances of dynamic social interactions within the particular geographic, social, cultural and political contexts that may influence the meanings assigned
to tourism (Berno, 1999; Hepburn, 2002; Santos & Buzinde, 2007).

Our research assumes an emic approach to consider the gaze of a diverse group of residents in eight villages of Madura, an island located off the northeastern coast of Java, the
capital city of Indonesia (see, Figure 1). The data for this study was collected at a time of profound change: when the opening of the Surabaya-Madura National Bridge (the Suramadu
Bridge) connected the previously isolated island to East Java. At the time of research,
Madura Island was emerging as a potential tourism destination, primarily for domestic visitors, with the host communities having had very limited experience of tourism.

The bounded geography of island destinations in Indonesia engender unique religio-cultural permutations that may not exist in other places (Geertz, 1966). On the
Indonesian archipelago Islam is the prominent religion, and the large diversity of traditional and ancestral island ethnic groups strongly influence how Islam is practiced
(Peacock, 1986). To understand the rise of tourism and what it means to residents in
the religio-cultural context of Madura Island, research requires the micro-examination
of the meaning making process at the same time as acknowledging the influences of
Islamic cultural praxis at play in this community. Consistent with a critical symbolic
interactionist approach, this study positions day-to-day interactions and meaning making within the complexities of the particular social and cultural context that may influence those interactions (Aksan, Kisac, Aydin, & Demirbuken, 2009; Santos & Buzinde,

Figure 1. Map of Indonesia highlighting the location of Madura Island.
(Source: CIA, 2018)

2007). The following literature review considers how religio-cultural contexts interplay with the host gaze, and describes how a critical symbolic interactionist framework helps unpack and illuminate this interplay.

2. Literature review

According to Amuquandoh (2010), an understanding of meanings and interpretations beyond perceptions requires a nuanced and in-depth examination of individuals and groups within a community. Recognition of historical and cultural contexts of resident societies is key (Nunkoo et al., 2013; Sharpley, 2014). For example, non-Western less developed societies have been found to view tourists and tourism differently, confirming that meanings are not only localised but also culturally influenced (Berno, 1999; Hepburn, 2002). Further, meanings are complex and contested, and can vary according to community roles (Cheung, 1999). A homogenised view of island communities misrepresents the population for not recognising the different interest groups at play (Mowforth & Munt, 2016). Given that this research focuses on the meanings of tourism in a devout Islamic island community, this culturally specific context warrants further discussion.

2.1. Religio-cultural contexts and Islamic destinations

Religio-cultural context refers to the overlap and juxtaposition of cultural and religious practices and is informed by Geetz's (1966) seminal work that focused on Islam in Indonesia. Indonesia is the largest Muslim country with close to 90% of the 209 million

Figure 2. The Surabaya-Madura (Suramadu) National Bridge.
(Source: iStock/Valens Hascaryo, 2019)

population followers of Islam (Jafari & Scott, 2014). Religion and culture are interwoven in Muslim societies; religion is an integral part of everyday life and the essence of identity (Hassan, 2007; Jafari & Scott, 2014; Zamani-Farahani & Henderson, 2010). Whilst there is significant difference across countries regarding the influence of values and beliefs of Islam, the *Qur'an* 'provides guidance in all aspects of human activity' including tourism (Jafari & Scott, 2014, p. 13). As Zamani-Farahani and Henderson (2010, p. 79) explain, society 'is ordered in conformity with the principles of Islamic law, which directly and indirectly affect recreation and travel'. Geertz (2000) notes that while broad-based conformity to Islamic teachings is evident, geographically isolated contexts (such as, those found in Indonesia) result in unique localised religio-cultural practices. A nuanced understanding of these practices is, therefore, essential when seeking to understand their influence on how meanings of tourism develop in such contexts.

Religio-cultural norms and values shape leisure and tourism choices and experiences (Jafari & Scott, 2014), as well as tourism industry operations and tourism destination policy making (Henderson, 2010). However, how these operate under particular contextual conditions – especially given that every Muslim country is a complex amalgamation of tradition, culture and religion – is often overlooked in tourism research. An exception is Ackerman's (2019, p. 406) recent discourse recognising place meaning as 'often limited by traditional dualisms of sacred/profane, pilgrim/tourism, and body/mind'.

An increased scholarly interest in touristic travel by Muslims explains Islamic tourism as religiously inspired travel 'primarily undertaken by its followers within the Muslim world' with an emphasis on pilgrimage (Henderson, 2010, p. 76). Religious tourism is a tenet of Islam, especially through pilgrimage (for example, the *Hajj* to Mecca is the fifth pillar of Islam in the *Qur'an*). The primary purpose of Islamic tourism is for historical, social and cultural experiences to, for example, mosques and shrines that emphasise 'the sacred goal of submission to the ways of God' (Din, 1989, p. 551). Individual motivations for Islamic tourism will not always be exclusively religious; Islamic travellers may seek 'similar leisure experiences to non-Muslims, albeit within parameters set by Islam' (Henderson, 2010, p.76).

As hosts and guests, Muslims are 'repeatedly enjoined to support *Fi-Sibilillah* (in the cause of God)' (Din, 1989, p. 551) seeking to encourage the responsible and congenial development of host-guest relationships (Din, 1989; Jafari & Scott, 2014). Although it has been noted that tensions may arise when Muslim residents and non-Muslim tourists intersect at destinations (Henderson, 2003; Henderson, 2010), there is little knowledge about the intersections of Islam, culture and tourism from a host perspective (Jafari & Scott, 2014). In the context of Madura Island, central to religious tourism is *silaturrahim*, an Islamic practice entrenched in Madurese culture. *Silaturrahim*, an Arabic word meaning 'brotherhood' or the 'bond of friendship' is enacted in various ways, and has been positioned as building communities, family reunions and gatherings of kinship, and kindness towards others (Efyanti, 2016).

Din (1989) explores community attitudes towards tourism in Muslim countries. His discussion of host-guest encounters found resident perceptions to be either positive or negative, with optimistic attitudes based on the economic benefits of tourism (for example, income and employment). Historically, orientalist pre-conceptions or tropes of post-colonial imagination have focused the gaze of Westerners to Islamic countries (Johnson, 2010). Yet as Din (1989) argues, this is often the starting point of negative perceptions in Muslim communities – particularly the view that western tourism is hedonistic and often violates Islamic norms. Islamic law 'deals with the whole of human conduct' (Jafari & Scott, 2014, p. 4) and laws governing behaviour influence Muslims as destination hosts (Din, 1989) and the 'conditions and obligations about religious observances... can pose dilemmas' for Muslims hosts (Zamani-Farahani & Henderson, 2010, p. 80). Fisher (2004) observes the demonstration effect in traditional destinations where social learning by youth affects behaviour which can disrupt and/ or challenge traditional value systems. Indeed, knowledge acquisition of social practices, consumption patterns, and other tourism behaviours, commonly trigger community reactions towards tourists and tourism in emerging destinations (Canavan, 2016; Fisher, 2004; Harrill, 2004; Lepp, 2008).

Academic writings have tended to speculate that the development of tourism in Muslim countries may lead to conflict over values and beliefs (see, for example, Din, 1989; Jafari & Scott, 2014; Zamani-Farahani & Henderson, 2010). Touristic experiences of Islamic living cultural heritage draw from social and cultural resources which, like tangible resources, can be depleted through exposure. Examples of tourists seeking experiences of authenticity in local culture and traditions are evident in the appeal of the burial practices of the Toraja of Sulawesi (Adams, 1984; Adams, 2018) and attendance at funeral processions for Western tourists visiting Bali (Wall, 1996; Yamashita, 2003). In her study at the Shrine of Shah-e Tcheraq in Shiraz in Iran, Johnson (2001, p. 53) reports on tensions that can exist between Islamic hosts and Western tourists reporting that a tour leader recognised 'the presence of anti-Western hostility even when it was not overtly shown due to Iranian custom of showing courtesy to strangers' (Johnson, 2001, p. 53). In these situations of conflict, host communities may mask overt expressions of true feelings when confronted with inappropriate behaviour as a coping strategy.

Whilst these studies provide insight into potential host-guest tensions, research investigating the host gaze and tourism in Muslim communities remains under researched (Jafari & Scott, 2014). To examine the multifaceted nature of tourism and the articulation of tourism by the host community, the question guiding this study maintains an emic perspective: *What does tourism mean to residents of Madura Island?* Traditional approaches to symbolic interactionism provide a theoretical frame for examining meaning making processes (Blumer, 1969). A critical turn in this theory acknowledges that meaning making must consider the specific cultural contexts within which these processes are located (Bianchi, 2009; Denzin, 1989). This critical approach is adopted in our study of the meanings of tourism from a host perspective in an emerging island destination.

2.2. Symbolic interactionism revisited

Symbolic interactionism is a social psychological approach that seeks to understand: the ways that people as sense-making beings use the meanings associated with symbols; and, the related impact these meanings have on behaviour. As a theoretical perspective developed by Mead (1962), symbolic interactionalism is a pragmatic approach to deciphering meaning making as a dialogic process between self and society. This approach examines how society influences the self: 'human beings act toward things on the basis of the meanings that the things have for them' and meaning is 'derived from, or arises out of, the social interaction that one has with one's fellows' (Blumer, 1969, p. 2). Central to the theory is that no individual stands alone because relationships are always developed with others (Lauer & Handel, 1977) and meanings are 'handled in, and modified through, an interpretive process' by an individual as they deal with the things they encounter (Blumer, 1969, p. 2). Accordingly, 'facts' are based on and directed by the interpretation of symbols, and these interpretations serve to guide actions (Aksan et al., 2009). People act according to a world they define (Charon, 1979) and they 'form meaning as a result of their own experiences' (Aksan et al., 2009, p. 903). Therefore, objects will have different meanings for different people (Amuquandoh, 2010) and will affect the ways in which individuals and societies behave towards an object (Xiao, 1997). As Blumer (1969, p. 11) explains, 'meaning sets the way in which he [sic] sees the object, the way in which he is prepared to act toward it, and the way in which he is ready to talk about it'.

Our study extends this micro-interactionist perspective by locating meaning making within a context where religio-cultural factors have significant influence. Early approaches to symbolic interactionism have been inextricably linked to grounded theory, a methodological approach that places importance on rich descriptions of interactions and how individuals draw meanings from objects in their daily lives (Blumer, 1969). However, such a micro-approach has been widely criticised for lacking critical interpretations of the social contexts that operate somewhat invisibly in shaping meaning making processes (Dennis & Martin, 2007; Denzin, 1989; Musolf, 1992). Therefore, more recently, researchers have revisited symbolic interactionism as a theoretical frame that can be used to more critically position day-to-day meaning making interactions within the context of broader sociocultural influences (Carter & Fuller, 2016; Handberg, Thorne, Midtgaard, Nielsen, & Lomborg, 2015).

Colton (1987) explains that it is through interpretation that the signs and symbols of tourism produce meanings which are affixed to the toured: places, peoples and cultures (see, also, Wearing, Stevenson, & Young, 2010). Symbols can appear as human (for example, the samba dancers of Brazil), as the built environment (such as, the pyramids), as the natural environment (such as, the hedonistic island paradise), and in a number of other forms. Following Colton (1987), this study employs an interpretive-qualitative research design. We examine the outward host gaze focusing on how residents symbolise tourism andtourists. In so doing, we investigate meaning making processes and how meanings are negotiated and interpreted. Given the importance of understanding the context within which meanings are made, the following section explains the unique geographical, historical, social, and cultural context of this study.

3. The study area

Madura Island is off the north eastern coast of Java, Indonesia (see, Figure 1), with a population of over 3.5 million people. Indonesia is home to around 300 ethnic groups influenced by geographic and topographical location, groups that are most often identified by the island on which they live (Javanese, Balinese, Sudanese, Madurese, and so on). The data for this study was gathered in 2009, five months after the opening of the Suramadu Bridge linking Madura Island with Surabaya in East Java. Madura Island presents an intriguing case study to examine initial meanings of tourism because, since the opening of the bridge to the time of writing (in 2019), the island continues to represent an emerging destination in the exploration stage of tourism development (Butler, 2006). Lonely Planet (2018) recently described Madura Island as an 'off the beaten track' destination that attracts only 'a trickle of tourists'.

The Suramadu Bridge is a mega infrastructure project (the longest bridge in South East Asia) that introduced a land route to the island previously only accessible by sea. Strohmayer (2011, p. 120) explains 'the most immediate nexus between architecture and mobility comes in the form of bridges'. Bridges are part of the urban fabric in myriad ways. The function of bridges in facilitating amenity has often been mentioned in island tourism research (see, for example, Andriotis, 2004; Bramwell, 2004, Joliffe & Smith, 2001), most notably in relation to increased access, increased tourist visitation and resident mobility, and increased economic viability. The Suramadu Bridge connecting Madura Island to Surabaya facilitates amenity in all these ways. The period of time following the opening of the bridge presented new possibilities for resident encounters with tourists and tourism and, in line with the focus of this article, encounters between people of different religio-cultural milieu. This study presents insight into the views of Muslim residents towards tourism thus addressing Zamani-Farahani and Henderson's (2010) concern that little is known about the effects of tourism on Islamic religio-cultural destinations. By identifying themes that underpin the meanings of tour-ism, a unique religio-cultural context to analysing the host gaze is revealed at a critical and historically significant time of change: when Madura Island was on the cusp of emerging as a tourism destination:

Given its enduring isolation prior to the opening of the Suramadu Bridge, Madura Island was described as an insular society with limited economic development, unemployment, poverty, and rapid migration to the Java 'mainland' (Rachbini, 1995; Van Dijk, De Jonge, & Touwen-Bouwsma, 1995). The opening of the Suramadu Bridge was described as a proud accomplishment of the Indonesian government whose goal was to boost the economy of Madura Island, including the development of tourism (Faisal & Harsaputra, 2009). Data on tourism arrivals to Madura Island were not avail-able at the time of research and continue to be unavailable. While country-wide arrival statistics are available, a breakdown of arrivals to the island remain non-existent. Empirical evidence gathered in this study found that tourism to Madura Island increased after the bridge opened, particularly domestic tourism from Java (Reindrawati, 2013). Visitors to the island can experience traditional culture unique to the Madurese, including tours of ancient palaces, shrines, tombs, religious tours of the *pesantran* (Islamic boarding schools), and to attend the annual bull races. Because of increased tourist activity in the town of Sumenep (in the immediate vicinity of the bridge), development swiftly followed with a tourist information centre, Islamic Centre, food court, cafes, souvenir stalls, parking area, playgrounds, and a mosque (Reindrawati, 2013). It is only very recently, in October 2018, that the Suramadu Bridge became 'toll-free' in a further attempt by the Indonesian government to boost the growth of Madura Island as a tourism destination (Wonderful Indonesia, 2019).

At the time of the bridge opening in June 2009, the local media identified pre-existing challenges to tourism, including low levels of support from local residents who reportedly viewed tourism as a corrupting influence threatening cultural customs and traditions (Faisal & Harsaputra, 2009). A complex relationship between Islam, politics and traditional life is practiced on Madura Island, and conserving traditions in religion and culture are extremely important (Hidayaturrahman, 2018). There is a reli-gio-cultural uniqueness of the Madurese - the philosophy of *Buppa, Babbu, Guru, Rato* - a complex social code explaining relationships of power, authority and compliance that is exclusive to Madura Island.

The Madurese embrace the philosophy of *Buppa, Babbu, Guru, Rato* as the founda-tion of life and a philosophy of leadership with defined layers of respect maintaining a culture of obedience (Sobri, 2017). This ladder of respect is referred to as *tangga kuasa*, defined as the hierarchy of reverence given to the four major figures in life: Father (*Buppa*), Mother (*Babbu*), teachers/religious leaders (*Guru*) and government leader (*Rato*). Inherent to the hierarchy is the normative rule of obedience, a key tene-ment of the teaching of traditional authority in Madurese community. As Sobri (2017, p. 147) explains, this teaching is only one of several cultural identities of the Madurese, others include 'the culture of shame, Islam, deliberation and consensus'. While it is beyond the scope of this paper to go into depth about the origins of these practices, it is important to note that whilst this philosophy is not Islamic *per se*, the interconnectedness between the ways Islam permeates life on Madura Island

Table 1. The research sites.

	Villages with tourism planned or implemented	No. of residents interviewed in village	Villages without tourism planned or implemented	No. of residents interviewed in village
Bangkalan Regency	Sukolilo Barat	6	Banyuajuh	6
Sampang Regency	Taddan	6	Prakam	6
Pamekasan Regency	Tanjung	6	Kacok	6
Sumenep Regency	Kebon Agung	6	Prenduan	6

evidences a close compatibility with traditional norms and values. Islam is 'a part of [Madurese] ethnic identity ... [and serves] as a reference of social behaviour in people's lives' (Sobri, 2017, p. 147). *Buppa, Babbu, Guru, Rato* is a normative construction where violations of observance will result in social and/or cultural sanctions (Sobri, 2017).

Thus *Buppa, Babbu, Guru, Rato* is a major influence on everyday life of the Madurese and it is reasonable to expect that this value system plays a role in influencing tourism planning, development and industry on the island. Moreover, the culture of compliance and obedience (adherence to collective norms and values) will, arguably, influence the ways by which residents assign meaning to tourism. The results of this study seek to uncover meanings assigned to tourism, and the factors that influence the perceptions of residents associated with, and disassociated from, tourism development on the island.

4. The research process

4.1. Data collection

The study participants were adult residents living in the four regions of Madura Island: the regencies of Bangkalan, Sampang, Pamekasan and Sumenep. A regency is a second level administrative division directly administrated under a province (Madura Island is in the province of East Java). Data were collected from November 2009 to January 2010 in eight villages (two in each regency): four villages had tourism development planned or already implemented, and four villages where there were no tourism plans or development (see, Table 1). The choice of villages was informed by secondary data analysis of regional tourism master plans, and local and national media, supplemented by data collected from Indonesian tourism offices (Reindrawati, 2013).

Purposive sampling was employed to select all participants in the study. The criterion used was that any participant must be permanent resident of one of the eight selected villages. A recruitment strategy was put in place that utilised the distribution of recruitment flyers and direct word-of-mouth recruitment through snowball sampling. The recruitment flyers were placed on community noticeboards in the eight villages. These flyers outlined the rationale and objectives of the research, and invited individual residents to contact the researchers if they wished to participate in the study. This approach aimed to capture a range of backgrounds and societal roles but, ultimately, the reach was limited to those who accessed community noticeboards and who were literate. Low literacy typically reflects low socio-economic status (Elley,

2001) and literacy rates are low on Madura Island. Thus, while the method was useful to identify a cross-section of the communities, only gaining access to the literate did limit the diversity of voices.

To overcome this limitation, as the intention was to capture a wide diversity of society in these locations, an interactive model of recruitment was developed that recognised the ways that components (in this case, the study participants) affect and are affected by each other (Maxwell, 2009). For these reasons, snowball sampling was also used to recruit participants and proved useful to attract individuals that would otherwise be hard to reach, or hidden, within the population. Working with the initial group of residents recruited, the reach was widened to encourage others to come forward. The researchers were mindful that a disadvantage of this recruitment strategy is that referrers could recommend others who hold similar views to their own, which further limits the diversity of responses.

A total of 48 participants ranging from age 19 to 70 years (median 37 years) were recruited. The majority were male (75%), a result that may be attributed to the strong patriarchal cultural system which supports male dominance and female subordination and a strong hierarchical social structure (Sobri, 2017). Notably, in the Madurese *Buppa, Babbu, Guru, Rato* philosophy, *Buppa* or Fathercomes first as the head of the family. Although the participants were not categorised into the *Buppa, Babbu, Guru, Rato* roles during the analysis, it was understood that this cultural system is the ethos of the Madurese and, as an integral part of everyday life, would influence the research process in terms of recruitment and responses. It could be argued that because of the strength of social hierarchy present in the social order of Madura Island, low levels of literacy (reflected with low social standing in most, if not all, cases) may have dissuaded potential participants of this category. Thus, the results need to be considered within the parameters that all participants in the study were literate.

In-depth, semi-structured interviews were conducted with the 48 individuals. They represented a broad range of employment: 40% were involved in tourism. This group was split into: (a) direct tourism and hospitality (23%), and (b) small business sellers of food, cloth, souvenirs, and other items to visitors (17%). The sample included a large proportion of teachers (25%) relative to the population of Madura Island, 16% were public officers, and the remaining 19% were from a variety of walks of life (unemployed, fisherman, farmer, house duties, and so on; see, Table 2).

The interview schedule included structured questions of demographics and open-ended questions about involvement in, and feelings about, tourists and tourism. Questions were asked about their knowledge of tourism, their perceptions of the effects of tourism, and interviewees were asked to provide examples of any positive and negative impacts of tourism on the island. They were also asked about their employment dependency on tourism, their roles in the community, and the influence their role may have on their feelings towards tourism. These questions were open-ended and designed to be broad enough to encourage participants to speak openly and express their views freely (Cresswell, 2003; Denzin & Lincoln, 2008). The interviews ranged between 45 minutes to four hours, providing a rich foundation of qualitative data. Since there are no fixed rules for the sample size in qualitative research, the interviews stopped at the point of 'redundancy' (Lincoln & Guba, 1985, p. 202).

Table 2. Details of interview respondents.

Occupation	Gender		Age group				No. of respondents
	Male	Female	19–29	30–40	41–50	51–70	
Teacher	8	4	7	4	1	0	12
Market Sellers	4	4	3	0	3	2	8
Village Leader/Officer	4	0	1	2	1	0	4
General Business/Trade	4	0	2	1	0	1	4
Fisherman	2	0	0	1	0	1	2
Farmer	2	0	0	2	0	0	2
Student	2	1	2	0	1	0	3
Travel Agents	2	1	0	1	2	0	3
Restaurant	2	0	1	0	1	0	2
Government Officer	2	0	0	2	0	0	2
Grave Officer	2	0	0	0	0	2	2
Hotel Manager	1	0	0	0	1	0	1
Factory worker	0	1	0	1	0	0	1
House duties	0	1	0	0	1	0	1
Unemployed	1	0	0	0	1	0	1
Total by Gender	36	12	-	-	-	-	48
Total by Age	-	-	16	14	12	6	48

Adler and Adler (1987) argue that the researcher role when undertaking qualitative studies must be explicitly considered and acknowledged as having potential impact on the research process. The team included researchers from both Muslim and non-Muslim backgrounds, including an Indonesian resident of Java who conducted the interviews. The balance of context familiarity with, and distance from, the research setting enabled a form of triangulation of the data. The interviews were conducted in Bahasa Indonesian and were recorded and transcribed, and then translated into English by the member of the research team who is a native speaker of Bahasa. While it is possible that there is bias in having only a single translator, this bias was explicitly acknowledged with the Indonesian researcher reflecting on her positionality through the use of a reflective journal (Li, 2011; Temple & Young, 2004).

4.2. Data analysis

The data were analysed inductively using open, axial and selective coding techniques. These techniques were well suited to the inductive process and focused on 'discovering patterns, themes, and categories' (Patton, 2002, p. 453). Open coding helped to identify and label initial conceptual patterns in the transcripts (Sarantakos, 2005). Coding was carried out using N-Vivo software, where the initial codes (labels) were derived from actual words or phrases used by the participants (Strauss & Corbin, 1998). Axial coding was used to identify central characteristics in common and relationships between the initial open codes (Patton, 2002). This analytical process is consistent with symbolic interactionism as the initial codes reflected the meanings individuals assigned to tourism, while axial codes provided a technique for considering broader social influences in meaning-making.

Selective coding was used to identify and remove any initial open codes that appeared unrelated to the main themes that emerged through the axial coding process (Charmaz, 2006). This coding process provided the opportunity to describe and synthesise the meanings of tourism from the participants' perspective, and to provide a mechanism for interpreting the broader cultural factors that influence meaning making. All researchers undertook independent analysis of the data. A final process of comparing and reconciling differences into tentative themes was essential in developing the final themes. Through this process five key meanings of tourism were observed as key themes (see, Table 3). In the sections that follow, the findings based on this analysis are presented.

5. Findings: the meanings of tourism

Rich data were gathered from the interviews highlighting a diversity of views. The participants discussed the impact of the tourism industry on everyday life, and how they felt about tourists, tourism, and tourism development. Five overarching themes were found: advancing enterprise, economic mobility, pilgrimage, moral decline and commodification (see, Table 3).

5.1. Advancing enterprise

One key meaning was advancing enterprise whereby tourism was perceived as an opportunity to develop small businesses (such as, food and souvenir stalls) or to expand already established businesses (including, restaurants and hotels). Here, individuals discussed economic gains provided by increased visitation, and an overwhelming support of tourism growth because their experience of tourism had a material impact on their lives. For example, a female resident who rents a fixed stall selling souvenirs at the Bangkalan entrance to the Suramadu Bridge reflected on the pecuniary benefits for herself and her family, 'I am happy to have tourism development... because it gave me and my mum the opportunity to open our business and make money. It is a really big relief to have a job'.

Tourism was viewed as an opportunity to develop small businesses in tourist areas for employment and income. As one souvenir seller pointed out, 'before I started selling souvenirs at the bridge... I was out of work... my aunt asked me to consider selling at the bridge... [because] we could make more money, which was too tempting for me to resist'. Field observations in this location also confirmed that tourist activity near the bridge was busy, with food and souvenir stalls set up on both sides of the entrance and exit gates to take advantage of passing trade. The informal economy was also active with mobile sellers walking around selling items to visitors.

Tourism as an opportunity for entrepreneurship, including opening larger scale tourism and hospitality businesses, was also evident. For example, increased visitation from Java had motivated one interviewee to open a Javanese restaurant at Camplong Beach. He described tourism, and his decision to open the restaurant, as 'life changing'. Prior to opening his business, he was a teacher, but now considers his primary occupation as restauranteur and teaching as 'a safety net occupation'. His restaurant appeared quite large and busy. His decision to change occupation was influenced by his lowly status as a temporary teacher with a small salary. Increased visitation provided him the opportunity to gain higher income, job security and respect as a businessman; and he reported confidence with his future prospects. Another

Table 3. The meanings of tourism.

Meanings	Signifiers of meaning	Examples (Respondent quotes M = male; F = female)
Advancing enterprise	TOURISM is an opportunity to develop businesses	Tourism development ... gave me and my mum the opportunity to open our business and make money. (F, 21, seller) This area used to be quiet. Now, many business opportunities exist in here. (M, 44, chef) I depend on my [restaurant] business. (M, 22, restaurant entrepreneur) Tourism development is definitely good for bringing profits to our hotel. (M, 41, hotel manager)
	TOURISM provides opportunities for employment and income	It really is a big relief to have a job. (F, 21, seller) The more people come in, the more income I will get. (M, 57, seller) Tourism gives me opportunities to gain income. (M, 59, seller) Tourism may become a way for locals to earn some money. (M, 33, teacher) Tourism can add income for local residents. (M, 42, teacher)
Economic mobility	TOURISM can bring a positive change to people's lives	I am happier now because I am not as poor as what I was. (F, 29, seller) My additional income through tourism helps me funding my household economy. (M, 52, fisherman) I am financially independent now. (M, 23, seller)
	TOURISM can improve an individual's social status	People in my village respect me because I can earn some money. (M, 44, chef) Working ... gives me higher status in my community. (M, 34, farmer) Plenty of people followed me and did the same thing. (F, 29, seller)
Pilgrimage	TOURISM is spiritual and an opportunity for sharing and strengthening Islamic values	We have to see tourism as God's scripture. (F, 24, teacher) Tourism should be based on cultural and religious values. (F, 19, teacher) Tourism is an opportunity for us to do recreation and to strengthen our religion. (M, 25, teacher) Enjoying the beauty of beaches means enjoying the bless of God. (F, 23, teacher) Tourism ... gives me opportunities... to show my respect to my ancestors. (M, 59, seller) Tourism is about silaturrahim, connecting with others. (M, 36, teacher) Silaturrahim should be number one in tourism. (M, 33, teacher) The aim for tourism is developing wide silaturrahim. (M, 57, seller)
Moral decline	TOURIST BEHAVIOURS AND ACTIVITIES contradict religious values	I know that sometimes men and women who are not married take a room together at the hotel. (F, 45, housewife) Visitors at the beach wear improper dress and get drunk.... it does not agree with my religious values. (M, 40, entrepreneur) Tourism is filled with negative things such as karaoke, hotels, night clubs, drunks. (M, 40, teacher) There should be separation between men and women for a swimming pool ... this separation does not exist.(M, 42, teacher) Swimsuits should be fully closed ... [an open swimsuit] contradicts with our religious and cultural values (F, 23, teacher)
	TOURISM conflicts with Madurese religion and culture	Tourism... is unacceptable to me and this pesantren environment. (F, 24, teacher) I just cannot support tourism because I grew up in this neighbourhood and it is a Pesantren environment. (M, 30, unemployed)
	TOURISM changes the behaviour of the younger generation	[Karaoke] is a bad influence on the younger generation and does not fit with our cultural and religious values. (M, 46, village officer) Visitors will bring their own culture then people here may copy. (F, 24, teacher) Local teenagers may get drunk. This can harm the whole local residents. (F, 19, teacher) Sometimes many young people get drunk. (F, 37, fish factory employee)
Commodification	TOURISM commercialises traditional culture and religion	We have to be careful that tourism may damage our culture. (M, 33, teacher) [Visiting the graves of ancestors] should not be commercialised otherwise our religious values will gradually disappear. (M, 46, teacher)
	TOURISM destroys traditional culture and religion	We do not want destruction of culture happening in Madura. (M, 42, teacher) Hadrah is now replaced by modern band; this is a signal of cultural destruction. People will forget our cultural values.(M, 33, teacher) Tourism may destruct our religious values. (F, 23, teacher) Tourism will bring outsiders in. This can cause people to lose their faith. (F, 24, teacher)

entrepreneurial interviewee in Taddan Village also stated that 'tourism development is definitely good for bringing profits to our hotel'.

However, entrepreneurial activities are simply not feasible for many residents of Madura Island where poverty is widespread and traditional agriculture is the economic mainstay. For instance, interviewees involved in primary industries expressed a conservative (and risk-adverse) view by expressing an intent not to be dependent on tourism for fear it would not provide financial security. For example, a factory employee explained tourism 'is in its early stages with not many visitor arrivals ... I am better off continuing to work in a fish factory ... [it is] a more secure form of employment'.

For the participants who viewed tourism as advancing enterprise, the meaning of tourism was influenced by increased economic capital (employment and income), but not all of the interviewees were so positive. Whilst residents, such as those above, expressed their feelings towards tourism excitedly, a lament for business adversity also emerged. This was particularly the case for the employees of a travel agency based at Kamal Harbour (an area that has been bypassed because of the location of the bridge). All travel agent employees acknowledged that the bridge threatened business not only because of its location but also because residents could now travel to Java independently by road and simply did not need their service: 'this business is impacted by the Suramadu Bridge. People used to pass Kamal, now they pass Suramadu. More people are going to Surabaya (Java). Consequently, here has become quiet'. This travel agency was losing custom. As a result, income declined and the employees we spoke to were concerned for their job security. This group of participants questioned whether tourism could provide business opportunities and secure employment as they had previously run a successful tourism business that had now failed because of the bridge development and increased independent mobility.

Yet, embracing the idea of tourism as a positive economic force emerged as a key theme, with tourism meaning advancing enterprise through the development of small and medium businesses. Of the study participants, eight defined their occupation as a 'seller', with a further 12 indicating their occupation as employment in the emerging tourism industry (as shown in Table 2). For these 20 residents involved directly in tourism enterprise, the industry was an empowering force to alleviate poverty and enhance individual status through economic gain and social mobility.

5.2. Social mobility

Tourism was viewed as an opportunity to change livelihoods through economic empowerment. Increased income through employment led to social mobility emerging as another key meaning for residents. Interviewees involved in small and medium tourism enterprises emphasised how tourism brought about a relief from poverty. For instance, one participant described how he 'used to be so poor' but is a travelling seller of traditional medicines with income putting him in a position to buy land.

Financial gains were viewed as increasing social capital, made interviewees 'happier' by providing them a sense of stability. Upward social mobility was evident in interviews with those individuals who found tourism to bring status and respect within their community. For example, a rise in her household income allowed one interviewee to better support her family. She explained that now that they were no longer considered poor, they held a higher status in the community: 'people in my village respect me because I can earn some money'.

Similarly, the two interviewees who worked at the *Asta Tinggi* Cemetery (the tombs of the royal family and a popular attraction for religious tourists) discussed their personal pride at being employed at the attraction, including the privilege of working at the graves, and how this led to their improved status within the community: 'I am so proud because working in here gives me higher status in my community'. In this example, employment at *Asta Tinggi* is tourism-related and consistent with Madurese religio-cultural values whereby tourism symbolises religious pilgrimage.

5.3. Pilgrimage

As discussed above, travel is encouraged in Muslim societies. Islamic travel as pilgrimage is spiritually purposeful, with its focus on gaining knowledge 'to make Muslims aware of the greatness of God' (Din, 1989, p. 559), to 'spread God's word, and to enjoy and appreciate God's creations' (Jafari & Scott, 2014, p. 7). A recurring theme in the interviews was that (domestic) tourism symbolised an opportunity for pilgrimage through which religion is enjoyed, shared and strengthened: 'As a Muslim, we have to be able to enjoy the beauty, and spread the words of God's scripture widely... tourism is a very good way of doing this'.

As the discussion on Islamic tourism,above, explains, associating and connecting with others is a central purpose of Islamic travel with *silaturrahim* commonly understood as bonding with one's family and society as well as getting in touch with oneself. The concept is consistent with the pillars of Madurese culture which places *Buppa* (father), *Babbu* (mother), close family ties and cohesive community as paramount to sociocultural order (Sobri, 2017). Participants discussed *silaturrahim* as meaning how tourism fosters the growth of human relationships. In this context, tourism symbolises opportunities for respecting and connecting with others: 'the aim for tourism is developing wide *silaturrahim*'.

Many of the tourist attractions on Madura Island are religiously significant and provide visitors opportunities for *silaturrahim*. In particular, tourists visiting Madura Island go to mosques and palaces, as well as the cemeteries and tombs of the royal family. The data revealed that visitation to the graves at *Asta Tinggi* Cemetery in Sumenep to be a form of religious pilgrimage that domestic tourists from Java undertake to show respect to their ancestors: tourism symbolises visiting the graves. Visitation provides an opportunity for the sharing of local cultural and religious values, and tourism an avenue through which culture and religion could be maintained and rejuvenated – a way to build social and cultural capital: 'tourism should be able to rejuvenate Madurese culture and religious values'.

However, a differentiation between the touristic activities of domestic visitors as compared to those of Western-style leisure tourism emerged as a theme. Concern was voiced that that tourism, particularly the perceived hedonism that Western-style tourism symbolised, would negatively impact the sociocultural order to threaten religious values and lead to moral decline.

5.4. Moral decline

The interviews revealed considerable trepidation about the potential conflict that could arise between Muslim residents and non-Muslim tourists. Western tourism was viewed as a profane practice and tourist behaviour as violation of social mores. Given the devout religiosity of the Madurese, these findings positioned religion as an over-arching influence on the meaning making of tourism by participants. Central to these concerns were negative meanings associated with the possibility of mass tourism, the potential influx of visitors of different faiths, and the perceived impact this would have on the very traditional Madurese society. These sentiments expressed a concern that tourism would weaken the Madurese social fabric through violating religio-cultural customs.

Specific embodied tourist behaviours and western-style tourist facilities were seen to symbolise the antithesis to Islamic values, with concern regarding swimming pools, specifically western swimwear, and women and men swimming together as examples. One participant stated 'a swimsuit should be fully closed. It just contradicts with our religious and cultural values if people wear an open swimsuit at a swimming pool', and another said 'there should be separation between men and women for a swimming pool. Unfortunately, this separation does not exist'. This particular issue was confirmed by the manager of a hotel in Sampang who explained 'it is still hard for the Sampang people to accept the existence of a swimming pool'. For some participants, the hotel itself was a symbolic exemplar of moral deterioration promoting objectionable behaviours and activities, such as, drinking and karaoke. One resident expressed very strong views: 'I don't like karaoke at the hotel ... it is a bad influence on the younger generation and does not fit with our religious and cultural values'. These sentiments reflect an adherence to an Islamic value system that bans alcohol, advocates conservative dress codes, and restricts fraternisation of the sexes. While domestic tourism was perceived to strengthen religio-cultural capital, Western tourism symbolised a threat to islander ways of life.

It should be noted that many participants had not actually been exposed to Western tourists and had not experienced these behaviours first-hand. Concerns about indecency were evidently hearsay and potentially based on stereotypes of Western tourism. For example, as one resident explained, 'people say that most of the visitors at the beach wear improper dress and get drunk'. And another participant, when expressing strong concern about tourism, actually questioned the interviewer to confirm his views saying, 'tourism is filled with negative things such as karaoke, hotels, night clubs, drunks, isn't it?'. These examples illustrate the difficulty of reconciling tourism with religious values, and fear of the destructive potential of Western tourism on Madurese culture. As Din (1989, p. 553) notes, touristic activities such as these in Islamic contexts are often seen as the 'roots of misdemeanour' and are not 'tolerated'.

5.5. Commodification

A range of negative social practices were raised by participants as impacts of tourism, these included crime and prostitution. However, a concern that elicited far greater frequency was the potential for tourism to lead to irrevocable cultural change. The theme of commodification emerged as interviewees discussed strong fears for tourism and its potential to weaken traditional culture and lead to commodification. Wearing et al. (2010) explain commodification as a function of tourist consumption, the tourist-as-consumer, which diminishes culture to a commodity that can be bought and sold. This view was most strongly voiced by teachers at *pesantren* (the Islamic boarding schools) who used strong language, such as 'cultural destruction' and 'cultural damage', to express their views on the meanings of tourism. For example, one teacher expressed grave concern for changes in the behaviour of Madurese youth that could result from interacting with tourists. Discussed in the context of *hadrah* (the traditional music), he explained that Madurese youth were not performing traditional music anymore: '*Hadrah* is now replaced by modern band. You know, this can be a signal of cultural destruction. People will forget our cultural values'. However, it must be noted that while they attributed this directly to tourism, it could have more to do with other outside influences. As Fisher (2004) explains, individuals will choose to change their behaviour depending on how their peer group responds to these changes and this does not necessarily mean they are 'demonstrating' tourists. In such instances, tourism may provide a convenient scapegoat for changes occurring for other social and cultural reasons.

A further concern about flaunting religious values were packaged tours to the cemeteries, particularly any tours that combined visits to the graves (sacred) with visits to the beach (profane). As noted by a *pesantran* teacher, 'tourism is an opportunity for visiting the graves and it should not be commercialised otherwise our religious values will gradually disappear'. From this perspective, the commercialisation of religious tours was seen to interfere with the concept of *silaturrahim* as a sign of disrespect to the ancestors. Another teacher bluntly stated that tourism 'is unacceptable to me and this *pesantran* environment'. When tourism symbolised commodification, fears for the modification or destruction of religio-cultural values were voiced.

Whilst there was strong resistance to tourism in its Western form, there was also an opposite view of excitement in the prospect of exposure to new cultures. As one participant said, 'the arrival of many visitors will allow us to learn different cultures, dialects and languages'. This exposure to outsiders was viewed as having the potential to 'make our culture richer' and by another as an opportunity to 'restore our culture'.

6. Discussion

The themes emerging from the analysis indicate that the meanings attributed to tourism by study participants were diverse and not easily categorised as negative or positive. This is consistent with previous qualitative research that recognises that meanings are not fixed: meanings are negotiated and contested (Amuquandoh, 2010; Berno, 1999; Hepburn, 2002; Lepp, 2008). However, recurring patterns were also evident. Factors such as increased social and economic mobility were important in early studies of the perceptions of tourism (especially in developing countries) and also emerged here as important influencers of the meanings the participants assigned to tourism. In part, this finding is reflective of the study sample and cannot be generalised and further research could examine the meanings of tourism for a broader sample of residents including those with limited literacy skills.

Another emerging theme contributes to the critics of Doxey's (1976) Irridex Model, to challenge perception studies that suggest host communities go through predictable stages as tourism develops in a destination. This study reveals that participant reactions towards tourism were mixed. For instance, euphoria was evident in the themes 'advancing enterprise' and 'economic and social mobility', and annoyance was clearly evident, especially perceptions of a decline of the moral fabric of Madura Island and negative impacts on Madurese cultural integrity. Whilst existing scholarly research tends to focus on well-established destinations where tourist interactions with local communities are commonplace, in this study tourism was (and still is) in its infancy and first-hand experiences of tourism were limited. Those participants who were not directly working in or around the tourism industry had only heard stories about Western-style tourism from the media and their community. These participants subscribed to social learning which emanates from reference groups within their communities, a stance that may be ascribed to serving 'as a symbolic identification for a culture group' (Colton, 1987, p. 354).

A recurring theme in the study findings was how meanings were influenced by the devout religio-cultural order of Madurese culture and society. Such findings are perhaps not surprising as scholars concerned with tourism in Muslim countries have already noted a lack of tolerance for what may be considered as normal tourist behaviour: as ideologically driven Western hedonism. For example, Jafari and Scott (2014, p. 4) state that Islamic law 'deals with the whole of human conduct, it covers matters that Western people would not consider law at all'. Islamic doctrine on whether certain food or drinks are permitted (halal), how dress codes are enforced, banning entertainment (such as, gambling), and regulating co-mingling of the sexes, are some of these restrictions. Further to this, male-female public displays of affection and physical contact are strictly controlled, including unmarried couples sharing rooms, dressing inappropriately, and so on (Zamani-Farahani & Henderson, 2010).

In our study, a critical approach to symbolic interactionism provides an excellent tool to uncover how social positioning influences viewpoints as they are manifested through social interactions guided by shared norms and values (Blumer, 1969) and while acknowledging localised cultural practices (Geetz, 1966). As discussed above, the philosophy of *Buppa, Babbu, Guru, Rato* reflects layers of respect in Madurese society. The findings reveal that *Guru* had particular sway and influence on what tourism means to participants in this study. *Guru* can be *tokoh panutan* (leader) representing the informal leaders within the community. Guru can also refer to *sesepuh* (respected person) or *kyai* (religious teacher). This study finds that the high level of reverence given to *kyai* (religious leaders) and *pesantran* (Islamic boarding schools) underpins support or resistance to tourism, particularly for those interviewees who had no direct contact with tourism. Given that tourism was only emerging on the island at the time of research, there is opportunity for a wider social enquiry to explore how to involve these leaders in tourism. For example, including *kyai* and *pesantran* teachers in tourism planning may have a positive impact on the industry as it develops, and on the meanings residents attach to potential tourism growth and tourist visitation.

Buppa and *Babbu* (mother, father/ancestors) were evidently less influential in shaping the meanings of tourism for study participants. However, the link between family, ancestry and Islamic life remains strong in Madurese culture. Previous research on tourism in Muslim societies recognises the potential of Islamic travel as one of the major areas of growth in global tourism (Jafari & Scott, 2014) and this potential was evident as the theme of pilgrimage emerged as a significant meaning of tourism. Jafari and Scott (2014, p. 7) note that travel is increasingly becoming acceptable in Muslim societies beyond pilgrimage, and they describe Muslims as 'avid tourists' who are 'encouraged to visit and to be visited by their Muslim brethren' (Din, 1989, p. 559). In the context of Madura Island, much of this pilgrimage was closely associated with visiting the graves of ancestors, a tradition that is closely linked to family life in Madurese culture.

The influence of *Rato* (government) was not overtly evident in the findings of this study. It is possible to interpret the meanings of tourism as 'advancing enterprise' and 'economic and social mobility' as evidence that the government's tourism growth agenda had some sway upon residents. Criticism of governments in developing countries, and the top-down approaches that drive an economic agenda around tourism is commonplace (particularly the lack of community consultation in tourism planning), and Madura Island (and more broadly Indonesia) is no exception (Mowforth & Munt, 2016; Tosun & Timothy, 2001). Whilst this study did not specifically explore the role of local elected tourism officials and their role in shaping the meanings of tourism, or the ways in which local variations in meaning can bear directly on participatory planning, further research in this area is warranted.

7. Conclusion

An understanding of the host gaze and the ways by which the host gaze is constructed and developed is essential to tourism development. Resident support for tourism will influence host-guest relations and the success of the industry. This research, that took place at a historically significant time of change for residents of Madura Island, addresses the call for more qualitative and interpretative accounts of the perceptions of tourism held by destination communities (Deery et al., 2012; Sharpley, 2014). The opening of the Suramadu Bridge a few months prior to the fieldwork led the highly isolated island to emerge as a tourism destination with inbound tourism activities focused primarily on domestic religious cultural tourism.

In an emerging destination, 'local resident perceptions of tourism may be based on limited, if any actual contact with tourists' (Sharpley, 2014, p. 39). The meanings of tourism for Madurese participants in this study were heavily influenced by *guru* (teacher/leader) and the moral frameworks underpinning the role. However, *guru* do not have material influence over tourism planning on the island. As an analytical tool, symbolic interactionism assists to explain why these meanings emerged, and how they manifested through social interaction with others in particular contextual conditions.

Amuquandoh (2010) argues that more interpretive theoretical and methodological traditions are needed to address the complex development and articulations of the meanings residents hold towards tourists and tourism development. This study illustrates how a more critical symbolic interactionist approach (Carter & Fuller, 2016;

Handberg et al., 2015) can be used as a theoretical lens for examining micro-interactions while recognising how macro-cultural, social and historical dimensions of host communities add complexity to the ways in which meanings are negotiated. And whilst the meanings of tourism within a community are heterogeneous and localised, the religio-cultural uniqueness of the Madurese provides a path to understand complexities in the relationships that influence meaning making and its negotiations in Islamic destinations, such as Madura Island. These findings highlight that nuanced religio-cultural local knowledge is an important factor in the formation of host attitudes and perceptions of tourism. This study provides the groundwork to apply this theory in research on other islands of the Indonesian archipelago and beyond.

Further research is warranted to study *ratu* (government leaders) and the role of Madurese tourism officials as influencers as meaning makers in tourism. Deeper insight into the roles of *Buppa* and *Babbu* would also add an important gendered dimension to the interpretation of results. Indeed, a limitation of this study is that other sources might verify the meanings of tourism expressed by the study participants. Further research could map these meanings against objective data, such as, economic impact data or crime data, adding value to symbolic interactionism as a framework to analyse tourism and island communities. Further exploration of local variations in meanings and how they bear directly on tourism planning and development in island destinations, such as Madura Island, is another area that deserves scholarly attention.

Disclosure statement

No potential conflict of interest was reported by the authors.

ORCID

Tamara Young (iD) http://orcid.org/0000-0001-8132-4194

References

Ackerman, J., (2019). Meaning-making in the course of action: Affordance theory at the pilgrim/tourist nexus. *Tourism Geographies*, *21*(3), 405–421. doi:10.1080/14616688.2018.1505942

Adams, K. M., Loyola University Chicago., & Sandarupa, D., (2018). A room with a view: Local knowledge and tourism entrepreneurship in an unlikely Indonesian locale. *Asian Journal of Tourism Research*, *3*(1), 1–26. doi:10.12982/AJTR.2018.0001

Adams, K., (1984). Come to Tana Toraja, "land of the heavenly kings": Travel agents as brokers in ethnicity. *Annal of Tourism Research*, *11*(3), 469–485. doi:10.1016/0160-7383(84)90032-X

Adler, P. A., & Adler, P. (1987). *Membership roles in field research*. Beverly Hills, CA: Sage.

Aksan, N., Kisac, B., Aydin, M., & Demirbuken, S., (2009). Symbolic interaction theory. *Procedia – Social and Behavioural Sciences*, *1*(1), 902–904. doi:10.1016/j.sbspro.2009.01.160

Amuquandoh, F. E., (2010). Lay concepts of tourism in Bosomtwe basin, Ghana. *Annals of Tourism Research*, *37*(1), 34–51. doi:10.1016/j.annals.2009.07.002

Andriotis, K. (2004). Problems of island tourism development: The Greek insular regions. In B. Bramwell (Ed.), *Coastal mass tourism: Diversification and sustainable development in Southern Europe* (pp. 114–132). Clevedon: Channel View.

Berno, T., (1999). When a guest is a guest: Cook Islanders view tourism. *Annals of Tourism Research*, *26*(3), 656–675. doi:10.1016/S0160-7383(99)00002-X

Bianchi, R. V., (2009). The 'critical turn' in tourism studies: A radical critique. *Tourism Geographies*, *11*(4), 484–504. doi:10.1080/14616680903262653

Blumer, H. (1969). *Symbolic interactionism, perspective and method*. Englewood Cliffs, NJ: Prentice Hall.

Bramwell, B. (2004). *Coastal mass tourism: Diversification and sustainable development in Southern Europe*. Clevedon: Channel View.

Butler, R. (2006). The concept of a tourist area life cycle evolution. In R. Butler (Ed.), *The tourism area life cycle: Applications and modifications* (Vol. 1, pp. 1–6). Clevedon: Channel View.

Canavan, B., (2016). Tourism culture: Nexus, characteristics, context and sustainability. *Tourism Management*, *53*, 229–243. doi:10.1016/j.tourman.2015.10.002

Carter, M. J., & Fuller, C., (2016). Symbols, meaning, and action: The past, present, and future of symbolic interactionism. *Current Sociology*, *64*(6), 931–961. doi:10.1177/0011392116638396

Central Intelligence Agency. (2018). Library: Indonesia Administrative Map. Retrieved 18/11/19 from https://www.cia.gov/library/publications/resources/cia-maps-publications/Indonesia.html.

Charmaz, K. (2006). *Constructing grounded theory: A practical guide through qualitative research*. London: Sage.

Charon, J. M. (1979). *Symbolic interactionism: An introduction, an interpretation, an integration*. Englewood Cliffs: Prentice-Hall.

Cheung, S. C. H., (1999). The meanings of a heritage trail in Hong Kong. *Annals of Tourism Research*, *26*(3), 570–588. doi:10.1016/S0160-7383(99)00006-7

Colton, C., (1987). Leisure, recreation, tourism: A symbolic interactionism view. *Annals of Tourism Research*, *14*(3), 345–359. doi:10.1016/0160-7383(87)90107-1

Cresswell, J. W. (2003). *Research design: Qualitative, quantitative and mixed method approaches* (3rd ed.). Thousand Oaks, CA: Sage.

Deery, M., Jago, L., & Fredline, L., (2012). Rethinking social impacts of tourism research: A new research agenda. *Tourism Management*, *33*(1), 64–73. doi:10.1016/j.tourman.2011.01.026

Dennis, A., & Martin, P. J., (2007). Symbolic interactionism and the concept of social structure. *Sociological Focus*, *40*(3), 287–305. doi:10.1080/00380237.2007.10571311

Denzin, N. K. (1989). *Interpretative biography*. Newbury Park, CA: Sage. doi:10.1093/sw/35.5.477-a

Denzin, N. K., & Lincoln, Y. S. (2008). Introduction: The discipline and practice of qualitative research. In N. K. Denzin & Y. S. Lincoln (Eds.), *Collecting and interpreting qualitative materials* (pp. 1–43). Thousand Oaks, CA: Sage.

Din, K. H., (1989). Islam and tourism: Patterns, issues, and options. *Annals of Tourism Research, 16*(4), 542–563. doi:10.1016/0160-7383(89)90008-X

Doxey, G., (1976). When enough's enough: The natives are restless in Old Niagara. *Heritage Canada, 2*(2), 26–27.

Efyanti, Y., (2016). NILAI-NILAI KEARIFAN LOKAL DALAM TRADISI SILATURAHIM MENJELANG RAMADHAN DI HAMPARAN RAWANG. *Islamica, 16* (1), 101–109.

Elley, W. B. (2001). Literacy in the present world: Realities and possibilities. In L. Verhoeven, & C. Snow (Eds.), *Literacy and motivation: Reading engagement in individuals and groups* (pp. 205–221). Mahwah, NJ: Lawrence Erlbaum.

Faisal, A., & Harsaputra, I. (2009). Suramadu bridge touted to boost economy, create jobs. The Jakarta Post, 11 June 2009. Retrieved from http://www.thejakartapost.com/news/2009/06/11/suramadu-bridge-touted-boost-economy-create-jobs.html.

Fisher, D., (2004). The Demonstration Effect Revisited. *Annals of Tourism Research, 31* (2), 428–446. doi:10.1016/j.annals.2004.01.001

Geertz, C. (1966). Religion as a cultural system. In M. Banton (Ed.), *Anthropological approaches to the study of religion* (pp. 1–46). London: Tavistock.

Geertz, C. (2000). Deep play: Notes of the Balinese cockfight. In L. Crothers & C. Lockhart (Eds.), *Culture and politics*. New York: Palgrave Macmillan.

Handberg, C., Thorne, S., Midtgaard, J., Nielsen, C. V., & Lomborg, K., (2015). Revisiting symbolic interactionism as a theoretical framework beyond the grounded theory tradition. *Qualitative Health Research, 25*(8), 1023–1032. doi:10.1177/1049732314554231

Harrill, R., (2004). Residents' attitudes towards tourism development: A literature review with implications for tourism planning. *Journal of Planning Literature, 18*(3), 251–266. doi:10.1177/0885412203260306

Hassan, R., (2007). On being religious: Patterns of religious commitment in Muslim societies. *The Muslim World, 97*(3), 437–478. doi:10.1111/j.1478-1913.2007.00190.x

Henderson, J. C. (2010). Islam and tourism: Brunei, Indonesia, Malaysia, and Singapore. In N. Scott, & J. Jafari (Eds.), *Tourism in the Muslim world: Bridging tourism theory and practice* (Vol. 2, pp. 75–89). Bingley, UK: Emerald.

Henderson, J. C., (2003). Managing tourism and Islam in peninsular Malaysia. *Tourism Management, 24*(4), 447–456. doi:10.1016/S0261-5177(02)00106-1

Hepburn, S. J., (2002). Touristic forms of life in Nepal. *Annals of Tourism Research , 29*(3), 611–630. doi:10.1016/S0160-7383(01)00070-6

Hidayaturrahman, M., (2018). Integration of Islam and local culture: Tandhe' in Madura. *MIQOT: Jurnal Ilmu-Ilmu Keislaman, 42*(1), 189. doi:10.30821/miqot.v42i1.477

iStock/Valens Hacaryo. (2019). Suramadu Bridge Stock Photos (1179313033), Retrieved 27/11/19 from https://www.istockphoto.com/au/photo/suramadu-bridge-gm1179313033-329940846.

Jafari, J., & Scott, N., (2014). Muslim world and its tourisms. *Annals of Tourism Research, 44*, 1–19. doi:10.1016/j.annals.2013.08.011

Johnson, P., (2001). An examination of risk within tourist experiences to the Islamic Republic of Iran. *Annals of Leisure Research, 4*(1), 38–57. doi:10.1080/11745398.2001.10600890

Johnson, P.C., (2010). Writing liminal landscapes: The cosmopolitical gaze. *Tourism Geographies, 12*(4), 505–524. doi:10.1080/14616688.2010.516397

Joliffe, L., & Smith, R., (2001). Heritage, tourism and museums: The case of the North Atlantic islands of Skye, Scotland and Prince Edward Island, Canada. *International Journal of Heritage Studies, 7*(2), 149–172. doi:10.1080/13527250119047

Kim, K., Uysal, M., & Sirgy, M. J., (2013). How does tourism in a community impact the quality of life of community residents?. *Tourism Management, 36*, 527–540. doi:10.1016/j.tourman.2012.09.005

Lauer, R. H., & Handel, W. H. (1977). *Social psychology: The theory and application of symbolic interactionism*. Boston: Houghton Mifflin Harcourt.

Lepp, A., (2008). Attitudes towards initial tourism development in a community with no prior tourism experience: The case of Bigodi, Uganda. *Journal of Sustainable Tourism*, *16*(1), 5–22. doi:10.1016/j.tourman.2006.03.004

Li, P., Ryan, C., & Cave, J., (2016). Chinese rural tourism development: Transition in the case of Qiyunshan, Anhui 2008-2015. *Tourism Management*, *55*, 240–260. doi:10.1016/j.tourman.2016. 02.007

Li, Y., (2011). Translating interviews, translating lives: Ethical considerations in cross-language narrative enquiry. *TESL Canada Journal*, *38*, 16–30. doi:10.18806/tesl.v28i0.1079

Lincoln, Y. S., & Guba, E. G. (1985). *Naturalistic inquiry*. Newbury Park, CA: Sage.

Lonely Planet. 2018. Indonesia: Pulau Madura. Retrieved from https://www.lonelyplanet.com/ indonesia/pulau-madura.

Maxwell, J. A. (2009). Designing a qualitative study. In L. Bickman and D. Rog (Eds.), *Applied social research methods* (2nd ed., pp. 214–253). London: SAGE.

Mead, G. (1962). *Mind, self and society: From the standpoint of a social behaviourist*. University of Chicago Press: Chicago.

Moufakkir, O., & Reisinger, Y. (2013). Gazemaking: Le regard – do you hear me?. In O. Moufakkir & Y. Reisinger (Eds.), *The host gaze in global tourism* (pp. xi–xvi). Oxfordshire, UK: CABI.

Moufakkir, O., & Reisinger, Y. (Eds.). (2013). *The host gaze in global tourism*. Oxfordshire, UK: CABI.

Moufakkir, O., (2011). The role of cultural distance in mediating the host gaze. *Tourist Studies*, *11*(1), 73–89. doi:10.1177/1468797611412065

Mowforth, M., & Munt, I. (2016). *Tourism and sustainability: Development, globalisation and new tourism in the third world* (4th ed.). London: Routledge.

Musolf, G., (1992). Structure, institutions, power, and ideology: New directions within symbolic interactionism. *The Sociological Quarterly*, *33*(2), 171–189. doi:10.1111/j.1533-8525.1992. tb00370.x

Nunkoo, R., & Gursoy, D., (2012). Residents' support for tourism: An identity perspective. *Annals of Tourism Research*, *39*(1), 243–286. doi:10.1016/j.annals.2011.05.006

Nunkoo, R., Smith, S. L. J., & Ramkissoon, H., (2013). Residents' attitudes to tourism: A longitudinal study of 140 articles from 1984-2010. *Journal of Sustainable Tourism*, *21*(1), 5–25. doi:10. 1080/09669582.2012.673621

Patton, M. Q. (2002). *Qualitative research and evaluation methods* (3rd ed.). Thousand Oaks, CA: Sage.

Peacock, J., (1986). The creativity of tradition in Indonesian religion. *History of Religions*, *4*, 341–351. doi:10.1086/463053

Rachbini, D. (1995). Conditions and consequences of industrialization in Madura. In K. Van Dijk, H. De Jonge, & E. Touwen-Bouwsma (Eds.), *Across Madura Strait: The dynamics of an insular society* (pp. 209–220). Leiden: KITLV Press.

Reindrawati, D. Y. (2013). *What does tourism mean to residents? An investigation of Madura Island, Indonesia* (PhD thesis). The University of Newcastle, Australia

Santos, C. A., & Buzinde, C., (2007). Politics of identity and space: Representational dynamics. *Journal of Travel Research*, *45*(3), 322–332. doi:10.1177/0047287506295949

Sarantakos, S. (2005). *Social research* (3rd ed.). Hampshire: Palgrave MacMillan.

Sharpley, R., (2014). Host perceptions of tourism: A review of the research. *Tourism Management*, *42*, 37–49. doi:10.1016/j.tourman.2013.10.007

Sobri, A. A. Y., (2017). Leadership values in Madurasee culture. *Advances in Economics, Business and Management Research*, *45*, 146–151. doi:10.2991/coema-17.2017.25

Strauss, A., & Corbin, J. (1998). *Basics of qualitative research: Techniques and procedures for developing grounded theory* (2nd ed.). Thousand Oaks, CA: Sage.

Strohmayer, U. (2011). Bridges: Different conditions of mobile possibilities. In T. Cresswell and P. Merriman (Eds.), *Geographies of mobilities: Practices, spaces, subjects* (pp. 119–135). Farnham, Surrey: Ashgate.

Temple, B., & Young, A., (2004). Qualitative research and translation dilemmas. *Qualitative Research*, *4*(2), 161–178. doi:10.1177/1468794104044430

Tosun, C., & Timothy, D. J., (2001). Shortcomings in planning approaches to tourism development in developing countries: The case of Turkey. *International Journal of Contemporary Hospitality Management, 13*(7), 352–359. doi:10.1108/09596110110403910

Urry, J., & Larsen, J. (2011). *The Tourist Gaze 3.0.* Sage: London.

Van Dijk, K., De Jonge, H., & Touwen-Bouwsma, E. (Eds.). (1995). *Across Madura Strait: The dynamics of an insular society.* Leiden: KITLV Press

Wall, G., (1996). Perspectives of Tourism in selected Balinese villages. *Annals of Tourism Research, 23*(1), 123–137. doi:10.1016/0160-7383(95)00056-9

Wearing, S., Stevenson, D., & Young, T. (2010). *Tourist cultures: Identity, place and the traveller.* London: Sage.

Wonderful Indonesia (2019). Discover Indonesia's latest destination: Madura Island across Surabaya. Retrieved 20/11/19 https://www.indonesia.travel/gb/en/destinations/java/surabaya/discover-indonesia-s-latest-destination-madura-island-across-surabaya.

Xiao, H., (1997). Tourism and leisure in China: A tale of two cities. *Annals of Tourism Research, 24*(2), 357–370. doi:10.1016/S0160-7383(97)80006-0

Yamashita, S. (2003). *Bali and beyond: Explorations in the anthropology of tourism.* New York: Berghahn Books.

Zamani-Farahani, H., & Henderson, J.C., (2010). Islamic tourism and managing tourism development in Islamic societies: The cases of Iran and Saudi Arabia. *International Journal of Tourism Research, 12*, 79–89. doi:10.1002/jtr.741

The integrated touristic villages: an Indonesian model of sustainable tourism?

Sylvine Pickel-Chevalier, I Komang Gde Bendesa and I Nyoman Darma Putra

ABSTRACT

The desa wisata terpadu policy was created in 1992 by the Indonesian government. Translated as integrated touristic villages, this model promotes an archetype of sustainable development adapted according to the characteristics of the local villages. Twenty-five years after the creation of this policy, it becomes relevant to examine its capacity to do so, by meeting the expectations of sustainable tourism, understood as a motor of global development and territorial integration. Because Bali remains the most important touristic destination in Indonesia, this study focus on this special case, and more especially on three villages considered as model examples: Penglipuran, Tenganan and Jatiluwih. For each, have been studying its economic sustainability, analyzing whether tourism brings local economic development; its social sustainability, evaluating the capacity of tourism to foster cohesion among the inhabitants by maintaining the traditional local organization; and its cultural sustainability, examining the complex effects of tourism on the preservation of local heritage. The methodology is based on a multi-case study, through a qualitative approach composed of 12 interviews with actors and inhabitants among the local population involved in tourism. Our results show that the three villages are successfully meeting the expectations of sustainable tourism by favoring economic growth that enables the local population to keep their community alive through community-based management that globally respects the traditional organization. However, their sustainability remains fragile and needs to be improved through an increasingly efficient socio-economic model. It includes more flexibility to involve young qualified inhabitants, without gender prejudice, in order to avoid the 'vicious circle' of a lack of qualified human resources limiting their capacity for economic growth. Those results may be of interest to researchers who are involved with tourism and sustainability issues, but also to institutions and professionals working on the establishment of sustainable models of tourism in Bali or elsewhere.

摘要

综合旅游村政策是印度尼西亚政府于1992年制定的。这一模式被翻译为综合旅游村落, 提出了一种符合当地村落特点的可持续发展模型。在该政策实施25年之后, 有必要审查其实现可持续旅游业预期的能力, 因为旅游业被认为是全球发展和领土一体化的动力。由于巴厘岛仍然是印尼最重要的旅游目的地，本研究将重点放在这个特殊的案例上，尤其是以彭丽浦兰、腾格南和贾蒂鲁瓦三个村庄为例进行研究。我们研究了每一个村落旅游发展的经济、社会及文化的可持续性：经济可持续性，分析旅游业是否带来了当地经济的发展;社会可持续性，评估旅游业保持传统的地方组织以促进居民凝聚力的能力；文化可持续性，考察旅游业对保护当地遗产的复杂影响。本文以多案例研究为基础，采用定性方法，访谈了12位参与旅游业的当事人和居民。我们的研究表明，这三个村庄都成功地实现了可持续旅游的预期，它们都促进了经济增长，实施了全球范围内推崇的尊重传统组织的社区管理，保持了社区的活力。然而，它们的可持续性仍然脆弱，需要通过一种更加有效的社会经济模式加以改进。它需要更为灵活地、不带性别偏见地让优秀的青年居民参与进来，避免由于缺乏合格人力资源限制其经济增长能力的"恶性循环"。这些结果可能会引起旅游和可持续发展研究人员的兴趣，也会引起致力于在巴厘岛或其他地方建立可持续旅游模式的机构和专业人员的兴趣。

Introduction

Bali is today a crossroads for domestic and international tourism that attracted over 8.6 million Indonesian visitors and more than 4.9 million foreign tourists in 2016 (Bali Government Tourism Office, http://www.disparda.baliprov.go.id/en/Statistics2). The latter come from Western countries – particularly Australia, Europe and North America – but also from Asia – China, Japan, Singapore, etc. Bali has in fact benefited from over a century of tourism development (Picard, 2010; Vickers, 2012), encouraging the redefinition not only of its economy but its societal organization (Hitchcock & Putra, 2007). In fact, tourism there has been boosted by the cultural and religious uniqueness of Bali – a small Hindu island within the largest Muslim country in the world, in terms of population. Tourism has taken advantage of what is available, yet has also changed its core offer. This tourism, which seems to have been an impelling force in Bali's shift towards modernity, has produced significant effects on its social, cultural and religious organization (Picard, 1992, 2010; Vickers, 2012), as well as on its environment (Pickel-Chevalier, 2017; Pickel-Chevalier & Budarma, 2016). The enormous increase in tourism in Bali since the 1970s has created a double-edged phenomenon, boosting economic growth while generating growing feelings of discontent in relation to capital-intensive tourism development. Sentiments of this sort were identified as early as the 1990s (Picard & Vickers, 2017).

These reflections fused with the new international questions on the fairness of global development that emerged in the 1970s, leading to the creation of the sustainable development paradigm in Europe (1987) and therefore that of sustainable tourism (1992), which began to interest researchers in the social sciences field (Butler, 1999; Cater, 1993; Hunter, 1997; Mowforth and Munt, 1998; Liu, 2003, etc.). It is interesting to note that the quest for a different model of tourism, seeking to rebalance tourism development, arose as early as 1989 in Bali. It resulted in the creation of the Bali Sustainable Development Project (BSDP). The project ran from 1989 to 1994 (Yamashita, 2016, p. 134) and emphasized traditional Balinese culture as the foundation of sustainable tourism on the island. It favored the establishment in 1992 of the *desa wisata terpadu* policy which the Indonesian government defines as (cited in Yamashita, 2003, p. 104):

> village areas which have an atmosphere reflecting the authenticity of the Balinese village in regards to social and cultural activities, everyday customs, buildings and the traditional use of space, which at the same time are able to provide the infrastructure, attractions, catering, and accommodation required for tourists.

Translated as 'integrated touristic villages', this model seeks to establish an archetype of sustainable touristic development adapted to the characteristics of local villages in Indonesia.

As such, our objective is to question, 25 years after the creation of this policy, its capacity to do so. Therefore, we propose to analyze the ability of the desa wisata terpadu to meet the expectations of sustainable tourism which we understand to be a motor of global development and territorial integration, posing a challenge to researchers in social sciences, and to geographers in particular in their study of communities interacting with their environment. We embrace Hunter's (1997, p. 860) notion that 'The remit of sustainable tourism is extended to consider the role of tourism in contributing to sustainable development more generally'.

Because Bali remains the most important touristic destination in Indonesia, we have focused our study on this special case. As of 2017, 44 villages were officially registered on the island by the Ministry of Tourism of Indonesia as belonging to this category. Not all of them are perceived to be successful. Although our ultimate objective is to study a wide range of villages, including those less successful ones in order to also examine the constraints in their development, we decided to start with the detailed analysis of three of the most famous, considered by local and national authorities as model examples: Penglipuran, Tenganan and Jatiluwih (Figure 1).

Our objective is to understand is which ways they are defined as 'successful', according to the double expectation of the desa wisata terpadu policy and the sustainable tourism paradigm. In this context, even if we generally adopt Farrell's (1999) 'trinity' definition of sustainability which posits the interpenetration of economic, social and environmental issues, in this study we focus only on the economic and socio-cultural effects of tourism in the villages. We can justify this choice, first, because of the definition of the desa wisata terpadu that prioritizes those issues over environmental ones; and second because we have already worked on the complexity of the tourism effect on nature in Bali, combining the two opposite phenomena of transformation and conservation (Pickel-Chevalier, 2017; Pickel-Chevalier and Budarma, 2016).

Thus, we question the ways in which the desa wisata terpadu can be an efficient model of sustainable tourism development in Bali, by examining for each village:

- *its economic sustainability*, analyzing whether tourism brings economic development to the villages, and challenges, or not, the previous traditional agricultural system;
- *its social sustainability*, questioning the capacity of tourism to foster cohesion among the inhabitants by maintaining, or on the contrary restructuring, the traditional local organization of the villages. We consider notably the evolution of the

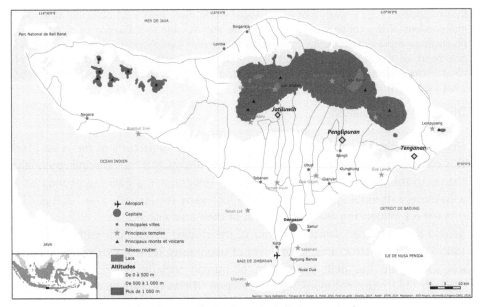

Figure 1. Location map of the three studied villages in Bali. Source: Authors.

role of women and the propensity of tourism to facilitate, or not, their emancipation;

- *its cultural sustainability*, studying the complex effects of tourism on the preservation of local heritage, questioning the seemingly contradictory double movement of conservation/reinvention of traditions.

The contribution to knowledge that our work offers lies in a better understanding of an attempt to create an Indonesian model of sustainable tourism development, with the ambition to meet both international expectations and respect local traditional society, through three original models. The results of our work may be of interest to researchers and students in geography and in the social sciences in general, who are involved with sustainability issues, and/or the socio-economic and environmental effects of tourism in Indonesia and in Bali in particular. It should also be of interest to institutions and professionals working on the establishment of sustainable models of tourism in Bali or elsewhere in the world, illustrating the complex appropriation of a western paradigm into non-western societies and the flexibility and understanding of local cultures that it requires.

Material and methods

The aim of our work is to provide an in-depth understanding of tourism in particular sites in Bali, comparing the official definition (*desa wisata terpadu*) and objective (a model of sustainable development adapted to the characteristics of the local villages) to field analysis. Our epistemological position is structuralist constructivism, defined by Pierre Bourdieu as:

By structuralism [...] I mean that in the social world there exist [...] objective structures independent of the conscience and will of the agents, able to influence or dictate their practices or representations. By constructivism, I mean that there is a social genesis, on one hand, of the schemes of perception, thinking and actions that are constitutive of what I name habitus; and on the other hand, of the social structures, and in particular what I call fields (Bourdieu, 1987, p. 5).

This position postulates:

- *First the need to take into account the cognition and subjectivity of the researcher.* In this context, our research is based on a cross-cultural and multidisciplinary analysis, thanks to the partnership between a French geographer, a Balinese economist and a Balinese anthropologist. This collaboration helps to relativize the habitus of the researchers influencing the construction of their study object.
- *Second the phenomenological relations of the studied populations* with physical, historical and social structures. In the field of geography, it means that 'The geographical spaces are the built production of human societies with natural materials, through their representations and techniques' (Di Méo, 2016, p. 1). This approach induces the importance of a dialogism between theoretical models and fieldwork that favors the understanding of the complexity of social phenomena (Le Moigne, 1995; Morin, 1986). In this context, we argue that Geography, that is 'neither idiographic neither nomothetic, since it is both' (Scheibling, 2015, p. 231) is in a privileged position to study both the physical and phenomenological relationships of societies to territories, but within a dialog with other disciplines that favor a better understanding of the complexity (Morin, 1986).

As such, to analyze the ability of the 'desa wisata terpadu' to be an agent of sustainable development in Bali, meeting both international expectations and the local needs, we based our work on a multi-case-study methodology (Yin, 2018). Our ambition is to use empirical evidence from the three different sites, to compare their differences and similarities, in order to build a more holistic picture. This method provides access to data through a wide variety of tools, mixing secondary data with primary material which we collected and analyzed ourselves. In this context, we combine historical and statistical analyses with the results of our qualitative survey and our observations in the three villages selected. Although tourism research includes a wide range of methods (Richards & Munsters, 2010), we award priority to a qualitative approach that engages with those involved in this policy at different levels. We have chosen a qualitative approach that enables a deep understanding of the behavior, the social practices, but in particular the mental representations of the actors we interviewed, from the people in charge to the residents. We did not undertake a quantitative survey as that would not have allowed such precision. Besides, this method requires a large number of answers to be relevant, whereas the parent-population of the three villages remains small.

For these reasons, we implemented a qualitative project including a total of 42 hours of in-depth semi-structured individual interviews at Sahid Institute in Jakarta (December 2016) and in the villages (March 2017 and March 2018) and with a total of 12 people. The interviewees were both digitally recorded to provide a register of all the answers and written down in notebooks for safety reasons (in case we had a technical problem with the recording). We examine the *integrated touristic village* policy, a top-down system which begins at the national decision-making level (Ministry of Tourism), from which it moves on to the local managers who are responsible for its application, and finally, the village residents it brings into the process. This led us to identify and interview the following social actors: (1) two representatives of the *desa wisata terpadu* policy working within the Ministry of Tourism in Jakarta, seeking to understand policy objectives and modus operandi, (2) nine village residents, among them five women, with diverse responsibilities in tourism development and (3) one Balinese tourist guide who takes tourists to the three villages, thus offering us an outsider's perception of what recent evolutions in tourism of this type offers.

Those interviewed are (to preserve their anonymity we have provided just the first capital letter of their name) – Table 1.

We have access to the Ministry of Tourism through the relationship between the Universities of Angers and Sahid, some of whose academics are involved with the *desa wisata terpadu* policy. We made an appointment by telephone with the community leader and tourism manager in Penglipuran in order to organize interviews with them in the village. The inhabitants, both men and women, who we interviewed in the villages, were selected randomly during our stay because they were involved in tourism activities at different levels. We chose this random method to provide a more representative range of answers (they were not pre-selected). The interviews were conducted in English when the respondents could speak English, or in Balinese with simultaneous translation into English by the Balinese researchers when they could not. Finally, Mr. K. was selected by the Balinese members of the team for his long experience as a tourist guide for both domestic and international tourists in Bali.

The above-mentioned interviews were combined with a total of around 150 hours of participant observation (a total of 4 days at each site, with overnight stays in Jatiluwih and Penglipuran), conducted on-site in March 2017 and 2018. The results were manually coded and analyzed theme by theme differentiating, according to the subjects, the national and local authorities; the inhabitants – men and women could have different questions – and the guide. The objective was to understand the societal and geographical organization of each village but also to experience their tourism offers, examining their ability to reach sustainability criteria while respecting local specificities, emphasizing their strengths, difficulties and limits.

Although we combined secondary and primary data in our research, the purpose of our results and discussion section is not to introduce any new literature, but rather to use previously reviewed and presented literature to defend and position the results of the study.

Results and discussions

Are the desa wisata terpadu villages economically sustainable?

The tourism development of traditional villages: three opening process patterns
We chose three villages that are considered successful by the Chief of the Jury for the desa wisata terpadu policy, Mr. K., according to their visitor numbers, but also their

Table 1. Interviewed persons and topics of their interviews.

1. Mr. K., 50 year old, male, Dec. 2016 – Jury Chief for the *integrated touristic villages* policy at the Ministry of Tourism, Indonesia.
Topic: The history of the policy; its objectives and global strategy.
2. Mr. P., 40 year old, male, Dec. 2016 – Facilitator for integrated touristic village development, Head of Tourism Department, Sahid Institute.
Topic: The selection criteria, management; difficulties of the desa wisata terpadu policy; the successful ones and using which criteria; the less successful ones and the constraints.
3. Mr. I., 60 year old, male, March 2017 – Community leader and Penglipuran resident, in charge of managing all operational activities in the traditional village.
Topic: History of the village; how administrative village (desa dinas) and traditional village (desa adat) laws are articulated; how tourism is managed in relation to both regulatory systems that are at work in the village; views on the strengths and weaknesses of the existing tourism model.
4. Mr. W., 30 year old, male, March 2017 – In charge of tourism management, under the supervision of Mr. I., and inhabitant of Penglipuran.
Topic: Village tourism statistics; tourism management and its articulation with customary law; the socio-economic transformations brought about by tourism; views on the strengths and weaknesses of the existing tourism model.
5. Mrs. S., 49 year old, female, March 2018 – Souvenir seller in Penglipuran.
Topic: Her work, age, status at home and in the village; her dependence on/independence from her husband for money/decision-making; her perception of the evolution of her role in the community, and in her family, thanks to her work; her perception of the evolution of women's status in the village thanks to tourism, now and in the future; the positive and negative effects of tourism on traditional culture and identity.
6. Mrs. O., 44 year old, female, March 2018 – Souvenir seller in Penglipuran.
Topic: Her work, age, status at home and in the village; her dependence on/independence from her husband for money/decision-making; her perception of the evolution of her role in the community, and in her family thanks to her work; her perception of the evolution of women's status in the village thanks to tourism, now and in the future; the positive and negative effects of tourism on traditional culture and identity.
7. Mrs. R., 41 year old, female, March 2018 – Owner of a restaurant and homestay in Penglipuran.
Topic: Her work, age, status at home and in the village; her dependence on/independence from her husband for money/decision-making; her perception of the evolution of her role in the community, and in her family thanks to her work; her perception of the evolution of women's status in the village thanks to tourism, now and in the future; the positive and negative effects of tourism on traditional culture and identity.
8. Mr. M., 30 year old, male, March 2017 – Rice paddy owner and farmer in Jatiluwith, deputy subak and tourist guide.
Topic: His work, age, status in the community and family; the socio-economic transformations brought about by tourism, including its impact on the division of labor; the evolution of the role of women and young people within traditional society; the local population's involvement in tourism management and engagement with external actors; the positive and negative effects of tourism on traditional culture and identity.
9. Mrs. A., 23 year old, female, March 2018 – Accountant for the Badan Pengelola Daya Tarik Wisata Jatiluwih (Tourism management organization) in Jatiluwih.
Topic: His work, age, status in the community and family; the socio-economic transformations brought about by tourism, including its impact on the division of labor; the evolution of the role of women and young people within traditional society; the local population's involvement in tourism management and engagement with external actors; the positive and negative effects of tourism on traditional culture and identity.
10. Mr. N., 50 year old, male, March 2017 – Tenganan village inhabitant and tourist guide.
Topic: His work, age, status in the community and family; the socio-economic transformations brought about by tourism, including its impact on the division of labor; the evolution of the role of women and young people within traditional society; the local population's involvement in tourism management and engagement with external actors; the positive and negative effects of tourism on traditional culture and identity.
11. Mrs. Y., 50 year old, female, March 2017 – Inhabitant of Tenganan, thread producer and weaver of Gringsing textiles.
Topic: Her work, age, status at home and in the village; her dependence on/independence from her husband for money/decision-making; her perception of the evolution of her role in the community, and in her family thanks to her work; her perception of the evolution of women's status in the village thanks to tourism, now and in the future; the positive and negative effects of tourism on traditional culture and identity.
12. Mr. T., 36 year old, male, March 2017 – Balinese tourist guide.
Topic: How accessibility and quality of services in the villages have evolved, as well as the behavior, satisfaction and dissatisfaction of the tourists who visit them.

respect for the policy which requires the conservation of traditional village organization. These three villages are also very famous among the Balinese population and have received various kinds of awards or recognition. Although they are differently organized, they have all maintained partial dependence on agriculture. Their inhabitants chose to open their villages to tourism several decades ago, leading them to establish a new, complex and delicate balance combining traditional and touristic cultures.

Penglipuran is a 'customary village'. According to Mr. K., there are two political bodies in Bali: the administrative villages (*desa dinas*) and the customary villages (*desa adat*). Administrative villages apply national laws, whereas customary villages are in charge of the preserving traditions, culture and religion. Penglipuran is located in Bangli regency in a mountainous region. It covers an area of 112 hectares composed of 45 ha of bamboo forest, 58 ha of farmland and 9 ha of settlements. The village is regarded as traditional, particularly due to the layout of houses, respecting the Balinese religion which is a syncretic blend of shivaique Hinduism, Buddhism, and previous local animism. Our observation allowed us to observer that the houses are characterized by their regularity, placed on both sides of the main street which boasts a narrow entrance adorned by a gate and houses that stretch back towards the rear. The entrances to 50 out of the 76 houses in the village are used as shops (Figure 2). Penglipuran was declared an integrated touristic village in April 1993. It is regarded as the most successful of all the integrated villages, estimated by community leader Mr. I. and Mr. W. who is in charge of village tourism management to welcome over 250,000 tourists a year – the number of tourist stays is estimated for each village, since the local tourism management does not always keep a precise account of tourist visits. This has resulted in the establishment of 30 private homestays and 3 guest houses which are run by the community. Tourist attractions in addition to the architecture of the village include, according to Mr. W., dance performances, dancing and gamelan classes, trekking up Mount Batur and the Penglipuran Festival. The village received several awards and notably the *Asia green homestay* in 2014. It was ranked among the three top tourist destinations in Indonesia in 2016.

Jatiluwih is both an administrative and customary village. It is located in a rice paddy area, situated in the bottom of the Batukaru Mountain in the Tabanan regency. It is famous as one of the emblematic sites of the traditional irrigation system, or *subak*, and was registered on the UNESCO heritage list in 2012 as the 'Cultural *landscape of the province of Bali: the subak system as an example of the Tri Hita Karana philosophy*' (http://whc.unesco.org/en/list/1194/). This listed system consists of a collection of 4 sites of rice terraces and their water temples covering 19,500 ha. It is worth noting here that the main objective of UNESCO classification is to conserve cultural and traditional social organization as well as the quality of the 'natural' landscape. The *subak* remains a living social organization, involving about 1200 water cooperatives and their populations, who manage the supply from each water source. Their continued existence is currently at risk. Jatiluwih village was selected to become an integrated touristic village in 1992. Its *subak* is amongst the oldest in Bali, mentioned as early as the 10th century in inscriptions, extending over 303 ha and including 562 farming households and 7 communities in 2015. It is the biggest *subak* in Catur Angga Batukaru and the one which has invested the most in its tourism dynamic, with the construction of accommodation options. According to Mrs. A., the accountant for tourism management in the village, Jatiluwih offers 5 homestays, 1 resort with 10 rooms and 5

Figure 2. Penglipuran, combining traditional layout with tourism accommodation and shops. Authors' photo, used with permission, 2017.

restaurants. Mrs. A. claimed that in 2016 Jatiluwih was visited by 213,509 tourists, whereas in 2017 the figure reached 250,973, representing an increase of 17.5%.

Lastly, there is Tenganan, which is also both an administrative and customary village. Located in the Karangasem regency and regarded as one of the most traditional Balinese villages, it was also selected to become a *desa wisata terpadu*. Recognized by European anthropologists prior to the 1970s as one of the island's most secluded societies, Tenganan became famous for maintaining the *Bali Aga*, considered to be the original Balinese culture that predates the Hindu-Javanese immigration waves beginning in the 9th century. Its characteristics emerge from the preservation of some of the original Austronesian elements apparent in its cultural traditions, especially concerning marriage and membership of the village circle: only those born in the village can become full members of the community and get married in the village. However, Mr. N. explained:

> This fact results in the problem of a decreasing population. In 1972, scientists came to conduct blood-tests to find the reason for this situation. They identified a genetic disease. Since that time, we have changed the law to allow marriage outside the village and organize a ceremony to allow them to be 'reborn' as a Tenganan inhabitant.

Besides, contrary to the rest Bali, the community is not led by a patriarchal system: 'men and women have the same rights today regarding life and land ownership' emphasized Mrs. Y. As such, the community leaders are not only men, but six couples (husbands and wives). As early as the year 1930, the isolated character of this village made it an attraction. According to the tourist guide Mr. T., tourists are attracted by the *Bali Aga* culture that still holds on to the original traditions and ceremonies of the ancient Balinese, and by their traditional handcrafts such as the famous *Geringsing* double ikat textiles. They are also interested in the maintenance of the traditional lay-out and architecture. Although the village has developed tourism activities for almost the last 90 years, their inhabitants have chosen the restricted variety. M. N. explained: 'There is no homestay in the village, to protect the culture and the life of the people, and not to disturb things too much. Visiting is ok but staying overnight is not allowed'. As such, there are no homestays available, to preserve the privacy of the villagers. According to M. N., they welcome around 30,000 tourists a year, with the biggest concentration in June and July at the time of the 'Pandan Battle' ritual tradition, consisting of friendly tournaments during a whole month of festivities.

The three villages offer different patterns of tourism development that depend on the choice of their community. Nonetheless, behind their diversity, their common characteristic is, according to M. P., their capacity to build tourism activities out of their traditions. Thus, our objective is to examine this process, since opening a living culture up to the public induces changes and evolution which can run deep in its attempts to reconcile the needs of the contemporary inhabitants and the expectations of the diverse contingent of tourists. The aim of these communities, as well as of the public authorities who work with them, is to use tourism to develop the villages, with the dual aim of favoring better living conditions for the inhabitants and helping them to maintain their traditional culture. We will now analyze if and how tourism has brought economic development to the studied villages.

Economic development through diversification

Despite their differences, the three integrated touristic villages studied here reveal some similarities in their social organization. They are more touristic sites than real destinations, by which we mean that they are more a place to visit than to stay. This is a definitive choice that has been made regarding Tenganan, as claimed by M. N., yet even in Penglipuran and Jatiluwih less than 10% of the tourists spend one night or more in the village. M. W., in charge of tourism management in Penglipuran, explained: 'Most of the tourists only spend one day visiting. Only around 5% or 10% spend 2 days and 1 night or more'. The average time spent visiting Penglipuran and Tenganan is, according to our observations, even less, between one and three hours, depending on whether they take a local tour guide or visit freely. In Jatiluwih, the average time spent is longer: as indicated by the guide Mr. T., tourists stay between 2 and 6 hours in general depending on the trekking option they choose – lasting from 45 min to 4 hours (Figure 3) – and because people often enjoy the accommodation options – restaurants and cafes before or after trekking in the paddy. Some stay overnight to make several treks.

Thus, tourism in the three villages remains limited, in accordance with the expectations of the *desa wisata terpadu* as well as the philosophy of 'alternative tourism' which expects tourism to remain a diversification of the traditional economy by contributing to its maintenance. In Penglipuran, according to M. I. the village community leader, 'Around 40% of the local population are farmers, 20% are government workers, 10% are cruise workers and 30% are tourism workers'. In Tenganan, the division of work is complex since families accumulate multiple activities. M. N. explained that one third of village land is private and two thirds belongs to the communities. As such, even if less than 20% of people own land and are solely devoted to farming, most have regular agricultural activities as tenant farmers on private land or as users of the community land. He confirmed that:

> around 30% of the villagers work in the production of handicrafts and most specifically in itak weaving, that is, making baskets from ata leaves or calligraphy on palm leaves called lontar. These producers can sell their products to the villagers who own shops in the main street of the villages, but also at outdoor markets or directly to the tourists from their own street stalls.

Thus, even if community leaders estimate that 30% of the population works in tourism (essentially shop-keepers and tourist guides), for most families it constitutes a secondary activity. The rest of the villagers (around 20%) work outside the village, in public and private areas.

In Jatiluwih, the community still lives by the *subak* system. Although not everyone works in the rice fields, the form of social organization that it imposes remains predominant. Furthermore, half of the 562 farming households are land-owners, holding property of different sizes. Agriculture continues to be the primary activity, yet has diversified. Mr. M. explained that rice production is still the number one activity, yet coffee, cacao and flowers are also produced. Tourism has become the main activity for some of the villagers who own the restaurants or resorts, but is still a form of diversification for most of the farmers offering homestays. Tourist guides are essentially farmers who are paid by the community to work for 15-day shifts before going back to the rice fields. Few of them, as yet, are actually able to take part in these activities, since not many of them speak English, and are thereby able to welcome those tourists who are predominantly international. As Mr. M. confided: 'Not all the farmers work in tourism in Jatiluwih, because not all the farmers can speak English. There are only five people working as guides in shifts'.

Tourism undoubtedly favors the economic development of the villages, allowing the maintenance of their population and even permitting slight growth since the second decade of the 21st century. Tenganan and Penglipuran each have around 230 families and Jatiluwih has more than 560 families. Tourism may not bring them wealth, yet it allows them to live in their village as part of the middle class, ranging from lower to higher. As such, Mr. N. from Tenganan said that the money he earns with his wife, he as a tourist guide and she as a producer and seller of gringsing to tourists, is enough for a good life in the village. Mr. I., community leader in Penglipuran, stated that: 'Tourism provides a positive impact for the economic development of the village; many of the villagers open small shops inside their houses, allowing them to reach middle-class positions'. However Mr. N. in Jatiluwih claimed: 'The quality of life for the farmers is poor or medium. Tourism brings better opportunities but people remain generally at a medium level'. This status is contingent upon the previous social position of the family, but also on its capacity to invest in tourism opportunities.

Our initial finding regarding the three cases studied, and which are considered 'successful', is that tourism brings economic development to the villages through

Figure 3. Tourist activity in Jatiluwih: trekking in the paddy thanks to the hiking trails. Authors' photo, used with permission, 2017.

diverse patterns that depend on local investment and strategies. Their economic sustainability remains, nonetheless, fragile: if tourism allows for a diversification of activities which provide income and an improvement in living conditions, they remain moderate, without bringing wealth to the local population. Besides, this economic development and redistribution created by the tourism development of the villages, also raises the question of its social sustainability. Does tourism help to generate cohesion among the inhabitants by maintaining/respecting the local traditional organization, or does it on the contrary generate restructuration, including the transformation of the role of women?

Does desa wisata terpadu preserve or restructure the villages? The social effects of tourism

A sustainable community-based tourism?

The three villages studied here are characterized by a community-based management style, following the rules of the customary village. It was in the wake of this traditional societal organization that, in the 2010s, formal tourism organizations remaining under community management were created. Thus, the *desa wisata terpadu* meet the definition of community-based tourism, characterized according to Mowforth and Munt (2016, p. 103) by its capacity 'to increase people's involvement and ownership of tourism at the destination end'. The three villages respect the essence of the concept, relying on the involvement of the local population in inviting tourists to visit their communities, generating income and employment. It also enables common benefits, since all villages use tourism development for, above all, community improvement. In each village, almost 60% of revenue from entry-tickets is retained by the communities for the organization of rituals and ceremonies. The rest is used for building mainten-ance in public areas and community activities, such as the regular organization of vil-lage councils. As Mrs. A., an accountant in Jatiluwih, explained: 'The money goes to the community organization for rituals and public activities, so the villagers do not have to pay for the cost of them'.

Tourism in the village is also based on the idea of offering tourists the possibility of discovering local traditions and lifestyles, even if the process of tourism conversion induces adaptation, as M. P., facilitator for integrated touristic village development recalls. Nonetheless, the ability to meet western standards of accommodation and services varies from one village to another. According to our observations, we can emphasize that in Jatiluwih, the restaurants facing the rice fields meet those standards, as does the resort. Homestays in Penglipuran function at a more basic level, providing only frugal services. Wi-Fi is available nowhere except the front office. In Tenganan, the services are even more limited. A phone service is available only at the front gate, for use in case of emergency.

The differences in situation from one village to the next arise from a combination of economic capacity and local resistance to the requests of foreign tourism compa-nies, as is the case in Tenganan. This situation seems to testify to the community's ability to control their tourism development, as suggested by Mowforth and Munt (2016). Nonetheless, negotiation is never uncomplicated. Tourism is a 'system of actors, activities and places' (Knafou and Stock, 2003, p. 931) that mobilizes a combin-ation of participants at every level, from global to local, including tourists themselves who, through their choices and activities, can be understood as co-producers of touris-tic sites. As such, the tourism development of the villages we studied further depends on the initiative of the public authorities. This impulse takes shape through communi-cation, equipment and accessibility. As Mr. P. confirmed:

> As integrated touristic villages, the three destinations have been included within Educational Tours, but have also relied on social networking with travel agencies. Besides, local governments have provided all of them with parking and safe roads in good condition in order to allow proper accessibility.

International institutions such as UNESCO may also play an important role, such as in the case of the village of Jatiluwih.

In this regard, it becomes clear that public authorities and international institutions are essential elements in the creation of a tourism project, providing scope through vision. However, without the deep involvement of the community, blueprints cannot go beyond mere good intentions. According to Iwahara (2016), the different 'alternative' tourism projects in Bali only succeed when locally appropriated and inte-grated into the previous village organization. In fact, according to M. K., only a few integrated touristic villages in Bali really work, and all of those that are successful can be characterized by a similar combination of actors, articulated through the strong contribution of the local population. Tourism management, as well as tourism companies inside the villages, is all owned by the residents, even if they are able to employ outside staff when the need arises, although local skills may not be up to par, as is the case for the restaurants in Jatiluwih. All decisions connected to tourism remain community-based, incorporating traditional forms of organization based on common decisions made during regular meetings. As Mr. N. from Tenganan explained:

> Bale agung is a meeting hall for the council, held every night, which the 6 main couples will attend. The meeting takes place from 8:30 pm. The agenda of the meeting is to solve any problem in the village's daily life, including tourism management.

Penglipuran and Jatiluwih have developed the same kind of daily organization, even if the structure of the banjar is different, with only male members.

The three integrated touristic villages we study here can be defined as community-based tourism. Nonetheless this status does not protect them from societal difficulties. As we stated earlier, tourism, like all other human activities, brings about socio-economic changes (Knafou and Pickel-Chevalier, 2011) that can create tensions. The first negative impact that all those we interviewed mentioned is 'the increasing competitiveness of the villagers which decreases harmony among the villagers' as Mr. I., community leader of Penglipuran, regretfully revealed. Indeed, besides the income generated from entry-tickets, which is reserved for the community, the inhabitants of the villages are allowed to have their own businesses. In this manner, tourism brings about wealth redistribution that has generated a socio-economic evolution. It changes the atmosphere of the villages, which may then be perceived as 'too commercial, with a different distribution of the economic profits that creates competition among villagers' complained Mr. N. from Tenganan.

Communities are aware of this situation and try to find innovative solutions to at least decrease competition between tourism business owners. As such, local tourist guides are booked through the front office in all three villages, in order to establish a rotation system between them. This same philosophy is applied in Penglipuran for the reservation of homestays, as Mr. W. explained:

> The village management has created a system called 'take turn' to prevent disloyal competition, especially for the reservation of homestays. Tourists who want to rent a room call or come to the front office and are given the homestay that has waited longest for a booking, in order to distribute rooms equally.

Furthermore, tourists who come to the villages on their own have access to all the houses that are open to tourism to buy souvenirs, but the ones who hire a local guide also follow the rotation system. Thus, if tourism inevitably brings social disparities to the villages, the question is above all, as Buckley (2012) reminds us, about what is 'acceptable' in terms of equality or inequality. In each village, the inhabitants have devised systems based on their own values and meant to promote an 'acceptable' balance for them, between customary ways and the inequality brought about by tourism. In this context, in order to maintain the traditional way of life, we observed that all three communities have concentrated tourism activity only in the main street. In Jatiluwih it is the main road, overlooking the rice fields, which is designed to receive most of the tourist infrastructure (accommodation, restaurants, parking areas, shops). In Penglipuran and Tenganan that do not have a view point of this kind, the tourist shops and services are located on the central street, whereas the rest of the village remains traditional and not necessarily welcoming for the tourists who dare to venture there – they can be politely accompanied back to the main street where they are supposed to be. In Tenganan, especially, we observed a clear desire to keep a distance between today's life and tourist activities which all need to stop in the evening.

Tourism and women's emancipation: a social improvement?

Tourism also breeds complex social evolution, such as that regarding the place of women in society. Traditionally, Balinese society remains patriarchal, with some rare exceptions such as Tenganan, where the village council is led by six couples. In the other villages, although Balinese Hinduism officially claims that men and women are born free and have the same rights and duties, in reality, social position varies considerably according to gender (Long and Kindon, 1997). The *desa adat* rules are based on oral or written codes (*awig-awig*) which can differ from one village to the next (Hitchcock and Putra, 2007). Nonetheless, the *desa adat* are all composed of several *banjars*, which are more social subdivisions than real territorial ones. According to Byczek (2016, p. 221), the banjars can be 'regarded as the most important reference group of the Balinese'. Yet these banjars are made up of married men, traditionally considered to be the head of the family. They meet at least several times a month, in order to oversee the religious and traditional life of the inhabitants. Women can participate by giving their opinion, especially to their husband, but are not able to make official decisions.

However, tourism is bringing about evolution in this arena. As observed in different countries (Cone, 1995; Moore & Wen, 2008; Sinclair, 1997; Swain, 1995), women who invest in tourism activities enjoy increased autonomy, which in turn slightly increases their social power, even if this does not mean actual equity. As stated by Sinclair (1997, p. 3): 'Women obtain some power by providing men with increased material resources, while men retain much of their power owing to the persistence of many facets of traditional gender roles'. As such, in the three villages studied here, and according to our observations and interviews, women rarely have supervisory positions yet, but shops, homestays and even restaurants are mostly female-managed (Figure 4). In our study Mrs. R. owns a restaurant and homestay whereas Mrs. O. and Mrs. S. are souvenir traders in Penglipuran. As for Mrs. Y., she is a geringsing producer who create cloth and textiles to be sold.

This situation flows from the fact that these types of establishment and activity are more or less directly attached to the home, traditionally the women's sphere. Thus, as Costa et al. (2017) argue social reproductive gender roles (taking care of the house and hosts) may influence productive roles (welcoming tourists). These activities give women the possibility to progress from the home-based informal economy to the formal economy, awarding them greater societal visibility. Nonetheless, even as business owners, women may remain under the tutelage of their spouse. As such, Mrs. S. said: 'I still depend on my husband to take decisions, especially about money', even if she earns her own from her business. The other women we interviewed made closely-related statements, but with some nuances. Mrs. N. explained that she can manage her own money, but only for specific activities. She explained to us that: 'I can use my money by myself, but only for daily needs. More specifically, I use around 25% for kitchen utensils, 25% for religious ceremonies and 50% for the venture capital of my

Figure 4. Woman in her shop selling Geringsing and souvenirs, on the main street of Tenganan, Authors' photo, used with permission, 2017.

business'. Mrs. R. claimed that she can manage her own money, then reconsidered and added: 'sometimes … ' Finally, Mrs. A., who is younger (23 years old, whereas the others are between 40 and 50), stated: 'I was given the full right to use the money I earned for my needs, but I still partly gave it to my family'. These statements reveal different types of behavior, and maybe an evolution according to the generation, but which still depend on the openness of the husband who can allow, or not, his wife to be more independent. However, all the women we interviewed considered that working in tourism has brought them greater consideration in the village and at home. Mrs. R. refers to these changes asserting, 'Now, my opinion is more taken in account!' They all testified that working in tourism has brought them more respect from their family and from the community. In addition, they think that tourism generally brings about an improvement for women in the villages, because it gives them more visibility and relative independence. As such, Mrs. S. emphasized 'tourism in my village results in better living conditions, especially for women because now women can be souvenir traders and run other businesses', whereas Mrs. R. claimed: 'Tourism is very good, because women can supplement the family income, and not always depend on the husband'.

Although gender prejudice persists – seen for example, in the preference for male guides, as it is not socially acceptable for a woman to be alone with foreign men – tourism activities accrue women a greater degree of social power, all the more so when combined with education, as demonstrated previously in other case studies (Tajeddini, Ratten, & Denisa, 2017). Education creates new opportunities to access formal sector jobs and even management roles, particularly within national and international companies. Today women may have access to the highest responsibilities in Indonesia, such as government ministries. In 2001, a woman became the President of Indonesia (2001–2004). This paradoxical situation shows the gap between the evolution of administrative and traditional life, the latter still attached to a patriarchal system (despite some exceptions, such as in Tenganan or in Minangkabau in Western Sumatra). The maintenance of this local tradition can also be detrimental to village wealth. According to all the respondents we interviewed, the main problem villages face comes from the lack of a workforce with professional tourism skills. As such, Mr. W. stated that their major problem in Penglipuran is 'the lack of human resources to work in the village because they cannot pay them high salaries. For now, there is no salary paid to the tourism managers in the village. Like me, they have to be volunteers, in addition to having another professional activity'.

Indeed the local young people, who go to big cities to study, most often choose to stay in the southern region of Bali. There they work for international and national tourism companies, enjoy higher salaries and more comfortable daily lives and conditions (Bendesa & Aksari, 2017). This is all the more the case for young women, who are able to attain higher social status through access to top positions in companies, whereas within the villages they are barred from *banjar* decision making (except in Tenganan). Thus, even if there are more tourism opportunities in the resort and restaurants in Jatiluwih than in the other villages, Mrs. A. confessed: 'In my opinion, the employment created in traditional villages is still limited. That is why, in my view, when someone, especially women, acquire higher education qualifications, they normally look for jobs outside their village'.

This skills drain is a crucial problem for the future of the village, since young educated villagers appear to be the key to allowing the community to work towards the construction of a local socio-economic balance, combining conservation and adaptation to the modern world. Their knowledge of customs, combined with tourism management skills, is important in this regard, as shown by the cases of Mr. W., SMK (vocational school) graduate, and Mr. M., who graduated from the Negeri Singaraja School. Yet, the temptation for young people to leave their native villages and emigrate to big cities with higher economic potential is all the more important in the cases we study here because the monetary returns on tourism remain low. This situation is exacerbated by the fact that between 45% and 60% of the entry ticket price goes directly to the region, leaving the community with the remainder. In order to escape from this situation, the leaders of Tenganan decided not to collect fees at the entrance. As Mr. N. explained: 'There is no revenue from tickets; there are no tickets, we only receive donations from visitors. The idea is to avoid the regional government tax from the revenue. The income goes solely to the village'. This system, which is not completely legal, is also risky since the community depends on the generosity of visitors, without any fixed prices. This complex situation weakens the social sustainability of the development model for the villages that are then at risk of being locked into a 'vicious cycle', with a lack of qualified human resources limiting their capacity for economic growth, and a lack of material wealth that encourages their inhabitants to leave.

Does tourism enhance or re-invent heritage? A combination of cultural tourism and touristic culture

Tourism and culture: a co-construction

Villages are characterized by a complex process involving the constant reconstruction of local societal models, combining conservation and innovation. This phenomena further identifies the ambiguous relationships between communities and their heritage. The latter is defined by O. Lazzarotti (2003, p. 692) as 'a set of attributes, performances and activities attached to a non-contemporary object […]'. This means that not everything is heritage: its determination results from collective choices, promoting construction of memory through the recognition of common milestones, as Richards (2000) has demonstrated. Based on a Western principle of linearity of time, this notion of heritage results in a distancing of the past in relation to the present as linked to the phenomenon of ring-fencing. The past is therefore fixed so as to be protected in its current state and shared with future generations. This choice to ring-fence memory requires complicated relationships with culture, defined as 'the grouping together of ideal products available in a given social reality' (Lussault, 2003, p. 216).

In some ways, heritage which fixes the assets of the distant past is then opposed to culture, enshrined in a contemporary time-frame and therefore subject to constant change, under internal but also external influences. The complexity of the relationship of the Balinese to their heritage (Picard, 2017; Vickers, 2012) comes from the fact that, although partially a legacy from a previous generation, it cannot be ring-fenced into the past, but remains a part of their contemporary culture. Thus, Balinese society illustrates the continuous process of reinvention of tradition, as in the concept developed by Hobsbawm and Ranger (2012). It is a process to which tourism contributes, through complex relationships. The dialectic between tourism and heritage, one feeding off the other (Richards, 2000) stems from the fact that tourism comes partly from the enhancement of the natural and cultural environment that it covets and transforms, due as much to modernization as to forms of preservation that are based on arbitrary fixations (Pickel-Chevalier, 2014).

Tourism as an ambivalent agent of cultural reinvention, questioning balinese identity

This ambiguous co-construction is very relevant in the three villages that we studied. Rather than threatening or enhancing local heritage, tourism helps to revitalize it, moving from the inspiration of legacy to the reality of reinvention. The village of Tenganan, for example, is notably famous for the production of geringsing, a textile created using the double *ikat* method with traditional natural colors. Geringsing is regarded by the Balinese as sacred cloth, endowed with supernatural properties to keep impurities and danger out of the village as well as protecting humans from baleful influences. As Mrs. Y. explained:

> Many people from other villages in Bali and from abroad come to here to buy geringsing, because it is used in ritual ceremonies, especially for the transition from one phase of life to the next, like baby birthing ceremonies, tooth filling ceremonies, and other rituals. It is also used in case of animal sickness. The color of geringsing makes it very sacred for healing and for protecting people from bad spirits. The word gering means sickness, and sing means no, so geringsing means 'no sickness'. It is made up of 3 natural colors: black that represents liquid; red for heat; and yellow for the air. The combination of all three in the pattern provides balance, keeping the three body element in harmony. We traditionally have 25 motifs, such as the Cakra motif, puppet motif, cempaka motif, tali dandan motif.

The quality of the weaving, reinforced by its mystical reputation, helps to spread the Geringsing's fame, now well known among the international tourist population. To meet increasing demand, the production process has changed, offering varying qualities at different prices. Mrs. Y. stated that:

> Originally to make geringsing, we needed two and a half years. If the first coloring is not good, we have to dye the thread several times to get the color, every six months. Now the drying process in the sun can be faster: we can make geringsing in only a few months, but the color fades, so we need to soak the thread many times to get a bright color. We have three different qualities at different prices, but each family has to keep one of very good quality for their own ceremonies.

This adaptation favors the continuity of local production, as heritage but also as a contemporary culture providing a living for nearly 50 families in the village (Figure 5).

This situation is also reflected in the Pandan Battle that has become the biggest attraction in the village. The tradition is based on friendly duels between all the male villagers, who fight each other armed with a tied packet of thorny 'pandan' leaves. According to tradition, participating in the Pandan Battle is an obligation for Tenganan males, and serves as a rite of passage into manhood for young men. Today this tradition has become doubly crucial for the inhabitants: in addition to its ritual meaning, it is also an important source of income for the village. According to M. N., it attracts around 300 tourists a day during the month-long ceremony. For this reason, the event has been re-thought and adapted to accommodate a large stream of visitors, as Mr. N. explained. Today, even foreign males may take part in the fights, as part of the game. This is an example of how tourism may favor the creativity of the local population, but not without a certain ambiguity, insofar as the Balinese are expected to display and perform their 'Balinese-ness' (Kebalian: Balinese identity). The latter, of course, is not a fixed entity, but rather the result of a long historical and continuous process of transcultural construction, fed from influences which are internal (communities leaders, Balinese intelligencia) but also external (Picard, 2010, 2017).

Penglipuran also provides evidence of this phenomenon. Firstly, the so-called typical architecture of the houses and the layout of the village which has attracted thousands of tourists as a 'traditional Balinese village' is actually the outcome of repairs made for President Suharto's planned visit in 1991 which in fact never took place (Yamashita, 2016, p. 135). This means that its aesthetic appearance is not the fruit of spontaneous historical evolution, but of a design that was made to fit expectations regarding a model of a 'perfect' traditional Balinese village, which today gives it its singularity and identity. This process is repeated with regard to village handicraft production. Today, inhabitants sell not only local products such as baskets made from bamboo or paintings on bamboo leaves, but also food and products which they buy in other markets to re-sell (fabric, coffee, food). That is why M.W. would like to encourage new creations from the inhabitants. He claimed:

> Villagers produce their homemade food such as potato donuts, herbal drinks and many other things for their own consumption and for the tourists. Sometimes they sell it outside the village such as in the market. But they buy a lot of handicrafts outside the village and resell them at home. These are all the same which is why we need to make more local handicrafts, through our home production system, with the dual purpose of attracting tourism and increasing local identification.

Figure 5. Woman weaving the famous geringsing in Tenganan. Authors' photo, used with permission, 2017.

These dynamics, which incorporate the invention of tradition, was initiated three years ago, around the Penglipuran village festival, a five-day culture and arts event organized in the month of December. According to Mr. I., the festival provides a better image of Penglipuran culture, even if it has been, in fact, created for the tourists.

This reinvention of culture, initially for tourism development but eventually reappropriated by the local population as a symbol of their pride, is also perceptible in the reshaping of the environment, from the productive land to the esthetic landscape. As such, the Penglipuran bamboo forest has been redesigned as a tourist walkway with the creation of paved paths through the woods and the marking out of different kinds of trees with explanatory signs. Jatiluwih village illustrates the most striking example of this territorial mutation by reconstructing the rice fields as a landscape. The fields are covered with trekking paths of varying lengths that run through the paddy (Figure 3). They all converge in front of the restaurants on the main street, offering a 'view over the rice paddy'. This means that the community has begun to re-imagine their farming land as a playground which requires an element of planning. This induces the villagers to combine their own farming perception of the fields (fertility, productivity) with the foreign one (external spectators), bringing together two divergent interpretations of the land – utilitarian versus scenic. Once again, we can here identify the complex effects of tourism: on the one hand it has severe effects on Balinese society and the environment, where many hectares of rice fields dramatically disappear every year under pressure from the building industry. On the other hand it has a paradoxical status as the major force behind the preservation of the rice paddy, redefined as a living heritage, a dynamic illustrated by its registration on the UNESCO world heritage list in 2012 as the 'Cultural landscape of the province of Bali'.

Conclusion

The objective of our study was to question the sustainability of the desa wisata terpadu. We chose a multi-case methodology to exploit the empirical material to try and build a more holistic picture in order to understand, through the villages officially considered as successful for a start, their organization and modus operandi. In this context, we looked at consecutively Pengpliuran, Tenganan and Jatiluwih, their economic, social and cultural sustainability, mainly defined as a contribution to economic growth, social cohesion and cultural enhancement.

Our results show the complexity of the effects of tourism, which are always plural and sometimes contradictory. First, we can agree that our three case studies are successful because they meet the expectations of both the desa wisata terpadu and sustainable tourism policy, being based on 'social and cultural activities, everyday customs, buildings and the traditional use of space', and at 'the same time [being] able to provide the infrastructure, attractions, catering, and accommodation required for tourists'. Their tourism development has brought income to the inhabitants that allow them to keep their community alive, as notably illustrated by the increase in their local populations. In addition, tourism in the three villages can be defined as community-based, respecting and integrating on the whole the previous social organization. We can argue that this achievement depends on the involvement of all the inhabitants. We observed that the three villages each proposed a singular pattern that has been collectively chosen in the village – according to the local organization that can include inequality in community decision-making, especially when linked to gender.

However, despite the apparent success of these so-called model examples of integrated touristic village, we can identify some limitations. First, if tourism brings about economic growth, it remains moderate. It is a diversification of activity that can enable the local population to reach middle-class status, but not wealth. As such, incomes are not high enough to persuade the young qualified generation to stay, and they are more tempted by making a career in the international resort in southern Bali. Yet, for the three villages, the lack of human resources is the main difficulty when it comes to securing the future of their community.

Second, we demonstrated that even within this 'sustainable design', tourism causes significant societal transformations. If the communities endeavor to maintain their traditional activities and ways of life, the process of opening villages up to the public requires changes – opening houses, transforming ceremonies, modifying practices that can even lead to a decrease in the original quality of products, etc. Besides, the investment of the local population in tourism in not homogeneous. As such, tourism creates a redistribution of wealth, and hence of social position, that engenders restructuring and new inequalities between families. This situation can become a source of tension, perceived in the three villages as a 'decrease of harmony' between the inhabitants.

Nevertheless, these transformations are ambivalent since they can also contribute to the sustainability paradigm, based on a western ideology of equality and individual liberty. As a matter of fact, tourism clearly results in the empowerment of women. Admittedly it remains limited, hardly ever leading to gender equality. However, women today contribute substantially to the development of tourism in their village through the creation of services (accommodation, catering and production of handcrafts) that are associated with their traditional activities (household management, production of cloth and utensils such as baskets, etc.) This situation gives them the possibility of opening their businesses and earning their own money. Even if it does not, in the traditional villages dominated by the banjar system, give them total autonomy, it provides them with more visibility and respect, a fact that they are deeply grateful for.

In addition, our study also reveals that the complexity of tourism is clearly perceived by the local population, and they understand both the necessity to develop this activity and the difficulties that it generates. In the three villages, the respondents demonstrated their awareness of the ambiguous intrinsic relationships between their traditional activities and ways of life and their tourism development. Tourism is, above all, for them an instrument for maintaining their village which will be threatened by desertification without the economic diversification provided by tourism. However, the relationships between tradition and tourism remain complex, echoing the difficulties of trying to unite the conservation of culture with openness to modernity. This ambition takes shape in different ways in the three villages, but it is also a dynamic motor for the revitalization of culture. The necessity to assert their local specific characteristics for economic purposes in the competitive tourism sector of Bali has led them to claim their distinctive identify which is, to a certain extent, a community and evaluative construction. In fact, such new creations are neither traditional nor 'fake'. Rather, they are the results of a living culture, and unique because they are co-produced by the local population and tourists, with a desire to perpetuate a social idea of Balineseness. The latter meets the expectations of the local population who unconsciously appropriate the image of themselves conveyed by tourists, and this thereby confirms the specific, ambiguous role of tourism as an agent of both transformation and conservation of their culture and heritage.

The study of these three villages, which are presented as successful, shows that the desa wisata terpadu can be defined as a mode of sustainable tourism which is well adapted to Balinese society in its diversity. A sustainability that nonetheless remains fragile and needs to be based on a socio-economic model with strengthened efficiency. It includes more flexibility to integrate young qualified inhabitants, without gender prejudice, in order to avoid the 'vicious circle' of a lack of qualified human resources limiting their capacity for economic growth, and a lack of material wealth that encourages their inhabitants to leave.

Disclosure statement

No potential conflict of interest was reported by the authors.

References

Bendesa, I. K. G., and Aksari, N. M. A. (2017). From agricultural to tourism hegemony: A deep socio-economic structural transformation, In S. Pickel-Chevalier (Ed.), *Tourism in Bali and the challenge of sustainable development* (76–102). Cambridge: Cambridge Scholars Publishing.

Bourdieu, P. (1987). Espace social et pouvoir symbolique [Social space and symbolic power]. In *Choses dites*. Paris: Minuit.

Buckley, R. (2012). Sustainable tourism: Research and reality. *Annals of Tourism Research, 39*(2), 528–546. doi:10.1016/j.annals.2012.02.003

Butler, R. (1999). Sustainable tourism: A state-of-the-art review. *Tourism Geographies, 1*(1), 7–25. doi:10.1080/14616689908721291

Byczek, C. (2016). Traditional livelihoods and community-based ecotourism. In I. D. Putra & S. Campbell (Eds.), *Recent developments in Bali tourism* (pp. 214–239). Denpasar: Buku Arti.

Cater, E. (1993). Ecotourism in the third world: Problems for sustainable tourism development. *Tourism Management, 14*(2), 85–90. doi:10.1016/0261-5177(93)90040-R

Cone, C. (1995). Crafting selves: The life of two Mayan women. *Annals of Tourism Research, 22*(2), 314–327. doi:10.1016/0160-7383(94)00079-4

Costa, C., Bakas, F., Breda, Z., Durão, M., Carvalho, I., & Caçador, S. (2017). Gender, flexibility and the 'ideal tourism worker'. *Annals of Tourism Research, 64,* 64–75. doi:10.1016/j.annals.2017.03.002

Di Méo, G. (2016). Une géographie sociale. Entre structures et représentations [A social geography. Between structures and representations]. *Cybergéo, Les 20 ans de Cybergeo.* Retrieved from http://journals.openedition.org/cybergeo/27761

Farrell, B.H. (1999), Conventional or sustainable tourism? No room for choice. *Tourism Management 20*(2), 189–191.

Hitchcock, M., & Putra, N. D. (2007). *Tourism, development and terrorism in Bali.* Hampshire: Ashgate Publishing.

Hobsbawm, E. & Ranger, T. (Eds.). (2012). *The invention of tradition.* Cambridge: Cambridge University Press.

Hunter, C. (1997). Sustainable tourism as an adaptive paradigm. *Annals of Tourism Research, 24*(4), 850–867. doi:10.1016/S0160-7383(97)00036-4

Iwahara, H. (2016). Sustainable tourism discourse and practice: A case study of village-ecotourism in southern Bali. In I. D. Putra & S. Campbell (Eds.), *Recent developments in Bali tourism* (pp. 193–213). Denpasar: Buku Arti.

Knafou, R., & Pickel-Chevalier, S. (2011). Tourisme et développement durable: de la lente émergence à une mise en oeuvre problématique [Tourism and sustainable development: from slow emergence to problematic implantation]. *Géoconfluences* (pp. 1–13). Retrieved from http://geoconfluences.ens-lsh.fr

Knafou, R., & Stock, M. (2003). Tourisme. In J. Levy & M. Lussault (Eds.), *Dictionnaire de la Géographie et de l'espace des sociétés* [Dictionary of Geography and Spaces Societies] (pp. 931–934). Paris: Belin.

Lazzarotti, O. (2003). Patrimoine [Heritage]. In J. Levy & M. Lussault (Eds.), *Dictionnaire de la Géographie et de l'espace des sociétés* (pp. 692–693). Paris: Belin.

Le Moigne, J. L. (1995). *Les épistémologies constructivistes [Constructivism epistemologies].* Paris: Presses Universitaires de France.

Liu, Z. (2003). Sustainable tourism development: A critique. *Journal of Sustainable Tourism, 11*(6), 459–475. doi:10.1080/09669580308667216

Long, V. H., & Kindon, S. L. (1997). Gender and tourism development in Balinese villages. In M.T. Sinclair (Ed.), *Gender, work and tourism.* London: Routledge.

Lussault, M. (2003). Culture. In J. Levy & M. Lussault (Eds.) *Dictionnaire de la Géographie et de l'espace des sociétés* (pp. 216–217). Paris: Belin.

Moore, S., & Wen, J. J. (2008). Tourism employment in China: A look at gender equity, equality, and responsibility. *Journal of Human Resources in Hospitality and Tourism, 8*(1), 32–42. doi: 10.1080/15332840802274429

Morin, E. (1986). *La Méthode, Tome 3, La Connaissance de la connaissance [The Method. Tome 3. The knowledge of the knowledge].* Paris: Le Seuil.

Mowforth, M., & Munt, I. (2016). *Tourism and sustainability: New tourism in the third world* (4th ed., 1st 1998). London: Routledge.

Picard, M. (1992). *Bali. Tourisme Culturel et Culture Touristique [Bali. Cultural Tourism and Touristic Culture]* Paris: L'Harmattan.

Picard, M. (2010). L'identité balinaise à l'épreuve du tourisme [The Balinese Identity in front of tourism]. *EspacesTemps.net, Travaux.* Retrieved from http://www.espacestemps.net/articles/identite-balinaise-epreuve-tourisme/

Picard, M. (2017). *Kebalian. La construction dialogique de l'identité balinaise* [Kebalian. The dialogical construction of the Balinese identity]. Paris: Cahiers d'Archipel.

Picard, M., & Vickers, A. (2017). Being Balinese in the face of tourism. In S. Pickel-Chevalier (Ed.), *Tourism in Bali and the challenge of sustainable development* (pp. 14–39). Cambridge: Cambridge Scholars Publishing.

Pickel-Chevalier, S. (2014). *L'Occident face à la nature* [The Western civilization in front of nature]. Paris: Cavalier Bleu.

Pickel-Chevalier, S. (2017). Can tourism enhance «nature» in Bali? Moving toward a new paradigm, through interculturation process. In S. Pickel-Chevalier (Ed.), *Tourism in Bali and the challenge of sustainable development* (pp. 132–160). Cambridge, Cambridge Scholar Publishing.

Pickel-Chevalier, S., & Budarma, K. (2016). Towards sustainable tourism in Bali. *Mondes du Tourisme, La troisième révolution touristique.* Retrieved from http://tourisme.revues.org/1187.10.4000/tourisme.1187

Richards, G. (2000). Tourism and the world of culture and heritage. *Tourism Recreation Research, 25*(1), 9–17. doi:10.1080/02508281.2000.11014896

Richards, G., & Munsters, W. (2010). *Cultural tourism research methods.* Oxfordshire: Cabi.

Scheibling, J. (2015), *Qu'est-ce que la géographie ?,* Paris: Hachette supérieur.

Sinclair, M. T. (1997). *Gender, work and tourism.* London: Routledge.

Swain, M. (1995). Gender in tourism. *Annals of Tourism Research, 22*(2), 247–267. doi:10.1016/0160-7383(94)00095-6

Tajeddini, K., Ratten, V., & Denisa, M. (2017). Female tourism entrepreneurs in Bali, Indonesia. *Journal of Hospitality and Tourism Management, 31,* 52–58. doi:10.1016/j.jhtm.2016.10.004

Vickers, A. (2012). *Bali: A paradise created* (2nd ed.). Singapore: Tuttle Publishing.

Yamashita, S. (2003). *Bali and beyond: Explorations in the anthropology of tourism.* New York: Berghahn.

Yamashita, S. (2016). The Balinese subak as world cultural heritage. In I. D. Putra & S. Campbell (Eds.), *Recent developments in Bali tourism* (pp. 116–144). Denpasar: Buku Arti.

Yin, R. K. (2018). *Case study research and applications* (6th ed.). Los Angeles: Sage.

Resilience and Non-Linear Change in Island Tourism

AMRAN HAMZAH & MARK P. HAMPTON

ABSTRACT *Perhentian Kecil, located off the east coast of peninsular Malaysia, is predominantly a small-scale tourism destination, specifically for backpackers and independent travellers. Against the context of an aggressive drive by the state government to remove small-scale tourism development in favour of formal and high-end resorts, this paper examines the local responses to the exogenous factors that had threatened the equilibrium, and hence sustainability, of the tourism systems on the island. The paper draws upon a longitudinal study with multiple visits over an extended period since the mid-1990s. Using insights from Resilience Theory, the paper argues that this island destination is an example of non-linear change rather than conventional resort evolution. The paper also discusses how the authors – as researchers – had to realign their research framework and approach to take into consideration the growing complexities of tourism development in small island destinations.*

Introduction

For many small islands, tourism is economically significant as a source of income and employment. In some insular areas such as the Caribbean, tourism accounts for over 75% of some countries' GDP (Graci & Dodds 2010). Islands, especially small islands, continue to fascinate and attract tourists (Royle 2001), and for tropical less-developed countries (LDCs) such as Malaysia with many offshore islands, developers and government planners see the potential to develop resorts. However, what of small islands that already host international tourism, albeit at a small scale and catering for backpackers? What issues and tensions might emerge as these small island destinations face significant change?

The Perhentian islands, off the east coast of peninsular Malaysia, have been a tourism destination since the late 1980s when backpacker tourists 'discovered' these islands. The two main islands, Perhentian Besar ('large Perhentian island') and Perhentian Kecil ('small Perhentian'), have experienced differing forms of tourism development. This paper focuses on Perhentian Kecil, which has remained broadly a small-scale tourism destination, specifically for backpackers and independent travellers. Against the backdrop of an aggressive drive by the Terengganu state government to get rid of small-scale tourism development in favour of formal and high-end resorts, this paper examines the local responses to the exogenous factors that had threatened the equilibrium, and hence sustainability, of the tourism systems on the island. In addition, this paper documents how the authors had to realign their research framework and approach to take into consideration the growing complexities of tourism development in small island destinations.

Modelling the Evolution of Tourism in Small Islands

Island tourism has a growing literature since the seminal work of Hills and Lundgren (1977) in the Caribbean, and Archer's (1977) work on economic impacts. The well-cited and highly influential model developed by Butler (1980) of the Tourist Area Life Cycle (TALC) suggested a stages approach to understanding resort evolution and proposed that resorts moved through 'exploration', 'involvement', 'development', 'consolidation' and, finally, 'stagnation'. For many destinations, the post-stagnation stages are the most crucial (or even problematic) since the model suggests that resorts may experience rejuvenation or may continue to decline. Since the 1980s, authors have applied Butler's TALC to islands (Weaver 1990; Choy 1992), and many others have researched environmental impacts and sustainability (Wilkinson 1989; de Albuquerque & McElroy 1992; Briguglio *et al.* 1996; Bardolet 2001; Gössling 2001). Research has also examined other geographical aspects such as the links between island ecotourism and economic development (Klak & Flynn 2008) and, most recently, small-scale tourism as a possible form of 'soft growth' for islands (Timms & Conway 2011). Much of the literature though concerns large resorts or mass tourism in islands, so small-scale tourism, particularly backpackers and independent travellers, has a smaller literature, with the main research located in South-East Asia, the predominant backpacker region (Cohen 1982; Wall 1996; Hampton 1998; Spreitzhofer 1998; Fallon 2001; Hampton & Hampton 2009; Hamzah 1995, 1997, 2007).

Spatial temporal or evolutionary models have largely been used to analyse the evolution of small-scale tourism (Butler 1980; Oppermann 1993; Agarwal 1997; Dodds & McElroy 2008). There have also been criticisms of the model (Choy 1992; Getz 1992), but its simplicity makes it an attractive tool to explain the evolution of resort destinations, especially those that started from an 'involvement stage' initiated by the local community.

Lately, researchers have argued that the TALC's linear narrative is unable to rigorously analyse the complexity of the interactions and forces shaping destination areas

(McKercher 1999; Farrell & Twining-Ward 2004, 2005; Cochrane 2010). These are the proponents of Resilience Theory, a model that was initially developed by Holling (1973) for the field of ecology, but has lately been applied to other disciplines, including tourism. The main difference between the four phases of Resilience Theory and the TALC is that the former describes the evolution of tourism systems in a destination area as a cycle or a loop instead of a linear progression. The four phases are 'reorganisation', 'exploitation', 'conservation' and 'release' (Holling 2001). *Reorganisation* represents the rapid change that usually takes place after a 'destabilising event', which is often manifested in the form of the regeneration of societal structures. *Exploitation* explains the creation of new systems or institutions accompanied by new cultural, political and social relationships. *Conservation* refers to the formation of a stable but rigid state through newly formed and interconnected structures and capital. Finally, the *release* phase occurs when the disturbance event(s) destabilises the existing rigid structures to produce rapid changes (Holling 2001: 394).

The use of Resilience Theory in tourism studies has been rather limited. Among the few attempts to use the model in the context of tourism development, Calgaro and Cochrane (2009) applied Resilience Theory to develop strategies to strengthen the tourism systems in Thailand and Sri Lanka after the 2004 Tsunami. Schianetz and Kavanagh (2008) developed tourism indicators based on Resilience Theory, and Nguru (2010) applied the model to explain the resilience of the tourism system in Kampung Cherating Lama, the pioneer 'drifter enclave' in Malaysia. According to Resilience Theory, local knowledge is important for resource management, which is often generated via a process of 'learning by doing' (Folke *et al.* 2005). This explains why local communities had been able to develop environmentally friendly 'drifter enclaves' by applying their knowledge and expertise in sustainable vernacular development (Nguru 2010). Nonetheless, Resilience Theory also does not deny that cultural knowledge should be complemented by scientific knowledge (Folke *et al.* 2005), which is crucial in moving up small-scale tourism development along the value chain.

In the context of tourism development, Cochrane (2010) suggested that Resilience Theory could be used to describe the four phases that a tourism system goes through in its development path. The 'release' phase is considered to be the equal of TALC's 'rejuvenation' stage, but prior to this phase, a 'destabilising event' usually occurs (such as tsunamis, bird flu etc.) that may result in the destination going through a temporary decline. This happens before the destination is then revitalised through the community's resilient actions, such as innovation and adaptation to changing market forces and strong leadership, which would ensure that the destination will not succumb to permanent decline but reinvent itself. In the same light, the revitalisation that occurred in Kampung Cherating Lama, according to Nguru (2010), was due to the fact that practical business knowledge was accumulated and exchanged, and this helped the local community in understanding the market forces and tourist demand despite their lack of formal education.

The Research

This paper is based on a longitudinal study that began in the mid-1990s, with later visits in July 2006, July 2008, May 2009 and June 2010. The initial fieldwork commenced in 1994 in the form of a series of preliminary visits to the island, and one of the authors stayed with the local residents at Kampung Pasir Hantu. The participant-observer approach was adopted as part of the researcher's overall methodology in understanding the dynamics of small-scale tourism development for their doctoral work. The aim of the initial fieldwork was to establish contact and gain the trust of the local community who were directly involved in the development and operation of small-scale tourism development in Perhentian Kecil. These visits provided valuable insights into the local response towards the advent of tourism on the island, which included the dynamics of their business operation, empowerment process and relationships with policy-makers and tourists.

During the mid-1990s, small-scale tourism development was confined to Pasir Panjang (Long Beach) on the east coast, and one author identified the forces that were shaping the entrepreneurial capacity of the local community, given their lack of education and capital. In addition, it was a timely opportunity to closely examine the dynamics of local community involvement in the early stage of tourism development in Perhentian Kecil. This coincided with the 'involvement stage' of Butler's TALC (1980), and the participant-observer approach adopted allowed an examination of the phenomenon from the perspective of the local population by gaining their trust through regular stays with the local community at Kampung Pasir Hantu.

From 2000 to 2005, both authors had separately visited Perhentian Kecil several times and had observed the gradual evolution in its physical development from basic A-frame huts to more comfortable chalets with better facilities. Informal interviews with key informants from the local communities revealed that investors from the mainland were either taking over some of the 'mini resorts' that used to be operated by the local people or were becoming business partners. In addition, small-scale tourism development had expanded to Coral Bay, on the opposite coast of Perhentian Kecil. The authors then got to know each other through their participation in international tourism conferences. Recognising that they were working on common subject matters within the same geographical area, the authors decided to embark on a joint longitudinal study to examine the economic, social and ecological dimensions of small-scale tourism development in Perhentian Kecil. Having established a good relationship with the local community at Kampung Pasir Hantu and the local operators at Pasir Panjang, it was decided to focus on the evolution of the small-scale tourism development on the island from the perspective of the local stakeholders.

The first field visit of the joint research was carried out in 2006 with the aim of establishing baseline data on the small-scale tourism development and operation both at Pasir Panjang (Long Beach) and Coral Bay. As noted earlier, the island at that time had been attracting investors from outside, which corresponded with the

TALC's 'development stage'. The methodology used was a blend of semi-structured interviews, site mapping, participant observation and formal questionnaires. The scope of the 2006 fieldwork mainly covered the operators' business profile, such as the nature of business, source of capital, human resource development, partnerships between local operators and outsiders, relationship with local authorities, future planning etc.

Due to financial constraints, field visits could not be carried out in 2007. After securing new funding, fieldwork was resumed in 2008 and two experienced local research assistants (RAs) were employed to help with logistics and to undertake some interviews and translate others. The RAs were qualified to Master's level in tourism and both had worked with the authors on previous projects. Prior to visiting the island, training was held to induct the RAs into the project, pilot the questionnaires and discuss the semi-structured interviews.

The 2008 fieldwork took a new dimension because the new state government had managed to 'introduce' a formal resort (Bubu Resort) that was supposed to pave the way for the transformation of Perhentian Kecil into a high-end resort destination (*The New Straits Times* 2006). Coupled with the development of a two-storey shopping arcade on Long Beach, these new developments were receiving negative response from the local community as well as tourists (especially through blogs). At this juncture, the authors were presented with the opportunity to examine whether strong exogenous factors would lead to a possible demise of the small-scale tourism development to make way for formal resorts ('decline stage' followed by 'revitalisation stage' according to Butler's TALC). Much to the surprise of the authors, the 2009 field visit revealed that the anticipated demise of the informal sector, though buy-outs did not occur. Instead, the small-scale operators showed great resilience and flexibility to adapt to the new development scenario that was taking place on the island without losing their market share.

At this stage, the authors decided to revisit the appropriateness and limitations of evolutionary models as well as seek alternative theories to explain the new phenomenon that was shaping up in Perhentian Kecil, created by the tensions between powerful exogenous forces and the resilience of the local tourism systems. Based on the literature, the authors were attracted to the potential application of Resilience Theory, having noted how it was successfully used by Nguru (2010) in the case of Kampung Cherating Lama, which had gone through a similar development path as Perhentian Kecil. Having started the longitudinal research with the aim of plotting the spatial temporal evolution of small-scale tourism development in Perhentian Kecil in a linear progression (as in Butler's TALC), the authors later realised that the complexities of the phenomenon implied that the original research questions had to be revisited and readjusted.

Resilience Theory presented the authors a tool to comprehensively examine the counter-reactions towards the exogenous factors that occurred from 2004 onwards. There were two exogenous factors, namely the state government's directive to remove budget accommodation and the relaxation of affirmative policies to protect *Bumiputra* (Malay) entrepreneurship. In addition, there was an endogenous factor in the form of negative media reports on the deteriorating state of the coral reefs around Malaysia's islands (*The Star Online* 2010). Although Perhentian Kecil performed better than the other islands in terms of coral condition, the poor sewage treatment system employed by the small-scale operators was identified as one of the main contributors towards water pollution and possible coral depletion (Reef Check Malaysia 2008). These exogenous factors, in tandem with the endogenous factor, could be interpreted as being 'destabilising events' with the potential of upsetting the equilibrium (and the fundamental sustainability) of the tourism systems in Perhentian Kecil.

To reflect the changing conceptual framework of this longitudinal study, the research questions had also been reviewed and realigned from those that were initially concerned with understanding the dynamics of small-scale tourism development/operation within an enclavic type of development to those that investigated their evolving role within an inter-connected tourist system shared with other key stakeholders, such as government agencies, formal resorts, tourism marketers, new investors and environmental NGOs (see Table 1).

Throughout the longitudinal study, the qualitative method was used in the form of participant observation and semi-structured interviews, with key respondents selected from chalet/resort operators, restaurant and shop owners, dive schools, transport operators, environmental NGOs, tourists and local government officials. In addition, respondents were asked to recommend who else might be interviewed on the island using the 'snowballing' technique to gain further entry to a given population of potential respondents.

Tourism Development in Perhentian Kecil

Within the emerging South-East Asia backpacker trail, the Perhentian islands are one of the 'honeypot' sites in northern peninsular Malaysia, along with Penang and the Cameron Highlands. Typically, backpackers enter Malaysia from southern Thailand (or travel north from Singapore) and then journey in a circuit between Penang via the Cameron Highlands and then to the east coast specifically to visit the Perhentian islands. Backpackers often stay on islands or at other beach resorts as mini 'holidays', as a break from harder travelling within their larger trips around the region (Hampton 1998). Backpacker enclaves have been discussed elsewhere (Lloyd 2003; Brenner & Fricke 2007), and spatial flows of backpackers are beginning to be analysed (Rogerson 2007).

The Perhentian archipelago lies about 20 km off the coast of peninsular Malaysia in Terengganu state. The island group consists of two main islands, Perhentian Besar (Big Island) and Perhentian Kecil (Small Island), plus some small uninhabited islets. The Perhentian islands are located in a marine park and visitors pay a small entrance

Table 1. Evolution of conceptual framework during longitudinal study

Year	Physical development	Research questions	Model used in conceptual framework
1995–2005	Organic growth of small-scale tourism development at 'drifter enclaves'	• How did the local community respond to the advent of tourism? • What was the role of related government agencies to nurture *Bumiputra* entrepreneurs? • How did the local operators develop their business skills and business knowledge to cater for changing tourist demand?	Evolutionary models (Butler 1980; Oppermann 1993) to explain 'involvement' stage
2006	Outsiders taking over 'mini resorts' but maintaining physical form/setting up business partnerships with locals	• What percentage of tourism development was in the control of the local community? • Without access to capital, was establishing partnerships with outsiders the only option? Who were the outsiders in terms of their relationship with the local community?	• Evolutionary models (TALC) to describe 'development stage'
2008	Introduction of formal resort (Bubu Resort) and construction of two-storey shopping arcade at Long Beach	• How did the local operators initially respond to the introduction of formal resorts and tourism facilities? • Were the local operators ready to compete against the new operators with sophisticated business models?	TALC in combination with basic principles of Resilience Theory (McKercher 1999; Farrell & Twining-Ward 2004, 2005)

(Continued on next page)

Table 1. Evolution of conceptual framework during longitudinal study (*Continued*)

Year	Physical development	Research questions	Model used in conceptual framework
2009	Development of two new resorts along Coral Bay (Senja and Shari-La)	• Did the introduction of the pioneer formal resort resulted in a comprehensive takeover of the small-scale tourism operators? • Did the small-scale tourism operators upgrade their facilities and services to compete against the formal resort? • What role did 'local champions' and community organisations play in protecting the local operators' market share?	Adaptation of Resilience Theory in tourism destination management (Cochrane 2010; Nguru 2010)
2010	Upscaling of business operation by small-scale operators and commitment to physical upgrading	• Did the local operators embrace modern technology to enhance their business operation and marketing? • What were the roles of local knowledge and kinship in harnessing the resilience of the local operators? • Was there a desire from the local stakeholders to work together to enhance the economic competitiveness and ecological sustainability of Perhentian Kecil?	Model development based on Resilience Theory (McKercher 1999; Farrell & Twining-Ward 2004, 2005) (Cochrane 2010; Nguru 2010)

fee of RM5 (approximately US $1.50). There is one main *kampung* (village), Kampung Pasir Hantu, on Perhentian Kecil with a resident population of around 1500 (Figure 1). By virtue of its inclusion in the *Lonely Planet* guidebooks, Perhentian Kecil is well known to international tourists, especially backpackers. It is the most visited backpacker destination in Malaysia and has the highest per capita expenditure, which can be mainly attributed to their expenditure on scuba diving (MOTOUR 2007). Ironically, few tourists are aware of the geographical location of Perhentian Kecil within Terengganu state, much to the chagrin of the state government. In 2010, 287,149 international tourists visited Terengganu, of whom 90% purposely went to the Perhentians and Redang Island without visiting any other attractions in the state (MOTOUR Terengganu 2011).

The two main Perhentian islands appear to have experienced quite different forms of tourism development. Perhentian Besar now has more upmarket resorts with both international and domestic tourism accommodation, whereas Perhentian Kecil has mainly backpacker tourists/small-scale tourism accommodation and presently only three mid-range resorts. Perhentian Kecil has two main beaches: Pasir Panjang or Long Beach (east coast) and Coral Bay (west coast). Different forms of accommodation, restaurants, dive operators and other tourist infrastructure exist on both beaches, but interestingly, differences between the two beaches are now beginning to appear. Long Beach is larger, has more facilities and many bars, and attracts younger tourists, being seen as the 'party beach'. Coral Bay is quieter and attracts slightly older tourists and more families. The tourist accommodation is generally small scale and low cost, consisting of simple wooden chalets or A-frame buildings, sometimes built on a concrete base. Local materials are used both for construction and for fitting-out. The budget prices are typically $10–25 per night. Coral Bay had one larger resort, although it is still a mid-market type of accommodation, but in 2008, another mid-market place opened with 100 rooms, mainly targeting domestic groups. Not surprisingly, given the basic facilities, backpackers and independent travellers are the main market segments (Hamzah 1995). At present, there are no booking systems for most island accommodation, so they rely entirely on 'walk-in' trade. Consequently, during peak season, tourists arriving later in the day may find that all the accommodations have been filled by arrivals from earlier boats, and commonly they either have to sleep the first night on the beach or return to the mainland (Hamzah 2007). However, the newer resorts use online bookings or have agents on the mainland.

There is a lack of official data on tourist arrivals, but Kaur (2007) provided an interesting comparison between the number of accommodation units on Perhentian Kecil and those in other destinations in Terengganu, revealing that for a small area of 15 km², there were 47 chalets on Perhentian Kecil offering 1140 beds. In comparison with other popular tourism destinations in Terengganu, only the capital city of Kuala Terengganu surpassed this, having 41 hotels/chalets offering 1747 beds, but covering a much bigger area of 605 km². In high season, the accommodation units at Perhentian

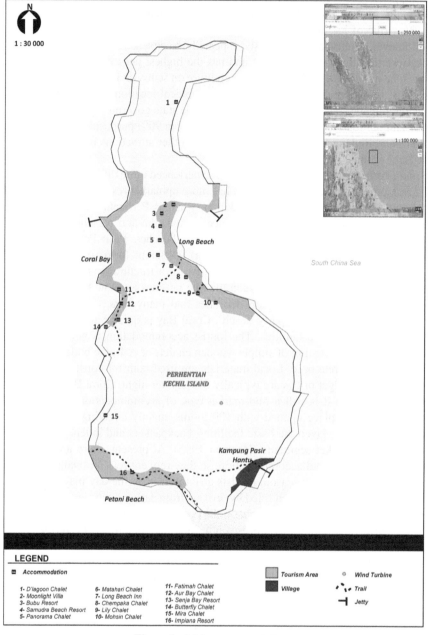

Figure 1. Main accommodation.

Kecil have a 100% occupancy rate. This raises a major question on the carrying capacity of the island. Carrying capacity threshold limits for Perhentian Kecil had been recommended by a study on coastal and island development commissioned by the Terengganu state government but they were not enforced (Sea Resources Management 2006). As noted above, the facilities are limited and somewhat basic. Rooms tend to have an attached toilet and simple shower. Some have air-conditioning, but most rooms just have a fan. There is some electricity, and chalet operators have their own generators, which run for limited hours during the evening. The more recent mid-range resorts offer better facilities and higher levels of comfort and service quality (Table 2).

The tourist infrastructure is basic, consisting of simple cafes and bars, limited – and relatively expensive – Internet facilities and some small shops. The island does not have any bank or automatic telling machine and has limited credit card facilities. The main tourist activities are scuba diving and snorkelling on the coral reefs and boat trips. The Bubu Resort offers parasailing, banana boat rides, kayaking and water skiing (Table 3).

Table 2. List of tourist accommodations on Perhentian Kecil

No	Accommodation	Number of units	No. of beds[a]	Location
1.	Rock Garden	32	64	Long Beach
2.	Bubu Long Beach Resort	39	78	Long Beach
3.	Chempaka Chalets	20	40	Long Beach
4.	Lemon Grass	20	40	Long Beach
5.	Simfony Chalets	28	56	Long Beach
6.	Matahari Chalets	30	60	Long Beach
7.	Moonlight Beach	28	56	Long Beach
8.	Panorama Chalets	31	62	Long Beach
9.	Lily Chalets	13	26	Long Beach
10	Mohsin Chalets	64	128	Long Beach
11	D'lagoon	64	128	Long Beach
12	Rajawali Coral	64	128	Coral Bay
13	Fatimah Chalet	11	22	Coral Bay
14	Aur Bay	10	20	Coral Bay
15	Butterfly Chalet	10	20	Coral Bay
16	Maya Beach Resort	12	24	Coral Bay
17	Senja Bay Resort	50	100	Coral Bay
18	Mira Chalet	8	16	Coral Bay
19	Shari-La Island Resort	71	142	Coral Bay
20	Petani Beach	5	10	Petani Beach
21	Impiani Resort	23	46	Petani Beach
	Totals:	562	1, 124	

[a]Estimated average two beds/room in each accommodation.
Source: Fieldwork notes.

Table 3. Tourist facilities on Perhentian Kecil

No.	Facility	Numbers of units: Long Beach	Numbers of units: Coral Bay
1.	Restaurant	7	6
2.	Multi-purpose shop	5	2
3.	Scuba diving shop	7	2
4.	Souvenir shop	3	1
5.	Batik/painting shop	1	—
6.	Mini shop	1	2
7.	Massage	1	—
8.	Bookshop	2	1
9.	Water taxi service	7	2
10	Snorkelling rental shop	5	2

Source: MOTOUR/UTM 2007.

The islands are accessed by speedboats from Kuala Besut harbour. Perhentian Besar has several wooden jetties, whereas until as recently as 2008, Kecil did not and so relied on small water taxis to transfer tourists from the speedboats to the shore. Interviews with water taxi boatmen showed that a circuit had emerged where the boatmen also worked in the Southern Thai islands in the Perhentians' 'off' (monsoon) season between October and February. However, with the completion of the two large concrete jetties on either beach (funded by the Ministry of Tourism Malaysia), the water taxi business disappeared and their services became redundant. Some had been forced to leave the island to look for alternative work elsewhere, while others had diversified into taking snorkelling trips for tourists or intra-island ferry trips.

Most of the food and drink required by the tourists were imported from the mainland. The islands do have some potable water supply from wells, but tourists prefer to drink bottled water. There are minimal medical facilities, and the only clinic is located at the local village, Kampung Pasir Hantu, and staffed by a paramedic and a midwife. There are no tourist police, and the newly constructed police station complex only has two regular policemen on duty. The state government has recently started preliminary work on the construction of a centralised water supply system for the island, and for sewerage, most accommodation units have septic tanks, which are emptied into the sea during the monsoon period. Solid waste and general garbage are regularly collected and shipped to the mainland by barge; however, this has been criticised, given that the large garbage bags often fall into the sea while being transported to the mainland. One resort operator commented that 'the private contractor has never bothered to reprimand his men for allowing some of the bags to fall off the barge. We suspect it is being done intentionally'. Since 2007, two wind powered turbines provide electricity to the villagers in the *kampung*, and the tourist operators still rely on their own diesel generators for electricity.

Analysis and Findings

Spatial Temporal Evolution of Tourism Development in Perhentian Kecil

Based on the longitudinal study that started from the mid-1990s, the evolution of tourism development in Perhentian Kecil was synthesised and initially described using Butler's TALC (1980) as the conceptual framework. Essentially, Perhentian Kecil has undergone three distinct stages of development: Stage 1: early 1990s until the mid-1990s, Stage 2: mid-1990s to early 2000s (until around 2003), and Stage 3: from around 2004 to date.

Stage 1: Early 1990s till Mid-1990s

This stage was characterised by the local response to the demand from tourism. The form of development was broadly 'organic', small-scale and unplanned. Arguably, the close-knit fishing community at Kampung Pasir Hantu, with little knowledge of the tourism business, became small-scale tourism entrepreneurs almost overnight. Perhentian Kecil was a relatively late starter and benefited from the exodus of backpackers from Cherating once domestic tourists began to overwhelm the 'drifter enclave' there (Hamzah 1997). Due to the remote location of the island, there was no government intervention, and the new operators provided their own capital, thus ensuring complete local ownership and control. All the pioneer operators were from the local *kampung* (village) and were mostly related to each other. Due to the lack of capital, the initial development was mostly in the form of A-frame huts.

Although the *kampung* had a formal headman, the actual leadership was assumed by a colourful village elder, Pak 'A'. Despite not holding any official post, Pak 'A' was instrumental in setting up a boat cooperative at Kuala Besut harbour to transport tourists to Perhentian Kecil. He also represented the villagers in meetings organised by the District Office and provided strong moral support for the villagers who wanted to venture into the tourism business.

During this stage, the fieldwork revealed that it was common for the foreign tourists to go about topless and many were engaged in 'hedonistic' practices such as excessive drinking, which is common in much international tourism. Despite being located in a conservative Islamic state, the local operators had surprisingly developed a high tolerance level to such practices as they were becoming increasingly dependent on tourism as their main source of livelihood. According to a pioneer operator, 'we regard the topless bathing and drunkenness as occupational hazards as long as they are carried out at Long Beach' (Long Beach is separated from the *kampung* by a rocky cliff). Even in the early days, the local operators were fast learners in terms of understanding tourist demand, behaviour and expectations. At the same time, the operators were also very protective of the traditional values in the *kampung*, and as much as 'hedonistic' behaviour was tolerated at their 'work place' (Long Beach), participant observation showed that most of the locals were outraged whenever a foreign tourist(s) strayed into their *kampung* to take photographs. As their 'local champion' and moral guardian, Pak 'A' made sure that none of the beach boys who flocked to Long Beach were from the *kampung* and this form of 'territorial coexistence' survived throughout the 'involvement stage'.

In essence, the 'involvement stage' was a steep learning curve for the local community, during which they were observed to be continuously learning new skills, such as foreign languages, culinary skills and bookkeeping etc. Interestingly, their culinary skills were mostly learned from backpackers, especially the art of making banana pancakes, which are still considered as being the now-iconic food for many backpackers. More importantly, they were comfortable adjusting to a new system brought about by the advent of tourism, without sacrificing their traditional values.

Stage 2: Mid-1990s to Early 2000s

In this stage, outsiders started to form partnerships with the locals, but the semi-structured interviews revealed that these 'outsiders' were mainly *Bumiputras* residing in the nearby mainland towns/cities of Kuala Besut, Kota Bahru and Kuala Terengganu. They often had family ties with the islanders and maintained the small-scale and low-density development as well as employed locals as the workforce. Rooms and other facilities were improved but were still basic and low cost. Many of these new operators also supplied in-house restaurants/cafes and dive shops. One group of investors said: 'We do not need new development here such as the Berjaya resort type [a large scale resort group in Malaysia], no need for concrete jetties, tourists here want to relax and enjoy the natural beauty of the island and they could go to Kuala Lumpur if they want to see modern resorts and development'.

The lack of access to micro-credit facilities was one of the main reasons why locals sought partners from outside the island. Although Malaysia has both a Special Tourism Fund and a Tourism Infrastructure Fund created by the Ministry of Tourism, these were mainly exploited by mainland developers. According to an official from the commercial bank appointed to handle these funds, islanders 'do not know how to write business plans and do not have the collateral' (land is often owned by many family members). Without access to micro-credit, they turned to outsiders, with the local headman sometimes acting as the land broker.

This stage could be interpreted as the beginning of TALC's 'development stage', but the pace of development slowed from 1999 to 2004, which coincided with the period when the conservative Islamic political party, Parti Islam SeMalaysia (PAS), took control of the state government of Terengganu. In fact, there was a lull in Perhentian Kecil during this period, given that PAS was not supportive of tourism, and directives to hotels/resorts to provide separate swimming pools for male and female guests scared away investors. During this stage too, the local operators had become confident businesspeople in their own right and started to educate guests on the need for proper behaviour. This was surprisingly effective since topless bathing practically ceased almost overnight and 'full moon parties' had to go underground.

Stage 3: 2004 Until Present Day

In 2004, the Barisan Nasional (National Front) won back the control of the Terengganu state government and tourism was again regarded as a major economic driver. This period also marked the arrival of Bubu Resort, a formal and Malaysian Chinese-owned resort – the first of its kind in Perhentian Kecil. Bubu Resort also introduced a new 'business model' that differed significantly from the unpackaged stays of most backpackers. The new model is typically a package of three days, two nights full board, boat transfer plus snorkelling trip for RM 299 (US $93). Following the model of the Laguna and Berjaya Resorts on Redang Island, as favoured by the state government, 'this new business model for the islands will set a new benchmark for resort operators to follow, we do not want chalets that are charging RM30/night' ($9.30) (a state tourism official).

Unlike other backpacker areas such as Bali or coastal Mexico, until this period, the island had not experienced foreign ownership, including the so-called 'developer-tourists' (Brenner & Fricke 2007). Bubu Resort is fundamentally different, being more capital intensive. It consists of three-storey, permanent concrete buildings and has Chinese-Malaysian owners. In addition, the entire workforce was sourced from established hotels in Kuala Lumpur and 'translocated' to the island. It also caters for the mass package market of East Asian tourists (Chinese, Taiwanese and Hong Kong people). An interview with a Terengganu state tourism official (pers. comm., 2009) revealed his preference for the business model introduced by Bubu Resort, which he claimed 'should trigger a new trend in resort operations on Perhentian Kecil, which the local operators have no choice but to follow'. The new business model is said to be similar to that practiced in Redang Island, which has succeeded in attracting an influx of East Asian visitors (ECERDC 2010).

Once Bubu Resort opened for business, there were intense initial reactions from the local operators on the island. One operator lamented: 'What can we do, they have strong political connections, even though they are not *Bumiputras* [literally: 'son of the soil' that is Malay]' (Chalet owner A). Another said: 'Now it is a free-for-all!' (a landowner). A pioneer operator added 'too much development and concrete, [the] government should control it' (Chalet owner B).

From the findings of fieldwork between 2008 and 2009, it could be surmised that the arrival of Bubu Resort was initially regarded by the local operators as a threat to their survival. On the other hand, the policy-makers in the Terengganu state government welcomed Bubu Resort and its 'new' business model as the right catalyst to transform Perhentian Kecil into a high-yield tourism destination. These conflicting aspirations therefore created tensions which were about to upset the balance of power and tourist systems that had gradually evolved in Perhentian Kecil and had been mainly created by the local response to unsophisticated tourist demand.

Exogenous Factors and Their Destabilising Effects

Ever since the Barisan Nasional (National Front) won back control of Terengganu from the opposition PAS in 2004, the state government has been aggressively promoting the redevelopment of the formerly neglected Terengganu islands into a high-end resort destination. In this light, the state government has also been making strongly worded statements in the local media against backpacker tourism on Perhentian Kecil, such as: 'We want to get rid of backpackers from Perhentian Kecil as they destroy the coral reefs. Instead we encourage the development of high end resorts which generate greater economic impact to the local economy' (*The New Straits Times* 2006).

In essence, the advent of Bubu Resort plus two other formal resorts at Coral Bay could be interpreted as a 'destabilising event' that could trigger the 'relapse' stage according to Resilience Theory (Cochrane 2010). Once the rhetoric that greeted the arrival of Bubu Resort had simmered down, the local operators went through a denial stage. When asked whether she would upgrade her establishment and level of service to compete against Bubu Resort, a pioneer operator was adamant: 'Why should I change? My children are well provided for and my loyal customers keep coming back?' Repeating the same question to the pioneer operator a year after the interview, a change of heart was detected when she admitted that 'we would like to upgrade and increase the number of chalets using our own money, in fact I have already paid someone to come up with architectural drawings a few years ago but he just vanished' (Chalet owner C).

During the 2008 and 2009 field visits, the authors heard many tourist complaints regarding the archaic 'first-come-first-served' system still being used by the local operators. The common response was succinctly given by a local operator: 'I'm not in favour of telephone or online booking, it's a hassle and tourists can always book through the dive shops which offer the service'. A year later, she simply said: 'I'm interested in setting up an online booking system' (Chalet owner D).

In 2006, the local authority started building a new two-storey concrete shopping arcade on Long Beach to the anger of the chalet owners, who mounted a substantial local protest. In terms of the TALC, this shopping arcade development, combined with the new Bubu Resort and state government's overall policy for the island, could be seen as perhaps being the beginning of a 'consolidation' stage. However, the construction went on despite attracting an inspection by the then Chief Minister of Terengganu. The main complaint against the shopping arcade was that it would significantly block the view to the sea, given its location on the beach reserve. A long-established operator said: 'We were not consulted over the construction of the shopping arcade, it's not that we are against it but it should not be located along the beach where it would block the open view to the sea'. The shopping arcade opened in 2009, but has significantly changed the visual quality of Long Beach, given that the concrete building did not conform to the human scale of the surrounding mini resorts as well as blocked the surrounding chalets' view of the sea. Despite this, the field visit in 2010 revealed that the adult children of the pioneer operators have since set up internet cafes and tourist information kiosks within the shopping arcade and were handling the online booking for their parents' mini resorts. Suffice to say that while in terms of Resilience Theory, the exogenous factors did create a 'destabilising effect' on the tourist systems in Perhentian Kecil, the local tourism industry managed to quickly adjust their operation to accommodate the recent changes without using a confrontational approach.

To facilitate the development of Bubu Resort in Perhentian Kecil – given its Chinese-Malaysian owner – the Terengganu state government had to take the radical step of exploiting loopholes in the National Land Code (GOM 1965), which stipulates that only *Bumiputras* (Malays) are allowed to own and develop Malay reserve land. Most coastal areas and islands in Malaysia are located on Malay reserve land, including Perhentian Kecil. It should be highlighted that this kind of affirmative protection gave rise to the organic growth of small-scale tourist development within the fishing communities along the east coast of peninsular Malaysia.

Although the whole of Perhentian Kecil is gazetted as Malay reserve land, the law cannot stop non-Malays/*Bumiputras* from getting involved in development, provided that it is carried out in the form of a joint venture or partnership with a local landowner. More often than not, the island landowners are paid a nominal fee to act as sleeping partners, or what is locally known as the 'Ali Baba' syndrome. Although this practice is rife on uninhabited islands, such as Redang, Lang Tengah and Tenggol, it has yet (until Bubu Resort) to penetrate Perhentian Kecil due to the presence of a sizeable (and proud) local Malay community on the island. Despite this, interviews with the operators revealed that 65% of the resorts are currently operated in the form of partnerships with outsiders from the mainland (Table 4). However as mentioned earlier, many of these partners are related to the locals. Bubu Resort was supposed to be a 'guinea pig', with the blessing of the state government to test the reaction (and resolve) of the local operators (pers. comm., a state tourism official, 2008). At the height of the Bubu Resort controversy, the local champion, Pak 'A', suffered poor health and eventually passed away in 2009. His demise left a vacuum in terms of leadership and organisation because until today, there is no formal organisation representing the local operators: 'We don't need one – the other operators are our brothers, sisters and sons. We are family and that is stronger than any formal organisation' (Chalet owner C). Participant observation revealed that the community reaction to the arrival of Bubu Resort was that it brought them closer together and sibling rivalries were put aside. They agreed to accept and accommodate Bubu Resort but pledged that they would not be part of any collaboration with non-Malays that could result in the proliferation of such resorts in the future.

Table 4. Ownership status of mini resorts on Perhentian Kecil

No.	Accommodation	Ownership		
		Local	Besut local	Outsider
1.	Rock Garden		✓	
2.	Bubu Long Beach resort			✓
3.	Chempaka chalets	✓		
4.	Lemon grass	✓		
5.	Simfony chalets			✓
6.	Matahari chalets	✓		
7.	Moonlight beach			✓
8.	Panorama chalets	✓		
9.	Lily chalets			✓
10.	Mohsin chalets			✓
11.	D'lagoon			✓
12.	Rajawali coral			✓
13.	Fatimah chalet	✓		
14.	Aur Bay			✓
15.	Butterfly chalet	✓		
16.	Maya beach resort			✓
17.	Senja Bay Resort			✓
18.	Mira Chalet			✓
19.	Petani Beach			✓
20.	Impiani resort			✓

Source: Fieldwork notes (2007).

Deteriorating Condition of Coral Reefs and the Resulting Change in Attitude

Besides the exogenous factors described earlier, there was also an endogenous factor that could have had a 'destabilising effect' on Perhentian Kecil, which is the deteriorating condition of the coral reefs around the island. Immediately after capturing back Terengganu from the opposition party in 2004, the newly installed Chief Minister instructed that the Terengganu islands should encourage the development of high-end resorts that are certified by Green Globe or the like so that tourists will pay premium rates to enjoy a world-class tourism experience (pers. comm., UPEN Terengganu, 2005). This sentiment was echoed in one of the tourism policies contained in the Terengganu state Structure Plan, which recommended 'the sustainability certification of resorts on the Terengganu Islands so as to attract Green and discerning tourists' (JPBD 2005).

Against this backdrop, media reports and reef monitoring studies carried out by environmental NGOs such as Reef Check Malaysia showed that the quality of coral reefs around Malaysian islands was deteriorating. Coral bleaching was also happening at an alarming rate, to the extent that several dive and snorkelling sites had to be temporarily closed by the Department of Marine Parks (*The Star Online* 2010). Prior to this, the Terengganu state government had been making bold press statements that blamed the deteriorating quality of coral reefs around Perhentian Kecil due to the budget establishments: 'We want to get rid of backpackers from Perhentian Kecil as they destroy the coral reefs ... ' (*The New Straits Times* 2006). The reef monitoring report published by Reef Check Malaysia (2008) vindicated the small-scale operators by concluding that the status of the reefs around Perhentian Kecil was better than that of reefs around the other islands, such as Redang and Tioman (larger-scale developments). However, the report also recommended that the poorly treated sewage problem from the chalets, using septic tanks, had to be addressed. During the 2008–2009 field visits, it was observed that these environmental NGOs were starting to work with the local operators in coming up with strategies and action plans to minimise negative impacts on the coral reefs. At the same time, the foreign tourists going to Perhentian Kecil were becoming more discerning and concerned about environmental sustainability.

During the earlier part of the longitudinal study, the local operators did not feel that their basic sewage treatment was causing water pollution and there had been no attempt to upgrade the existing system, although the government was introducing a centralised treatment system for the village. The 2010 field visit added questions on the willingness of the local operators to adhere to sustainability certification. The majority (92%) said that they were willing to participate in any sustainability certification exercise but could only afford to pay RM 1000 ($313) per resort. The majority also felt that the government should take the lead and subsidise the bulk of the cost, and suggested that the enforcement should be in the form of self-regulation by their local organisation, despite the fact that they had yet to set up a formal association.

Discussions and Conclusions

This paper raises a fundamental question: Is the island now reaching a 'tipping point'? In other words, has Perhentian Kecil reached the moment that could be identified as being when the destination changes from small-scale backpacker tourism to a very different form of tourism development? In essence, the 'tipping point' would also imply the transfer of local ownership and control to outsiders, which could lead to the marginalisation of the local community and potentially negative impacts on the fragile island environment due to overdevelopment. In terms of Butler's (1980) evolutionary TALC model, the findings of the longitudinal study have shown that tourism development in Perhentian Kecil had moved into the 'development' stage, with some characteristics starting to appear from the 'consolidation' stage.

The question can also be raised whether the path along Butler's S-shaped curve is inevitable or are local operators, as the weaker stakeholders – or 'prey' according to Cochrane (2010) – resilient enough to accommodate the changes to the tourist systems brought about by government policy and the arrival of 'predators' such as Bubu Resort?

The organic growth of small-scale tourism development on Perhentian Kecil mirrors the conceptualisation by Oppermann (1993), who identified the primary role of the informal tourism sector in establishing 'drifter' enclaves along the coastal areas of LDCs. Oppermann (1993) also argued that as such enclaves move along the TALC (Butler 1980), they are neither overwhelmed nor displaced by the formal sector but continue to exist alongside the latter. This parallel yet separate existence was originally postulated by Cohen (1982), but Oppermann (1993) suggested that as a competitive, attractive and strategically located enclave evolves into a major destination or hub with heavy investment from the formal sector, the informal sector also moves out of its enclavic nature to become part of mainstream tourism, albeit without losing its distinct informal features. This evolution process appears to be similar to the early stages of many other backpacker destinations in the region, such as Gili Trawangan in Lombok, Indonesia, in the early 1990s (Hampton 1998) or the Southern Thai islands in the early 1980s (Cohen 1982).

The earlier part of the longitudinal study presented the authors with the opportunity to closely examine the dynamics of small-scale tourism development as it gradually moved from Butler's 'involvement stage' to the 'development stage'. One interesting finding concerned the 'learning-by-doing' process (Folke *et al.* 2005), which the local operators went through to compensate for their lack of formal education and training. Ahmad (2005) discovered that the same process was adopted by most fishing communities along the coastal areas of Malaysia, and that the practical knowledge accumulated through this process was shared between the chalet operators within the community.

The arrival of Bubu Resort appeared to bring significant change to the existing tourism system in Perhentian Kecil. Previously, the island seemed to have a fairly uncomplicated tourism system where local family members met the young backpackers' basic needs and this demand was manifested in the form of small-scale, low density development that also had minimal environmental impacts. However, the arrival of Bubu Resort had initially threatened to upset this equilibrium. For the paper's authors, the research problem and questions became more complex at this stage. This then called for the linear narrative based on Butler's TALC (1980) to be revisited. Despite its limited application in tourism studies, Resilience Theory would be able to complement TALC to better understand the complexities of the scenario brought about by the advent of Bubu Resort, and more so, the forces behind it. At this stage, Perhentian Kecil exhibited outward signals of tourism systems that were trapped in transition, in the form of antagonistic reactions from the local community and foreign tourists, as well as 'trial by media' arguably mainly driven by the state government.

Explicitly, both the federal and the state government were trying to scale up coastal and island tourism development along the value chain, as exemplified by the high-value/high-yield tourism rhetoric in various tourism plans and policies that included Perhentian Kecil (e.g., see JPBD 2004; Sea Resources Management 2006;

ECERDC 2007; JPBD 2008; PEMANDU 2010). As a consequence, affirmative policies to protect *Bumiputra* ownership and control, as embedded in the country's New Economic Policy, are being compromised to make coastal and island tourism more competitive and lucrative. In the same light, protectionist measures created by the local planning authority are under pressure of being removed, and to be replaced by a forced commitment to sustainability certification with the view that eco-labelling will increase the island's competitive edge (ECERDC 2007).

It remains to be seen whether the small-scale, locally owned accommodation at Perhentian Kecil will withstand government intervention and new market forces to maintain their identity and market share. Interestingly, since the arrival of Bubu Resort in 2004, the anticipated wave of takeovers, similar to what had happened in neighbouring Redang Island once a large-scale resort (Berjaya Resort) was introduced, has yet to materialise at Perhentian Kecil. It should be pointed out that Redang Island was uninhabited before the advent of tourism, whereas Perhentian Kecil had a sizeable and resilient community.

The situation in Perhentian Kecil resembles the development path that Kampung Cherating Lama experienced, when the arrival of two formal resorts in the late 1980s (Butler's 'development stage') signalled an inevitable transformation of Malaysia's pioneer 'drifter enclave' into a formal resort destination. In applying Resilience Theory to the case of Kampung Cherating Lama, Nguru (2010) discovered that the local operators' ability to adapt to changing market demand and 'kinship support' rather than government intervention were instrumental to their survival once their main market segment, which were the backpackers, left *en masse* for Marang and, subsequently, Perhentian Kecil.

The study findings also support the contention by Dahles (2000) that small-scale tourism operations are more flexible and respond better and swiftly to changes in the marketplace. By using Resilience Theory to describe the impact created by Bubu Resort, it could be said the 'old tourism systems' that had been in place since the advent of tourism had been destroyed. In retrospect, the 'old tourism systems' were already showing signs of becoming irrelevant to current tourist demand, such as the archaic 'first-come-first-served' system and the conviction that small-scale tourism development does not contribute towards environmental degradation. Bubu Resort set a higher standard of service and a business operation that optimises the use of information technology. After an initial reluctance, the local operators too embraced modern technology by getting their adult children to set up Internet cafes and handle online bookings, thus fulfilling the changing expectations of modern-day backpackers (Hampton 2010). Their commitment to responsible tourism principles is now evident in their willingness for their establishments to obtain sustainability certification.

Instead of being taken over and marginalised by large, corporate resorts, the local operators are making a significant contribution towards the creation of a new tourist system in Perhentian Kecil. Community leadership that used to be provided by a 'local champion' has now been assumed by an informal community organisation with the desire to represent and move up the small-scale establishments along the value chain. It is anticipated that a formal tourism association may soon be established, with Bubu Resort as a member.

With better organisation and a sustainable business model, the relationship with government agencies should also improve, which should pave the way for strong multi-stakeholder partnerships to be formed. In turn, this will also enhance access to MOTOUR's Special Tourism Fund as a way of incentivising local operators to move up the value chain. To surmise, the tourist systems in Perhentian Kecil are in the process of being reinvented, having recovered from the shock created by the forces behind Bubu Resort, which should lead to a more sustainable development path.

Perhentian Kecil has many lessons for other LDCs that have embraced island tourism as a catalyst for development. The evolution and life cycle of similar enclavic tourism developments have been deconstructed in the past mainly using spatial temporal models, of which Butler's TALC (1980) had provided a practical framework. While writers such as Choy (1992), Getz (1992) and Agarwal (1997) have criticised the application of Butler's TALC, proponents of Resilience Theory (McKercher 1999; Farrell & Twinning-Ward 2005; Lepp 2008) concur that even though the TALC is considered too linear to analyse the complexity of tourism destinations, its six stages provides a symbiotic interface with the four phases or loops that are considered to be more effective and realistic in analysing this complexity.

By incorporating Resilience Theory towards the end of the longitudinal study, another dimension could be added to the research by capturing not only the physical evolution but also the social construction of the tourist space in Perhentian Kecil (Phillimore & Goodson 2004). There had been the risk that by applying TALC throughout the longitudinal study, the research might have become stuck in a 'comfort zone' without questioning the appropriateness of using a positivist line of enquiry throughout. A mechanistic attempt to equate the evolution of tourism development with the various stages of Butler's TALC would have been a futile exercise once the dynamics of small-scale tourism development on the island had been comprehensively investigated, although approaches are still common (see Graci & Dodds 2010). In the final analysis, the longitudinal study not only produced a new perspective of the evolution of small-scale tourism development but also became a form of rite of passage for the authors as researchers.

Acknowledgements

The research on which this paper reports is associated with two projects, one funded by the Ministry of Tourism, Malaysia, and the other by the British Council (PMI2 Project funded by the UK Department of Business, Innovation and Skills [BIS]) for the benefit of the Malaysian Higher Education Sector and the UK Higher Education Sector. The authors are grateful for the Ministry's assistance, particularly Dr Junaida Lee Abdullah, but the views expressed here are not necessarily those of the Ministry,

BIS or British Council. We would also like to thank Che Wan, JD, Joern, Lngesh and Shima for their assistance with fieldwork, as well as the interview respondents who generously gave their time. The usual disclaimers apply.

References

Agarwal, S. (1997) The resort cycle and seaside tourism: An assessment of its applicability and validity, *Tourism Management*, 18(2), pp. 65–73.

Ahmad, G. (2005) Small firms network in tourism and hospitality: Chalet firms and its owner-managers network, unpublished doctoral dissertation, University of Strathclyde, Glasgow, 2005.

Archer, B. (1977) *Tourism, Multipliers: The State of the Art* (Cardiff: University of Wales Press).

Bardolet, E. (2001) The path towards sustainability in the Balearic Islands. in: D. Ioannides, Y. Apostolopoulos, & S. Sonmez (Eds) *Mediterranean Islands and Sustainable Tourism Development*, pp.193–213 (London: Continuum).

Brenner, L. & Fricke, J. (2007) The evolution of backpacker destinations: The case of Zipolite, Mexico, *International Journal of Tourism Research*, 9(3), pp. 217–230.

Briguglio, L., Butler, R., Harrison, D., & Filho, W. (Eds) (1996) *Sustainable Tourism in Islands and Small States: Case Studies* (London: Pinter).

Butler, R. (1980) The concept of a tourist area cycle of evolution: Implications for management of resources, *Canadian Geographer*, 24, pp. 5–12.

Calgaro, E. & Cochrane, J. (2009) *Comparative Destination Vulnerability Assessment for Thailand and Sri Lanka* (Stockholm: Stockholm Environment Institute).

Choy, D. (1992) Life cycle models for Pacific island destinations, *Journal of Travel Research*, 3, pp. 26–31.

Cochrane, J. (2010) The sphere of tourism resilience, *Tourism Recreation Research*, 35(2), pp. 173–185.

Cohen, E. (1982) Marginal paradises: Bungalow tourism on the islands of Southern Thailand, *Annals of Tourism Research*, 9, pp. 189–228.

Dahles, H. (2000) Tourism, small enterprises and community development. in: G. Richards & D. Hall (Eds) *Tourism and Sustainable Community Development*, pp. 154–169 (London: Routledge).

de Albuquerque, K. & McElroy, J. (1992) Caribbean small island tourism styles and sustainable strategies, *Environmental Management*, 16, pp. 619–632.

Dodds, R. & McElroy, J. (2008) St Kitts at a crossroads, *ARA Journal of Travel Research*, 1(2), pp. 1–10.

ECERDC (East Coast Economic Region Development Council) (2007) *East Coast Economic Region (ECER) Master Plan* (Kuala Lumpur: ECERDC).

ECERDC (East Coast Economic Region Development Council) (2010) *Development Plan for Kampung Penarik Mainland Coastal Tourism Development and Setiu Wetlands State Park, Merang Setiu Terengganu* (Kuala Lumpur: ECERDC).

Fallon, F. (2001) Conflict, power and tourism on Lombok, *Current Issues in Tourism*, 4(6), pp. 481–502.

Farrell, B. H. & Twining-Ward, L. (2004) Reconceptualising tourism, *Annals of Tourism Research*, 31(2), pp. 274–295.

Farrell, B. H. & Twining-Ward, L. (2005) Seven steps towards sustainability: Tourism in the context of new knowledge, *Journal of Sustainable Tourism*, 31(2), pp. 109–122.

Folke, C., Hahn, T., Olsson, P. & Norberg, J. (2005) Adaptive governance of social-ecological systems, *Annual Review of Environment and Resources*, 30, pp. 441–473.

Getz, D. (1992) Tourism planning and destination life cycle, *Annals of Tourism Research*, 19, pp. 752–770.

GOM (Government of Malaysia) (1965) *National Land Code (Act 56)* (Kuala Lumpur: Government of Malaysia).

Gössling, S. (2001) Tourism, economic transition and ecosystem degradation, *Tourism Geographies*, 3, pp. 430–453.

Graci, S. & Dodds, R. (2010) (Eds) *Sustainable Tourism in Island Destinations* (London: Earthscan).

Hampton, J. M. & Hampton, M. P. (2009) Is the beach party over? Tourism and the environment in small islands: A case study of Gili Trawangan, Lombok, Indonesia. in: M. Hitchcock, V. T. King & M. Parnwell (Eds) *Tourism in South East Asia Revisited*, pp. 206–308 (Copenhagen: NIAS Press).

Hampton, M. P. (1998) Backpacker tourism and economic development, *Annals of Tourism Research*, 25(3), pp. 639–660.

Hampton, M. P. (2010) Not such a rough or lonely planet? Backpacker tourism: An academic journey. in: K. Hannam & A. Diekmann (Eds) *Beyond Backpacker Tourism: Mobilities and experiences*, pp. 8–20 (Clevedon: Channel View Publications).

Hamzah, A. (1995) The changing tourist motivation and its implications on the sustainability of small-scale tourism development in Malaysia. Paper presented at the World Conference on Sustainable Tourism, Lanzarote, Spain, April 24–29.

Hamzah, A. (1997) The evolution of small-scale tourism in Malaysia: Problems, opportunities, and implications for sustainability. in: M. J. Stabler (Ed) *Tourism and Sustainability: Principles and Practice*, pp. 199–217 (Wallingford: CAB International).

Hamzah, A. (2007) ICT for tourism SMEs: A partnership building approach. Paper presented at the UNCTAD Asia-Pacific e-Tourism Conference, Kota Kinabalu, Malaysia, March 13–14.

Hills, T. & Lundgren, J. (1977) The impact of tourism in the Caribbean: A methodological study, *Annals of Tourism Research*, 4, pp. 248–267.

Holling, C. S. (1973) Resilience and stability of ecological systems, *Annual Review of Ecology and Systematic*, 4, pp. 1–23.

Holling, C. S. (2001) Understanding the complexity of economic, ecological and social systems, *Ecosystems*, 4, pp. 390–405.

JPBD (Jabatan Perancangan Bandar dan Desa Semenanjung Malaysia) (2004) *Rancangan Tempatan Daerah Kuantan 2004–2015* (Kuala Lumpur: JPBD).

JPBD (Jabatan Perancangan Bandar dan Desa Semenanjung Malaysia) (2005) *Rancangan Struktur Negeri Terengganu 2005–2015* (Kuala Lumpur: JPBD).

JPBD (Jabatan Perancangan Bandar dan Desa Semenanjung Malaysia) (2008) *Rancangan Tempatan Daerah Besut 2008–2020* (Kuala Lumpur: JPBD).

Kaur, C. R. (2007) Ecotourism in Malaysia's marine parks: Principles, issues and the effects of 'green washing' practices. Paper presented at the 5th Asia Pacific Ecotourism Conference (APECO) – Marine Ecotourism: Emerging Best Sustainable Practices and Success Stories, Merang, Malaysia, October 27–28.

Klak, T. & Flynn, R. (2008) Sustainable development and ecotourism: An Eastern Caribbean case study. in: E. L. Jackiewicz & F. J. Bosco (Eds) *Placing Latin America: Contemporary Themes in Human Geography*, pp. 115–136 (Lanham, MD: Rowman & Littlefield).

Lepp, A. (2008) Attitudes towards initial tourism development in a community with no prior tourism experience: The case of Bigodi, Uganda, *Journal of Sustainable Tourism*, 16(1), pp. 5–22.

Lloyd, K. (2003) Contesting control in transitional Vietnam: The development and regulation of traveller cafes in Hanoi and Ho Chi Minh City, *Tourism Geographies*, 5(3), pp. 350–366.

Mckercher, B. (1999) A chaos approach to tourism, *Tourism Management*, 20(4), pp. 425–434.

Ministry of Tourism (MOTOUR) (2007) *About Malaysia*. Available at http://www.virtualmalaysia.com/visit_malaysia/index.cfm?sec=1 (accessed 16 August 2010).

Ministry of Tourism (MOTOUR) & Universiti Teknologi Malaysia (UTM) (2007) *Study on the Contribution and Potential of Backpacker Tourism in Malaysia* (Kuala Lumpur: MOTOUR Kuala Lumpur).

MOTOUR Terengganu (Ministry of Tourism Malaysia Terengganu Office) (2011) *Terengganu Tourism Statistics 2010* (Kuala Terengganu: MOTOUR Terengganu).

Nguru, A. I. (2010) Resilience in tourism business: A case study of Cherating Lama Village, Pahang, unpublished Master's Tourism Planning thesis, Universiti Teknologi Malaysia, Skudai.

Oppermann, M. (1993) Tourism space in developing countries, *Annals of Tourism Research*, 20(3), pp. 535–556.

PEMANDU (Performance Management and Delivery Unit) (2010) *Economic Transformation Programme (ETP): A Roadmap for Malaysia* (Kuala Lumpur: Prime Minister's Department).

Phillimore, J. & Goodson, L. (2004) (Eds) *Qualitative Research In Tourism: Ontologies, Epistemologies and Methodologies* (London: Routledge).

Reef Check Malaysia (2008) *Coral Reef Monitoring Report* (Malaysia: Reef Check Malaysia Bhd.).

Rogerson, C. (2007) Backpacker tourism in South Africa: Challenges and strategic opportunities, *South African Geographical Journal*, 89(2), pp. 161–171.

Royle, S. (2001) *A Geography of Islands: Small Island Insularity* (London: Routledge).

Schianetz, K. & Kavanagh, L. (2008) Sustainability indicators for tourism destinations: A complex adaptive systems approach using systemic indicator systems, *Journal of Sustainable Tourism*, 16(6), pp. 601–628.

Sea Resources Management (2006) *Terengganu Coastal and Islands Study* (Petalaying Jaya: Sea Resources Management).

Spreitzhofer, G. (1998) Backpacking tourism in South-East Asia, *Annals of Tourism Research*, 20(4), pp. 979–983.

The New Straits Times (2006, October 2) Perhentian shifting focus to high end tourists, p. 25.

The Star Online (2010, April 10) *Tourism Ministry Give the Thumbs Up on High End Redang*. Available at http://thestar.com.my/news/story.asp?sec=nation&file=/2010/4/10/nation/6028886 (accessed 10 April 2010).

Timms, B. & Conway, D. (2011) Slow tourism at the Caribbean's geographical margins, *Tourism Geographies*. doi: 10.1080/14616688.2011.610112.

Wall, G. (1996) One name: Two destinations: Planned and unplanned coastal resorts in Indonesia. in: L. Harrison & W. Husbands (Eds) *Issues in Tourism: Case studies in Planning, Development and Marketing*, pp. 41–57 (Chichester: Wiley).

Weaver, D. (1990) Grand Cayman Island and the resort cycle model, *Journal of Travel Research*, 2, pp. 4–15.

Wilkinson, P. (1989) Strategies for tourism in island microstates, *Annals of Tourism Research*, 16, pp. 153–177.

Conclusion

Richard Butler, Michelle McLeod, and Rachel Dodds

The special issue of *Tourism Geographies*, Vol. 23, Iss. 3, on which this volume is primarily based, had three main themes, tourism life cycles, system decline and resilience. Interwoven with these is, perhaps inevitably, the concept of sustainability. Ideally, a sustainable (in the broadest sense of the term) tourism life cycle diminishes, if not removes the issue of system decline, and encourages the development of resilience. This latter concept involves adapting to and recovering from generally unanticipated shocks to the system, whether this be solely the tourism system or the complete environment of any island (Berbés-Blázquez & Scott, 2017). The initial call for papers, which comprise this volume was made in 2017. While in normal circumstances, a period of a few years might produce some change in the patterns of tourism and its associated development, instead, the impacts resulting therefrom the period from 2017 to the present saw massive and dramatic changes in tourism and other phenomena because of the COVID-19 pandemic and the subsequent no or reduced tourism activities. While for some islands, such as Boracay, Phi Phi, and of course, Venice, one of the issues which had emerged in the pre-COVID era was the problem of overtourism (Dodds & Butler, 2019; Mihalic, 2020; Milano, Cheer, & Novelli, 2019). This problem, however, disappeared totally as a result of the shut-down of tourism which began in 2019. King-Chan, Capistrano, and Lopez (2021) drew attention, in their chapter of this volume, to the potential environmental impacts from increasing numbers of tourists. Several of the chapters noted issues such as cultural change emerging as a result of tourism pressures, but these were more indicators of problems which might increase in severity in their respective areas if tourist numbers continued to increase. As has been seen, however, for the first time in global history, tourism worldwide came to a virtual complete halt because of the COVID pandemic and the associated restrictions or prohibitions on travel (Gössling, Scott, & Hall, 2020). For island destinations, tourism is impossible without air and sea travel as a bridge (Vanderpool-Wallace, 2018).

One could have argued that islands might have been spared the worst impacts of the pandemic by virtue of their very existence as islands, lands physically separated, for the most part, from mainlands and large populations. As we noted in the Introduction 'The distinction of being an island has been an attractive context for tourism researchers, with the context being viewed as a laboratory. Hall (2010) argues that islands are "natural laboratories" for the observation and study of tourism because of its bounded nature. With the possibility of a bounded island research area under study, the advent of tourism on an island takes a particular path' (McLeod, Dodds, & Butler, 2021, p. 362). It is too soon to conclude whether islands were more fortunate than their mainland competitors in tourism with respect to tourism in the COVID-19 era and after the pandemic, but some comments in this respect can be made.

Some islands and island nations were initially successful in utilising their islandness to self-impose a blockade on visitors as the pandemic and its effects began to be realised, and in this regard, remoteness of these islands helped. New Zealand, for example, closed its borders to all visitors, both tourists and absent citizens, early in 2020, and apart from a short period in 2021 when a 'bubble' was created allowing travel between New Zealand and Australia, the closure has been maintained until the end of 2021 at least. While for a long time this policy was successful in keeping those islands clear of COVID-19, eventually some cases were recorded and as vaccines had not been acquired and mass inoculation had not taken place during the period free from infection, lockdowns were imposed and travel restrictions maintained. This meant that international tourism to New Zealand has ceased almost entirely for two years at the time of writing (late 2021) and the domestic tourism industry also was locked down since the first outbreak. The tourism and hospitality industries there have suffered greatly as the relatively small domestic population is insufficient to keep the industry healthy, a common island condition has been discussed in general in several chapters. Other South Pacific islands such as Fiji failed to ensure a complete blockade, and have suffered greatly as a result, with the limited medical services on those islands becoming overtaxed and near collapse, and with next to no indigenous tourism to counter the loss of the international market. Allowing limited tourist access to selected minority affluent populations in Fiji's case produced the worst of both worlds, inadequate custom for the industry and a severe outbreak of the pandemic. In the Bahamas, with no precedence or clear tourism policies, a complete shutdown of tourism activities came with challenges of reopening and management of the ongoing pandemic (McLeod, 2021). Other islands, such as the Hawaiian Islands, did allow visitors but were not equipped to deal with the outbreaks and did not adequately consider their local residents in this decision making (Crist, 2021; McDonagh, 2021). Whatever, the circumstance, it is clear that islands have not fared as well as hoped.

What effect COVID-19 will have on island tourism in general, and specific islands, is hard to tell at this time. Much of the research that has been published on the impacts of COVID-19 is speculative for obvious reasons, as there is no parallel for comparison. The Spanish flu, the closest global comparison, was both more fatal and quicker acting than COVID-19 but was much more contained in its spread because of the limited transport and tourism industries at the beginning of the twentieth century (the main Spanish flu outbreak was 1918–19). COVID-19 has effectively closed both international and domestic tourism in most countries (UNWTO, 2020), while most crises in the recent past have affected international tourism primarily or solely. From the point of view of islands, as noted above, domestic tourism is rarely of great significance compared to the international component, and most island tourism facilities are geared to overseas visitors and their preferences, tastes and incomes. Apart from the massive loss of income and employment during the pandemic, there is also the unknown future effect of what a break in tourism and tourism-related development will have on future tourism development (Butler, 2021a). While most parts of the world suffered a break in international tourism during the Second World War for example, some countries have benefitted from such conflicts (Müller & Hoppler, 2013), but in the current situation all islands face severe problems. Most island tourism enterprises do not have the large capital reserves some multinational tourism industry players possess which could be used to furlough staff and tide establishments over the period of no customers. Many insular enterprises, like the islands on which they are located, are small, and tend to operate from year-to-year or even month-to-month, and complete closure is something which few could plan for and in many cases, few could survive.

Sustainability and resiliency of tourism sectors on islands must be built on adaptable frameworks of policy and planning to ensure the political will for tourism development continues. Diversification is a topical agenda with islands setting in motion plans to diversify tourism economies into other sectors. The importance of setting up new policies that will steer the course towards tourism recovery has to be mapped out and involve a stakeholder collaborative process. Partnerships are the way forward. For example, in the Caribbean a multi-agency platform facilitated advocacy, information sharing and capacity building activities to bring back Caribbean tourism.

A break in tourism has long term effects, not only because of closures and loss of attractions during and immediately following the pandemic, but also in terms of preventing an ongoing process of repair, renovation, reinvestment, and redevelopment in destinations (Jordan, 2000). The effects of a break in tourism in the Balkan countries is one of the few cases that has been documented (Šulc, 2014), and even there, with mainland transportation systems and widespread access to continental European markets, the impacts were severe and lasted for several years before tourist numbers were restored and some potential development did not take place (Vojnović, 2012). In this volume Bangwayo-Skeete and Skeete (2020) illustrate, using Barbados and Grenada, two SIDS, the extent of resilience to external shocks. Given the ongoing fall-off in visitor numbers, travel restrictions and adjustments to health protocols, island destinations have to ensure resiliency through strategies such as slow tourism (Walker & Lee, 2021) and market diversification, and market and product development strategies (Weaver, Tang, Lawton, & Liu, 2019). A prolonged reduced level of tourism activities will create pivoting activities with the resultant loss in fully competent and equipped tourism businesses and employees.

If there are any positives in this scenario, it may be found in the natural resilience of many island populations, as noted in several papers and the generally small scale of operations. In our introduction we noted that 'building resilience means gaining the capacity to adapt to and successfully manage changes in the dimensions and nature of tourism' (McLeod et al., 2021, p. 1) and COVID-19 has certainly presented a major change (Sharma, Thomas, & Paul, 2021), hopefully temporary in nature, in tourism to islands. Closures of facilities, disastrous though they may be to specific operators, may represent opportunities for potential competitors, and those with access to even limited capital may be able to quickly open replacement facilities at a comparable scale for visitors. That is quite unlike the situation in some large-scale urban tourist destinations marketed to mass tourists which would need large capital investment to reopen or replace closed facilities. Many islands are, sadly, used to suffering crises and disasters and recovering quickly from typhoons, cyclones, floods and storms and even volcanic eruptions, sometimes by basing resilience on tourism development (Becken & Khazai, 2017). In some cases such phenomena (e.g. volcanic eruptions) become tourist attractions in themselves over time, as in Iceland currently, and potentially in Las Palmas in the future, and what is often called the 'island spirit' sees resilience speedily put into practice. Unlike natural disasters or armed conflict (Buultjens, Ratnayake, & Gnanapala, 2017), the COVID-19 pandemic has mostly left infrastructure, including transportation, undamaged and available to be reused when demand is restored. To island destinations this is particularly important, because as discussed in some of the papers, access to islands is perhaps the key consideration to any hope of a successful tourism industry.

Lastly, there is the issue of safety and security (both real and perceived) from COVID-19 for visitors (Karl, 2018). It is likely that as the pandemic diminishes in impact and in perceptions, tourism will resume quickly to many destinations, as has been the case following many other disasters and problems (Isaac, Çakmak, & Butler, 2019), but the key issue will be which ones. During the pandemic the pattern of visitation changed, with priorities being given to tourists being able to reach a destination and return home without being subject to quarantine, and thus the journey to and from destinations assumed as much or even more importance than any specific destination itself (Butler, 2021b). This represented a radical, if presumably temporary, change from the traditional trip model (Clawson & Knetsch, 1966). It can be assumed that the normal priorities in destination choice will resume in the post-pandemic period, but the issue of perceived safety is likely to remain an issue (Li, Nguyen, & Coca-Stefaniak, 2020). The changing perceptions of travel and tourism markets and dynamic responses to the evolution of the COVID-19 pandemic remain an ongoing challenge. Long-haul travel is necessary to reach remote islands and without the effective support of the travel trade, tourism recovery will be delayed.

Those destinations which either avoided the pandemic, like New Zealand and some other Pacific Islands, or which appear to have handled the pandemic well and displayed good medical facilities and levels of care, like the Canary Islands, Iceland, and some islands in the Caribbean, may well benefit strongly from a positive image and immediate availability. Some destinations with limited medical facilities (a potential perceived problem should the pandemic re-emerge) or which earned a negative reputation (justified or not) because of their handling or mishandling of the pandemic, may suffer for some years. Such negative images may remain until the market in general has decided a new outbreak is unlikely, or until memories and perceptions have faded and changed. In general, islands will be perceived as victims of the pandemic rather than agents of it, and it is likely that their traditional markets will return more speedily than in the case of some other destinations, for example in mainland locations. For those islands with a high degree of dependency on mass tourism and/or cruise passenger traffic, much will remain beyond their control in the post-pandemic era, just as it was before COVID-19. The major carriers and cruise lines will make decisions on resuming tourism to island and other destinations based on their own priorities rather than the needs of those destinations. To at least some islands off the European coast many air carriers were quick to resume their services as quarantine and lockdown restrictions were removed at the end of the summer of 2021. The desire and the need to regain their markets were undoubtedly the decision-making factors in such situations. More remote islands may have to wait longer for what were normal services to be resumed.

When, rather than if, tourism is resumed to island destinations, a key question will be in what form tourism will return (Sharma et al., 2021). There have been a range of opinions expressed (see *Tourism Geographies* 2020, vol. 22, no. 3) arguing that the cessation of tourism during the pandemic should be taken as an opportunity to change the focus of tourism to a more sustainable model and form. Some calls for major refocusing of tourism (Everingham & Chassagne, 2020; Higgins-Desbiolles, 2020) displayed a viewpoint in line with other arguments that the concept of success in tourism should be based more on quality of life than purely economic criteria (Dwyer, 2021). Whether such arguments will hold water in the rush to restore tourism to economically hit destinations, both island and mainland, is hard to say and probably relatively unlikely. This is because given the numbers involved in mass tourism, which show no signs of declining despite many calls for sustainable tourism, and whether such a trend would be beneficial to all island communities is hard to say (Brouder et al., 2020; Hall, Scott, & Gössling, 2020). If there is a successful move towards a more sustainable form of tourism and if communities do change their perception of what success in tourism means by reducing the traditional narrow emphasis on economic priorities and continuous growth, then island tourist destinations, many of which base their appeal on their natural environment, their cultural heritage and their way of life, may find that their post COVID-19 future may be relatively bright.

References

Bangwayo-Skeete, P. F., & Skeete, R. W. (2021). Modelling tourism resilience in small island states: A tale of two countries. *Tourism Geographies, 23*(3), 436–457.

Becken, S., & Khazai, B. (2017). Resilience, tourism and disasters. In: R. W. Butler (Ed.) *Tourism and Resilience* (pp. 96–102). Boston, MA: CAB International.

Berbés-Blázquez, M., & Scott, D. (2017). The development of resilience thinking. In R. Butter (Ed.), *Turism and Resilience*, 9–20. Wallingford: CABI.

Brouder, P., Teoh, S., Salazar, N. B., Mostafanezhad, M., Pung, J. M., Lapointe, D., . . . Clausen, H. B. (2020). Reflections and discussions: tourism matters in the new normal post COVID-19. *Tourism Geographies, 22*(3), 735–746.

Butler, R. W. (2021a). COVID-19 and its potential impact on stages of tourist destination development. *Current Issues in Tourism*, 1–14. https://doi.org/10.1080/13683500.2021.1990223

Butler, R. W. (2021b). COVID-19: Impacts on the changed and changing nature of the tourism journey. In P. Callot (Ed.), *Tourism post Covid-19: Coping, negotiating, leading*. Montauban: Forestié.

Buultjens, J., Ratnayake, I., & Gnanapala, A. C. (2017). Sri Lankan tourism development and implications for resilience. In R. W. Butler (Ed.), *Tourism and resilience* (pp. 83–95). Wallingford: CABI.

Clawson, M., & Knetsch, J. L. (1966). Economics of Outdoor Recreation. *Baltimore: Johns Hopkins Press. Natural Resources Journal, 8*(13), 738.

Crist, C. (2021, 24 August 2021). Hawaii discourages tourists as COVID-19 rates rise. *WebMD.*

Dodds, R., & Butler, R. (2019). *Overtourism: Issues, realities and solutions* (Vol. 1): Walter de Gruyter GmbH & Co KG.

Dwyer, L. (2021). Resident well-being and sustainable tourism development: the 'capitals approach'. *Journal of Sustainable Tourism*, 1–17. https://doi.org/10.1080/09669582.2021.1990304

Everingham, P., & Chassagne, N. (2020). Post COVID-19 ecological and social reset: Moving away from capitalist growth models towards tourism as Buen Vivir. *Tourism Geographies, 22*(3), 555–566.

Gössling, S., Scott, D., & Hall, C. M. (2020). Pandemics, tourism and global change: a rapid assessment of COVID-19. *Journal of sustainable tourism, 29*(1), 1–20.

Hall, C. M., Scott, D., & Gössling, S. (2020). Pandemics, transformations and tourism: be careful what you wish for. *Tourism Geographies, 22*(3), 577–598.

Higgins-Desbiolles, F. (2020). Socialising tourism for social and ecological justice after COVID-19. *Tourism Geographies, 22*(3), 610–623.

Isaac, R. K., Çakmak, E., & Butler, R. (2019). *Tourism and hospitality in conflict-ridden destinations*. Abingdon: Routledge.

Jordan, P. (2000). Restructuring Croatia's coastal resorts: Change, sustainable development and the incorporation of rural hinterlands. *Journal of Sustainable Tourism, 8*(6), 525–539.

Karl, M. (2018). Risk and uncertainty in travel decision-making: Tourist and destination perspective. *Journal of Travel Research, 57*(1), 129–146.

King-Chan, M. S. E., Capistrano, R. C. G., & Lopez, E. L. F. (2021). Tourists really do behave responsibly toward the environment in Camiguin Province, Philippines. *Tourism Geographies, 23*(3), 573–598.

Li, J., Nguyen, T. H. H., & Coca-Stefaniak, J. A. (2020). Coronavirus impacts on post-pandemic planned travel behaviours. *Annals of Tourism Research, 83*(1), 102964.

McDonagh, S. (2021, 15 August 2021). Hawaiian overtourism: Residents beg tourists to stop visiting amid post-pandemic boom. *Euronews.*

McLeod, M. (2021). The Bahamas: Tourism Policy Within a Pandemic COVID in the Islands: A comparative perspective on the Caribbean and the Pacific (pp. 219–230). Singapore: Springer.

McLeod, M., Dodds, R., & Butler, R. (2021). Introduction to special issue on island tourism resilience. *Tourism Geographies, 23*(3), 361–370.

Mihalic, T. (2020). Concpetualising overtourism: A sustainability approach. *Annals of Tourism Research, 84*, 103025.

Milano, C., Cheer, J. M., & Novelli, M. (2019). *Overtourism: Excesses, discontents and measures in travel and tourism.* Wallingford: CABI.

Müller, H., & Hoppler, A. A. (2013). Tourism in a neutral country surrounded by war: the case of Switzerland *Tourism and War* (pp. 119–131). Abingdon: Routledge.

Sharma, G. D., Thomas, A., & Paul, J. (2021). Reviving tourism industry post-COVID-19: A resilience-based framework. *Tourism Management Perspectives, 37*, 100786.

Šulc, I. (2014). Tourism Development and Stagnation of Korčula Island in the Model of the Tourism Area Life Cycle. *Hrvatski geografski glasnik, 76*(2), 61–84.

UNWTO. (2020). *100% of global destinations now have COVID-19 travel restrictions.* Retrieved from www.unwto.org/news/covid-19-travel-restrictions

Vanderpool-Wallace, V. (2018). Island travel transportation. *Tourism Management in Warm-Water Island Destinations: Systems and Strategies,* 11–26.

Vojnović, N. (2012). Stagnation of a tourist destination: the example of the City of Pula. *Hrvatski geografski glasnik, 74*(2), 113–128.

Walker, T. B., & Lee, T. J. (2021). Contributions to sustainable tourism in small islands: an analysis of the Cittàslow movement. *Tourism Geographies, 23*(3), 415–435.

Weaver, D., Tang, C., Lawton, L., & Liu, Y. (2019). Cultivating the Chinese market through destination loyalty: enhancing resilience in the Maldives. *Tourism Geographies, 23*(3), 552–572.

Afterword

Anthony Clayton

This special issue on island tourism resilience has addressed some of the most critical dilemmas facing the small island nations of the world. It is hard for small islands to compete in areas such as agriculture or manufacturing, as they are limited by transport costs and small domestic markets. Some have developed positions in niche markets, but many are now stuck in the middle income trap, without the human capital, technical and innovative capacity to compete in high value-added markets. A couple have become rich by exporting oil, but the climate crisis signals the need to start shutting down most of the fossil fuel industry. Some have moved successfully into services; a few have become wealthy in offshore banking and financial services, but some of these are now being squeezed by anti-money laundering measures. Partly as a result, the majority have come to depend largely on tourism. The tourism sector accounts for almost 30%, on average, of the GDP of the Small Island Developing States (SIDS), but in some cases it is far more (over 50% for the Maldives, Seychelles, St. Kitts and Nevis and Grenada). The most tourism-dependent economies in the world are all small island nations, and some of those rely on the income from tourism for most of their foreign exchange, tax revenues and employment. This can be a dubious bargain for the host nations, as the benefits from tourism are very unevenly distributed; tourism generates high demand for scarce water and for imported energy and materials, so it can be a costly industry for islands to support, while the profits typically accumulate in low-tax jurisdictions elsewhere. Cruise tourism is an especially poor bargain for the islands, as most of the passengers that get off the ship are funnelled into gift shops and tourist experiences that the cruise lines also own.

The Covid-19 pandemic has resulted in millions of deaths and trillions of dollars in economic losses. The tourism-dependent island economies have suffered particularly badly, with record falls in revenue and no alternative way to service external debt and pay for imports. In most of these cases, the countries have slender foreign reserves and cannot access additional debt because they are already highly indebted, with a narrow economic base that cannot generate the additional revenues needed to repay additional loans. The average external debt of the SIDS is nearly 75% of their GDP, and is now close to 200% in some of the most tourism-dependent countries.

The international development agencies are calling for billions of dollars in concessionary loans for the tourism-dependent island economies, coupled with external debt suspension or relief programmes, but donor nations will find this hard to justify against a background of urgent demand for government support for domestic businesses. There are also challenging questions as to why most SIDS did not use the revenues from tourism to develop other sectors of their economy, reduce their extreme level of dependence, build sovereign wealth funds or pay down external debts, and in some cases there is a history of bad decision-making, mismanagement and extensive corruption that has contributed significantly to the current crisis.

This is therefore a moment of truth for the industry. Some will want to get back as quickly as possible to business as usual, but it would be wiser to reflect on the tourism model, and develop the international accords and legislative and regulatory frameworks needed to build greater resilience into every aspect of the industry and of the small nations that have come to depend upon it.

Index

Note: Figures are indicated by *italics*. Tables are indicated by **bold**. Endnotes are indicated by the page number followed by "n" and the endnote number e.g., 20n1 refers to endnote 1 on page 20.

For Product Safety Concerns and Information please contact our
EU representative GPSR@taylorandfrancis.com Taylor & Francis
Verlag GmbH, Kaufingerstraße 24, 80331 München, Germany